2003

Parenting in Canada

Human Growth and Development

Mary K. Cunningham, PHEc

Eva Meriorg, PHEc

Laura Tryssenaar, PHEc

THOMSON

NELSON

Australia   Canada   Mexico   Singapore   Spain   United Kingdom   United States

THOMSON

NELSON

Parenting in Canada: Human Growth and Development
First Edition
Mary K. Cunningham, PHEc
Eva Meriorg, PHEc
Laura Tryssenaar, PHEc

Director of Publishing
David Steele

Publisher
Carol Stokes

**Executive Managing Editor,
Development**
Cheryl Turner

**Program Manager and
Developmental Editor**
Marilyn Wilson

Inhouse Program Manager
Leah-Ann Lymer

Editorial Assistant
Kim Toffan

**Executive Managing Editor,
Production**
Nicola Balfour

Senior Production Editor
Joanne Close

Copy Editor
Dianne Horton

Proofreader
Linda Szostak

Production Coordinator
Sharon Latta Paterson

Creative Director
Angela Cluer

Interior Design
Sarah Battersby

Cover Design
Ken Phipps

Cover Image
Getty Images/Kaz Chiba/Taxi

Composition
Erich Falkenberg

Photo Research
Maria DeCambra

Permissions
Maria DeCambra

Printer
Transcontinental Printing Inc.

**National Library of Canada
Cataloguing in Publication Data**

Cunningham, Mary, 1949-
   Parenting in Canada : human growth and development / Mary Cunningham, Eva Meriorg, Laura Tryssenaar.

Includes index.

ISBN 0-17-620196-3

1. Parenting—Canada—Textbooks.
2. Child rearing—Textbooks.
I. Meriorg, Eva II. Tryssenaar, Laura
III. Title.

HQ755.7.C86 2003   649'.1
C2003-901398-7

Acknowledgments

There are many who I need to thank. My sincerest gratitude goes to my husband, Al, for his patience, forbearance and for all those times the dinners he cooked got cold. To Carol and Ian, and their new beginning families: without you I would know little about parenting or grand parenting. Your stories are in this book and will continue to provide me with the passion and compassion to teach others. Last but not least, my thanks goes to the Social and Global Studies staff and my students at Don Mills Collegiate. All of you made essential contributions to this book.

Mary K.Cunningham, PHEc

Thanks to my husband and soul mate Eamonn O'Dowd, whose love inspired me to want children in my life. His quiet encouragement and unwavering support have allowed me to work on this text. Thanks to my children, Eadonn and Jordanna, who continually excite, motivate, hearten, and challenge me. They have taught me that parenting is the most important and rewarding job there is. Finally, I would like to thank my parents, Endla and Ernst Meriorg for giving me the love of learning, the self-confidence, and the perseverance to complete important projects such as this.

Eva Meriorg, PHEc

Thanks to my daughter Miriah, who has been my own case study, and my husband Bill Armstrong for giving me the space, time, and support to complete this project. I am grateful to the many parenting students along the way who have taught me the importance of parenting education, and to my mentor Beverley Cowan, a family studies textbook author who advocated for parenting education long before it became a school subject.

Laura Tryssenaar, PHEc

List of Reviewers

Advisory Committee

Jane Bertrand
Atkinson Centre for Society and
  Child Development
Department of Human Development &
  Applied Psychology
OISE/UT

Dr. Robert Glossop
Executive Director of Programs and Research
Vanier Institute of the Family

Bev Murray
Canadian Home Economics' Association

Sharron Richards
Children's Aid Society of Toronto

Dr. Carol Crill Russell
Invest in Kids

Dr. Otto Weininger
Child Psychologist

Ontario Reviewers

Adora Achtenberg
Thunder Bay

Jane Atal
Aurora

Penny Ballagh
Toronto

Carole Booth
Burlington

Patricia Cibinell
Thunder Bay

Sue Dalton
Owen Sound

Denise Kelly
Guelph

Helen Miller
Ajax

Donna Pree
St. Catharines

Suzanne Robertson
Mississauga

Anne Sabourin
Arnprior

Pat Taylor
Owen Sound

National Reviewers

Sharon Anderson
Montaque, PEI

Judy Chan
Vancouver, BC

Merle MacDonald
Canning, NS

Eunice Martin
Esterhazy, SK

Lorraine Pollock
Sussex, NB

Jenell DeFehr Wiebe, B. H.ECOL., B.ED.
Winnipeg, Manitoba

Aboriginal Content Review

Rocky Landon
Kingston, ON

Equity Review

Mary Anne MacArthur
Mississauga, ON

Table of Contents

Introduction

Dear Student,

The authors invite you to explore the world of parents and children. This textbook is intended for secondary level courses in parenting and human development, but it will be of interest to anyone who enjoys children and wants to learn more about them. Children are everywhere, and in the future, you will come in contact with them in many aspects of your everyday life, whether or not you become a parent. Knowing about children will help you understand them, communicate effectively with them, and foster positive relationships with them.

Most parenting and human development courses have similar goals—to help you gain critical knowledge about human development and to prepare you for parenthood. These courses encourage you to better understand children and to care for them in the best ways possible. Different questions, exercises, activities, and research opportunities are used in different courses. Your teacher will direct you to the sections of this textbook that you will need to use in the particular course you are taking. You may find that other features and topics not covered in your course are interesting to read as well, and may be helpful for future careers, part-time jobs, or baby-sitting.

The features in this textbook use different approaches to help you learn about parenting, living and working with children, and human development. They include articles, theories, statistics, case studies, career capsules, and advice from some of the many experts and organizations dedicated to the well-being of children. The text also explores human and family development and examines many issues of importance for parents, caregivers, and anyone in our society who is involved with children.

We recommend that you think carefully about what you read, and question and analyze the points that are raised, especially as you begin to apply what you learn to your ongoing interactions with children. Children are fascinating and fun to be with. Learning about them can be most rewarding and enjoyable.

Sincerely,

Mary K. Cunningham, Eva Meriorg, and Laura Tryssenaar

Using the Textbook to Study Children

This textbook addresses a wide range of information about human development and parenting in a social context. It is designed as a social science textbook that examines children, childhood, parenting preparation, the nature of children and their growth and development, the nurturance of children through their socialization, and the big picture of society and the influences on children from beyond the family.

The textbook is divided into seven units:

Unit 1 **Parenting in Canada** provides an overview of research methods used to study children and their development;

Unit 2 **Historical and Cultural Perspectives** examines children and childhood in Canada in the past and studies the universal nature of childhood among cultures;

Unit 3 **The Circles of Life** investigates children in the family setting and the various relationships that involve children;

Unit 4 **Children in Your Future** explores the decision to become a parent and the importance of planning for parenthood;

Unit 5 **The Nature of Children** is the study of human growth and development from infancy, through early childhood, and into later childhood and adolescence;

Unit 6 **Nurturing Children** examines the socialization of children as the primary role of families and the range of parenting practices in the raising of children;

Unit 7 **Children in the Global Community** investigates the role of society in the lives of children, the world beyond the family that influences children, and investing in the future of children.

Features of This Textbook

- Each unit opens with an explanation of the focus of the unit, and a list of chapters within the unit.
- Each chapter opens with a list of expectations that shows what you will learn in the chapter. **Important Terms** is a list of glossary words found in the chapter. **Chapter at a Glance** lists the main topics of the chapter.
- **Checkpoints** are questions throughout the chapters that allow you to test your recognition and understanding of facts and concepts.
- **Connections** are questions that help you to apply information and ideas to situations.

- **What the Experts Say** provides up-to-date information from professionals who work with children.

- **Parenting Skills** gives information and shows competencies that can be directly applied to caring for, working with, or building relationships with children.

- **Talking Parenting** shows how parenting ideas can be applied to everyday life.

- **Margin Notes** give further details, summaries of information, and quotations about parenting.

- **Boxed Sidebars** present detailed, vital information related to the main text.

- **Case Studies** provide examples of situations and problems that involve children.

- **Career Capsules** focus on work that involves children in some way. You will explore a diverse array of careers that involve both direct and indirect work with children.

- Each chapter concludes with a **Chapter Summary**, consisting of:

  - **Chapter Highlights**, a summary of the main points of the chapter;

  - **Review and Extend Your Learning**, questions and activities. Icons identify whether the question or activity uses the following skills: Knowledge/Understanding **K/U**, Thinking/Inquiry **T/I**, Communication **C**, Application **A**;

  - **Research Opportunities**, presents situations for further investigation;

  - **Issues Analysis**, explores issues related to topics in the chapter.

- The **Appendix** on page 463 contains material from *What a child will be depends on you and me: A resource kit for a child's first five years*, produced by Invest in Kids, a not-for-profit organization. You will be asked to refer to this material in Chapter 12.

- Difficult terms and concepts are boldfaced throughout. Their definitions are located in the **Glossary** on page 478.

- A comprehensive **Index** is located on page 486.

Selected References

Ambert, A. M. (2002). *Divorce: Facts, causes, and consequences* [Electronic version]. Ottawa, ON: The Vanier Institute of the Family.

Baumrind, D. (1971). Current patterns of parental authority. *Developmental Psychology Monographs*, 2, 4(1), 1-103.

Bibby, R. W. (2001). *Canada's teens: Today, yesterday, and tomorrow*. Toronto, ON: Stoddart.

Brazelton, T. B. (1983). *Infants and mothers: Differences in development*. New York, NY: Dell.

Brazelton, T. B. & Greenspan, S. I. (2000). *The irreducible needs of children: What every child must have to grow, learn, and flourish*. Cambridge, MA: Perseus Books.

Bullying: Myths, facts and strategies for reducing it. (n.d.). Retrieved May 21, 2003, from http://www.the-family-centre.com/Telescope/Bullying1.htm

Carter, B., & McGoldrick, M. (Eds.). (1988). *The changing family life cycle: A framework for family therapy* (2nd ed.). New York, NY: Gardner Press.

Coloroso, B. (1989). *Winning at parenting…without beating your kids*. Littleton, CO: Kids Are Worth It Press.

Coloroso, B. (1994). *Kids are worth it*. Littleton, CO: Kids Are Worth It Press.

Dreikurs, R. & Stolz, V. (1964). *Children: The challenge* (1st ed.). New York, NY: Duell, Sloan & Pearce.

Dworetzky, J. P. (1993). *Introduction to child psychology* (5th ed.). St. Paul, MN: West Publishing Co.

Galinsky, E. (1981). *Between generations: The six stages of parenthood*. New York, NY: Times Books.

Gardner, H. (1999). *Intelligence reframed. Multiple intelligences for the 21st century*. New York, NY: Basic Books.

Gibson, E. M. (2002). *The challenge of difficult children: Elaine M. Gibson's insights on parenting*. Retrieved May 21, 2003 from http://www.elainegibson.net/parenting/threeplan.html

Gilligan, C. (1982). *In a different voice: Psychological theory and women's development*. Cambridge, MA: Harvard University Press.

Gopnik, A., Meltzoff, A., & Kuhl, P. K. (1999). *The scientist in the crib: What early learning tells us about the mind*. New York, NY: Morrow/Avon.

Invest in Kids. (2001). *What a child will be depends on you and me: A resource kit for a child's first five years*. Toronto, ON: Invest in Kids Foundation.

Jaffe, P., Wolfe, D. A., & Wilson, S. K. (1990). *Children of battered women*. Newbury Park, CA: Sage.

Kohlberg, L. (1984). *Essays on moral development, vol. II: The psychology of moral development*. New York, NY: HarperCollins.

Kronby, M. C. (2001). *Canadian family law* (8th ed.). Toronto, ON: Stoddart.

Ledingham, J. (1994, August). *The effects of media violence on children* [Electronic version]. Ottawa: National Clearing House on Family Violence, Health Canada.

McCain, M., & Mustard, F. (1999). *Early years study: Final report*. Toronto, ON: Children's Secretariat, Government of Ontario.

Prentice, S. (2000, June 20). The case for public child care in Manitoba. *Fast Facts: Canadian Centre for Policy Alternatives-Manitoba*.

Ritts, V. (1999). *Infusing culture into parenting issues: A supplement for psychology instructors*. Retrieved May 21, 2003 from http://www.stlcc.cc.mo.us/mc/users/vritts/culture.htm

Tannen, D. (1990). *You just don't understand: Women and men in conversation*. New York, NY: William Morrow and Company.

Vanier Institute of the Family. (2002, Spring). Family voices: Living with disability. *Transition*, 32, 4.

Weinhold, B., & Weinhold, J. (2000). *Conflict resolution: The partnership way*. Denver, CO: Love Publishing Company.

Weininger, O. (2002). *Time-in parenting*. Toronto, ON: Rinascente Book Inc.

Unit 1 Parenting in Canada

This unit explains how children are studied in formal and informal ways. Social scientists study children to learn about their behaviour, how they grow and learn, and the patterns they follow in their growth and development. You will gain the knowledge and skills necessary to study children using a number of sources. As well, you will learn about gathering, interpreting, and presenting information about children.

KEY INSIGHTS:

- Studying children increases parent effectiveness.
- The study of children enables those who live and work with children to be effective in their roles.
- Studying older children and adolescents prepares one for parenting or working with this age group.
- Social science research can clarify issues and enhance knowledge regarding human growth and development.

Unit at a Glance

Chapter

1

The Study of Children

By the end of this chapter, you will be able to:

- use appropriate social science research methods

- demonstrate an understanding of how to access information for research purposes

- organize and analyze both quantitative and qualitative data

- compile and present the results of research

Important Terms

anthropology
ethics
family studies
human ecology
hypothesis
informed consent
interdisciplinary study
primary research
psychology
public domain

qualitative research
quantitative research
research question
scientific method
secondary research
social science
sociology
style guide
theory

Why Study Children?

Children are cute, interesting, endearing, lovable, delightful, silly, challenging, precious, but also curious, frustrating, and very tiring. As babies, they are totally dependent, yet they end up as independent adults in their own right. Each developmental stage has its own characteristics and must be examined on its own.

Figure 1.1
Play is an important part of childhood.

How do you know what children are like if you never study them? Any time you play with children, watch children, listen to children, care for children, or talk to children, you are studying them in an informal way. By taking courses in parenting, child care, or child development, you are choosing to study children in a more formal way.

Ten Important Reasons for Studying Children

1. To learn more about the child you were.
2. To find out how children think and behave.
3. To understand human growth and development.
4. To strengthen your relationship with the children already in your life.
5. To prepare you for future community, social, and work situations that involve children.
6. To give you confidence when children are placed in your care.
7. To be able to identify and take action against child abuse.
8. To see the world through the eyes of a child.
9. To be the best parent you can be someday.
10. To understand the contributions of your own parents to your growth and development.

There are many reasons for studying children. As you read more about them, spend time with them, and research different topics concerned with them, you learn a great deal about how they think and behave. When you study children, you will understand them better, and you will understand yourself better. Most teenagers will become parents in the future. Learning about children of all ages and stages will help you care for children now and prepare you for the lifelong responsibility of parenthood or caring for children in your future.

Social Sciences and the Study of Children

Social science is the study of human society, human thought, human culture, and human behaviour. Because humanity is so complex, social science includes several different disciplines. There are three main disciplines that involve the study of parenting.

■ Social science is the study of:

Human society

Human thought

Human culture

Human behaviour

- **psychology**, the scientific study of behaviour and the human mind
- **sociology**, the systematic study of human relationships within social organizations
- **anthropology**, the study of the lives and cultures of human beings

The social sciences also include **family studies** or **human ecology**. This is the **interdisciplinary study** of individuals and their families using anthropology, sociology, and psychology, along with the social sciences of economics and political science. Family studies also includes some aspects of the humanities disciplines of religion, philosophy, law, and education.

Social scientists have studied children for a long time, and for many reasons. Children grow and change so quickly and in such distinct ways that they are excellent subjects for the study of human development. The study of children makes it possible to learn how humans acquire language, form relationships, use their mind, develop and master skills, and cope with a complex world. By taking a course in parenting, child care, or human development, you, too, become a social scientist. You will be conducting social science research with a focus on children.

Expectations of Teenagers, 1992–2000

Do you expect to... (% indicating "Yes")		1992	2000
Career	Pursue a career	96	95
	Get the job you want when you graduate	83	86
	Have to work overtime to get ahead	41	44
Family	Get married	85	88
	Stay with the same partner for life	86	88
	Have children	84	92
Success	Own your own home	96	96
	Be more financially comfortable than your parents are	77	79
	Travel extensively outside Canada	73	72

From *Canada's Teens: Today, Yesterday, and Tomorrow* (p. 200), by R.W. Bibby, 2001, Toronto: Stoddart Publishing.

Figure 1.2
Most teenagers envision having children at some time in the future. Learning about children now can lead to better parenting and family relationships.

Social Sciences

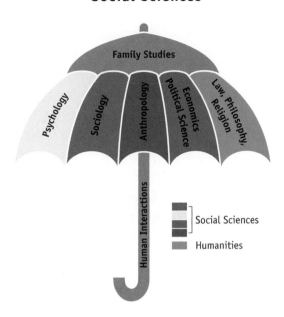

Figure 1.3
The social sciences are made up of these disciplines.

■ *Anthropology is the science which tells us that people are the same the whole world over—except when they are different.*
— Nancy Banks-Smith

Figure 1.4
Children are lovable and challenging.

What the experts say

ROBERT GLOSSOP

Robert Glossop, the Executive Director of Programs and Research at The Vanier Institute of Family in Ottawa, answers the following question.

What role does social science research play in the work of The Vanier Institute of the Family?

In 1965, The Vanier Institute of the Family was established to promote the well-being of Canadian families. Using research, we identify and try to under-stand patterns in how families are formed, what they do, and how they feel. Once we have an accurate description of these dimensions of family life, we identify the personal challenges and public policy issues that emerge from these trends so that Canadians can together better understand how to support today's families.

It is probably fair to say that research on its own cannot really strengthen families, but it is also fair to say that any attempt to strengthen families not based on reliable research is bound to fail. So, if a government or agency wants to change public policy to help families, they should do their research first.

Studying the family is very multidisciplinary. Social historians show us that there is no such thing as "the" family by recording how families have changed in adapting to the consequences of social, technological, economic, and cultural forces across cultures and through history. Sociologists have discovered much about how families both mirror and strengthen their environments. Psychologists and social psychologists have taught us much about how families interact to shape the individual identities that guide us in our roles as workers and citizens.

Perhaps the biggest change in families has to do with the fact that 70 percent of couples who are raising children need two incomes to make ends meet, and both men and women today are expected to provide financially and emotionally to sustain their households and make a home.

Research also reveals that these changes are not simply accidental. In the middle of the last century, most men and women had a pretty good idea of what was expected of them. People today do not have the same kind of easily understood gender roles. Changes in both the workplace and our expectation that our living standards will rise have left a lot of us trying to figure out our roles. What does it mean to be part of an egalitarian family in which men and women both work, share the work around the house, and together teach and nurture their children? There has been some progress in trying to figure out our new roles, but it has been slow and there is still a long way to go to adapt to these major changes.

Some people think parenting is instinctual and does not need to be researched. I do not think parents have ever just relied on their instincts. Parenting does not really come naturally. We have all heard the phrase: "...it takes a community to raise a child." Well, it is also fair to say that it takes a community to guide parents. Most societies have always understood that the job of caring for and raising the next generation of citizens is far too important to leave to the parents alone. That is why, in the past, parents were supported and, yes indeed, instructed in how to be a parent by members of their faith, their community, and their parents and other relatives.

More recently, parents have also been able to rely upon the lessons of research to guide them. These emphasize the crucial importance of strong attachments between parent and child, the essential role of stimulation in the early years for cognitive, social, and emotional development, and the factors that determine child outcomes, like adequate incomes and community supports.

In the end, sound parenting depends essentially on the respect we demonstrate for the child, the extent to which we are willing to devote ourselves and our resources to him or her, and the consistency with which we express both our expectations and our affection.

■ One research method is not superior to any other. The method you choose will depend on what you hope to learn.

Children are the future of every family and every society. They represent the connection between generations. What you learn about children can influence your relationship with the children in your life right now and in the years to come. What you learn about children can help to make Canada a stronger and better place because today's children will become the teachers, decision-makers, and parents of tomorrow.

Research Methods

Observation: Record what you see and hear when observing children.

Participatory Observation: Play or interact with children while observing them.

Personal Interview: Talk to an expert about children.

Phenomenology (Life Story): Listen to someone describe a unique experience with children.

Survey: Ask several people the same questions about children.

Historical Research: Check out information about children in historical documents.

Official Statistics: Find out what government records or population breakdowns say about children.

Review of Literature: Summarize what a number of authors/theorists have written about children.

Ways of Learning about Children and Parenting

Researchers use many different methods to gather information about children. One research method is not superior to any other, and the method you choose will depend on what you hope to learn. Good researchers are impartial, open-minded, and objective, and use the research methods as outlined, keeping personal prejudices out of their research.

Observation

Researchers can learn a great deal by watching and listening to children. They use one-way mirrors when they do not want or need to be seen by the children they are observing. Researchers record their observations in several ways. They use

- observation checklists if they are looking for a particular series of behaviours that can be checked off on a list
- anecdotal reports, which can be either detailed written descriptions of everything a child says and does, or tape recordings in which they describe everything they see and hear
- videotapes that can be made and then analyzed later

Observers must be objective and record only what they see and hear. Later on, they can be more subjective when they analyze and interpret their observations.

Figure 1.5
By observing children, social scientists learn how humans use their minds, develop and master skills, and cope with their complex environment.

Participatory Observation

In participatory observation, researchers interact with the children and participate in their activities. A researcher may wish to ask questions to discover what they are thinking or to learn whether they are able to perform certain tasks such as counting, hopping, or identifying colours. Researchers can record their observations in checklists or written descriptions, again keeping subjective interpretations separate from the details observed. Later, they can analyze their observations for interesting patterns or compare their findings with developmental patterns identified by other theorists or researchers.

Personal Interview

A child may be interviewed with parental permission. The researcher prepares an interview schedule with specific questions and sets out to find the answers. Questions may range from "How old are you?" or "What grade are you in?" to "How do you feel when someone takes something of yours without asking?" The interviewer develops the questions in advance and writes down the answers word for word or makes a tape recording of the interview and then transcribes or writes it out afterward. Researchers can use their interview notes to compare the information they have gathered with the opinions, theories, and findings of others.

Phenomenology (Life Story)

Social scientists often use phenomenology, the attentive examination of a particular life experience, to study the lived experiences of children and families. For example, they use the story of the parents' experience to examine a phenomenon such as raising a child with a physical disability, or living with a child who has Fetal Alcohol Spectrum Disorder (FASD), or experiencing the tragedy of Sudden Infant Death Syndrome (SIDS). They tape-record and then transcribe conversations with the parents. This enables researchers to identify and examine common themes and to gain an understanding of what it is like to live through the experience. The story can be told by itself or framed with information from research studies and demographics. Phenomenology is a very powerful way of doing social science research.

Survey

Researchers generally use surveys to get information or data from a large number of people. Survey questionnaires can gather numbers, facts, and

Figure 1.6
A survey is an effective tool to gather data about facts and opinions.

opinions fairly quickly. "How many four-year-olds are enrolled in junior kindergarten in your board?" "What is the favourite activity of three-year-olds and four-year-olds in your day care?" Researchers can record the results of a survey in a chart or a graph for easy comparison. Because a respondent must read and complete the survey, it must be given to an adult who will record the observations. Therefore, it may not be the most suitable method for gathering information from children.

Historical Research

Researchers can use many sources to learn about children in the past. Diaries, historical novels, family, religious institutions, and school records, old photographs and paintings of children, old letters, and stories told by men and women who were children themselves many years ago are excellent ways of learning about children in the past. To use such resources objectively, researchers must use the same questions to examine each resource and guide the research. They can then prepare and interpret extensive notes that look for both trends and patterns and atypical examples.

Official Statistics

Census data, school records, and other official records depict the size, composition, and demographics or distributions of human populations. Sometimes, these numbers are converted to charts, graphs, or tables to show changes over time in such measures as birth rates, fertility, infant mortality rates, or family income. Statistics Canada collects demographic data about population trends in Canada. This information is available for researchers studying children and the family and can be examined to determine trends, patterns, and features that are relevant to the topic being researched.

Review of Literature

Research studies and human interest articles in books, textbooks such as this one, magazines, electronic media, and print materials make it possible to gather a variety of information on a topic. The researcher reads the literature and either paraphrases the information (takes notes in his or her own words), or copies direct quotes word for word. When paraphrasing or quoting an author's work, a researcher must credit the original author. **Style guides** show how to do this properly. After gathering information from a number of sources, the researcher reviews the literature for common topics and uses subheadings to organize what each author contributes to the understanding of the topic. The researcher notes both opposing views and similar views.

The style guide that is used most often in the social sciences is the *Publication Manual of the American Psychological Association*, referred to as the "APA Style Guide." Your teacher, school, or local library may have a copy.

Career Capsule

RESEARCHER

Tasks and Responsibilities

When information of any type or for any purpose is needed, researchers know how to find it. They can skillfully navigate the huge amounts of information available through the Internet, databases, newswires, trade publications, and public records. They know how to evaluate sources, check facts, and sometimes conduct interviews with experts, government officials, and other specific segments of the population. Then they write up summaries or analyses of their findings.

Consulting firms, governments, and corporations rely on skilled researchers to find and organize information on markets, government regulations, new technologies, and industry trends. In addition to collecting and organizing materials relating to the business or government department, many "special librarians" do research for managers, executives, and government officials. They may also monitor industry news or government activities and circulate news clippings or reports.

Work Environment

Researchers work for banks, consulting companies, corporations, and various sectors of government. They usually work in offices and spend much of their time on the computer. Most are employed full time and work regular office hours. Independent researchers, sometimes called "information brokers," work on a contract basis. Because information brokering is a new field of work, these researchers may have to work hard to identify potential clients and sell their services.

Education and Aptitudes

To become a researcher, the minimum requirement is a bachelor's degree. Most research jobs, however, require a master's degree, either in an area related to the organization's work, or in library and information science. Library and information science programs teach advanced manual and electronic research methods, as well as methods for interpreting, organizing, and storing records, materials, and data.

❖ Checkpoints

1. What are the components of social science?
2. Describe three ways in which observations about children can be recorded.
3. Explain the ways in which surveys, official statistics, and historical research can be used in social science investigations.
4. Select three research methods and explain the characteristics of each one that would help to ensure that the researcher remained objective.

Conducting Social Science Research

Because social science is a discipline with diverse interests, many different kinds of research are acknowledged, and the research takes on many different forms. At one time, social science research was conducted using only the scientific or experimental method, because that was the accepted way to do research. The **scientific method** follows the format that many students use to write up science experiments. It includes a purpose, **hypothesis**, method, results (data), analysis, and conclusion.

The scientific method has been used more often in some social science disciplines than in others. In psychology, experiments on human subjects were often translated into statistical data. How many first-born children go on to higher education? How often does a child go around an obstacle rather than knock it over? Sociologists and anthropologists also used experiments, but some were more interested in what led first-born children to choose higher education, or why some children and not others avoided obstacles. Detailed descriptions of behaviour and theories about what motivated the behaviour were more important than the number of occurrences.

Quantitative research is experimental research that results in data such as numbers, measurements, and statistics. It is sometimes limiting without **qualitative research,** which is the story or description of what those numbers, measurements, and statistics mean in human terms, and can provide a much-needed dimension. If the question is, "Have birth rates changed in Canada in the past two decades?", then data produced by quantitative research will do the job. However, if the question is, "Has the childbirth experience for new parents changed in the last two decades?", then qualitative research that describes the experiences of new parents will be more appropriate.

Quantitative and qualitative research both have advantages and disadvantages. Sometimes one is preferred over the other, but sometimes they are both used in the same research project. The kind of

■ Based on what you've learned so far, what do you think of this quote? *After all, the ultimate goal of all research is not objectivity, but truth.* — Helene Deutsch

The Research Process

1. Identify the problem, topic, or issue.
2. Do some preliminary research to determine your interests and the existing views and theories about your topic.
3. Take a position and formulate a research question.
4. Gather information and/or data using the method or methods that offer the best answers.
5. Organize, summarize, and analyze your information.
6. Develop your argument.
7. Conclude by explaining how your research answered your research question.

research method chosen usually depends on the goals and preferences of the researcher. The **research question** that the social scientist hopes to answer often suggests the best research method to use.

How to Formulate a Research Question

The research question is a question that a researcher answers by gathering specific information. Choose a topic of interest and think about what you want to learn about that topic. Conduct preliminary research by reading about the topic, learning about existing theories, or talking to others who know a great deal about the topic. The research question will narrow the topic by asking something specific, but your preliminary work will give you an idea of the kind of research you would have to do to answer the question. Refine the question you want to answer, and then decide where you will go to find the information you need to answer it.

A good research question is about something important that can be looked at from different perspectives and cannot be answered with a "yes" or "no" answer. For example, "Does a crying baby bother parents?" does not generate research because the answer could be "yes" or "no." "How do parents react to crying infants?" is a question that requires further research before you can answer it. You would need to talk to a number of parents, or you would need to read other research studies or articles that have already examined the same concern.

A Good Research Question

- asks exactly what you want to learn
- cannot be answered with a "yes" or "no" answer
- can be answered only by gathering information

Possible Research Questions and Methods

Topic	Possible Research Question	Possible Research Methods
Child Care	• What kind of child care was available to parents in Canada in the late 1800s? • What problems do single parents face in finding childcare?	• historical letters and documents • historical novels • archives • personal interviews • life stories • books, magazine articles
Poverty	• How is child poverty managed in Canada? • What is it like for a child to live in poverty? • How do newspapers report and describe poverty?	• demographics and statistics • public records • review of literature • life story • personal interviews • newspaper articles
Child Development	• What is the relationship between talking and reading to babies and their future success in school?	• review of literature • personal interviews with parents • school records

Figure 1.7
The research question often suggests the best research method.

❖ Connections

1. For two of the research questions in Figure 1.7, choose a title for the research and suggest three sub-topics that would be relevant for examining the topic.
2. For the following research questions, what research method or methods do you think would be most appropriate?
   - What are the immediate and long-term effects of prenatal smoking on a child?
   - What are some of the challenges a parent faces when raising a child with Attention Deficit Disorder?
   - How can parents solve sibling rivalry problems?

Organizing and Analyzing Research Information

People conduct research for many different reasons. Buying a car, planning a trip, or deciding what jobs to apply for all involve some kind of research. The kind of research you do and the depth of research you undertake both depend on why you are doing the research.

Students are expected to do different kinds of research. Think about the research projects you've done over the past few years. Have you needed facts about a topic so that you could create a poster or design a pamphlet or media campaign? Have you had to look something up in the library or on the Internet and share the information with the class? Or have you had to do extensive research for a written report or a major research essay? In any of these projects, you have gathered relevant information to inform your audience about your topic and convince them that you have accurately and objectively reflected your research. In each case, you should follow some important steps for gathering, organizing, and analyzing your information.

Gathering Information

After you know the research question you want to answer, you should decide how to find the information you need to answer the question (see Figure 1.9 on page 15). If you ask people about their experiences or their expertise and record your conversation or interview, you are conducting **primary research**. If you use print material, you will need to take notes or photocopy and highlight key points. By reading and recording what other researchers have already discovered or reported, you are conducting **secondary research**. If you gather artifacts such

Figure 1.8
You are conducting secondary research when you read and record what other researchers have reported.

as letters, diaries, or old newspaper articles, you could photocopy them if they are not too fragile, or you could keep them in a file and make detailed notes on what you learned from them. The important thing is to gather enough information to answer your research question in a convincing way.

Plagiarism

Whatever source you use to gather information, you must always acknowledge your source. Failure to do so results in plagiarism, or passing off someone else's ideas or work as your own. Plagiarism is a serious offence, and the punishment might be a zero evaluation on your assignment or the loss of a credit in the course. At colleges and universities, it can mean being expelled altogether.

To prevent plagiarism, always keep a record of where you found your information. A style guide will tell you exactly how to reference your sources in your research presentation. Every kind of source has different requirements. Books by a single author, books by multiple authors, magazine articles, Internet sources, newspaper articles, videotapes, audiotapes, and radio programs, to name a few, are each referenced in a unique way. Keep a record of your sources with the information that you gather so that you do not have to look everything up again when you compile your research and cite your sources in a reference list or a bibliography.

If you are using the *Publication Manual of the American Psychological Association*, you will find the instructions for how to reference your sources correctly in the section entitled "Elements and Examples of References in APA Style." The style manual is updated regularly, so be sure to work from the latest edition. The fifth edition, published in 2001, includes rules for citing electronic media sources.

What Information Is Important?

One problem that social science researchers face when they gather information is deciding whether they are gathering facts or opinions. Both facts and opinions are used in social science research. Facts are important for making research convincing. Opinions can be useful for raising questions and exploring concerns through research. When using an opinion, it is important to be clear about whose opinion it is and whether the opinion is based on personal experience or is informed by research. When you are factual, the opinions you share are more convincing.

■ Keep a record of where the information came from so that you can give credit to the person or source. In social science research, you must acknowledge any idea that is not strictly your own. This not only gives credit to other authors but also provides support for your own research findings because it shows that others share your view.

Techniques for Gathering Information

Sources of Research Information	Ways to Gather Information
Print Materials: books, magazines, newspapers, journals	• Photocopy and highlight key ideas, noting the complete source details on each page you copy. • If you cannot photocopy, take detailed notes on the information that is most important for answering your research question, citing the complete source at the top of each page. • Copy convincing quotes word for word, in quotation marks, noting the page number in brackets. • Write in your own words other information that is important to your topic but that does not need to be quoted directly.
Human Subjects	• Use audiotapes to record personal interviews, and then transcribe or write out what you hear on the tape. • Use videotape to record interviews or observations (with participants' permission), and then take notes as you replay it. • Take detailed notes, complete checklists, or both, when observing others. Record exactly what you see and hear, not what you think it means. • Design questionnaires or surveys that are clear and easy to answer, and that clearly measure what you intend to measure.
Electronic Media: Web Sites, Internet	• Select the relevant text, and copy the information to a word-processing file. • Select and copy the exact Web site address, and add it to the information in the word processing file. • Print out copies, and highlight the important information. • Cut and paste the quotes you want into a working file, keeping the required source information with each quote.

Figure 1.9

Whether you use primary or secondary research, the important thing is to gather enough information to answer your research question in a convincing way.

Fact or Opinion? How do you know?

When conducting research, it is important to distinguish between facts and opinions.

Facts are items of information that can be demonstrated to be true. They are often based on scientific research, physical evidence, or numeric data. For example: "71% of teenagers are living with their mothers and fathers" (Bibby, 2001, p. 54).

Opinions describe peoples' attitudes, feelings, and thoughts about a topic. Opinions are less exact because they are based on personal viewpoints. For example: "People have a right to medical care."

How often people share an opinion can be measured. For example: "92% of teenagers agree that people who cannot afford it have a right to medical care" (Bibby, 2001, p. 191).

Quick Quiz

Determine which of the following statements is fact and which is opinion:

1. According to Statistics Canada, two out of five marriages end in divorce.
2. According to single mother Alison Ouimet, being divorced can negatively affect your quality of life.
3. The divorce rate in Canada is lower than the divorce rate in the United States.
4. Fetal Alcohol Spectrum Disorder has been shown to affect one in 100 live births.
5. Parenting a child with a developmental delay challenges the parents' marriage.
6. The thought of parenting was scary but it turned out to be incredibly joyful.
7. Muscular dystrophy is a genetic condition affecting male children.

Answers: 1. F 2. O 3. F 4. F 5. O 6. O 7. F

Analyzing Information

After you gather information, you need to make sense of it for the research project you are completing. What does it mean to analyze information? It means looking at your information in different ways. You could study, scrutinize, consider, evaluate, question, explore, probe, or check out your information. You can do this while you are gathering information to determine what is important and necessary for your presentation and what should be discarded.

Depending on the purpose of your research, you can analyze your information to answer some or all of the following questions:

1. What information is most convincing?
2. What information should be kept and what should be discarded?
3. What patterns are taking shape?
4. What themes, topics, or categories are emerging?
5. What headings and subheadings does the information fall into?
6. What viewpoints can be supported by the information?
7. What arguments can be made?
8. What is missing?
9. What generalizations can be made from your research?
10. What conclusions are taking shape?

After you have analyzed your information and determined how you will use it, you can begin to organize it into one of many different formats.

Organizing Information

Whether you are writing a report, putting together a group presentation, poster presentation, a major research paper, or just sharing your

■ Use headings to organize written, visual, or oral presentations. In addition, your presentation should have an introduction, conclusion, and list of references.

findings with the class, you will need to organize your work to make it interesting, coherent, and convincing.

Organizing your Research Presentation

- **Introduce your topic**. Use your introduction to get the attention of your audience and provide an overview of the topic. Explain why your topic is worthy of research, and outline what you will be exploring in your research.

- **State the research question**. In the introduction, let the audience know the research question, the methods used to gather the information, and what you hope to convince the audience about your research.

- **Analyze**. Examine your information so that you can organize, interpret, and summarize it. You may choose to use charts, graphs, or spreadsheets for your quantitative data. Grouping themes or summarizing subtopics is useful for analyzing qualitative data. Compare your findings. Look for relationships between the information you have gathered and the research question, and explain it in an interesting way.

- **Organize**. Present your ideas in an order that makes sense. Does your information fall into different categories? Does it follow a pattern from most important to least important, from historical to present day, from societal to personal? Use headings to group related information.

- **Give details**. Use specific examples from your research by paraphrasing, quoting your sources, or showing the steps you followed to gather first-hand information.

- **Cite your sources**. Cite your sources throughout your presentation and at its end using a method suggested by a style guide such as *The Publication Manual of the American Psychological Association*. Here is a single example of a source that is cited in the presentation:

"Some 71 percent of young people say they receive a high level of enjoyment from their mothers, while 62 percent say the same about their fathers" (Bibby, 2001, p. 24).

The source reference (author, date, and page) follows the quotation mark but appears before the end punctuation. The complete reference to any source cited in the presentation must be noted in the documentation at the end of the presentation. Movie credits do this, and so does a "References" list or "Works Cited" list. In

■ **Organizing Your Research Presentation**
1. Introduce your topic.
2. State the research question.
3. Analyze.
4. Organize.
5. Give details.
6. Cite your sources.
7. Explain.
8. Present a conclusion.

Figure 1.10
Make sure you have given the audience a clear understanding of your topic.

this case, the complete citation for the sample quote is as follows: Bibby, R.W. (2001). *Canada's teens: Today, yesterday, and tomorrow*. Toronto, ON: Stoddart Publishing. (In APA style, you only capitalize the initial word in the title.)

- **Explain**. Explain your points in your own words to show that you are thinking about what you have researched.

- **Present a conclusion**. Leave your audience with a clear understanding of your topic and what you learned from your research. Summarize how your findings answer your research question. You need an ending that ties up any loose ends and brings your research to an end.

Communicating Social Science Research

After you gather, organize, summarize, and analyze your information, you can present your social science research in a variety of ways.

Ways to Present Research

Research Paper. A research essay or journal article not only describes the research process but also make connections among a number of sources of information to argue a point and convince the audience of a certain position.

Written Report. A report generally outlines the process, information gathered, analysis, and conclusion using clear headings and clear and concise terms. Written reports can take many forms, including a newspaper or magazine article or a report to a committee or an organization.

Oral Report or Presentation. The researcher talks about the topic, describes the research process, and uses the information gathered to explain how the research question was answered. Audiovisual material may be included to make the presentation or report interesting to the audience. Introductions and conclusions are still very important in an oral presentation.

Poster Presentation. A poster display is a visual presentation that includes clear headings, point-form information, analyses, and conclusions written or typed in large print that can be read from a distance. Eye-catching visual details such as charts, graphs, graphics, and pictures help present the information that was gathered to answer a research question.

Multimedia Presentation. The researcher chooses from a number of technological methodologies, including video or digital video recordings, Web pages, slide or tape presentations, or audio recordings, to name a few. The information gathered is introduced, analyzed, and organized for the presentation, and concluded in a way that brings the audience to a clear understanding of how the research question has been answered.

Group Presentation. Any of the above forms can be used or combined, but more than one person is involved in the research process. Each person in the group can take on a different responsibility to contribute to the whole process. One person could be the expert in layout and design while another person could have a speaking role.

This textbook provides numerous research opportunities to expand your knowledge on various topics. The possibilities for communicating your research range from simple to complex. Some research can be done quickly by surveying the members of your class, questioning a parent or relative, or observing children in your community. Other kinds of research require more time for reading, taking notes, organizing information, and putting together the final presentation. Research gives you the opportunity to explore many different topics, issues, and theories and learn more about parents and children.

❖ Checkpoints

1. After you have gathered and analyzed information from your research, what steps should you follow to organize and communicate the information?
2. What role does a style guide such as the *APA Style Guide* play in how you communicate research information and prevent plagiarism?
3. Name and describe some of the ways in which you might effectively communicate the results of your research.

Ethical Considerations during Social Science Research

Whenever social science research is done using human subjects, complex ethical questions arise. When doing this type of research, the researcher must get **informed consent** from the subjects before conducting the study. They must be informed of all aspects of the research, and they must give their consent, usually by signing an agreement. If children are involved, they are not old enough or mature enough to give this consent, and it must be obtained from their parents or legal guardians.

Consideration must be given to whether the social science research could cause emotional or physical harm to those studied. Research subjects must be informed of the complete scope of the study and any possible consequences. Only then can they be asked to give informed consent.

■ When using human subjects, the researcher must obtain informed consent.

Research professionals generally describe behaviour that they consider morally desirable when conducting research. These professional standards are called **ethics**. In his book *Introduction to Child Psychology* (1993), J.P. Dworetzky created a list of children's rights in relation to social science research. His "A Child's List of Rights" is an example of the ethical principles for research with children. When planning your research for this course, review this list and ask yourself whether your research conforms to these guidelines. If the answer is "yes," your research is off to a good ethical start. All good social science research must place the best interests of the research subjects ahead of any experimental goals or personal gain.

Ethical Standards for Research with Human Subjects

A Child's List of Rights

1. No matter how young the child, he or she has rights that supersede the rights of the investigator.
2. Any deviation from these ethical principles requires that the investigator seek consultation in order to protect the rights of the research participants.
3. The investigator should inform the child of all features of the research that may affect the child's willingness to participate, and the investigator should answer the child's questions in terms appropriate to the child's comprehension.
4. The informed consent of parents or of those who act *in loco parentis* (e.g., teachers, superintendents of institutions) similarly should be obtained, preferably in writing. Informed consent requires that the parents or other responsible adult be told all features of the research that may affect their willingness to allow the child to participate. The responsible adults should be given the opportunity to refuse without penalty.
5. The investigator may use no research operation that may harm the child either physically or psychologically.
6. If concealment or deception is practised, adequate measures should be taken after the study to ensure the participants' understanding of the reasons for the concealment or deception.
7. The investigator should keep in confidence all information obtained about research participants.
8. The investigator should clarify any misconceptions that may occur during or after the research.
9. When, in the course of research, information comes to the investigator's attention that may seriously affect the child's well-being, the investigator must make all arrangements necessary to assist the child.
10. If, during the research, any previously unforeseen consequences of an undesirable nature should occur, it is incumbent upon the researcher to correct these consequences or redesign the experimental procedures.
11. When experimental treatment is believed to benefit the children, the control group should be offered the same or similar beneficial treatment.
12. Every investigator also has the responsibility to maintain the ethical standards of his or her colleagues.
13. Teachers of courses related to children should present these ethical standards to their students.
14. The research must be scientifically sound and significant.
15. The research should be conducted on animals, human adults, and older children before involving infants.

❖ Connections

1. What might be unethical about each of the following kinds of research?
   - Parenting students are asked to use a child's first and last name in a report they write based on observations of the child's behaviour in a play group.
   - Children in Grade One are videotaped by high school students for a class presentation.
   - A student wants to study the effect of name-calling on children in child care.
2. Describe the ethical considerations facing researchers who might be doing any of the research projects described in Figure 1.7 on page 12.

Talking Parenting

Tina Morrison is a mother of two children and is expecting another child. She describes how the latest research in parenting and child development has affected her and her family.

There is a lot of information "out there" about prenatal care, child development, and parenting. I try to look for up-to-date, reliable sources of information when making decisions that will affect my children. I read about proper nutrition, exercise, and rest and how important they are to my baby. I have been trying to keep away from refined sugar and satisfy my "sweet cravings" with fresh fruit. I also try to rest as much as I can by putting my feet up for a few minutes periodically throughout the day. This really gives me the energy boost I need to look after the kids at the end of the day. Although I love to run and roller-blade, I now stay away from high-impact exercise and prefer walking and swimming to keep healthy and strong while I am pregnant. I am a firm believer in technology and science and I opt for every test there is to confirm the health of my baby. The most difficult time during this process is waiting for the results.

I have done lots of reading about the major developments in what is known about children and how their brains develop. I read the *Early Years Study* and I now know why the first six years are so important to the health and well-being of children. As a result of this report and other current research, I have participated with my children in

Figure 1.11
Tina and her children, Martina (6) and Colton (2)

some wonderful programs at the local community centre. Music and play have been the focus of these programs. Learning and playing go hand-in-hand but this does not always have to be in "structured" programs. To ensure the best development for our children, my husband and I try to make learning and play a part of our routine. We love to sit on the floor and play with Colton and Martina every day knowing that, by having fun with them, we are fostering brain development, learning, and healthy emotional relationships.

Studying Theories and Issues

Research has already been done by social scientists that provides the background for a study of theories and issues. This textbook provides many opportunities to study theories and issues that are important for understanding parents and children.

Studying Theories about Children

Any practice, whether it is teaching, investing, marketing, or parenting, is based on theory.

A **theory** is an explanation or view of events, behaviours, or situations that make them easier to organize and understand. Some theories are based on years of experimental research, while other theories are based on speculation about events that occur and follow the same pattern over and over again. All theories have an element of truth in them, and that is why they are accepted or embraced. Good theories are widely held. They can stand the test of time and be embraced for a long time. A good theory accurately predicts reality. Sometimes, however, a theory loses its following because it no longer seems true, or it is replaced with other theories that do a better job of explaining something.

Theory also plays an important role in research. A researcher may challenge existing theories, or use them to guide and support a particular research project. Research sometimes adds a different perspective to a theory, or may come up with something entirely new.

Case Study: Dr. Benjamin Spock

Dr. Benjamin Spock was a famous doctor whose own theories about child rearing changed over his long career. He first published *Dr. Spock's Guide to Baby and Child Rearing* in 1945, and went on to publish eight editions. His early advice helped parents of several generations handle everything from cleaning the navel, to teething, toilet training, handling nightmares, disciplining, and just plain raising children. The more recent editions, however, acknowledged the importance of emotional well-being, and began to focus on the ever-increasing social problems families face such as divorce, single parenting, and stepparent relationships.

Questions

1. Describe a research study that could be used to develop a theory about toilet training.
2. Why would parents trust Dr. Spock's theories rather than developing theories of their own?

When studying parenting and human development, many theories are considered. There are theories about what to eat during pregnancy, or how to handle the pain of childbirth. There are theories about how to maximize a baby's brain development, promote language development, or teach toilet training. Theories help us make sense of the many situations involving parents and children. Some theories are more credible than others. You may develop some theories of your own as you study children, or as you try out some of the theories mentioned in this textbook in your own interactions with the children in your life.

Figure 1.12
Dr. Benjamin Spock (1903–1998) was a pediatrician whose theories about child care helped to guide parents around the world.

Studying Issues

Life is complex. That is as true for children as for adults and, as a result, issues or concerns may arise. An issue is a problem that parents or children, or both, face. Some issues such as child care, poverty, and child abuse and neglect are explored in detail in this textbook. Some will be explored through the research you will do in the course.

When issues are explored in the **public domain** (on television, in the media, and in public debates), we sometimes get a distorted view. There are often problems associated with studies as quoted in newspapers and explored in the media. The quality of the research may be unknown, the reporter may use only the newsworthy results to complete the study, or conclusions may be based on a small sample size.

When examining various issues, it is important to be open-minded as well as critical, and to focus on reliable sources.

Issues involving children require careful consideration. You may be faced with some of the same issues that face many children and families in your own life, now or in the future. Issues can be studied and analyzed to make them less of a threat and transform them into a problem that can be understood or solved.

Steps in an Issue Analysis

1. Define the issue (e.g., teen pregnancy).
2. Identify who is involved in the issue (e.g., both teen parents and their parents).
3. Consider the position each person holds and why (e.g., his parents want her to give the baby up for adoption, he wants her to marry him, she wants to drop out of school to raise the baby, her parents want her to stay single and stay in school).
4. Determine current views that are held on the issue, and identify whose position these views support (e.g., a teen parent can stay in school and raise a child at the same time).
5. Locate additional research or information from reliable sources that supports the different views (e.g., statistics regarding how many teen mothers get married, give their children up for adoption, or raise their children alone).
6. Identify the argument in favour of each view.
7. Determine which view you hold and why.

❖ Connections

1. Make a list of issues or concerns that you think are important for children, adolescents, and parents in our society today. Select one, and conduct an issue analysis using the steps outlined above.

Figure 1.13
Whether you are beginning or continuing your study of children and parents, you will learn about the children in your life today and in the future. You will expand your knowledge and understanding and find many ways to make connections between what you learn and the real world of human development and parenting. Enjoy the next step on your journey.

Chapter Summary

Chapter Highlights

- This chapter introduced you to the study of children through the eyes of a social scientist.
- There are many reasons for studying children, particularly if you have children in your life now, or will have children in your life or career in the future.
- Social scientists examine children through observation, participatory observation, personal interview, phenomenology (life story), survey, experimentation, historical research, a review of literature, or official statistics.
- The social science research method begins with a research question that is answered by gathering relevant information. The information, which is analyzed, organized, and summarized, can be presented in a variety of ways.
- Besides conducting research, social scientists examine a variety of issues and theories relating to children.
- Many issues and theories are presented in this textbook, which has been designed to cover a range of information about parenting and human development in a social context.

Review and Extend Your Learning

1. Reread the letter from the authors in the Introduction to this book. Write a letter to them explaining what you are studying, why you chose the course, and what you hope to learn. **C**

2. Why is it beneficial to study children? Identify the ways in which you can personally benefit from studying children. **K/U A**

3. Describe the discipline of social science. Investigate how it is similar to or different from other disciplines. **K/U T/I**

4. Take a tour of this text. Look at the unit openers and chapter openers to get an idea of what each chapter is about. Refer to the Introduction if you need to. Write a brief synopsis of what you will learn by using this text. **K/U C A**

5. Identify the organizers and features contained in this text. Plan a list of strategies to use them to help you in your own learning process. **K/U A**

6. Using a topic of interest to you, discuss the differences that quantitative and qualitative research would contribute to the analysis of the topic. **K/U** **A**

7. Social science research uses a variety of methods. Formulate a research question to demonstrate this social science approach. **T/I** **A**

8. Research studies are published in scholarly journals such as the *Canadian Home Economics Journal*. Journal articles are available online and from local libraries. Locate a research study in a journal, and identify the headings used to organize the study. Discuss your findings with another student. Compare the organization of your research study to his or hers. Do they follow the same format? **T/I** **C**

9. Reread "What the experts say" on page 5.
   a) Select quotes from the article that support Robert Glossop's theory about sound parenting practices.
   b) What role does research play at The Vanier Institute of the Family? **K/U** **T/I**

Research Opportunity

10. Find the Statistics Canada Web site on the Internet, and then find an example of official statistics from the most recent Canadian Census. Suggest a research topic that could make use of the statistics you find.

Unit 2 Historical and Cultural Perspectives of Childhood

This unit provides a rich foundation and background for learning about children and childhood. The history of childhood is examined, as is the world of play. You will discover how observing children at play adds to your knowledge and understanding of them. This unit also looks at the many ways that parents and children are influenced by Canada's rich cultural and religious diversity.

KEY INSIGHTS:

- Children and childhood have changed throughout history.
- Play is essential for development.
- Play enhances human growth at all stages of life.
- Cultural heritage shapes children and child-rearing practices.
- Culture and heritage influence how children are raised and valued around the world.
- Children and parents are influenced by cultural and religious diversity.

Unit at a Glance

Children and Childhood: A History

By the end of this chapter, you will be able to:

- examine the historical roles of children in families and society

- identify a variety of historical, social, and cultural differences in children

- explain various historical global influences on children and childhood

- identify and evaluate various child-rearing practices and beliefs and parenting techniques practised in the past

Important Terms

adolescence

bride price

chattels

childhood

dowry

midwife

parenting

rite of passage

Chapter at a Glance

What Is Childhood?

All humans go through a period of time known as **childhood**. According to the dictionary definition, childhood is the state or period of being a child between infancy and **adolescence**. It is a time of play and of rapid growth, incredible learning, and mastery of skills for daily living. In childhood, individuals also discover where they belong in their families, communities, and country.

Childhood is considered a special time of life in Canada today. Children are protected and kept apart from adult society in many ways. Most are kept from the adult realities of birth, death, jobs, unemployment, and daily hardships. They have few responsibilities or roles in the adult world. They play at home, go to child care, or attend school, where they are grouped with children their own age.

Childhood was not always this way in Canada. In earlier times, it was much harder to distinguish children from adults. They were an integral part of adult society.

Figure 2.1
Children are smaller than adults. Their facial features are less formed, their hair softer, their hands pudgier, and their voices higher. Their behaviour and activities set them apart from the adult population.

Children and Adolescents Throughout History

Canada's early history is based on two stories. One is the story of the Aboriginal peoples who were the country's first inhabitants and knew its wilderness. The other is the story of the Europeans who explored and settled what was for them an unknown country. Even though the groups were different in many ways, they shared an understanding of what it meant to struggle for survival each day of their lives. This reality shaped the lives of their children.

Aboriginal Childhood and Adolescence

Before the arrival of Europeans, Aboriginal populations existed in areas from the Arctic Circle to the tip of South America. They lived in kin groups with strong and separate identities and distinct languages. Many Aboriginal peoples were nomadic hunters and gatherers and followed the migration patterns of wildlife. Whether they were coastal, woodland, plains, northern, or southern peoples, they had one goal in common: survival.

The daily tasks of hunting animals, gathering edible plants and seeds, fishing, planting, food storage, or food preparation were all necessary for survival. Men and women had distinct roles to play. Besides

Figure 2.2
Many Inuit women today follow the tradition of carrying their infants on their backs. In the past, this method kept infants from harm while their mothers worked.

■ Older Aboriginal children were expected to care for their younger siblings.

hunting, trapping, or fishing, men took responsibility for making the weapons and tools needed to secure food. As bearers, women carried food back to the camp or belongings to the next location. They prepared food, dug roots, picked berries and nuts, and dried fish, meat, and fruit for winter survival. Caring for young children was an integral part of the day's work. Whether it was a sling, a shawl, a backboard, or a pouch, infants were carried while mothers continued to do the work required for the survival of their community.

Historically, children were valued in Aboriginal cultures and treated with respect. A child was as much a member of the community as an adult. The birth of a child tied families more closely to their ancestors. Children were not a burden because child care was often a collective task in the kin group. Everyone contributed to nurturing and socializing children. The elderly within the community played the valued role of sharing their wisdom with the young and guided them in the spiritual and ritual customs of their culture.

Aboriginal children experienced independence, which was highly valued. Their behaviour was directed through the telling of moral tales, and was held in check or corrected by the shame associated with disappointing the larger group.

Talking Parenting

Aboriginal Child-Rearing Practices

Rosemary Forbes describes what she has learned about traditional child-rearing practices in her Aboriginal community. This article originally appeared in *Child Care Focus,* a magazine produced by the Manitoba Child Care Association.

I was born and raised on the Lake St. Martin Reserve about 300 kilometres north of Winnipeg. I was one of thirteen children born to my mother who is still living on the reserve. When I was a young girl, my mother taught me how to care for my younger brothers and sisters. I am a mother and a grandmother now, and I am teaching and encouraging my daughters in the traditions of Aboriginal child rearing.

One of the most effective ways of helping a newborn or one-year-old baby to sleep is to wrap them snugly in a flannelette blanket. The arms should be placed crosswise or straight down, then wrap them tightly, but not too tight. This tightening of the wrapping makes a baby feel secure and warm. It also promotes muscle building and spine firmness. This wrapping serves the same as the Tikinagan—a straight board frame, but the Tikinagan also serves as a socializing tool. It holds the baby up for a period of time, and the baby observes people and things around him or her. The Tikinagan is widely used up in Northern Manitoba in the St. Theresa Point area, although very few are used in Winnipeg.

My mother still makes wrap-arounds, moccasins that are made like mukluks, but with a slit in the front with two long strips of leather to tie on the foot. When a baby starts to walk and is able to wear shoes, it is a tradition of some Native mothers to put wrap-arounds on their babies. These wrap-arounds make walking easier and help to keep the feet warm. Our Native mothers believe a baby's foot should be comfortable when walking. The wrap-arounds stay on the baby's feet, even for babies who do not keep their shoes on.

To make house cleaning faster, my mother used to make a hammock in the bedroom. It served for nap time for the baby while the housework had to be done. The baby would sleep for two hours. The hammock was made of fisherman's string and two large spikes that were inserted in the wall across from each other. The string (double-lined) was tied across and hung down in a large loop about four to six feet (120 cm to 180 cm) off the floor. A flannelette blanket was put on the overlapping string. A pillow was put in between the two strings to make a soft cushion to lie on. The baby was put on this pillow and was tied with a flannelette diaper folded like a triangle to keep her or him in place. The baby was then swayed back and forth until she or he fell asleep.

My mother also used cloth diapers. They were made of flannelette material. Pampers were not heard of when I was helping my mother bring up my younger siblings. Flannelette diapers are less expensive and they are easy to wash. I encourage my daughters to use cloth diapers on their babies.

Rosemary Forbes has worked as a trainer, teaching self-awareness in places such as Yellowquill College. She holds a Native Human Service Certificate.

As male children grew old enough to spend time away from the female caregivers, they joined their fathers, uncles, and other male elders in the daily pursuit of food and the production of necessary implements. Female children joined the women in food preparation, carrying, gathering, and making blankets, clothing, and adornment. Older girls also cared for younger children. The roles of male and female were clearly delineated as part of the socialization process. Male children imitated and learned the male role, while female children imitated and learned the female role. There was a smooth transition between boy and man, girl and woman.

The transition from childhood to adulthood was fairly rapid. Boys achieved adult status when they were able to complete a task of adult significance, such as killing a moose. Girls became adults when they began menstruating. In many groups, depending on their religious and cultural beliefs, rituals and ceremonies marked the significant event that symbolized the transition to adulthood. Social scientists call the ceremonial recognition for achieving adulthood a **rite of passage**.

Marriage was the next step after puberty was reached. The wishes of the parents and elders of the community prevailed. The elders chose a young person's spouse and either a **bride price** or **dowry** was paid. A bride price was either a token or goods given to the father of the bride by the groom as a form of payment for the bride. The dowry was goods or property given to the groom's family in return for marrying the bride. After the marriage ceremony and celebration, the newly married couple, likely 14 and 16 years old, took their place in adult society.

■ After the marriage ceremony, the new couple took their place in society.

❖ Checkpoints

1. Describe the roles played by Aboriginal women and men in the past.
2. Give examples of ways in which the lives of an Aboriginal boy and girl were different.
3. How did Aboriginal children move from childhood into adulthood?

The European Experience

Canada's primary European settlers, the French and the English, brought with them their laws, religion, language, culture, and respective histories. Paintings of family life in Europe before the settlers' migration to Canada provide a rich source of information about many aspects of their life, including how children were viewed and treated. The paintings can be found in museums and art history books.

From 1200 to 1500

Paintings between 1200 and 1500 depicted children as miniature versions of adults. They were dressed and looked like small adults. The role of children in society at that time was not separate from that of adults. Children participated in all areas of adult life. They were expected to work with adults in whatever capacity they could and were present at births, deaths, sick beds, parties, and festivals. They were essential beings who, if they died in childhood, were replaced by the next child that came along. Many parents tried not to love and adore their children because many died of illness and disease in childhood.

Before the 1500s, some children in Europe were seen as the property or **chattels** of their fathers and could be killed, abandoned, or even sold into slavery. They were typically beaten for their misdeeds. They did not receive a formal education, but learned the family trade or worked in the kitchen or stables of other families in the community for their food and lodging.

From 1500 to 1800

After 1500 and the spread of Christianity, the outlook for children in Europe changed dramatically. The Christian view was that children had souls so they should be protected and instructed in the "right way." Paintings from the 1500s to the 1800s reflect this change. Infants were much more cherubic and angelic looking and were often shown in the arms of their mothers. Although still dressed in adult clothing, children were painted with childlike features and were shown participating in activities resembling games and play.

From 1800 to 1900

By the 1800s, there were distinct differences between the children of the upper classes and the children of the poor. Schooling, private tutoring, and religious training were available for the wealthy. Lower class children were not given a formal education in schools. They worked alongside adults, and, as Europe became more industrialized, many became factory workers. Children were valued for their size. They could fit under machines where they set up yarns for weaving and carpet-making, or cleaned and oiled fittings. Industrial accidents involving small children were not uncommon. In England, orphaned, abandoned, and poor children were often rounded up and used as chimney sweeps. They were just the right size to climb up the inside

Figure 2.3
In paintings between 1200 and 1500, children were depicted as small adults.

Figure 2.4
Because of their size, small children were useful in the textile industry. They worked long hours in dirty and unsafe conditions. Illness and accidental deaths were common.

of a chimney and clear it of soot and obstructions. Many died from falls, from the excessive heat of the bricks, and from getting stuck in the narrow confines of the chimney.

Toward the late 1800s, the industrial era was in full swing. Mechanization improved so much that children and youth were no longer needed in factories. Without jobs, idle young people became a problem for society. The solution was to get children off the streets and into schools. Children of the lower classes had a chance to better themselves as more educational opportunities became available. Churches were the first to provide schooling, followed by the government. By the end of the 1800s, most children in Britain and Europe attended school, and compulsory education was promoted in many countries.

❖ Checkpoints

1. Describe the lives of children in Europe from 1200 to 1800.
2. How did industrialization change the lives of European children?

❖ Connections

1. Contrast the lives of children in Canada today with those of European children in historical times.
2. Propose some reasons why the attitudes of adults and parents toward children in historical times are different from those held by adults and parents today.

A History of Children in Canada

By the late 1600s, French settlers had established small communities in Quebec, where men significantly outnumbered women. To generate a population in the New World, the king of France, Louis XIV, offered transportation and a dowry to any woman who was willing to go to New France to find a husband. Starting in 1663, more than 700 women arrived in Canada to become wives and mothers. Some were as young as 13 and 14 and came from orphanages in France. They became known as "les filles du roi" or "daughters of the king." By 1671, the governor, who was determined to increase the French population, penalized bachelorhood. Many French Canadians today can trace their roots to these marriages. The plan was successful, and as more and more children were born in the New World, many hands became available to do the work of clearing the land, building shelter, and preserving food to survive the harsh winters.

Settlers from the British Isles also started to arrive in North America in the early 1600s. Their population grew quickly. They settled mainly in the Thirteen Colonies along the Atlantic seaboard in territory that later became the United States. Some landed and settled in the Maritimes.

Many of the original settlers came to the New World to escape religious persecution. They were strongly influenced by their strict Protestant religious faith, which shaped their child-rearing practices. Parents believed that if you spared the rod, you would spoil the child, so discipline involved physical punishment. Children could not speak until spoken to. They were expected to work with their parents from sunrise to sunset. Because idle hands invited the work of the devil, girls were encouraged to sew or embroider, and boys were given the job of polishing shoes, mending harnesses, or whittling and carving in their free time. A strong work ethic helped the British settlers survive in the New World.

When the Thirteen Colonies gained their independence from Britain and became the United States, the colonists who remained loyal to Britain moved to what is now Canada in return for free farmland. These colonists were called the United Empire Loyalists, and included Black Americans and Aboriginal people. The Loyalists settled mainly in the Maritimes and Upper Canada (known today as Ontario) and formed the first large non-Aboriginal population in these areas. They brought their own customs of family interaction and child rearing with them.

For the families arriving in the New World, survival was difficult. They often looked to the Aboriginal peoples for ways to hunt, fish, and prepare and preserve food, as well as how to care for children. More freedom and less punishment were modelled to encourage independence and self-reliance in children. As with their Aboriginal counterparts, the children of settlers had distinct male and female role models. Girls worked with their mothers and took over child-care roles as they got older. The boys helped their fathers cut down trees, break the ground, plant crops, hunt, trap, and fish.

Figure 2.5
The women sent to New France by King Louis XIV to become wives for the early settlers were called "les filles du roi" or "daughters of the king."

■ Survival in Upper Canada was difficult for the United Empire Loyalists.

The Role of the Church

The Roman Catholic Church played a large part in the lives of the French Canadian settlers. It provided much direction in the religious education and socialization within the community. Schooling soon became a concern in the New World. Jesuit brothers and Ursuline nuns sent out from France were the first to set up and teach in the schools in the new colony. In addition to basic lessons, girls learned to sew and embroider, while boys learned Latin with the hope that some would go into the priesthood. Marriage or entering a religious order were the two options for girls. Every French Canadian family was expected to produce at least one nun and one priest in every generation. The eldest son in each family was expected to look after his parents in their old age by forming an extended family with them.

A Story of a Real Canadian Pioneer Family in New France

François-Pierre Cherrier immigrated to New France in 1732 from Metz, in eastern France. Almost continuous war in this part of France drove many to the New World. His uncle, a parish priest south of Montreal, welcomed the young man, who became a storekeeper or merchant.

Shortly after arriving, François-Pierre met and married Marie Dubuc. They had nine children—four boys and five girls. One girl died in infancy. The rest of the girls married and, amongst them, produced the first mayor of Montreal (Dénis-Benjamin Viger), the first bishop of Montreal (Jean-Jacques Lartigue), and the leader of the Lower Canada Rebellion (Louis-Joseph Papineau).

The boys received a Jesuit education in a time where few people could read and write. The eldest son followed his great-uncle into the priesthood. Two younger sons became land surveyors. Another son, Joseph-Marie, became a cooper or barrel-maker and married Marie-Josephte Gate Bellefleur in 1777, when she was about 17. Marie-Josephte had at least 12 children from 1777 until 1800 when she died, aged 40. Joseph-Marie's older children likely helped by looking after their younger siblings. There is some evidence he remarried a younger woman after his first wife's death. Early Quebec was no place for a widower with 12 children. Later, Joseph-Marie and his siblings looked after their elderly parents when one of a series of economic depressions ruined the livelihood they had earned as merchants. Today, their descendants can still see evidence of the child rearing and family patterns of their French Canadian ancestors.

❖ Checkpoints

1. Describe a typical childhood in early French Canada.
2. What roles did the family, church, and education system play in raising children?
3. How closely did the Cherrier family follow the French Canadian family traditions described in the chapter?

❖ Connections

1. Reflect on the role of religion in family life and education in Canada today.
2. How do the roles of male and female children in early Canada compare with the roles of male and female children today?

Families in Pioneer Canada

Settlements soon grew and spread across Canada. Besides the French, English, Scottish, and Irish settlers, people of other origins began to make Canada their home. As early as 1775, Black families came to Nova Scotia and southern Ontario to escape American slavery, although some were also bought and sold as slaves in Canada. Male Chinese of all ages came to Canada to build the Canadian Pacific

Origins of the Canadian Population, 1881–1911

Origin	1881	1901	1911
Aboriginal	108 547	127 941	105 611
Austrian	-	10 947	44 036
Belgian	-	2 994	9 664
Black	21 394	17 437	16 994
Chinese	4 383	17 312	27 831
Dutch	30 412	33 845	55 961
English	881 301	1 260 899	1 871 268
Finnish	-	2 502	15 500
French	1 298 929	1 649 371	2 061 719
German	254 319	310 501	403 417
Greek	-	291	3 614
Hungarian	-	1 549	11 648
Irish	957 403	988 721	1 074 738
Italian	1 849	10 834	45 963
Japanese	-	4 738	9 067
Jewish	667	16 131	76 199
Polish	-	6 285	33 652
Russian	1 227	19 825	44 376
Scandinavian	5 223	31 042	112 682
Scottish	699 863	800 154	1 027 015
Ukrainian	-	5 682	75 432
Others	59 293	52 314	80 256
TOTALS	4 324 810	5 371 315	7 206 643

Adapted from Statistics Canada publication "Historical Statistics of Canada," Catalogue 11–516, 1983

Figure 2.6
The population of Canada became increasingly diverse between 1881 and 1911.

Railway. Later, Chinese families followed the gold rush and settled along the West Coast of Canada. At the beginning of the 20th century, Ukrainian, Polish, Hungarian, Dutch, and other families from Europe welcomed the opportunity to obtain farmland in the western provinces and establish their own communities. People came from Finland to northern Ontario to work in the logging industry and settled primarily in Port Arthur and Fort William, which later joined to become the city of Thunder Bay. In some cases, entire families arrived together. In other cases, the men came first and the women and children followed.

Case Study: Neesha's Heritage

"See, there it is!" Neesha was excited about showing her history fair project to her grandmother. She watched her grandmother adjust her glasses and look at the display. Gramma Brown read the bold letters declaring A History of Blacks in Canada. She looked attentively at the family photographs. There was one of herself on her wedding day in 1941, wearing the cream-coloured suit and flowered hat that she wore to church for many years afterwards. Her husband looked so serious and dashing in his uniform, about to go off to the war that made her a widow. Her parents stood proudly beside her, and her own grandmother who told her all those stories, stood stooped over leaning on her cane, but looking so pleased.

Then she carefully read the stories that Neesha had typed up for the display; the stories she had heard as a young girl, of how her own grandmother came to Canada as a slave of a rich British colonist who settled in Mount Royal, Quebec. Her grandmother had worked long hours, washing laundry by hand, scrubbing oak floors, emptying chamber pots, serving meals, and washing dishes. Late in the evening, she collected her two children from O'Mama who was too old to work up at the house. Then she went back to the cabin she shared with her little family. Her grandmother knew about the problem of balancing work and family a hundred years or more before it became a popular sociological issue.

Neesha waited happily as her grandmother read of the struggle of the first Blacks in Canada to form a community. Gramma admired the map showing the location and dates of Black settlements. Then she followed the flow chart with her gnarled old fingers, that showed the progression of Blacks coming into Canada, first as slaves, then as those fleeing slavery in the United States, and then more recently as immigrants from the Caribbean and other countries around the world. She nodded as she read of the contributions of Blacks to Canada, and finally, she read every word in Neesha's essay, "The Role of Black Canadians in the Founding of Canada."

Gramma Brown touched the first-place ribbon tacked to the display and heaved a great sigh. "That sure is something, Neesha," she said, tears shining at the corners of her eyes. "It makes me feel like I really belong!" Neesha hugged her and said, "You know Gramma, that means more to me than any first-place ribbon ever could."

Questions

1. What role did slavery play in the history of Black Canadians?
2. How does Neesha's grandmother's story compare to the challenges that are faced by parents in Canada and throughout the world today?

For families who came to Canada before the 1900s, life expectancy was low and infant mortality was high. Penicillin had not been discovered and did not become widely available until after the Second World War. Epidemics of typhus, diphtheria, smallpox, and tuberculosis often wiped out entire communities. Babies were born at home, either with or without the help of a **midwife** (a local woman who had years of experience delivering babies) or a relative or neighbour.

As with the children in Europe, those who did survive infancy worked with their parents on farms or in the family trade or business. Public schooling became available in most provinces in the 1800s. Except in Quebec, where French was the first language, children in public schools across Canada were expected to learn to speak, read, and write English. They could speak their language of origin in the home, but they faced discrimination if they spoke it outside of the home. These first-generation Canadian children provided an important link between the customs and culture of the New World and those of their immigrant parents. Often, young children were used as translators for their parents who spoke neither English nor French. These children learned about financial and legal worlds long before their English- or French-speaking counterparts.

❖ Checkpoints

1. Based on the "Origins of the Canadian Population" chart, which ethnic group formed the largest number in 1881? in 1901? in 1911?

2. What do the statistics tell us about the effect of immigration on family life in Canada?

3. How long has your family been in Canada? How far back in Canada's history do your family stories go? If your family is new to Canada, what is your family history? Share and compare family histories with your classmates.

Canadian Orphans and Street Kids

By the mid- to late 1800s, cities in Canada began to grow rapidly. Families that left their harsh rural existence with the hope of finding paid employment in the cities often found that their lives were not easier. Every bite of food had to be purchased from their wages. Often, male children left school to find some means of making money to help out. Jobs as shoeshine boys, paper boys, and delivery boys earned them only a small amount of money. To complicate matters, many children lost parents to illness, disease, or accidents before they reached their teen years. There were some orphanages, and relatives were sometimes able to take them in, but quite often they ended up on their own or even in prison. Children living on the streets became known as street urchins, waifs, strays, or guttersnipes and were considered a menace to society.

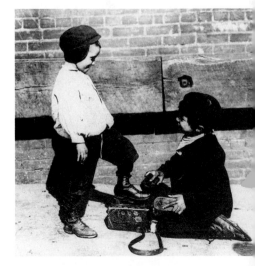

Figure 2.7
In the 1880s, neglected children were very visible on the streets of Toronto. Some tried to survive by working as shoeshine boys.

Because children living on the streets had little or no education or training, they were unlikely to find a paying position. Those who did work for wages earned so little that it barely paid for food, let alone lodgings. In winter, the situation became dire, and many died of exposure or had their feet amputated because of frostbite. Young women also began to move to the cities to find work in service positions. Some worked for well-to-do-families, but those who could not earn their keep often turned to prostitution.

Youth unemployment became a problem. As in Europe, the answer was schooling. High schools became more common in the early 1900s when more and more children between the ages of 13 and 16 stayed in school. Street children gained skills in reform schools and training schools. In the end, most provinces made schooling mandatory for children up to 16 years of age. This kept young people out of the work force and off the streets while providing them with the education and training needed for employment. According to Margaret Visser in an article for The Vanier Institute's *Transition* magazine (December, 1990), the term "teenage" was first used on March 11, 1921. A journalist for the *Daily Colonist* in Victoria, British Columbia, is credited with creating the term, and, subsequently, its use spread widely.

❖ Checkpoints

1. In the mid- to late 1800s, children were often orphaned. Outline some of the ways orphaned children lived.
2. How did the rise of cities in Canada affect the lives of families and children?
3. Why did schooling become important?

❖ Connections

1. Throughout history, schooling has played various roles in the lives of children. Compare the role of schooling for children today with the role of schooling in the late 1800s and early 1900s.
2. Historically, the purpose of schooling was to prepare children for the work force. Is this still true today? Explain.
3. To what extent does the problem of street kids continue in today's society?

Parenting and Child Care in the Past

The word **parenting** is a relatively new term in our vocabulary. In the past, child rearing was the term used to describe what parents did. A parent's job was to feed, clothe, care for, and guide his or her children, so that they could become good citizens, good workers, and parents of the next generation. How parents did that job depended on their culture, their religious beliefs, and their experiences as children. The effectiveness of child-rearing practices was not an issue of particular focus for families or societies. Child rearing was taken for granted and was considered an integral part of life and family function.

Large families, harsh conditions, and religious values led many new Canadians settling this country to use strict discipline and physical punishment to make their children behave. Raising children was a private venture. Parents expected children to "mind" or obey them and any other adult in the community. Speaking only when spoken to was the basic rule for most children. Although religion, social expectations, and local customs set the norms for how parents raised their children, there was also a belief that the way in which parents raised their children was their own business.

Parents learned how to raise their children from their own parents or from other family members. Their own childhood experiences were their guide to how they raised their own children. Experts on how to parent in those days were family members, friends, and members of the community. Then, during the 1800s, a new medium for learning how to parent appeared: women's magazines. Often, men advised women on how to manage the problems that came with raising children.

How parents cared for their children became much more of a public concern after scientists learned more about how to prevent disease and illness. By the end of the 1800s, the public health movement in Canada was gaining momentum. Ontario was the first province with a health board, but other provinces soon followed. Sanitation and hygiene were the focus of the health board. How families handled human waste and promoted cleanliness were major issues. It became the duty of public health officials to educate families, as well as doctors and teachers. Vaccinations became available for smallpox, and families were expected to enforce quarantines to prevent diphtheria epidemics. Books that instructed parents on how to prevent illness and disease became popular. In Ontario, Adelaide Hoodless pioneered the teaching of domestic science to women in schools so that they

■ In many families in the past, children were expected to be "seen but not heard."

Figure 2.8
Access to health care is an integral part of parenting in Canada today.

would know how to feed and clothe their families and protect them from disease. She took up this work because her infant son had died from drinking bacteria-laden milk.

❖ Connections

1. In the 1800s, what resources did parents have to help them raise their children?

2. Go back in time to the late 1880s, when radio and television have not yet been invented. Many Canadians cannot read or even speak English. Your job as a health official is to educate as many Canadians as possible about the importance of sanitation, hygiene, and vaccination. What is your plan?

Expert Advice for Parents

After it became acceptable to teach parents how to protect their children from illness and disease and reduce infant mortality, it also became acceptable to instruct them on how to manage their children. In the late 1800s and early 1900s, a growing interest in Sigmund Freud's psychoanalytic theories relating adult behaviour to early childhood experience gave rise to experts who felt it was their duty to tell parents how to raise their children. Some of what was written at the time seems humorous now, yet it did influence entire generations of parents and children. As information became available about the role parents could play in improving quality of life for children, it became socially acceptable to provide families with guidance on how to improve their child-rearing practices.

One such expert on child rearing was Henry P. Chavasse. His guide, published in Toronto in 1880 by Willing and Williamson, was an example of the kind of instruction directed at parents, mothers in particular, during this time. The title of the book, which does not leave any doubt about its intent, is *Advice to a Mother on the Management of Her Children and on the Treatment on the Moment of Some of Their More Pressing Illnesses and Accidents*. According to Chavasse, the task of child rearing fell squarely on the shoulders of mothers. He wrote:

> The care and management, and consequently the health and future well-doing of the child, principally devolve upon the mother; 'for it is the mother after all that has most to do with the making or marring of the man.' (1880, p. 2)

Chavasse divided the book into three parts. The first dealt with infancy and included suggestions for hygiene under such titles as

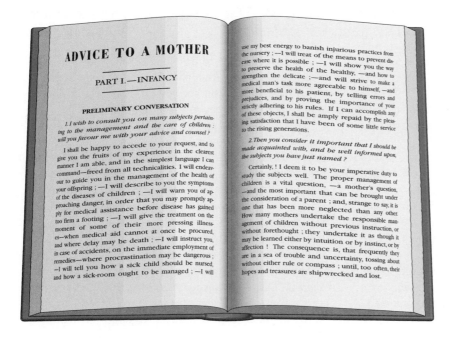

Figure 2.9
In his book, Chavasse directed his child-rearing advice at the mother.

Ablution, Management of the Navel, Vaccination, Dentition, Diet, Exercise, Sleep, The Bladder and the Bowels, and Ailments and Diseases. The second part focused on childhood and included the usual topics of Sleep, and Exercise and Diet, as well as Education, Amusements, Warm Baths, and Warm External Applications. The final section was called Boyhood and Girlhood. It focused on older children and adolescents, although there was no label for adolescents at the time. Again, the usual hygiene topics were covered, as well as Household Work for girls and Choice of Profession or Trade for boys.

Today, advice and guidance on how to raise children is extensively available. Popular magazines, some devoted specifically to parenting, contain the latest advice for parents. There are literally thousands of books available on subjects ranging from "how to raise an intelligent child" to "how to teach your teenager about money." Research into child-rearing practices of parents over the past 50 years supports specific practices for parents that may enhance the development of children.

Today, parents look for sources of information and inspiration. Many experts provide information to parents about child rearing. Parents must decide who has the most relevant and reliable information. One such expert is Kathy Lynn, a parenting educator.

Figure 2.10
Kathy Lynn is a parenting educator from British Columbia.

Canada's Leading Speaker on Parenting and Family Issues

The following material is excerpted from www.parentingtoday.ca.

Kathy Lynn is Canada's leading advocate for children, parents, and families, and the most recognized parenting educator in the country.

Over three decades of speaking to parents and professionals about kids and families, Kathy has helped thousands of moms and dads become better parents and has made a big difference in the lives of Canada's children. She is now host of *Parenting Today*, a weekly one-hour interview and phone-in radio program on CKNW in Vancouver.

In her keynote addresses to parent groups and members of the helping professions, her work on television and radio, and her newspaper and magazine columns, Kathy inspires parents to re-dedicate themselves to raising their children.

"All parents want to do a better job of raising their kids," says Kathy. "Grandparents want to help as well. When they come to me for advice or support and it works back home, they're delighted and so am I."

Kathy's career in parenting education began when her children were young and she sought help for the day-to-day challenges of raising children. There was very little professional help available, so she trained as a parenting educator and began leading parenting classes. She now devotes much of her time as a professional speaker for conventions, workshops, and seminars for school groups, parents, and professionals in British Columbia and across Canada.

She is a regular weekly contributor on the *Bill Good Show* on CKNW in Vancouver and has a daily parenting advice spot on NW News, for the Corus Entertainment Network. She also writes regular columns for *Today's Parent Magazine*.

Child Care in the Past

Canada was primarily a rural nation for many years. The majority of Canadians lived on farms or properties large enough to support a family. Women had their daily work to complete on the family farm. Housework, pumping water, laundry, gardening, food preparation, food preservation, weaving, sewing, knitting, and even tending poultry were some of their usual jobs. They cared for their children, finding ways to manage the household chores while keeping their children in sight yet out of the way. The cradle and later the playpen were used to contain small children while the daily tasks were being completed.

Family members were called upon if, for some reason, child care was needed. Grandparents often lived nearby or even in the same home. Boys who were not old enough to spend the whole day with fathers helped with household chores and watched younger siblings. Daughters, sisters, sisters-in-law, cousins, or aunts could usually be called upon to help with child care. In cases where family was not close by, a neighbour could be asked to help out. Most children were cared for in their own homes. Child care as we know it did not exist until the Second World War, but the local school provided a place for children over the age of five.

Figure 2.11
In the past, children who needed care were often looked after by relatives in their own home. Today, it is common for children to be cared for by professionals in child care outside the home.

In certain circumstances, outside help was necessary. Having a hired girl was often the solution. Girls as young as 10 were hired as mother's helpers. Some were orphans who were grateful for food and a place to sleep in exchange for caring for children and doing housework. Others came from large families or poor families and used their small wages to help out at home. Girls often came from farms into towns and cities, hoping for better prospects. Not all hired girls were treated well, and few were paid well. They put in long hours, did the heavy work, and were sometimes beaten as punishment for working slowly, overlooking a task, or breaking a dish. The opposite was also true. Some hired girls were well cared for and felt like members of the family.

Since the post-war economic expansion in the 1950s, women have entered the work force in increasing numbers. Families rely more and more on the income of two parents to meet their needs. Since both parents often leave the home for paid work and many children are cared for in formal child-care settings outside the home, the number of people required to provide child care has increased dramatically. Today, formal education is often necessary to become a recognized child-care worker.

Children in Canada Today

What are children like today and how have they changed? By observing children in a classroom or community setting, by having conversations with children of different ages, and by reading research studies, it is possible to get a good picture of what children are like today.

Children no longer work from dawn to dusk in the shadow of their parents and spend far more time at play than at family chores. Schooling and education have changed significantly. By law, children are expected to attend school regularly from age 4 until 16 years of age, and many are expected to complete high school and go on to higher levels of education. They achieve adult status later in life, marry later, and spend more years in the company of others the same age than children did in the first half of the 1900s.

Some social scientists are now suggesting that, in reality, children are not isolated from adult society. In fact, because of graphic media images, video, television, and computer games, they are definitely exposed to all aspects of the adult world from a very early age. Sex, birth, and especially death are everyday events in what they see in the media. Children today experience stress levels far above those of

■ *Children haven't changed. Childhood has.*
— Barbara Oehlberg

Figure 2.12
Canadian children today spend most of their time learning through play.

children as recently as 20 or 30 years ago. Evidence of this is found in *The Progress of Canada's Children 2001*, the fifth in a series of annual reports from the Canadian Council on Social Development, which monitors the well-being of children, youth, and families, and includes recent studies that reveal some interesting information about the lives of children today. Highlights from this report appear below. Although childhood in Canada today has changed a great deal from the past, children and families continue to experience similar challenges as well as new and different challenges.

Highlights from *The Progress of Canada's Children 2001*

- Most school-aged children have close friends. In addition, 92 percent of pre-teens and young teens feel they have someone other than their friends that they can talk to if they have a problem; 86 percent said they could talk to their mother.
- Feelings of pressure for good grades have increased for older students. Twenty-six percent of female Grade 10 students reported "feeling a lot of pressure from school work" in 1998, an increase of 24 percent over 1994. Twenty-one percent of their male counterparts reported similar feelings.

- Most school-aged children have mothers who work outside the home. Nearly 80 percent of women with school-aged children were in the paid labour force in 1999. Over the last two decades, this figure jumped by 42 percent, with most of the increase occurring in the 1980s.
- Family income level affects children's recreation. Sixty percent of children from very poor homes "almost never" participate in supervised sports, compared to 27 percent of their counterparts from well-off homes.

Chapter Summary

Chapter Highlights

- Historically, children of Canada's Aboriginal peoples had definite male and female roles, were nurtured by the entire community, and were disciplined with moral tales and group disapproval rather than punishment.

- The French and English who settled Canada came from a world that did not appear to have much affection for children and did not differentiate between children and adults before the 1500s. Children fared better in the centuries that followed.

- After coming to Canada in the first waves of migration to the new world, children provided much-needed labour on farms and in family trades.

- Education soon became an important element of raising children in Canada. Historically in New France, French priests and nuns taught children.

- In the late 1800s, cities solved the problem of street children with trade schools, elementary schools, and, later, high schools.

- A period of adolescence slowly emerged as children in their teens were kept out of the labour force through compulsory education. Farm labour and domestic service were the options for those not attending school.

- As health and sanitation became important, parents came under greater scrutiny. Information and education regarding child rearing has evolved from being a family responsibility to a societal issue.

- For children in Canada today, some changes are obvious, but their well-being, health, education, and job prospects are still a concern.

Review and Extend Your Learning

1. Define childhood. How has the experience of childhood changed throughout history? **K/U**

2. Children have been viewed differently in various cultures. Compare the historical experience of childhood in Canada's Aboriginal peoples with that of the European experience. **T/I C**

3. Describe some ways in which childhood in the past was different for upper- and lower-class children. **K/U**

4. Identify the reasons there were many orphans in the past. Why is this not the case today? **K/U A**

5. Caring for their children has always been the primary responsibility of parents. Where and how did parents learn how to do this in the past? **K/U**

6. Describe the conditions and events that have led to the popularity of "parenting experts." **K/U T/I**

7. Compare early advice given to parents with the type of advice that is common today. **K/U A**

8. Write a description of an imaginary day in the life of a street kid or a hired girl in the late 1800s or early 1900s. **K/U C**

Research Opportunities

9. Using the material in this chapter as a starting point, develop a research question that focuses on the history of childhood in Europe or in another culture of your choice. Locate two other sources that can help answer your research question. Write a two-page report on your findings, citing your sources within your report and at the end of your report.

10. Locate the oldest "how to parent" book, magazine, or pamphlet you can find. You could ask a family member or neighbour if they have saved one, check the Internet for historical documents, or go to your library or community archives. Answer the following questions:

    a) How old is the resource?

    b) How are parents depicted?

    c) What were the major concerns for raising children at that time? In what ways has advice for children changed?

Issue Analysis

11. Analyze highly publicized cases of child neglect or parental abuse reported by the media to determine how the statement "The way neighbours raised their children was their own business" is viewed in Canada today.

12. Debate whether today's children are protected and kept apart from adult society.

The Universality of Childhood Play

**By the end of this chapter,
you will be able to:**

- outline some of the common aspects of childhood and the experiences of young children in cultures throughout the world

- explain the strategies that encourage age-appropriate behaviour in children's play

- describe play environments that provide conditions for optimal child development

- reflect on your own practical experiences involving children

Important Terms

active play

associative play

cognitive development

cooperative play

emotional development

exuberant play

imaginative play

intellectual development

observation protocol

onlooker play

parallel play

physical development

play therapy

quiet play

social development

solitary play

symbolic play

temperament

Chapter at a Glance

Figure 3.1
Play is universal.

What Is Play?

Children the world over engage in play. They play for the sheer enjoyment they get from their activity. As they use toys and play games, children learn and develop. Children also find out about their culture and the world around them as they play. Observers can learn much about children, their behaviour patterns, and their development simply by watching them play. Observation enables us to step inside the world of children and find out what we ourselves have forgotten.

If you watch children at play anywhere in the world, you will see something interesting. You will see concentration, intensity, and determination. You will see frustration, and you will see delight. For children everywhere, play is a very serious enterprise. In fact, as Friedrich Froebel, a 19th century educational theorist pointed out, "Play is the work of children."

What Is Play?

- Play is educational. It enables children to learn about themselves and the world around them.
- Play provides an opportunity to make important choices and to problem-solve in a very real way.
- Play allows children to use their imaginations and to re-enact familiar behaviours.
- Play is a special place where a child straddles the realm of reality and fantasy. It can be seen as a bridge between the inner world of imagination and the outer world of reality.

- Play offers a familiar routine and a comforting ritual. Some children change environments frequently, by moving, going to different child-care situations in a given day or week, going from one parent's house to another's in shared custody arrangements, or even when travelling with families on vacation.
- Play is a way to work out the frustration and conflicts they may experience from developmental changes.
- Play is a way of making friends no matter where you go.

Play is the work of children.
— Friedrich Froebel

Play: A pleasurable activity engaged in for its own sake, with means emphasized rather than ends. Play is not usually engaged in as a serious activity and is flexible in that it varies in form or context.

Play is a normal process in human development. It provides children with the means to make sense of their world, learn, grow, and continue to find pleasure and enjoyment in toys, games, and playful interaction with others. Children everywhere move forward in their development as a direct result of the experiences they encounter. Their play is both intense and effortless. Babies are fascinated by their fingers and toes and develop in many ways by playing with them. In North America, parents sometimes intervene to improve on nature. Little slippers and mittens in contrasting colours with faces and even sound effects are used to encourage infants to extend their development.

Play and Human Development

The Invest in Kids Foundation is a national non-profit organization that was established for the single purpose of promoting the healthy development of children from birth to age five. The foundation emphasizes that children need to play to grow and develop properly. The three components of effective parenting and caregiving for children up to age five or six are

- play
- comfort
- teaching

Providing play opportunities suitable for each stage of development is an important part of all parenting and care for young children.

As you have already learned, babies the world over enter the realm of play with the discovery of their own hands and feet. As their fingers and toes come into their line of vision, they become objects for play. Babies who have recently discovered their hands and feet are fascinating to watch. They stare intently at them, wave and kick them, and even put them in their mouths. They spend several periods of time throughout the day engaged with their hands and feet.

After babies discover their hands and feet, reaching and grasping are the next step. As they reach out and grab at objects other than their own feet, parents everywhere feel a need to put an object into the little hands. The object may be as complex as a multicoloured intricately designed plastic rattle, or as simple as a piece of wood that has been smoothed on the edge of a stone. Whether the toy is elaborate or simple, if it keeps the child's interest, it is engaging that child in learning.

Moving on to the next level of play happens just as naturally. When is the best time to move on to the next level of play? Children will let you know. At a new level of development, children show that they are ready for the next type of play. They demonstrate their developmental readiness by turning their interest to a new toy or object, or by using a familiar object in a new way.

Play Is Learning

Play is much more than simple amusement. It is the classroom for learning about life. Children engage in play using all of their senses. They see, touch, feel, listen, and smell. When they play, they are

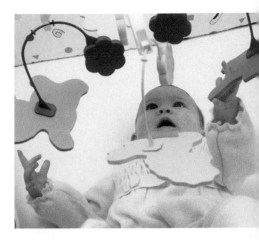

Figure 3.2
Babies learn to reach out and grab objects.

■ Play is much more than simple amusement. It is the classroom for learning about life.

thinking, problem solving, planning, and experimenting. They are scientists, finding out how the world works. They imitate and practise the roles of father, mother, older sister or brother. They imagine a whole range of careers, from firefighter, jet pilot, nurse, animal trainer, and hairdresser, to actor, artist, baker, carpenter, or astronaut. They have conversations, resolve arguments, and accomplish great feats, all in the course of a morning.

Play supports children in all areas of their development. When children use their bodies to catch balls, jump, and run, they are enhancing their physical development. Puzzles, games, and other creative pursuits support intellectual development. Pretend games and dramatic play allow children to develop socially and emotionally. Not all play involves rules, but it does have comforting rituals. Children practise their physical, verbal, and social skills over and over again, without being aware of it. As they master various levels of skill and understanding, they move on to more complex types of play.

Play Therapy

Play has been acknowledged and used as a way to understand a child's spirit or mind. Child psychologists and other child-care professionals use **play therapy** to discover hidden emotions, frustrations, fears, anger, and hostility in children. In the simplest terms, the play therapy professional has a child play with certain toys or objects in a playroom—toys like a dollhouse and a family of dolls, cars, and trucks. The therapist observes and takes note of how the child plays and what the child is saying during play. After several sessions, common themes and recurring patterns are identified. The therapist becomes more aware of the child's underlying problems and may then involve the parents or caregivers in making changes that will help resolve any issues.

Figure 3.3
The great outdoors provides opportunities for children to engage all their senses—to see, touch, hear, and smell the world around them.

Play Is Discovery

Not all play needs to be organized or arranged for children. The great outdoors is an adventure in itself. A park, a backyard, a municipal trail, or a schoolyard can offer varied experiences. Safety demands that parents supervise outdoor play, but, even better, if parents are able, they can join children in poking the ground with a stick, rolling down a hill, making angels in the snow, or following the trail left by a snail.

Interacting with nature offers many opportunities for play. Even in the city, parents can take children on nature walks to find out how plants, birds, and squirrels make their homes. In older European cities, children play soccer or catch in courtyards or squares, which are paved with cement or cobblestones. They float sticks in puddles left after the rain. They run and climb and invent many different ways to play.

Watch children at play and pay attention to the toys they prefer at different ages. Observe how children of various cultures play. Read the age recommendations on the labels of toy packages to see which toys children play with at different stages of development. Remember what you liked to play with when you were younger, and see whether you still have your favourite toy. Get down on the floor and play with children. By doing so, you will relearn what play is all about, how it feels, how it sounds, how it makes sense of the world in which children live.

Play Is Culture

Play is also an expression of culture. The toys and games used most often in a culture embody its values. In urban North America, for example, technology and numeracy are highly valued. Toy computers, cash registers, and calculators bring the world of business and commerce into the playroom. In hunting and gathering societies, spatial skills are highly valued, so games involving accuracy over a distance, such as throwing sticks and hitting targets, are popular. In societies in which language and linguistics are highly valued, books, alphabet blocks, paper, and writing tools are found in most homes. No matter what country, region, or province, children everywhere make their way into the adult world through the doors of play.

Play also reinforces the stereotypes in a society. There is often heated discussion in the playroom about which roles boys and girls can and cannot take on in play. Children reproduce in play the stereotypes they have seen on television, even if their experiences in their own families are very different. Violence, death, and dying find their way into play, no matter how vigilant parents and caregivers might be. Unless their play becomes a danger to others or affects their behaviour in a negative way, children should be allowed to explore and resolve feelings about all aspects of life. After all, playing should also be fun.

Play Is Music, Art, and Drama

Play is also an opportunity for children to explore art, music, and drama. Children everywhere have discovered that if they add water to dirt, they can mould and shape it into many different things. Children draw with sticks or markers. They make sounds, perhaps by banging on things or by blowing on a blade of grass between their thumbs. Many games involve singing or music such as London Bridge or Ring Around the Rosie. Finger games and action songs integrate singing with body movement.

Figure 3.4
In Canada, language and linguistics are highly valued. Paper and writing or drawing tools are readily available to most children.

■ In the past, Aboriginal children were constantly developing the necessary skills to survive. Play was often an opportunity to practise these skills.

Figure 3.5
Children sometimes try out adult roles when they play dress up.

Childhood is a time when children should sing or role-play without self-consciousness. They enjoy dressing up in old clothes and costumes and becoming make-believe characters ranging from mothers and fathers, to doctors, firefighters, or movie stars. At the same time, they are trying on the roles of the adults in their lives. Pretend play, such as wearing a firefighter's helmet, as well as creative activities provide an excellent foundation for introducing children to the pleasures of music, art, and drama.

❖ Checkpoints

1. How does play contribute to human development?
2. How can play be therapeutic for children?

Toys and Human Development

A toy is an object that holds a certain fascination for the person playing with it. In our society, toys are generally manufactured. We most often recognize toys by their shape, their colour, and the fact that they are primarily made from plastic, for durability. However, for a child, anything can be a toy, as long as it engages the child in a focused activity.

Toys are readily available for many children in Canada. Often, relatives and friends buy toys for the new arrival as soon as a pregnancy is announced. Adults, it would appear, like toys just as much as children do. Toys that are outgrown by older children are put away for the next child. Some families even have toys that have been handed down from one generation to the next.

Parents and relatives often buy toys that children are not ready to play with. A basketball for a child who is too small to bounce a ball is going to sit on the shelf. A puzzle with too many pieces, a game with too many rules, or an outdoor play centre that is too difficult to climb will cause frustration and will have to wait until the child is ready. Similarly, after children have mastered a particular skill, they will leave behind the toys, games, or activities with which they once spent so much time. The rattle will be discarded, the push toy abandoned, and the pedal car given up for a tricycle. The world of play changes with every new phase of physical, emotional, and **cognitive development**.

Early childhood educators, parents, caregivers, and baby sitters all need to know which toys are appropriate for which age group.

Suitable Toys for Children

The following guide suggests some toys suitable for each age group. There are many other toys with similar functions, not listed here, that may also be suitable. Always keep toy safety in mind.

The Hand to Mouth Stage (birth to 1 year)
Colourful objects, toys that rattle, musical toys, soft toys to cuddle

The Toddling Stage (1 to 2 years)
Push-pull toys, ride-on toys, large balls to roll and fetch, toys to manipulate, bang on, stack, and sort

The Exploring Stage (2 to 3 years)
Picture books, large-piece puzzles, sandbox with bucket and shovel, toys for water play, wagons, doll strollers

The Pretending Stage (3 to 4 years)
Pop-up books, dress-up clothes, housekeeping and workshop centres, toy phone, dolls and accessories

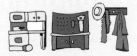

The Creative Stage (4 to 6 years)
Storybooks, costumes, modelling clay, finger paints, art centre, toolbox, craft supplies, building materials, puppet theatre, tabletop sports games

The Active Stage (6 to 10 years)
Skates, skis, scooters, bicycles and related protective gear, craft kits, science kits, battery-operated toys, cookbooks

The Mastery Stage (10 to 14 years)
Hobby supplies, sports equipment, computers, board games, mental challenges, mystery books

Fortunately, many resources available in print or electronic form, or both, provide this information. For instance, the Invest in Kids Web site gives concise and easily understood information.

Professionals and others who serve children in some way also require an understanding of the relationship between play and child development. In a medical clinic, a dental office, a restaurant, or even a hair salon, you see a positive difference if suitable toys and activities for children are provided. If nothing is provided for children, they will find a way to make their own toys. Tables, magazines, car keys, napkins, forks and spoons, and their own fingers, arms, and legs become useful in occupying their time.

Toys Around the World

In many countries of the world, children play with the same toys as children in North America. But what about children in countries where poverty, famine, and war have made it impossible to acquire the kinds of toys we take for granted in the rest of the world? How do these children play?

Adults and children in countries around the world have no difficulty making toys out of some of the most basic materials. In Japan, for example, paper is folded in such a way that when you blow into a small opening, it expands to form a ball. Children pat the ball back and forth until the air comes out, then it is again blown up. In countries where trees are abundant, toys are carved from wood. Where stones are available, dyes and etchings transform them into dolls, balls, and animals. Toys can be made from non-toxic plant materials that are carved, woven, painted, and dried into many things, ranging from dolls, to swords, to musical instruments. Old clothes, discarded household items, animal bones, strips of cowhide, and cardboard boxes are just a few of the materials that have been fashioned into toys. Even though they are not the kind of toys seen in holiday gift catalogues, store flyers, or advertisements on television, they involve children in play with purpose and energy.

Figure 3.6
This father and his children are playing with a box. A box can have great play value. One popular use is as a puppet stage.

❖ Checkpoints

1. Discuss the connection between stages of development and the use of toys.
2. Describe the types of things that children play with when "manufactured" toys are not available to them.
3. Outline the similarities and differences in what children play with around the world.

❖ Connections

1. Find a toy or a picture of a handmade toy. How was it made? How is it used? How does it compare to a commercially produced toy? Talk to some families to find out whether they have any handmade toys for their children.

2. Imagine you have been delayed on a train for three hours with a three-year-old child and a five-year-old child. What play materials would you use?

3. Describe a household object that you played with as a child.

Games and Human Development

Games are a form of play. A game is generally played the same way every time, whereas a toy is an item that can have a different purpose with each use. For example, children can stack blocks one day, build a block house another day, and turn the blocks into a long train on yet another day. Games are sometimes associated with older children who have outgrown many of their toys. That is because games often have rules and require the co-operation of two or more people. Parents play games with their children, and children of all ages play games with each other.

> ■ Games are the most elevated form of investigation.
> — Albert Einstein

Games for Babies and Toddlers

Games for babies generally involve the baby and one other person. Patty-Cake is a game played in many cultures. The singsong that goes with it may vary, but the aim is the same: to get the child to clap in time to the words. The rule for Patty-Cake is that the words and the actions follow the same patterns every time. The repetition of words is important for language development, while clapping delights the child as he or she is able to copy someone else. Clapping also helps a child develop a sense of rhythm.

When the baby has developed to the stage that she or he can stand up, the caregiver can introduce games such as rocking the child gently on the lap or jumping to music. These engage the whole body and further expose the baby to music and rhythm. After the baby has developed the understanding that things still exist when they are out of sight, Peek-a-Boo is guaranteed to delight both the baby and the caregiver. This game helps develop the baby's memory, thinking, and perception.

Toddlers who are playing games can follow only simple rules. Watch a group of two-year-olds playing Duck-Duck-Goose and you will find that they have no idea what the rules are. They love to run around the outside of the circle but have no intention of sitting down

Figure 3.7
Babies enjoy and learn from playing Peek-a-Boo.

Figure 3.8
Children playing Four Corners need to follow the rules of the game.

Figure 3.9
Most Canadian communities have organized sports for school-age children.

in the vacant space. Taking turns is not a concept that is understood until around four years of age, so several children might all get up and run around the outside circle. Even with patient explanation, two-year-olds are unlikely to get it right, which can be frustrating for the person who has organized the activity. The organizer needs to be patient and realize that as thinking abilities become more advanced, children become capable of learning and following rules. Everyone will have more fun if games for young children are kept simple.

Games for Preschoolers

Once a child has learned to follow instructions and can walk and run with confidence, games like Hide-and-Seek, London Bridge, Follow the Leader, and Simon Says are very popular. Dancing to music and action songs such as "Head and Shoulders, Knees and Toes" and "The Wheels on the Bus" contributes to a child's sense of personal autonomy and fosters self-awareness. Children not only experience enjoyment, but they also learn important concepts such as the relationship between the leader and the follower or the pursuer and the pursued. They explore a range of feelings in the safe context of a game that has a beginning and an end. They may experience the fear of not being found in Hide–and-Seek, the delight of catching someone in a game of Tag, or the frustration if they do not follow instructions correctly in a game of Simon Says.

Games for School-Age Children

Like toys, games do not suit children until they have achieved the stage of development that allows them to physically handle the skills of a game and intellectually understand the nature of its rules. By about the age of six or seven, children have gained enough control over their bodies to engage in demanding organized sports such as soccer, baseball, or hockey. They now have a much better grasp of complex rules and enjoy both following and challenging the rules of the game. Much of the time and effort spent in playing games at this stage goes into establishing rules and arguing over who has and who has not followed those rules. At this stage, games sharpen skills and interests, build interpersonal relationships, and enhance confidence.

Organized sports are a form of game playing that appeals to children in the middle years and adolescence. Team players are trained in skills and strategies. Rules are carefully followed and are enforced by umpires and referees. Players wear uniforms. Wins and losses are counted, and championships are declared. Following rules for any situation is a skill that game playing initiates and reinforces.

Games for Teens and Adults

During the teen years, game playing provides recreation and enjoyment, builds peer relationships, and improves proficiency in numerous skill areas. Games that require mental challenge such as board games, card games, and some computer games become more popular. Recreational games requiring particular skills, such as golf, curling, or bridge, may be pursued into adulthood. Adults also enjoy games as a form of play. Playing games continues to provide recreation, interaction, and mental stimulation, and contributes to lifelong well-being.

Games Around the World

Games are found in every culture of the world. Children play variations of the same games at the same age in many different countries. Figure 3.11 on page 60 outlines the kind of games that are universal.

Canada's Aboriginal children played games passed down from one generation to the next. Some of these games exist today. For example, Aboriginal children in some areas used a stick to roll a hoop made from bent willow along the ground. In a painting from the early 1500s called *Children's Games* by Pieter Bruegel the Elder, you can see a boy playing this same game. Lacrosse, which is still played in Canada today, was a traditional game for some Aboriginal peoples, such as the Iroquois, Algonquin, Passamaquoddy, and Ojibwa. The Huron played a kind of bowling game in which a rock was rolled to knock over a pile of rocks some distance away. Today, children of all cultures find their own amusements.

❖ Checkpoints

1. Suggest reasons children might spend less time playing outdoors now than they did 10 or 20 years ago.
2. Make a list of games you liked or still like to play. What type of game is each one? What did or do you learn from each of your favourite games? What skills are developed? Share any of your favourite games that are not on the list with the rest of the class.
3. Play helps children to develop physically, intellectually, socially, and emotionally. Examine the list of games around the world in this chapter. Describe the areas of development that each game enhances.
4. Explain how development relates to learning the rules of a game.

Figure 3.10
Lacrosse is a game played with sticks and a ball. It was a traditional game for some Aboriginal peoples.

Common Games Around the World

Type of Game	How It Is Played
Chasing Games	One person chases others. **Examples:** Tag, Capture the Flag, Hide-and-Seek
Games Played with a Ball	The ball is kicked. The ball is hit with a stick. The ball is thrown and caught. **Examples:** Soccer, stickball, catch
Circle Games	One person in the middle of or outside a circle must do something that involves others in the circle. **Examples:** Duck-Duck-Goose, Marbles
Playing House	Playing house is a universal activity in which boys and girls participate. They practise the role of mother or father, or brother or sister, and re-create the activities involved in everyday life.
Mental Games	Play guessing games. **Examples:** I spy with my little eye..., Who Touched Me?
Sensing Games	Recognize someone or something by touch. **Example:** Pin the Tail on the Donkey
Strength Games	Individuals or teams match strength. **Examples:** Arm wrestling, tug-of-war
Jumping Rope Games	Someone turns a rope, or swings it around while others jump over it. **Example:** Skipping
Square Jumping	Take turns jumping in the middle of squares drawn on the ground. **Example:** Hopscotch
Pretending Games	Play at adult work roles such as nurse, firefighter, or teacher are versions of pretend play.

Figure 3.11
Which of these games did you play when you were a child?

❖ Connections

1. Choose an age group, and then design a play centre that includes toys and games that allow children to learn and create in a variety of ways.

2. Describe the toys, games, or materials that would be included in your centre, and explain how they might be used.

3. Make a toy or game for the play centre out of household materials.

Career Capsule

CHILDREN'S ENTERTAINER

Tasks and Responsibilities

Entertainers may be musicians, clowns, magicians, actors, or other live performers who help children use their imaginations and see the magic and fun in life. The performances of children's entertainers need to be clear and simple for children to enjoy them. As a children's entertainer, you write your own material and maintain your own costumes and props.

Work Environment

An entertainer's work environment varies with the role played. A clown or magician may perform at a child's birthday party or neighbourhood fair. Musicians may appear in larger venues like concerts or community centres. Some children's entertainers visit schools; others go to hospitals and do shows in the children's wards. Most children's entertainers begin by working part-time and function as entrepreneurs in charge of their own success.

Education and Aptitudes

A good entertainer likes children and likes to be with them. An ability to enjoy life the way a child does is important. A good sense of humour is also helpful. A children's entertainer must be creative to be able to develop fresh new acts, songs, or activities. Education and training for children's entertainers may vary from community interest courses and self-study to university degree programs in drama, dance, music, or fine arts.

Identifying Patterns of Play

If you are ever responsible for supervising a play group or even a family get-together with many children, it helps to know that not all children play the same way. Play becomes more complex and sophisticated as children grow and mature physically, socially, intellectually, and emotionally. In a classic study done by Mildred Parten in the early 1900s, patterns of play were identified. Children today still exhibit the same types of play behaviour. Parten observed the following types of play among children of various ages:

1. Children play by themselves during **solitary play**. Babies and very young children often engage in solitary play, but children of any age can play by themselves from time to time, particularly when no playmates are available. A baby playing with her feet or a toddler waking up from a nap and amusing himself with an activity centre on the side of the crib are demonstrating solitary play.

Figure 3.12
Children engaged in associative play share toys and talk.

Patterns of Play
- solitary play
- onlooker play
- parallel play
- associative play
- cooperative play
- symbolic play
- imaginative play

2. Children standing and watching other children play are engaging in **onlooker play**. This is common in toddlers as well as some preschoolers. In this activity, children may be learning how to play by observing others before joining in the activity themselves. A child with a shy temperament is more likely to engage in onlooker play than a child who is more outgoing.

3. When children play side by side with different toys or activities, they are engaging in **parallel play**. This type of play is common from 18 to 30 months of age. At this age, the child seems to enjoy being in the company of other children but plays alone. For example, children often play side by side in a sandbox with little or no interaction. Each child is intent on a personal activity. Sharing toys is very difficult at this age, because the concept of how to play with the same toy is intellectually beyond children.

4. A child who plays with others and shares toys is engaging in **associative play**. This is a social type of play. It is usually observed in children who are about three years of age or older. By age three-and-a-half, children often start to talk a great deal as they play in association. They may start to form relationships with some friends they seem to like better than others. Two four-year-old girls sharing their teddy bears or dolls are engaging in associative play.

5. **Cooperative play** is a type of social play in which children play together in structured games that have rules. To participate in cooperative play, children must have reached a stage of development in which they are intellectually able to understand and accept rules. At the beginning, adults or older children are almost always involved in the organization of these kinds of games. As children reach six or seven years of age, they are able to initiate games on their own. Examples of cooperative games include Hide-and-Seek or Tag.

6. **Symbolic play** refers to a spontaneous type of play that children of all ages enjoy. Symbolic play involves the use of toys or objects to represent something entirely different. A hairbrush pushed around on the floor may be symbolic of a car or train. A plastic building block becomes a piece of toast. A spoon may become a comb for doing one's hair. Even when a child does not have an extensive vocabulary, this kind of play shows a sophisticated understanding of concepts.

7. **Imaginative play** is a kind of dramatic play. Examples of this kind of play include playing house, taking on adult work roles, or make-believe play outside on the climber, in the sandbox, or with

cardboard boxes. Imaginary play can bring together several other kinds of play. When children pool their imaginative ideas and agree on what certain toys or objects represent, they are engaging in symbolic play and cooperative play at the same time.

Parenting Skills

Parents, caregivers, or early childhood educators need to understand how children play at different stages of development. For example, they could structure the play area so that it is easier for the child to play with or side by side with other children instead of scolding a child who is developmentally unable to share a toy. Likewise, if some children are developmentally ready for cooperative play and enjoy interacting and sharing with each other, expecting them to play quietly side by side would be unrealistic.

Temperament and Play

Every child is born with a unique **temperament**. Some children are very quiet and passive and are content to watch the world from the sidelines. Others are alert and interactive. Some are very sensitive, easily overstimulated, and easily irritated, while others are eager to try everything and never slow down. Temperament affects children in many ways. For example, it determines what soothes them best and affects their eagerness to experience new things.

The kind of play a child prefers is also closely related to his or her temperament. Because play groups, child-care centres, preschool class-rooms, and baby-sitting situations generally involve children with a wide range of temperaments, caregivers must include several kinds of play, in addition to providing safe and appropriate places to play.

Places to Play

Quiet play requires a small area, such as a corner of the room or under a table, where a child can go to play alone or with a very small group.

Active play requires more space like a playroom or family room where movement, interaction, and manipulation take place.

Very active and exuberant play requires lots of space, such as a gymnasium or outdoor play area where children can safely run, chase, tumble, and yell.

What the experts say

MARY PADDEN

Mary Padden, a play therapist, answers the following question.

How is play related to child development?

For young children, play can serve as a tool to get control and understanding of their world. Play also provides the opportunity for creative self-expression and the development of individuality.

Often, a soft toy or blanket is the first external object to which the child develops a close attachment. In a way, the object is a tool to assist the child in separating from the mother and venturing out into the world. It is an instrument of comfort. It becomes a symbol used to control anxiety, often as a buffer to fear. At times, the child may use it as an instrument of fancy and illusion, or in a dialogue with an imaginary friend. The chosen toy assists in the active imagination, creativity, and the process of play. It also aids in affirming a sense of security and self. So that "teddy" or "blankee" is extremely important. It is the first playmate that the child will independently choose.

It is also important to acknowledge that a child cannot play unless the environment is safe, contained, and secure. If there is a sense of belonging and structure within which the child can play, then it is possible for the imagination to surface. One of the most significant aspects of the creative process and play is a sense of trust.

The process of imaginary play is often a rehearsal—an attempt to gain mastery and understanding of an emotion or event. The creative materials or toys used provide the tools for practice. It is only in playing that a child is able to be creative and to use his or her personality for self-discovery.

Play is a special place where a child straddles the realm of reality and fantasy. It can be seen as a bridge between the inner world of imagination and the outer world of reality. To children, their toys often become extensions of themselves. Play provides an opportunity to make important choices and to problem-solve in a very real way.

Figure 3.13
Often a soft toy or blanket is the first external object to which the child develops a close attachment. It aids in affirming a sense of security and self.

❖ Checkpoints

1. How could the ability to identify the patterns of play help a baby sitter supervise a group of three preschool children? Support your answer with descriptions of at least three play patterns.
2. Outline the differences between quiet and active play. Give examples of each.

Playing Safely

It wasn't that long ago that all children could play freely outside their homes. Out in the country, children explored and played in fields, ponds, woods, barns, apple orchards, and dirt piles. Children lucky enough to live near a lake or beach went wading, paddling, fishing, or swimming as soon as the water was warm enough. In the city, children had backyards, green spaces, and parks, but they also played in alleys, vacant lots, and railway yards. They hung out at gas stations or work sites where they could watch all the activity. Although many dangers lurked in the neighbourhood, playing unsupervised was common. Children were warned to be careful but caregivers expected that cuts, scrapes, and pinworms were all in a day's play.

Today, parents are warned of the many dangers of unsupervised play. They are aware that water is polluted, soil may be contaminated, and child molesters lurk where children play. Every year, children are injured or die while at play. Children have been suffocated by collapsing sand, or smothered in a toy chest or in an abandoned refrigerator. They have been killed when playing with loaded and unlocked guns or killed or injured by a land mine, a relic of an adult war. They have been backed over by vehicles, crushed by farm equipment, or fallen to their death from high places. The cords in their coats or snowsuits, or even the strings on the blinds in their bedrooms can be lethal.

Children are vulnerable to accidents and injury in almost every play setting. Even properly constructed playground equipment can be dangerous. Here is an article by Health Canada about playground safety.

Playground—Danger of Strangulation

Each year in Canada, thousands of children get hurt on playground slides, monkey bars, or swings. Some children have died when their clothing or drawstrings got caught on playground equipment or fences. Some children have died when they became entangled in ropes or skipping ropes attached to playground equipment. Loose clothing, hoods, scarves, drawstrings, mitten cords, ropes, and skipping ropes can all strangle a child.

Safety Tips
- Remove cords and drawstrings from children's hoods, hats, and jackets.
- Tuck in all clothing that can get caught on playground equipment.
- Have children wear a neck warmer instead of a scarf.
- Take off bicycle helmets before children use playground equipment. Bicycle helmets can get trapped on equipment and strangle a child.
- Make sure children do not tie ropes or skipping ropes to slides and other playground equipment.
- Supervise children on the playground.
- Teach children how to use playground equipment and play safely.

Consumer Product Safety Bureau, Health Canada, 2003 ©. Reproduced with the permission of the Minister of Public Works and Government Services Canada, 2003.

The loss or injury of a child will affect a family forever. After any incident, new safety regulations are developed to prevent the same tragedy from happening again. But children are carefree and often play without thought of danger. It is up to parents, teachers, and other adults to take action to provide children with safe play environments, supervise play, and warn children of danger.

❖ Checkpoints

1. In what ways has play been made safer than it was in the past?
2. List six guidelines for safe playground play. For more information on playground equipment, contact the nearest Product Safety, Health Canada office in your province or territory.

❖ Connections

1. Take a walk in your neighbourhood. Visit the local playground. Speculate about the ways in which children might be hurt or vulnerable to danger in these play environments.
2. Describe ways to teach children how to avoid danger when playing outdoors.
3. Describe your own childhood experiences of play in terms of the quality of the toys and games and the level of safety that was experienced.

Figure 3.14
What could an observer conclude from this picture?

Observing Children at Play

Have you ever watched a baby play with an object or a toy? The baby might look at the object intently, move it, turn it over, bang it, chew on it, and even smell it. From these observations, we can determine which senses are being used. We can even guess what the child might be learning from the experience, especially if the actions are followed by a reaction.

Because young children are preliterate, observation, or watching, listening, and paying attention to what children say and do is the most direct and effective way to learn about them. Social scientists such as sociologists, psychologists, and anthropologists use observation to study and reach conclusions about their subjects when their subjects are unable to answer questions or fill out surveys.

Where to Observe Children

Children can be observed casually within many aspects of your everyday life; at the mall, at a religious institution, at a family get-together, at the doctor's office, or at the library. To see children at play, you could go to a child-care centre or a playground, or you could visit them in their own homes. One of the best ways to observe children is to organize a play group or play school that includes a number of children for comparison.

Obtaining Consent

Any time children are observed formally to provide information about their development or for class discussion, parents must be informed and must give their permission. A letter outlining who is observing, why they are observing, when they will be observing, and what they hope to accomplish from the observation must be provided to the parents. When parents sign a permission form, they are giving **informed consent** for their child to be observed and for notes to be made for a report based on the observations. Children under 16 cannot provide their own informed consent.

■ Informed consent and assurance of confidentiality are critical before research can begin.

Confidentiality must also be ensured. Any oral or written reports should not use the full name of the child you have been observing. Use phrases like: "I observed a three-year-old boy I will call Seth," or "Child A crawled under a table and said… ." If you are using a checklist, use the child's initials, first name, or Child A and Child B. Confidentiality is also observed if you do not identify the children involved as you discuss your observations with friends or family. Some child-care settings require that you sign an Oath of Confidentiality if you will be working with or interacting with children.

In addition, when you create a videotape, anyone who appears in the video must give permission for you to use his or her image if it is being shared in a public setting, such as a classroom or a parenting group.

How to Observe Children

Professionals use different techniques to observe children. Children should not be aware that they are being observed in a formal sense, as this may encourage them to act out or to withdraw. Observing their most usual and natural behaviours offers the best picture of what children are like and what they are capable of doing, and it often provides us with some evidence about how children think. Professionals watch for clues to their physical, verbal, intellectual, social, and emotional development. They pay attention to what children are able to do well physically, how well they can talk and what they say, how they behave, who they interact with, what makes them happy, what makes them sad.

■ Sociologists, psychologists, and anthropologists use observation to reach conclusions about their subjects.

Methods of Observation

Many methods can be used in the observation process. The type of information required will determine the observation method selected.

Participant Observation

By getting right down on the floor and playing with children, you become a participant in their play. Younger children may hand you toys or just talk to you while they play. Older children might involve you directly by, for example, asking you to take on a role, pretending they are feeding you, or asking you to throw a ball. Taking notes while you are playing may interfere with the activity; therefore, it is best to write down what you saw the child do or say as soon as possible after the play period is over.

Observing from the Sidelines

If you stay in the background or watch a given activity from the sidelines, children often forget that you are there. As they continue with their play, you can take notes, complete a checklist, or speak into a hand-held tape recorder, outlining what is happening in your line of vision. You record the behaviour and the conversation as it happens and make your interpretations later.

Observing Through One-Way Mirrors

Some child-care centres, child development classrooms, and therapist offices have one-way mirrors. To the children in the playroom, these look like mirrors, but they are actually windows that enable researchers to observe children at play.

Because children do not see the observer, they play naturally and normally. The viewing rooms are equipped with speakers that pick up the sound from the playroom. Notes can be taken and video recordings can be made without the children's knowledge.

Videotaped Observation

Videotaping is advantageous because it allows you to rewind and review what the children said and how they behaved. You can make notes from the video, or the video can be used as a starting point for discussion. Behaviours or events that you might not notice in the room may become obvious as you view a video.

Videotaping does have limitations, however. You may miss something important just outside the camera range, or children may be self-conscious when being videotaped.

❖ Connections

1. What are the advantages and disadvantages of the four methods of observing children?
2. How could you combine observation methods?

What to Observe

There are endless questions you can use to guide your observations of children. How do they get along with other children? What interests them? What frustrates them? By using an **observation protocol**, a formal tool for recording observations, you will be able to focus your attention on what to observe. An observation protocol is a list of questions to ask or a list of details to which you need to pay attention.

For example, to learn about **physical development**, you observe children's balance, height, and weight, as well as their large muscle use (running, climbing, throwing), or small muscle use (writing, turning pages). To learn about **social development**, you observe how children play together, whether they share, take turns, invite others to play, or talk socially with others. To learn about **emotional development**, you would observe whether they are sympathetic to other children, whether they cry easily, what makes them happy, sad, angry, or excited. To learn about **intellectual development**, you observe their ability to speak, listen, follow directions, count, and identify colours, and any actions or other abilities that indicate what they know and what they do not know.

How to Record Observations

You use different kinds of records to record observations based on the setting and what you want to observe. For example, if you are looking to see which particular abilities are present, a checklist will do. If you want to keep track of changes in behaviour or attitudes, an anecdotal record would be better.

Figure 3.15
This participant observer is learning about intellectual development by playing a numbers game with children.

Running Record

Simply record what you see and hear as it happens, along with the time of each observation. Do not include any interpretations of what you see and hear. They can be noted when you reflect on your notes later.

Anecdotal Records

An anecdote is a story. It describes events and behaviours in detail as they unfold. You may wish to include your thoughts on why things are happening, and reflect on your notes later to determine what you have learned.

Observation Checklists

An observation checklist presents a list of abilities, such as hops on one foot, identifies colours correctly, identifies shapes correctly, or throws with accuracy. The list is developed according to the types of behaviours being investigated. As observer, you merely check off the behaviours you observe for a given child.

Interpreting Observations

When Billy throws play dough at another child, you do not know whether he was angry, upset, or experiencing some other emotion. You can record that Billy said, "I hate you," and threw play dough. If you say he was upset, it may be true, but it could be an inaccurate observation if the child was play-acting. Observing that the two children immediately break into giggles suggests that the second interpretation is the more accurate one. Accurate interpretations depend on how clearly you record your observations.

The more you know about child development, the more accurately you will be able to interpret your observations. Books, articles, videos, or online resources can help you get a better idea of what your observations mean. By observing children, paying attention to how they work, play, act, talk, and behave, you will have a much better idea of what can and cannot be expected of children of different ages and stages of development.

Chapter Summary

Chapter Highlights

- In many ways, children are the same the world over. They all follow a similar pattern of development, and they all learn through play.

- Play is many things. All forms of play prepare children for their role in society, and contribute to their ongoing development.

- Toys—whether they occur in nature, are hand-made, or are manufactured—are the tools used by children everywhere when they play.

- The type of toy a child prefers relates to his or her stage of development and should be suited to his or her capabilities.

- Games are a form of amusement that follows rules, which need to match a child's mental and physical abilities.

- Some games, or variations on the same game, are found in most societies around the world.

- Children have the right to a safe play environment. Safety must be kept in mind when choosing toys, planning play activities, or organizing games.

- Play patterns and temperaments can be identified in a play setting.

- By observing and interacting with children at play, you can determine their developmental process, identify how play contributes to learning, and become better able to understand and appreciate them.

Review and Extend Your Learning

1. In your own words, explain the meaning of the phrase "Play is the work of children." **C**

2. Why is it important for parents and caregivers to understand the relationship between stages of development and appropriate toys, games, and play environments for children? **K/U**

3. What are the similarities in and differences between toys and games? **K/U**

4. Evaluate a toy or game, identify the age of the child for which it is designed, and explain how it contributes to the child's development. **K/U** **T/I**

5. Explain how play is an expression of culture. **K/U**

6. Examine the Chart of Temperaments. Outline the types of play that might be most suitable for the various temperaments. Give reasons for your answers.

7. Outline some of the reasons and benefits of observing children at play. Discuss how this information may be personally useful to you. **K/U** **C** **A**

8. Go to a local playground and observe the children in action. Select an appropriate method to record your observations and present to the class what you learned from your observations about child development. **C** **A**

Research Opportunities

9. Conduct historical research by talking to elderly members of the community or searching for literature on games and activities of the past. Find out what was meant by "parlour games." Find out why parlour games were played, and learn the rules of one. Introduce the parlour game to your class.

10. Locate Canadian statistics for the most common accidents or deaths, or both, among toddlers, preschoolers, and school-age children. Create a chart or graph to illustrate your findings.

Issue Analysis

11. Many children today, especially in cities, are not allowed outside to play as freely as their parents did when young. Even if children are in the yard, their parents worry about abduction and watch them. Children are not allowed to go to the park without the supervision of a parent or caregiver. If they are latchkey kids, they are expected to lock themselves in their home and wait for the adults to return from work. They often watch television or play computer games instead of playing actively outside. Comment on the possible effects of this change in the play patterns on children. How might it affect their growth and development?

Chapter

4

Children and Their Cultural Heritage

By the end of this chapter, you will be able to:

- describe the common experiences of young children in various cultures throughout the world

- explain the various types of social and cultural differences in child behaviour

- identify a variety of global influences on children and families

- outline the role society plays in the lives of children

Important Terms

androgynous names
boarding schools
child labour
counter culture
covert rules
culture
egalitarian

kibbutz
matriarchy
mother tongue
nickname
overt rules
patriarchy
shared authority

Chapter at a Glance

What Is Cultural Heritage?

Canada has a culture that in itself embraces many cultures. Bilingualism and multiculturalism have helped to define what it means to be Canadian since the *Official Languages Act* became law in 1969, and Canada's multicultural policy was adopted in 1971. Canada includes diverse peoples whose cultural heritage continues to be an important part of their Canadian identity.

Cultural heritage and how it is interpreted in families and social groups differs widely throughout Canada and the world. Parents begin transmitting their unique culture to their children even before they are born. The expectations they have for their unborn children, their religious beliefs, the prenatal practices they follow, and how they get their homes and lives ready for a new baby all have cultural significance.

What is culture? **Culture** is far more than food and festivals. It is part of the essence of a person. Some sociologists define culture as a population's behaviour patterns, arts, beliefs, and institutions. Many customs that arise from a culture are passed from one generation to the next. Culture shapes your daily experiences, your inner emotions, and the way you present yourself to the world. It encompasses your past, present, and future. Ethnicity, religion, language, values, attitudes, and beliefs are all elements of culture, as are practices and behaviours that are followed by Canadian society in general, and by groups within our society.

Culture defines where you are comfortable in the world. For example, if you were a girl from a culture in which female children and women were not allowed to run, how comfortable would you feel when asked to run four times around the school track in a physical education class? If you were a boy from a culture in which boys and men were discouraged from crying, how comfortable would you be if you were moved to tears by a significant emotional event like a memorial service for a classmate?

Culture shapes an individual's personality and world view. Everyone is influenced by his or her own culture, as well as the culture of others. Your friends, your classmates, the children you observe and work with, and people of all ages in your community share their culture through everyday interactions. Culture adds character to a community and uniqueness to relationships.

Figure 4.1
Culture often determines how parents-to-be prepare for the birth of their baby.

■ *Culture is simply how one lives and is connected to history by habit.*
— Leroi Jones

Culture and Child Rearing

Child rearing is essentially a cultural activity. There are many different approaches to child rearing, yet it appears that cultures the world over share some expectations for their children. Whether male or female, children are expected to demonstrate an ability to follow instruction and display some degree of responsibility, nurturance, achievement, self-reliance, and independence.

Figure 4.2
For many North American parents, their children's educational achievements are of major importance.

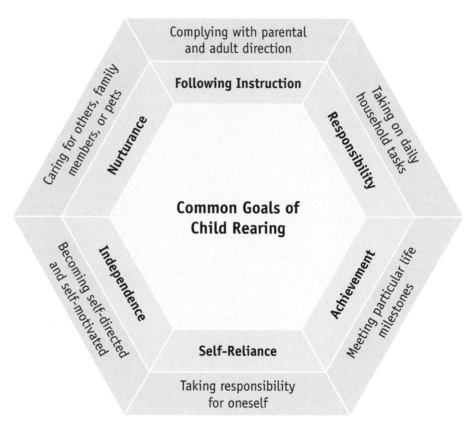

Figure 4.3
Cultures the world over share these expectations of their children.

These areas of achievement for children do not all receive the same amount of energy at any given time. Some will be more important than others depending on the child's age, ability, and circumstances, yet each is addressed by parents throughout the child's life.

Parental Authority

Culture has a significant influence on the power structure in families. Power and how it is perceived affects the roles and responsibilities of parents, children, and others in the community. Power distribution in families generally takes one of three common forms. They are as follows:

- **patriarchy** (male dominance)
- **matriarchy** (female dominance)
- **egalitarian** or **shared authority**, which features the sharing of power between the adult leaders in the family

Gender-based family roles in marriage, family relationships, and parenting practices reflect the power structure in families. For example, patriarchy has been common for centuries around the world. Today, it occurs in many cultures in Canada and elsewhere. It is often rooted in and supported by religion, which has a strong influence on the roles and responsibilities of men and women in society.

In male-dominant societies, men are often the leaders in the religious community as well as in the family. In a male-dominant household, the man has responsibilities as the principal breadwinner, decision-maker, and disciplinarian. The female role is to assist the head of the household by maintaining the home, nurturing the children, and, in many cases, acting as the mediator between father and children. Male children follow in their father's footsteps, while female children become the next generation of nurturers and mediators.

Matriarchy is less common throughout the world than patriarchy and often exists because the males in the society are largely absent. Shared authority is a relatively new sociological model to which many western societies appear to be moving.

■ Although patriarchy has been common in families, the sharing of power is increasing.

Figure 4.4
The way a family passes food around a table is a reflection of their cultural beliefs.

Rules for Behaviour

Religious and cultural beliefs often influence family rules, parental discipline, and guidance. Families have both overt and covert rules for parental behaviour and for children's behaviour. **Overt rules** are clearly stated. For example, "In this family, we all go to grandma's for dinner every Sunday" is an overt rule. **Covert rules** are implied or understood without being discussed. Passing food to the head of the house before you take food yourself may be a rule that has never been stated, but

Figure 4.5
Children need an authority figure in their lives who provides direction and guidance.

because everyone does it at every meal, it continues to be followed. An overt rule is easier to challenge and change. Imagine the reaction of the family if you challenged or broke a covert rule that has been embedded not only in your family, but also in your entire culture.

Discipline

Although Canada has laws against physical abuse, some cultural groups continue to believe in the use of strict discipline and physical punishment for children. Authoritarian parents have many rules and harsh punishments, and they demand obedience. Parents who were themselves raised by authoritarian parents sometimes take the opposite approach and become permissive, allowing their children to set their own rules and avoiding confrontation at all costs. Parental choice of discipline is strongly influenced by cultural and religious beliefs, personal experience, and prevailing practices. A notable current trend is a movement away from both authoritarian and permissive discipline styles in favour of a more democratic approach.

Guidance

All children need the guidance of an authority figure in their lives. They need to know that there is at least one person in their life who can answer their questions, who will make a difficult or important decision when necessary, and who has the capability and power to meet their needs, and will do so. Children need someone in their lives who they can count on to have the last word, who they can trust to point them in the direction they need to go, and who gives them support along the way. The person who assumes this role is often determined by culture. It may be one or both parents or a guardian. In some cultures, elders in the community fill that role. A trusted grandparent, a tribal elder, or a religious leader may be the authority figure who provides the guidance for both the parents and the children.

❖ Connections

1. Identify some of the overt and covert rules in your family that have been influenced by your culture. Compare your family rules with other students' family rules for similarities and differences.
2. Conduct a library or Internet search into a male dominant culture that exists in Canada. Write a comparison of the roles and responsibilities of men, women, and children in that culture with those in your own family.

Transmitting Cultural Heritage to Children

Cultural identity is shaped by the practices of a group, family, or individual. Culture is highly dependent on learning. Children are immersed in the daily practice of their family's culture in their homes. Some families choose to teach their children specific aspects of their culture, but all children learn and absorb their culture through their five senses every day of their lives. Your experiences of touch, sight, sound, taste, and smell have all contributed to the transmission of your cultural heritage to you, and have shaped you as a person.

The Role of Language in Culture

The expression **mother tongue** refers to the first language that you learn. It is the language that a baby hears from birth. As an infant is held, nursed, soothed, sung to, and played with, the mother's voice is usually the one the infant hears most often. A baby who is only a few hours old is able to distinguish the mother's voice from that of a stranger. Dads are not left out, either. Very young babies have been known to turn toward the sound of their father's voice. Babies who are distressed have been known to calm down readily when the father talks to them.

Language, then, is the first dimension of the child's culture transmitted by parents. The immediate and intense response by infants to language and song encourages parents to respond with more words, more talk, and more singing. Every culture has versions of baby talk, nursery rhymes, and baby songs. Many second- and third-generation Canadian children can recite some baby songs and verses in their grandparents' language.

Oral traditions are a part of every society. Storytelling transmits culture in many families. Moral tales, folk tales, and old-fashioned family stories are often told to children to provide an understanding of their background and how things are done in a particular culture. Grandparents and great-grandparents have stories and memories from long ago and they love to share these with the children in the family. These stories provide the connection to the cultural heritage of the family.

Music is also a way of transmitting culture. It speaks in ways that words do not. People around the world make music in many different ways. The instruments used to make music have regional and ethnic origins. Many cultures have influenced the music that you listen to on a regular basis. The term **counter culture** has been used to describe music preferred by different groups within society that is different from

Figure 4.6
A young baby can recognize his or her parents' voices.

▪ *Everything can change, but not the language that we carry inside us, like a world more exclusive and final than one's mother's womb.*
— Italo Calvino

or opposite to the mainstream. The music you listen to today is likely different from the music your parents listened to at your age, but it is also different from the music you listened to five or ten years ago.

Figure 4.7
Marta Kivik and her daughters

Talking Parenting

Marta Kivik is the mother of two teenagers, Erika and Andrea. She explains the importance of Heritage Language programs.

Heritage Language programs in a country where almost every language in the world is spoken—and certainly in Toronto, where over 100 languages are spoken—are important to children whose roots are in a small country such as Estonia. The population of Estonia is 1.5 million, half the population of Toronto. Because linguists predict that in 100 years, more than 50 percent of the world's languages will have disappeared, it is extremely important that children be given the chance to learn and maintain the language of their ancestors. Learning another language expands brainpower, gives students an understanding and conception of what other languages are like, and, therefore, helps them learn much more easily.

The only place our children met other Estonian kids was in the Estonian Heritage Language classes they attended each week. It was important to make this experience as interesting as a "Canadian" classroom so that the kids would want to attend. The Estonian school programs taught not only language and history, but also folk dancing, singing, folklore, handicrafts, games, traditions, and so on. Kids who joined kindergarten at age three are now well into their teens and twenties, having maintained the friendships through their "unique" cultural similarity. Now when I go out with my daughters, we specifically speak Estonian in stores, restaurants, and other public places, either because it is fun to be different, or because it allows us to have a private conversation in public.

The participation in Heritage Language programs has worked hand in hand with our insistence on speaking Estonian at home, especially when the children were young. It has given them the opportunity to decide whether they want to pursue the study of Estonian language, history, and culture, or, in fact, another language and culture. And, who knows, maybe my children will want to "go back" to Estonia to work or study, as have many other young people whose interest in their heritage has been rekindled since Estonia regained independence in 1991.

A family's religion also has a language of its own. The language of religious rituals, liturgies, prayers, readings, chants, or observances is very important, dating back hundreds or thousands of years. Children learn the language of their religion from their parents, schools, and places of worship. A child acquires parental beliefs from both their conversations and their practices.

❖ Connections

1. Have someone from a different culture teach you a children's song in his or her own language and share the experience in class.

2. Describe to one of your classmates a childhood song that you remember. Identify what was fun or interesting about the song, and explain what makes it memorable.

Transmitting Culture Through Touch

From the moment of birth, how an infant is held and touched is very closely tied to culture. In Canadian hospitals, it is fairly common practice for the mother to hold a newborn immediately after birth. In some cultures, infants are held face to face, while in others, the infant is held facing the world. Some infants are held closely and caressed often, some are swaddled or wrapped tightly in blankets, and some are carried in slings close to their mothers' body. In Canada, many parents of both sexes carry their infants in baby carriers close to their bodies. Kissing and cuddling of infants is natural in many cultures and frowned upon in others.

Breast-feeding, the closest form of human touch, is also tied to culture. In some cultures, women never consider anything but breast-feeding, and continue to nurse their children well into their second or third year of life. Breast-feeding has not always been the first choice for new mothers, however. The practice of having a wet nurse breast-feed children of the upper classes is one that survived in many cultures from antiquity into the early part of the 20th century. The wet nurse was often a working class woman who had nursed children of her own or whose own child had died and, rather than letting her breast milk dry up, hired herself out to nurse the children of the wealthy. Many wet nurses continued to serve their clients for years. Being selected to be a child's nurse was considered good fortune, because it provided the woman with a higher standard of living.

Figure 4.8
Kissing infants is natural in many cultures but unacceptable in others.

Figure 4.9
Sharing special foods during a celebration defines and teaches about the importance of that cultural or religious event.

Food as Culture

Food embodies all of the senses. The taste and smell of traditional food, how it looks, how it feels in your mouth, and the sounds that are made in its preparation and eating are all closely linked to cultural identity. Canada celebrates its cultures through cuisine. Children learn the food of their own culture long before they try the foods of others. One child may prefer hot spicy foods while another cannot tolerate them.

One of the last things given up by families coming to Canada is their familiar and traditional food. Recipes are handed down from generation to generation, some in written form, others by word of mouth. In some families, men prepare the special dishes of their culture, while in other families, men are discouraged from being in the kitchen. You may find that at certain times of the year, or in certain situations, you long for a particular kind of food that has been a part of your childhood. When the snow first falls, or when you have been away from home, there is only one kind of food that will do. Soup just like grandma's, a freshly baked pita bread, or a warmly scented curry are examples of comfort foods that might bring back the warmth and contentment associated with your own culture.

The growing interest in the foods of other cultures and the range of festivals and restaurants featuring the food of other nations have led to an appreciation of diversity and a multi-ethnic enjoyment of food. It is not unusual for pizza to be served in a Chinese household or curry to be served in a Ukrainian household. It is in religious festivals and family celebrations, however, that cultural foods find a prominent place. Food has different meanings for different people, and as children become aware of the cultural practices that involve food, they learn its symbolic meaning.

❖ Checkpoints

1. Name and describe the components of culture.
2. How do family stories and storytelling transmit culture?
3. How is breast-feeding related to the transmission of culture?
4. Describe the ways in which food is connected to culture.

❖ Connections

1. List foods that have cultural significance for your family.
2. When and why are these dishes served? Describe how you feel when you eat these foods.

Visual Expressions of Culture

Through observation and practice, children learn about their own culture and religion, as well as those of others. Ways of doing things, religious practices, and family rituals can be observed by children on a daily basis. Washing hands, lighting candles, standing up for elders, showing respect, lining up, or saying prayers or chanting are examples of daily practices that children observe and imitate. Knowing how to behave as other family members do makes a child comfortable within a cultural framework.

Children also see the clothing and dress associated with their own culture. Canada is a country that includes people of all nations. For many families, being able to preserve their culture is often the incentive for coming to Canada. Any major Canadian city provides a wide spectrum of cultures, evident in clothing that ranges from head coverings to national dress. Some children are encouraged to wear the clothing representing their culture every day. Some wear it only for festivals and special family events, while others see it as an interesting part of their past and choose western dress for every occasion.

Culture is also evident in home decor, family heirlooms, and special mementos from past generations. A family religious book or artifact, a set of ivory chopsticks, Delft blue tea cups, great-grandfather's rocking chair, or a tartan wall hanging are just a few examples of family treasures that may be displayed.

We can learn a great deal about the values, beliefs, and practices of cultures in Canada and around the world from works of art. Paintings, carvings, sculpture, and other artifacts and crafts illustrate customs and lifestyles. What artists see and feel in their culture is reflected in their art. Works of art may depict religious symbols or rituals, human and family interactions, or beloved landscapes of a culture. Individuals may have a preference for a certain kind of art because of cultural influences that begin early in life.

Figure 4.10
Traditional dress is one way of defining culture and demonstrating traditions.

Parenting Customs and Folklore

Every culture has its rituals, practices, and folklore. What is customary for some cultures could either be very similar or completely alien in other cultures. The same is true for parenting: some cultural practices are seen everywhere, while others are unique.

Naming Children

A child-rearing practice found in every culture is the naming of children. A name is a legal requirement in Canada. A child's name must be registered with the province or territory by a certain date after the child is born, and then a birth certificate is issued. But who names the children, how they are named, and when they are named can vary widely. Naming ceremonies can be extravagant.

The naming of children is a serious issue. The name will have to suit the child from birth to old age. What is appealing for a toddler might not be so desirable when a person is eighty. Some people believe that you have to see the child before you can tell whether the name fits the child. Others expect the child to fit the name they have chosen. They may even call the baby by name before birth.

Names are powerful. They are a part of a person's identity and may affect the development of personality. Besides or instead of their given name, people are often called by a **nickname**, which may be a variation on or shortened version of their name (Liza for Elizabeth; Jack for John), but could be based on anything: for example, Sunny for someone who is either always happy or always grumpy, or Rock for someone who is an unbeatable goaltender or a cave explorer. A nickname can be a sign of affection or a source of great embarrassment. Some people hate their nicknames while others use their nicknames exclusively. Many famous people have changed the names they were given at birth for something more comfortable, catchy, or memorable.

❖ Connections

1. (a) What is the full name you were given and why was it given to you?
   (b) Does your name have a particular meaning?
   (c) Who else in your family, class, or neighbourhood has the same name? Why were they given that name?
2. What are your current top three name preferences for a girl and top three names for a boy? Explain why you like these names.
3. Why might your preference for babies' names change by the time you have children?

Historical records show that names were so important in some families that they gave more than one child in the family the same first name. Because infant mortality rates were so high, a later-born child was often given the name of a sibling who had died in infancy.

In this way, families were more likely to be able to keep a name in the family and have it passed down.

Factors to Consider When Naming Children

Gender: Most cultures have definitive male and female names. **Androgynous names** (names that do not connote male or female) are also possible. Madison and Courtney can be used for both boys and girls. Some names like Sean and Shannon are the male and female versions of each other. In the past, Valerie and Tracey were both men's names. Today, they are more often girls' names.

Religion: Every religion has names of particular significance that have been given to children. In Christian cultures, for example, children are frequently named after saints.

Family Tradition: Many cultures have a practice of naming children after family members. In some cultures, a male child is named after his father's father, and a female child after her mother's mother. For example, male and female children in Muslim families are named after their respective grandparents.

Popularity: Names go through cycles of popularity. Often, children are named after celebrities. In the 1950s, many Canadian girls were named Marilyn after Marilyn Bell, who was the first woman to successfully swim across Lake Ontario. Names also fall out of favour. Elvira and Elmer are names that were once common in Canada but are less common today.

Associations: Names are often associated with famous people. Some are the names of highly respected heroes, such as Terry Fox, while others have lost favour with society because of negative associations. In North America, Adolf has rarely been used for boys since the time of Hitler.

Meanings: Some parents determine the meaning of the name before choosing it for their child. For example, Brian and its female form, Brianna, both mean "strong."

Initials: Parents sometimes consider the word spelled by the initials of a child's name. The initials for "Alexander Reid Tryssenaar" might be more acceptable than the initials for "Reid Alexander Tryssenaar."

Naming ceremonies vary from culture to culture. In some cultures, a child does not officially have a name until the name is registered with the state. In others, the child does not have an official name until after the naming ceremony. The ritual of naming can be as simple as telling the rest of the family the name chosen for the child, or as elaborate as having a religious or cultural ceremony attended by many, followed by a great celebration.

Respect for Elders

Many cultures, including North American Aboriginal and Asian cultures, encourage and promote a deep respect for their elders. They recognize the important role of elder family members in transmitting culture and family history. In these cultures, family and community members traditionally look to the elderly for guidance based on the wisdom that comes from years of living, working, and experiencing life's changes.

Figure 4.11
Elders are deeply respected in Aboriginal cultures in Canada.

The Role of Elders in the Inuit Culture

In *Inuit Way: A Guide to Inuit Culture,* authors discuss the important role grandparents play in the Inuit culture.

Elder family members continue to play an important role in family life and are treated with great respect. They are considered wise and important sources of knowledge about the past. They are sought out for their storytelling and advice on many issues. Children are still taught to be very respectful towards their elders, to greet them before anyone else, try to anticipate their needs, and not to express knowledge towards their elders unless they are asked.

Also present in many Canadian families, however, is a cultural element that does not reinforce respect for elders in their children. A more egocentric focus, rather than an intergenerational focus, may lead to the defiance of authority and an increase in elder abuse.

Other Child-Rearing Customs

Here are some child-rearing customs used in various parts of the world:

In Israel, the **kibbutz** is a form of communal living. Families live together on a kibbutz and focus on some area of economic development, particularly farming. Men and women work side by side every day. Prior to the 1970s, children were housed together and educated apart from their families. Sometimes children would secretly go back to their parents' compound to spend a night. By 1970, many kibbutzim allowed the children to stay with their parents at night and on weekends and be cared for communally during the day.

In England, many children are sent to private **boarding schools** around the age of eight. They live at the school, where their days and evenings are structured around lessons, schoolwork, sports, and related educational activities. Boys and girls do not attend the same schools. Some go home on weekends, while others go home only on holidays. Although there are local schools, there is a long-standing tradition, especially in the upper classes, to send children away to school.

Most North Americans follow a practice that would be considered unusual in other cultures. Our babies sleep alone in bassinettes, cradles, and cribs, often from the first day of life. This would be considered cruel in cultures in which infants sleep with their parents, often until two years of age. As more research is done on the long-term effects of this custom, more parents in western societies are embracing the practice of sleeping with their babies.

Families in Canada often continue practices that originated in other countries around the world. There are as many ways of raising

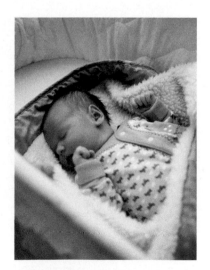

Figure 4.12
In North America, it is customary for newborn babies to sleep alone in a crib or bassinette.

children as there are cultures and, regardless of the method, most children turn out to be healthy, contributing members of every society of the world. Some cultures follow practices that may seem unusual to some, but, in general, a family or cultural group wants the best for its children. Superstitions, beliefs, and social preferences may yield interesting differences, but the desire for children to grow up successfully is the aim of every culture.

■ All cultural groups want their children to be successful. Many have cultural practices related to living a successful life.

❖ Checkpoints

1. Outline some of the factors related to the naming of children.
2. How might respect for elders be transmitted to children in Canada today?
3. What child-rearing practices have been used in your family's history?

The Universal Rights of Children

At Disney World in Florida, there is a boat ride that takes you on a journey around the world. As you float down the river, you pass by display after display of beautiful dolls no more than one metre tall, while a chorus of children's voices sing "It's a Small World After All." The dolls are dressed in the national costumes of the countries they represent. They skate, they dance, they swing, they do acrobatics, they ride donkeys, they play musical instruments, and they whirl and twirl. Except for their eyes and the colour of their skin and hair, they are all identical. Same shape, same size, same smile on their faces. Surrounded by flowers, rainbows, colour, and light, it is indeed a small, beautiful, and completely unnatural world—a fantasy.

You have likely seen pictures of children from around the world. Although they come in many different sizes, eyes, skin, and hair colours, they are alike in many ways. Unfortunately, their world is not always beautiful, and they do not always have a smile on their faces. While in some countries, all children are highly valued, seen as the future of the country, and treated with equality and respect, not every country values all children in the same way. In some places, boys are valued more highly than girls. Female infanticide (the killing of infant girls) is still practised in some parts of the world. Children should have the same rights around the world, but they are not all treated with the same care and respect. Some children in Canada and around the world still face abuse, deprivation, malnutrition, abandonment, and child labour.

Because we can connect with children around the world through satellite, Internet, and television programming, it becomes easier to consider the global welfare of children. In 1979, during the International Year of the Child, the United Nations initiated a declaration on the rights of children. On November 20, 1989, the United Nations adopted *The Convention on the Rights of the Child*. It has 54 Articles that outline the rights of children and the responsibilities of nations to protect and uphold the rights of every child. By December 31, 1995, 185 countries had ratified the Convention. Canada was among the first to declare that as a country we accept the articles to be children's rights and the country's responsibility.

Highlights of *The Convention on the Rights of the Child*

The Convention defines a child as a person under 18 unless national law recognizes that the age of majority is reached earlier. Key points from the Convention are listed below.

The United Nations continues to advocate for children everywhere.

Every child has a right to:
- life, survival, and development
- a name and nationality from birth
- not be separated from their parents, except by competent authorities for their well-being
- the highest attainable standard of health
- an education and dignified treatment in schools
- rest, play, and equal opportunities for cultural and artistic activities
- freely enjoy their own culture, religion, and language

Disabled children have the right to special treatment, education, and care.

All countries are responsible for:
- providing parents with appropriate assistance and developing child-care institutions
- protecting children from physical or mental harm and neglect, including sexual abuse or exploitation
- providing parentless children with suitable alternative care
- carefully regulating the adoption process to provide safeguards and assure legal validity if and when adoptive parents intend to move a child from the country of birth
- providing health care to all children, placing emphasis on preventive measures, health education, and reduction of infant mortality
- protecting children from economic exploitation and from work that may interfere with their education or be harmful to their health or well-being
- protecting children from the illegal use of drugs and involvement in drug production or trafficking
- efforts to eliminate the abduction and trafficking of children
- ensuring that children involved in infringements of the penal law shall be treated in a way that promotes their sense of dignity and worth, and aims at reintegrating them into society
- making the rights set out in the Convention widely known to both adults and children

Career Capsule

ACTIVIST

Tasks and Responsibilities

Activists are hired by organizations to educate and to raise funds. Many do their job purely out of love and dedication. They spread information in an attempt to influence public opinion to create change. Although some activists do things like chain themselves to trees to prevent logging, many others sit at desks all day making phone calls to raise money for causes such as women's shelters and endangered species. If someone is fighting for any type of change, that person is an activist. Activists can be paid or volunteer.

For an activist, it is important to know and understand the media. A children's activist is paid to write speeches, policy briefs, letters, and press releases. He or she develops a relationship with the press and does interviews to raise awareness of the cause.

Work Environment

Whether a person is out in the field or behind a desk, being an activist can be tough work. A lot of time may be spent walking the streets, knocking on doors, or investigating databases. Even the leaders of large activist organizations spend a lot of time on the phone with media and financial backers. If the activist's cause occurs across a large geographic area, he or she might have to travel to various locations or sites.

There are no set hours for an activist. He or she usually just does what it takes to get the job done. If the cause needs more money to stay afloat, or more support to more forward, the activist has to keep working until the job is done. There is no extra money for overtime work. Activists get paid out of the organization's budget, and the salaries are generally low.

Education and Aptitudes

Experience and talent dictate where an activist's future leads. Activists can often use their experience to get jobs in other areas that pay more but may not provide the same satisfaction.

There are no formal requirements to become a professional activist. People with all sorts of experience and educational backgrounds become activists. The most important characteristics are passion and perseverance. A post-secondary education may be helpful, and experience with marketing, law, media relations, or community development would definitely be an asset when seeking an activist role. For people looking to make a career out of activism, prior involvement with activist organizations will lead to roles with greater responsibility.

Children in Conflict and Poverty

Children are often victims in many countries, including our own, and do not have the rights they deserve. Circumstances beyond the control of families, communities, and entire nations have left children in grim conditions in many countries throughout the world.

Many families in Canada are refugees and survivors of war, and so understand war from personal experience. Others have family members who fought in one of many conflicts such as the two World Wars, the

Figure 4.13
Many children lose their families through acts of terrorism and war.

Korean War, the Vietnam War, Ireland, the war between Iran and Iraq, civil wars in the territories of the former Yugoslavia, or the wars in Afghanistan. In contemporary times, there is always a war or civil conflict somewhere in the world. These conflicts continue to affect families and their children. Canada sends peacekeepers to many countries, and we open our doors to refugees and children of war from many different countries. Children around the world have lost homes and families to war, terrorism, and civil uprisings. Orphanages are filled to overflowing in many countries to provide shelter to children whose parents have been killed, or who have been separated from their parents.

Poverty is by far one of the worst problems in the world, despite huge initiatives to stamp out world hunger. Debt-ridden countries use their best lands to raise cash crops for export to other countries. These crops include coffee, sugar, cocoa, bananas, and soybeans. The money disappears into private hands or is used to pay off national debt, while ordinary families farm the poorest lands or work for the lowest of wages wherever they can. Famine and poverty go hand in hand with overcrowding and malnutrition. Many children in the world do not receive enough food to sustain life. In Central America and South America, some children actually live in the city dumps, where they search for food, and create whatever shelter they can from the garbage they find.

Increasing numbers of street children are a problem throughout the world. Children are orphaned, leave families, or are sent to cities to fend for themselves, where they end up on the streets, looking for any way they can to survive. Prostitution and HIV is a growing problem among older children and adolescents in some countries. There is sometimes little hope of them surviving beyond their teen years. Children born to these street children are often orphaned early in life and face an early death from AIDS contracted from their infected mothers. Some countries face the loss of a whole generation of people and wonder how they will survive as a nation.

Child labour in developing countries is another concern. Some children are able to get work because they will accept lower wages than adults. Many Canadian and American companies, particularly in the clothing industry, set up factories in developing countries where women and children are eager to work for as little as twenty-seven cents an hour. Clothing and athletic shoes, handbags, rugs, embroidery, and household articles are just a few of the items produced using child labour. Working conditions in many of these countries do not need to meet the same standards as in North America. Poor lighting and ventilation, and long hours take their toll. Children have little chance of having a better life than their parents.

Case Study: Craig Kielburger

 In April 1995, Craig Kielburger became aware of the problem of child labour and the exploitation of children from a newspaper article on the front page of the *Toronto Star*. The article told of the death of child labourer Iqbal Masih. Kielburger, who was 12 years old at the time, was shocked at the cruel life and death of Iqbal. He researched the issue of child labour and organized his friends and class-mates to form Free the Children. He also organized a trip to South Asia that received media attention.

On that trip, he accompanied social activists who rescue children enslaved in bonded labour. The activists returned the malnourished and mistreated children to their friends and families. Kielburger's campaign caused individuals and community and government leaders to respond to this global problem. His continued work concerning child labour and exploitation resulted in a nomination for the Nobel Peace Prize in 2002.

Questions

1. Give reasons supporting Kielburger's nomination for the Nobel Peace Price.
2. What reasons may people Kielburger's age give for not becoming involved in the issues of developing countries?

Child Poverty in Canada

Some children live in poverty in Canada. Their environments may be different from those of children in other parts of the world, but their situations and hardships are often similar. Many families need the help of food banks and charity organizations to feed and clothe their children. Some families have lost their homes and possessions, and survive on the streets with the nation's homeless.

Global Awareness

As our global awareness increases, taking action to improve the lives of children in Canada and around the world becomes more important. How can you help? Students are making a difference everywhere. Some of the ways that students have taken action include supporting a child in need through direct donations, participating in fund-raising for famine relief, and boycotting products produced by companies that employ children.

❖ Connections

1. What aspects of children's rights interest you? How informed are you about children's rights? Find out how you could be active regarding children's needs and rights in Canada and around the world.
2. Check your library or do a Web search for a list of social justice organizations, such as Amnesty International, that work to improve the lives of children around the world. Share examples from your list with your class, with an explanation of how each organization helps children.

What the experts say

PEDRO BARRATA

Pedro Barrata, the Ontario Chair of Campaign 2000, answers the following question:

What can you tell us about child poverty in Canada?

The latest statistics show that we are failing to address the issue of child and family poverty in Canada. Between 1989 and 1998, the number of poor children increased 43 percent across the country. That number nearly doubled in Ontario during the same time period.

More and more families are also living far below the poverty line. In fact, the average poor family lives almost $9500 below the poverty line. This is the reality for many families, including those on social assistance and Employment Insurance benefits, as well as families who are working in minimum wage jobs with little security and few benefits. Families frequently cycle in and out of poverty and their position depends on a variety of factors, including their employment, housing situation, availability of supports such as child care, disability, and other factors. The way to prevent a "cycle of poverty" is to make sure that families have the supports that they need during difficult times. Without a strong safety net, families are much more vulnerable to falling into poverty.

Being poor in Canada means a child may experience hunger, but also means that a child may miss out on feeling safe, on a warm home or clothing, or on social events such as birthday parties, treats, school trips, or playing sports. A healthy start in life has a long-term impact on the well-being of children. Children who live in poverty encounter more hurdles to healthy development and are at an elevated risk for a wide range of negative outcomes in their health and well-being. We also know that children experiencing poverty are less likely to participate in organized sports and recreational activities, and they are less likely to live in safe neighbourhoods, risking exposure to environmental contaminants. To be poor is to be denied the opportunities to participate and share in the growth of a prosperous society. The ability of children to progress through each stage of development depends upon the range of resources and opportunities contributed by families, communities, and the broader society. An environment that nurtures inclusiveness requires a supply of good jobs that enable caregivers to support their families. Families and children also have a right to economic security; early childhood development services, and child care; affordable, secure housing; and accessible post-secondary education.

Chapter Summary

Chapter Highlights

- Child rearing is a cultural experience.

- Parents transmit their culture to their children from the moment they are born.

- Children absorb their culture through what they hear, how they are touched, and from what they see, smell, and taste on a regular basis.

- All cultures have customs associated with raising children, including the naming of children and teaching them to respect elders.

- Child-rearing practices can vary around the world.

- *The Convention on the Rights of the Child* states that all children around the world have the same rights.

- Some children around the world and in Canada experience abuse, deprivation, malnutrition, abandonment, or child labour.

- By developing a global awareness, action can be taken to support social justice for children everywhere.

Review and Extend Your Learning

1. Describe the many ways in which child rearing is a "cultural" activity. **K/U** **T/I**

2. Review Figure 4.3: Common Goals of Child Rearing. Identify the reasons that all cultures share these goals. Suggest reasons why some cultures may emphasize some of the goals more than others. **T/I** **A**

3. Explain how child rearing differs according to a family's authority patterns. **K/U** **C**

4. Make a list of names with which you are familiar. Analyze which factors may have been considered when selecting these names. **T/I**

5. Examine the list of children's rights as described in *The Convention on the Rights of the Child*. Explain how each right could be achieved and who would contribute to the achievement of that right. **T/I** **A**

6. Describe the impact of poverty on children and families. Explain why child poverty is considered one of the worst problems in the world today. **K/U** **T/I**

7. Survey students in your community using a questionnaire to determine their knowledge of child poverty in Canada. Compare their answers to the information in the Pedro Barrata interview and present them to the class. **T/I** **C**

8. Conduct an Internet search about child labour issues. Present your information as a formal report. **T/I** **C**

Research Opportunities

9. Interview a student in your school or a person in your community who was not born in Canada, or whose parents or grandparents were not born in Canada.
   a) What expectations does his or her culture have for newborns?
   b) What religious or cultural rituals are related to the birth and naming of children in this culture?
   c) How does the family prepare the home for a new baby?
   Pose three other questions about how culture is transmitted in the family.

10. To build your phenomenological research skills, gather family stories from your own family or another family you know that illustrates a specific cultural parenting belief or practice followed in the culture. Write a detailed description of the phenomenon, noting why and how it is practised, where and when it originated, and what makes it unique. Share what you have learned with your class.

11. Conduct a Web search to determine which countries have not ratified *The Convention on the Rights of the Child*. What are the legal implications for countries that do not support the rights of children? After researching this information, write a personal reaction statement.

Issue Analysis

12. Analyze the problems and possibilities of raising children when the parents represent two or more cultures.

Unit 3 The Circles of Life

The focus of this unit is the place of children in families and how families with children change over time. Families provide children with their identity and have a key influence on their lifelong well-being. You will learn skills and strategies that promote healthy relationships and positive interaction with children.

- Communication skills enhance relationships with older children and adolescents.
- Positive relationships that contribute to development depend on effective relationship skills and strategies.

KEY INSIGHTS:

- Families may vary, yet they all contribute to the developmental potential of children.
- Children rely on their unique families and are influenced by them throughout their lives.
- Families and parenting challenges vary as children grow and change throughout the life cycle.
- Healthy parent-child relationships are the basis for optimal development.
- Strong relationships and healthy interaction with children are essential for parents, caregivers, and those who work with children.

Unit at a Glance

Children and Families

By the end of this chapter, you will be able to:

- analyze the characteristics of families and compare the changing needs of individuals and families throughout life

- evaluate management strategies that promote self-discipline in children and adolescents

- identify causes and consequences of child abuse and family violence, and assess impact of abuse and violence on families, caregivers, and those who work with children

- identify social and cultural variations in family forms

- outline strategies that ensure safe, non-violent environments for all children

- recognize the stages and transitions within family life cycles

Important Terms

autonomy

beginning family

contracting family

expanding family

family

family development

family life cycle

family meetings

family of orientation

family of procreation

generational cycle of violence

human development

major decision

minor decision

Chapter at a Glance

How Do Children Fit in Families?

According to government statistics, more than 330 000 babies are now being born in Canada each year. Each of these children comes into the world with the biological, social, and emotional supports of two or more pre-existing families. Each child may also belong to many other families throughout his or her lifetime. Biologically, each child has inherited a chromosomal package at conception from both the sperm and egg that will determine the child's physical make-up. Socially, each child arrives in a family that already has a social status, a culture, and one or more languages, and that lives in a rural or urban community in a particular geographical location. Emotionally, each child may be loved and wanted, viewed with indifference, or rejected by one or more family members.

Figure 5.1
A child may belong to many types of families throughout his or her lifetime.

What Is a Family? Some Definitions

The Vanier Institute of the Family defines **family** as "any combination of two or more persons who are bound together over time by ties of mutual consent, birth and/or adoption or placement. Together they assume responsibilities for variant combinations of some of the following: physical maintenance and care of group members; addition of new members through procreation or adoption; socialization of children; social control of members; production, consumption, distribution of goods and services; and affective nurturance—love."

Statistics Canada defines family as "a married couple (with or without children of either or both spouses); a couple living common-law (with or without children of either or both partners); or a lone parent of any marital status, with at least one child living in the same dwelling."

Families are often described as a circle. Your family existed long before you were born and will continue long after you die. It has no beginning and no end. The family into which you were born, or your **family of orientation**, is the family that nurtures, provides for, and instructs you. The family that you generate in the future, the **family of procreation**, is the one in which you will nurture, provide for, and instruct. Each family is a circle, and in you, two circles representing your parents' families overlap. Throughout your lifetime, you will likely belong to many different kinds of families, and their influence will be felt in many ways.

Canadian Families Come in All Shapes and Sizes

There is no one Canadian family. For some, it may be a mother, father, two kids, and a dog, and for others, like Thu Thuy on page 97, it may

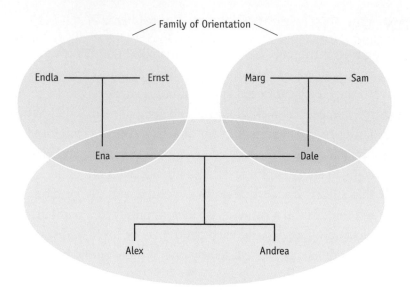

Family of Orientation

Endla —— Ernst   Marg —— Sam

Ena ————————— Dale

Alex   Andrea

Family of Procreation

Figure 5.2
You can identify families of procreation and orientation by looking at a family tree.

mean a mother, father, and siblings in another country, plus an adoptive mother here in Canada. What do families look like in Canada? Some are big, and some are small. Some are related by blood and others are connected by marriage, adoption, or choice. Same-sex couples appear in every family form in which heterosexual couples

Family Forms and Configurations

Adoptive family	One that accepts the legal responsibility of raising a child or children of other biological origins.
Childless couple	Sometimes called "child-free." A couple who shares a household without children.
Extended family	All your relatives, either living or deceased.
Family of friends	A close-knit group that shares a sense of family.
Foster family	A family that offers temporary care for children until they can return to their own family, or be placed into an adoptive family.
Lone-parent family	One parent and his or her children.
Nuclear family	Two parents and their child or children.
Recombined family	Sometimes called a blended or reconstituted family. A family re-formed through remarriage. May include either stepfamily members or half-siblings.

Figure 5.3
Which family configurations include children? Are some forms more common in certain populations in Canada? In your opinion, is this list complete?

appear. For example, a nuclear family can have two mothers or a mother and a father. Figure 5.3 on page 96 describes several configurations of Canadian families.

None of these types of families is new to Canadian society. In the 1950s, the nuclear family was the most prominent family form. It was the form that was idealized by the media and Canadian culture, to the point that even an extended family living in one household came to be seen as unusual. Yet, before the invention of penicillin and its worldwide availability in the late 1940s, fathers and mothers often died before their children were grown. Single parents raised children; remarriage was commonplace; stepfamilies were formed; and distant relatives or family friends raised children.

> ◼ *Happy families resemble one another; but each unhappy family is unhappy in its own way.*
> — Leo Tolstoy

Case Study: Thu Thuy's Story

Thu Thuy was born in Vietnam, where she lived with her mother, father, and siblings. They were so poor that just finding enough to eat was a daily challenge. Some families abandoned their children, while others tried desperately to find ways to improve life for their children. When Thu Thuy was eight years old, she was given the opportunity for a new life. A French Canadian woman from Quebec City wanted to adopt her! So Thu Thuy left her own family in Vietnam and came to live with her new mom, a single career woman, who found it easier to adopt a child from Vietnam than from Canada.

The first year was difficult for both Thu Thuy and her new mother. Everything was new for Thu Thuy. She was not used to wearing shoes and had no idea what pajamas were for, since she was used to sleeping in the same clothes she wore all day. The weather, especially the Quebec winter, was a big adjustment, too.

Thu Thuy has made the most of her life in Canada. She quickly learned to speak French, has made many friends, and does well in school. She trains 14 hours a week in gymnastics with the encouragement of her mom, who is a gymnastics instructor. She is learning to speak English, and after she completed Grade Seven, she spent two weeks on a student exchange in Ontario in July 2001. She still writes to her family back in Vietnam and sends them gifts and money from time to time. When she is older, her mother will take her back to Vietnam to see her Vietnamese family. Being part of a new family in Canada has changed Thu Thuy's life.

Questions

1. Thu Thuy has two families. Draw overlapping circles with stick figures to illustrate her families. Put Thu Thuy in the centre where the circles overlap. How many circles are there? Who would be in each circle?
2. Throughout your lifetime, you will likely belong to many different kinds of families, and their influence will be felt in many ways. Explain how Thu Thuy's new family has influenced her.

❖ Checkpoints

1. Outline the similarities and differences in the definitions of family given by The Vanier Institute and Statistics Canada. Why do you think there are differences in these definitions?

Families in the 20th Century

In 1901, about seven out of ten families were composed of a married couple with children. Close to 14% of families at the beginning of the century were led by lone parents, eight out of ten of whom were widows or widowers. As such, lone-parent families were almost as common in 1901 as they were at the end of the century. The main difference is that in 1901 more were caused by the death of one of the parents.

— *The Vanier Institute of the Family*

2. Compare and contrast the roles within the family of orientation and the family of procreation.

3. Throughout your lifetime, you will likely belong to many different kinds of families, and their influence will be felt in many ways. Explain how Thu Thuy's new family has influenced her.

Is one type of family form optimal for children? Children have been raised successfully in all kinds of families. Children have also been victimized and abused in all kinds of families. It is not the form that a family takes but the dedication and commitment to children that determines its success in nurturing the next generation.

"Out of 100 Families" (Family Types), 2001

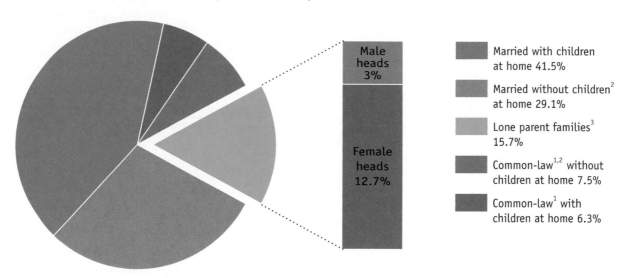

Male heads 3%

Female heads 12.7%

Married with children at home 41.5%

Married without children[2] at home 29.1%

Lone parent families[3] 15.7%

Common-law[1,2] without children at home 7.5%

Common-law[1] with children at home 6.3%

[1] Common-law couples are not legally married.

[2] Married and common-law couples without children at home are couples who have never had children, as well as "empty-nest" couples whose children have grown up and left home.

[3] A lone-parent family is headed by a single parent and has one or more children living at home.

Note that for all families with children at home, only children who have never been married are counted.

Adapted from the Statistics Canada Website, http://www.statcan.ca/english/census01/teacher's_kit/activity6.cfm, Handout 1: The Changing Canadian Family, Family Structure 2001 Census

Figure 5.4
Compare the differences among types of families in 1901 and 2001. Explain the nature of these differences.

Quick Quiz

Identify the family forms described in each situation below:

1. The Coghlins are expecting at least 300 people at their family reunion this year.
2. Sometimes it is often hard to say good-bye when a child you have grown attached to can go back to his or her own family.
3. Although Kasha and Toni are not related, they were both excited with the birth of their half-sister.
4. Emily and her mom have been a two-person family since Emily was born 17 years ago.
5. Mario and Ethel make up for not having kids of their own by sharing their warm hearts with nieces, nephews, and the neighbourhood kids.

Answers: 1. Extended family   2. Foster family   3. Stepfamily
4. Lone-parent family   5. Childless couple

Career Capsule

PHOTOGRAPHER FOR CHILDREN AND FAMILIES

Tasks and Responsibilities

Photographers that specialize in taking pictures of babies, children, and families are among the many kinds of specialized professional photographers. These photographers may work directly for families or take commercial photographs for business. They must be familiar with the nature and behaviour of children of different ages to be able to take photographs that expertly portray the essence of their clients.

No matter which area of specialization, a photographer must have knowledge and expertise with different types of cameras, lighting, camera settings, and film processing.

Work Environment

Children's photographers usually work in a private studio or at department stores with a photography studio, or they could travel from mall to mall or school to school working a short time in each place. They may also travel to the client's home or work "on location" in a large commercial studio if doing shots for print advertising. Child photographers may also work as employees of large companies that specialize in taking school photographs for graduation or yearbooks.

Education and Aptitudes

There are no specific educational requirements for becoming a photographer, although a college diploma in photography or a university degree in fine arts specializing in photography would be good preparation for a full-time career in the field. If you wish to run your own business, some courses in marketing and business studies would be advantageous.

All photographers require good communication skills and an approachable, friendly manner. They need to be able to relax their clients so that they can photograph them at their best. Photographers who specialize in children should genuinely like children and enjoy being around them. They should also understand the importance of play and be familiar with how children and adolescents of various ages are apt to behave.

Figure 5.5
The extended family includes both the family of orientation and the family of procreation.

Families Grow and Change

A family portrait is rarely a true representation of a family. The artificiality of a family portrait is evident in many ways. The individuals are posed, they generally smile, and they take great care in what they are wearing. A family portrait does not show the dynamics of interactions that occur within that family. The camera can never capture which child got scolded, who caused trouble, who told a great joke, or who showed their love in a special way that day. The portrait freezes the family briefly in a time and place. The moment after the portrait is taken, the family is already changing. The children are growing and maturing, the adolescents are slowing in physical growth but continuing to grow in intellect and maturity, while the parents may be showing some early signs of aging. It is just another family in the ever-changing circle of life.

The changes known as **human development** occur most spectacularly at the beginning of life. The most rapid change takes place in the short time between conception and the end of the first year of life. From a fertilized egg the size of a pinhead, a person who can practically walk, talk, and give hugs has emerged.

Although each person develops at an individual rate, a common pattern of development exists. At birth, children are totally dependent

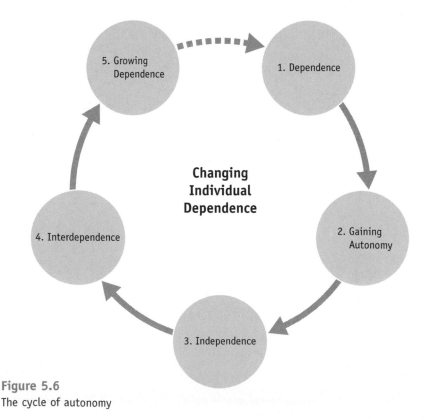

Figure 5.6
The cycle of autonomy

on others for meeting their needs. By 18 months, most children exhibit some desire for **autonomy** or wanting to do things on their own. As children develop physically, intellectually, socially, and emotionally, they take more and more steps toward independence. Interdependence becomes the focus of adulthood as lasting relationships with spouses, co-workers, employers, and children evolve. At times, you are dependent on them while at others, they are dependent on you. In later life, many individuals begin to lose some of their physical, intellectual, social, and emotional capacity. They may become more and more dependent on their own children and others. Some come full circle and in many ways are like children again.

Families, too, follow recognizable patterns of development. In Canada, families are strongly identified by the presence of children, even though not everyone has children. Therefore, the most basic pattern of **family development** focuses on children and evolves in three phases: the beginning family, the expanding family, and the contracting family. Later in this chapter, you'll learn about family life cycle theory, which identifies six family stages.

Figure 5.7
The most rapid human development occurs from conception to the age of one.

❖ Connections

1. Think about your extended family or a friend's extended family. Identify which form is represented by each of the families within the extended family. For example, you may have a cousin who lives in a lone-parent family or a great-aunt and uncle who are a childless family.
2. Speak to a parent—your own or someone else's. Ask them to describe the ways in which their family of orientation has influenced their family of procreation in terms of values, beliefs, and practices. You could ask about discipline, education, family traditions, and the like.

The Beginning Family

The **beginning family** is the stage during which steps are taken to start a family. Selecting a partner to become the other parent of your children is a first step in beginning your family. In Canada, as in much of western civilization, emphasis is placed on dating and courtship rituals, which often result in a commitment that can sustain the effort of producing and raising children.

For many Canadians, the commitment to become partners is symbolized by a marriage ceremony that gives couples the opportunity to

Figure 5.8
How will I know if he will make a good father? How will I know if she will make a good mother?

declare publicly that they intend to commit to each other. Whether in a religious ceremony or in a civil ceremony conducted by a justice of the peace, marriage is the institution most Canadians recognize as the one in which children will be born and raised. Some Canadians make less formal commitments but are no less dedicated to their children.

Another step in beginning a family is to plan and prepare for children. Whether a couple waits several years to have a child, or whether an unplanned pregnancy occurs, the couple has nine months to think ahead and plan for the baby's arrival. A first pregnancy is a critical time for looking forward to your role as a parent. In the past, the father often felt excluded, but today there are books written for the expectant father, and there are opportunities through local prenatal classes to meet and talk with other dads, both experienced and novice. When adopting, a couple must plan ahead, because the screening and waiting process can take a long time.

The birth or adoption of a first child is a major event. The life that individuals and couples have before the child arrives changes forever. Today, fathers are expected to be part of the birth process and become attached to their newborns from their first breath. The totally dependent new little person is now the focus of the beginning family. Parents have much to learn about caring for their infant, many questions to ask, and lots of anxieties and special moments to share with one another.

■ Family development involves three phrases:
• Beginning Family
• Expanding Family
• Contracting Family

Expanding Family

The next phase, known as the **expanding family**, begins when the second child arrives. Having more than one child is the norm in Canada. A second child in the family means many things: more diapers, less time for everything, more fatigue, and more people to share special family times. Easing the extra responsibility is that having done it all before, parents feel more confident in caring for subsequent children. There is definitely a difference between having a child and having children. Finding child care for one child is a challenge. You pay twice as much for two children, even though your own salary does not increase, and you may have children in two different child-care settings.

Family Size?

The freedom to have more than one child is sometimes taken for granted in Canada. We do not have laws limiting the number of children, nor do we have a cultural preference for a particular gender of children, as in some other countries. There are, however,

Figure 5.9
Many Canadians have more than one child.

Female Infanticide

The following material is excerpted from *Case Study: Female Infanticide* (2000) by Adam Jones.

The phenomenon of female infanticide is as old as many cultures, and has likely accounted for millions of gender-selective deaths throughout history. It remains a critical concern in a number of developing countries today, notably the two most populous countries on earth, China and India. In all cases, specifically female infanticide reflects the low status accorded to women in most parts of the world; it is arguably the most brutal and destructive manifestation of the anti-female bias that pervades "patriarchal" societies. It is closely linked to the phenomena of sex-selective abortion, which targets female fetuses almost exclusively, and neglect of girl children.

a number of factors that influence when the first child is born or how many children you might choose to have.

Culture and religion often influence the form that families take, as well as the size of families. In some ethnic and religious communities, big families are expected. Some religions discourage contraception, so larger families may be the result. For some couples, however, having more than two children is not a desirable choice.

Couples and individuals whose income is not adequate to support children may choose to delay or limit the number of children they have. By abstaining or using reliable methods of birth control, they are able to prevent the conception of children. Economics has often affected birth rates. During the Great Depression of the 1930s, the birth rate in Canada decreased significantly.

Peers and family members can also influence decisions on family size. If all your friends are having children, it might influence you to start a family, too. If you have brothers and sisters who are starting their families, it might encourage you to have children so the cousins can be friends. If it is typical for newly married couples among your friends and family to delay having children or to limit the number of children they have, you may feel pressured to follow that pattern as well.

The *Toronto Star* article "Women Putting Off Motherhood Even Longer Now" on page 104 indicates that current studies show a trend among Canadian women to wait to have children until after they have established a career. Other goals such as buying a house, travelling, or finishing a diploma or degree might come before starting a family. The older a woman is, the fewer child-bearing years she has left, so, naturally, the fewer children she could have if she delays parenthood until her 30s or 40s. Because women and men both experience a significant decrease in fertility as they age, couples who delay having children may experience difficulties in conceiving children.

Figure 5.10
If a couple has friends who are starting families, they may feel encouraged to start one, too.

The Challenges of Expanding Families

As the family continues to grow in size and age, family life becomes more complex. In the expanding phase, children are growing up, making friends, going to school, and becoming more independent. Their world is expanding, which makes family life more complicated. Frequently, both parents work at this stage, because the family's financial needs are growing as well. The expanding stage can be very stressful for parents as well as for children.

Parents must have good management, discipline, communication, and decision-making skills to handle the challenges of the expanding family. Children of all ages can be assigned chores and given increased responsibility for contributing to the family as they get older. Teaching children to share in the work of the family can reduce some of the stress on parents. Children as young as 18 months show an interest in "helping out" and can begin with easy tasks such as picking up toys. As family challenges arise, parents must develop effective family management strategies and hone their problem-solving and decision-making skills.

Women Putting off Motherhood Even Longer Now

by Marlene Habib, *The Toronto Star*, May 11, 2002

Penny Shore, a Toronto-based parenting educator, says a range of financial, emotional, and social factors should be taken into consideration when planning a family, or it would be like "jumping into parenthood without a parachute." Shore acknowledges, however, that one of the most burning questions for women is, "Do I interrupt my career to have a child?"

"The 'baby maybe' question is serious," says Shore, creator of ParentSmart Books and head of an international advisory council on parenting.

Women are more inclined than ever to delay hopping on to the mommy track, usually for financial or career reasons. As well, while fertility rates decline as a woman ages, new reproductive technologies are options for women choosing to start a family later in life.

The Statistics Canada survey notes the 27.1 average (age) of a first-time mother is up from 25.7 in 1986. This is not surprising, given the rise in women aged 25 to 44 in the workforce from 49.7 percent in 1976, to 78.2 percent in 1998.

More women work out of necessity because of increases in the cost of living and divorce rates, and they have more career choices and high-income opportunities. As well, changes in the workplace protect their jobs so they can take maternity leave.

But only moms and their partners know best about what works when it comes to family planning, says Shore.

(Karen) Wilson, for one, says she doesn't think she has as much energy as she would have had if she became a mother earlier.

"At the end of my work day, I'm pretty stressed and try to cram in dinner and quality time and bath and bedtime. That can be taxing," says Wilson.

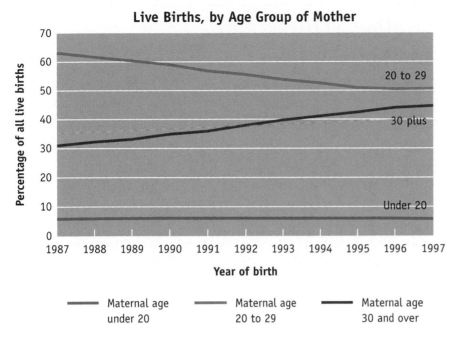

Live Births, by Age Group of Mother

20 to 29

30 plus

Under 20

Year of birth

Maternal age under 20   Maternal age 20 to 29   Maternal age 30 and over

Adapted from the Statistics Canada Web site, http://www.statcan/Daily/English/990616/d990616b.htm

Figure 5.11
Women are increasingly starting their families at age 30 or older.

The family may continue to expand even as the oldest child reaches adolescence. Siblings may compete for parents' attention, and younger children may envy the freedoms enjoyed by older children, while older children complain how easy the younger ones have it. It is a long way from the day when the first child was born.

Challenges of the Expanding Years

The expanding years offer growth and development, but they also offer new or additional challenges:

- juggling work and family life
- car pooling
- finding reliable baby sitters
- finding quality child care
- extra expenses
- not enough money, time, or energy
- crowded rooms, living spaces
- jealousy
- sibling rivalry
- keeping on top of homework

- TV and media violence
- preteen mood swings
- adolescent work schedules
- sleepovers
- taking care of pets
- getting kids to after-school activities
- family health concerns
- not enough time
- looking after grandma and grandpa
- children's independence needs
- difficulties at school
- bullying
- peer pressure

Figure 5.12
Family meetings can help to make family life more manageable.

Parenting Skills

Family Meetings

Parents sometimes need to look for ways to make family life less stressful and more manageable. One technique, recommended by Dr. Thomas Gordon who is known for his work on parent effectiveness training, is to schedule **family meetings** to complete a weekly calendar of activities and create a job board. Ideally, the family meets each week at a scheduled time, chooses a chairperson, follows an agenda, and gets input from every family member.

Weekly activities, such as hockey practice, swimming lessons, heritage language class, mom's exercise class, dad's school council meeting, and going out for pizza are all written down. Then daily and weekly chores, such as walking the dog and doing the dishes, are scheduled for each family member. Problems with the previous week's schedule are taken into account, and concerns that involve the whole family, such as who is going to give up a bedroom for Grandma's visit, are discussed. This way, the confusion of family life becomes the concern of the whole family, not just that of one person. A pattern for family meetings needs to be firmly established in early childhood. Most families, however, organize their family activities in an informal or less structured way.

Figure 5.13
In the contracting family stage, children begin to leave the family.

The Contracting Family

The final phase is the **contracting family**. In this stage, the family becomes smaller while older children grow more independent and begin to leave the family. For some families, this stage can be prolonged over many years, while young adults continue their education beyond high school. Great-grandparents may have reached the end of their life, and grandparents may become more dependent on their adult children. However, the circle of life continues when the next generation of children begins their own families. Each new family goes through its own expanding phase, as grown children and their spouses and children add to the extended family.

❖ Connections

1. Consider which developmental phase your family is in. How is it similar to or different from the phases that your classmates' families are in?

2. How many children are in the biggest family you know of today? How many children did each of your great-grandparents have?

3. What causes stress in your family? Consider ways in which you might help to relieve that stress.

Parenting Skills

Solving Problems with Decision-Making

Problems that arise in the expanding family fall into two categories: those that require a major decision and those that require a minor decision. A **major decision** is one that may require a substantial outlay of money or that may affect the life of one or more family members. Where should we live? What activity would be best for my child: hockey, dance, or swimming? How should we deal with a defiant child? How do we handle teenagers who want to stay home alone? A **minor decision** does not involve a significant outlay of money, and it does not affect anyone's life in a critical way. Should we have hot cereal or cold cereal for breakfast? Should we do the laundry today or tomorrow? Should we wear a jacket or not? Parents need to put far less energy into the minor decisions and use a more careful approach for the major ones.

There are five important steps in handling major decisions or problems:

Figure 5.14
Deciding where to live is a major decision.

POWER Decision-Making: A Five-Step Model

Step 1	Define the Problem.
Step 2	List the Options that are available.
Step 3	Weigh the advantages, disadvantages, and possible consequences for each option.
Step 4	Eliminate all but the best choice, and then act on it.
Step 5	Re-evaluate your decision as circumstances change. If it is not working, go back to Step 1.

This five-step method allows parents to consider carefully all the choices available to them, and imagine the outcome or consequences for each possibility. The needs of everyone involved, the costs, and the long-term effects should all be taken into account before making a commitment. Then, when the decision is made, the results are usually effective.

❖ Checkpoints

1. Describe the transitions into and out of the three phases of family development.
2. Analyze some of the factors in a couple's decision about family size.
3. Illustrate how you would solve a family problem using the POWER decision-making model.

Family Life Cycle Theory

The belief that individuals, families, or even societies follow a pre-dictable pattern is called developmental theory. In family studies, the view that the family generally follows a pattern of development is called family life cycle theory. Life cycle theory comes from the study of the family and pays attention to the similarities among many families.

Social scientists Betty Carter and Monica McGoldrick have developed a model that is often used in the social sciences to describe the family life cycle. Rather than the three stages of the beginning, expanding, and contracting family, they see six stages in the **family life cycle**:

- between families (young single)
- new couple
- family with young children
- family with adolescent children
- launching
- family in later life

As individuals and families move from one stage to the next, their needs change. What was important at one stage is not as important at another. The work of the family at each stage is to meet the needs of every family member. Figure 5.16 on page 110 identifies some of the changing needs of individuals and families throughout the life cycle.

Life Cycle Issues

Family life is both rewarding and challenging. Every stage of the life cycle has typical concerns and anxieties:

1. Young singles worry about their future, their identity, and their place in the world.

Stages of the Family Life Cycle

6. Family in
Later Life

1. Between
Families

5. Launching

2. New Couple

4. Family with
Adolescent
Children

3. Family with
Young Children

Figure 5.15

Social scientists Betty Carter and Monica McGoldrick believe that families tend to go through a six-stage model of the family life cycle. Teen pregnancy, separation, divorce, or death are family life-cycle disruptions that can happen in any family and alter its course. Although the six-stage model of the life cycle does not describe every family, it does provide a framework for making sense of families. Can you identify other variations or patterns that are not consistent with the six-stage model?

Changing Life-Cycle Needs

Stage of Life Cycle	The Individual Needs to...	The Family Needs to...
Between Families (Young Single)	Establish one's independence. Choose and implement career strategies. Form a lasting relationship (mate selection).	Encourage and support the young adult. Continue to nurture other children who have not left home.
New Couple	Maintain personal identity within the relationship. Plan for the role of a future parent.	Learn to live as a couple. Plan for future children. Achieve independence from families of orientation.
Family with Young Children	Child: Receive care, comfort, and instruction. Parent: Learn to parent. Find time for personal fulfillment.	Nurture and care for children. Maintain couple commitment. Balance work and family.
Family with Adolescent Children	Adolescent: Establish an identity. Adult: Acknowledge individuality of adolescents. Face middle-age issues.	Keep lines of communication open. Maintain connections between generations.
Launching	Young adult: Experience various roles. Older adult: Find self-fulfillment without children at home.	Encourage young adults to become independent. Become a couple again. Maintain communication with young adults.
Family in Later Life	Older person: Maintain health, wellness, and independence. Maintain connections with family members. Adjust to the loss of a life-long partner.	Family members: Support and maintain aging family members. Learn from the wisdom of older family members.

Figure 5.16
Each stage of life has unique characteristics and challenges.

2. New couples are concerned with their in-laws, their finances, and the stability of their relationship.

3. Families with young children have numerous worries: how to care for infants, toddlers, and preschoolers, postpartum depression, discipline, and child care.

4. Families with adolescent children have concerns about peer pressure, schooling, stepfamilies, discipline, and personal safety.

5. Launching families are facing mid-life crises, the cost of post-secondary education, and being sandwiched between the needs of their children and those of their parents.

6. Families in later life face the concern of aging, bereavement, ill health, and growing dependency.

A concern or issue at any stage can become a crisis. Whenever a family faces a crisis, family members need to examine the relevant issues carefully. They can take steps to make family problems less difficult—for example, learning about family life challenges before they happen can be helpful. Books, magazines, and educational media are good sources of information. Talking to family members, friends, or professionals may provide answers to many questions. It is impossible to predict what a family will face in the future, but there are opportunities to take courses and learn about living in families and raising children long before crises occur.

Cycles within Families

Families are circles within circles. You may have heard the expression "what goes around, comes around." Many things recur in families. It may be a family name that shows up generation after generation. It may be a unique talent that is passed from grandparent to grandchild. It may be a trait or tradition passed down from father to son, mother to daughter, father to daughter, or mother to son. On the positive side, strong, healthy families are cyclical, promoting and producing healthy families in their own right. Cycles are not always positive, however. Violence and poverty are two conditions that sociologists recognize as recurring from one generation to the next. These negative cyclic situations are detrimental to the functioning of families but may be difficult to stop.

The Cycle of Violence

Individuals who grow up in families in which they see or experience abuse often repeat this pattern in their own families. This is known as a **generational cycle of violence**. Because families live their daily lives in the privacy of their own homes, family violence may be a well-kept secret. Some religions or cultures believe it is the right of parents or male authority figures to dominate children. Such behaviours may be seen as abuse by others in Canadian society.

Violence toward children is not an easy cycle to break. Education is available to help those who work with children to identify the signs and symptoms of abuse. Canadian law requires individuals to report known or suspected child abuse or neglect to police or child-welfare authorities. Shelters and programs support women and children who have been abused. However, the cycle of violence will be broken only when the men and women who victimize children admit that they are abusive and seek help to change their behaviour. Children who have

Figure 5.17
One of the best choices you could make is to take a parenting course.

Figure 5.18
Some traits, talents, and traditions are passed on from generation to generation. This photograph shows three generations of farmers.

witnessed or experienced abuse require counselling so that they do not repeat the behaviour as adults.

The following article about violence against women was published by the Peel Committee Against Woman Abuse in November 2000.

How Are Children Affected by Exposure to Woman Abuse?

Children depend upon their parents for their physical and emotional needs and for security and protection. Abuse against a parent creates an environment that is tense, full of fear, and unhealthy. When children see their mother being abused by her partner, they may learn that:

- violence is okay
- violence is a way to resolve conflict
- violence is an effective way to gain power and control over others
- violence is a normal part of a relationship

Children can be directly or indirectly affected by seeing their mother being abused:

- They may also be directly abused by the abuser—verbally, physically, emotionally, and/or sexually.
- They may be abused if they try to intervene to protect their mother.
- They may be placed in the middle by one of the parents, which can be confusing and difficult.
- Being exposed to abuse, even if they are not directly harmed, is a form of abuse.

Children exposed to woman abuse are affected on many levels:

- emotionally (anxiety, anger, depression, low self-esteem)
- physically (difficulty sleeping, eating, or both; health problems)
- socially (poor social skills, peer rejection)

- cognitively (development delays, poor school performance)
- behaviourally (aggression, tantrums, immaturity)

The impact of abuse on a child may be affected by:

- the age of the child
- the developmental stage of the child
- how long the abuse has been happening
- how serious the abuse is
- the support the child receives

The Cycle of Violence

Children who are exposed to abuse have an increased chance of being abused or being abusive, or both, as an adult. Boys whose fathers abused their mothers have 1000 times greater likelihood of abusing their partners as adults than sons of non-violent fathers (Strauss, Gelles, Steinmetz, 1980). Children may learn that violence is an acceptable way to resolve conflict in the family and in relationships. It is important to recognize that not all children who are exposed to woman abuse become abusive or get involved in an abusive relationship as an adult; however, the likelihood is greater. Many factors, such as support and professional intervention, can help break the cycle.

The Cycle of Poverty

Families living in poverty do not have the money or resources to meet the necessities of life. In some families, poverty is another cycle that is difficult to break. Stories are told of children who escape poverty as adults, largely through their efforts in obtaining an education or through some amazing good fortune. The reality for many Canadian children born into poverty, however, is that they repeat the cycle with their own children. Lack of knowledge, skills, and opportunities for those living in poverty continue to perpetuate the cycle.

Campaign 2000

Campaign 2000, founded in 1991, is a diverse cross-Canada coalition of more than 80 groups committed to monitoring the implementation of the 1989 all-party House of Commons resolution to end child poverty in Canada by the year 2000. This Canadian coalition believes that poverty is a social measure, more than a tally of the basic survival needs of children and their families. The coalition is committed to creating an inclusive society that will ensure a place for every child with safe, secure housing; adequate income security policies; high quality, affordable child care; and accessible public education, health and recreation and cultural services. The coalition affirms that decent jobs are essential to enable families to support themselves.

Campaign 2000 issues an annual Report Card on Child Poverty that provides an update on trends with respect to child poverty. In 2001, Campaign 2000 issued its ninth annual report card, which indicated that while the rate of child poverty, at 19 percent, remains high, the rate decreased for the second year in a row. But it is important to remember that in 1989, only one in seven children lived in poverty, while the most recent statistics show that about one in five children lives in situations that are substantially worse off than average.

The Importance of Families for Children

A family is the foundation of a child's life. Children are born with a human potential that develops according to childhood and family experiences, particularly as a result of the quality of parenting that they receive. Families encourage development and provide children with a strong sense of identity. Before they can talk, babies recognize the members of their family and form strong attachments with each family member. Some of the most memorable moments a person experiences are with the family. Parents and siblings model behaviour and teach important skills. A healthy family is the best gift a child could have.

You have taken an important step in strengthening families by learning more about parents and children. You are learning to improve and develop the skills that contribute to a healthy family, from communicating and listening, to learning where to get help with parenting problems. Strong families will produce strong families. Continue to look for the strengths and enjoyment in families, including your own.

The following article, by Ben Schlesinger (1998), appeared in *Transition*, a magazine published by the Vanier Institute of Family.

Strong Families: A Portrait

by Ben Schlesinger

Though novelists and family researchers have traditionally been more interested in the troubles and turmoil of unhappy families, we stand to learn more from happier, stronger families. By studying the common elements in their lives, we may find the keys to strengthening all of the families whose lives we touch.

The family is alive and well at the end of the twentieth century despite widely published reports that it is an outdated social institution. In fact, the family as an institution is remarkably strong. Carlfred Broderick says it is **the** toughest evolutionary human structure and will outlast every other organization. Clearly, the evidence shows that the family bears more of the burden of individual human survival, and also of the transmission of civilization and culture, than any other social structure.

Of course, some flesh-and-blood families are not as strong as the institution we call "the family." What makes some families stronger and healthier than others? Why do some function better than others? The literature on family strengths has many answers. Let's start by defining what researchers are looking for when they try to identify "family strengths."

Family strengths are relationship patterns, intrapersonal and interpersonal skills and competencies, and social and psychological characteristics that:

- create a sense of positive family identity;
- promote satisfying and fulfilling interaction among family members;
- encourage the development of the potential of the family group and individual family members;
- contribute to the family's ability to deal effectively with stress and crisis; and
- contribute to the family's ability to be supportive of other families....

Healthy Families

A Canadian pioneering study by Westley and Epstein nearly thirty years ago examined the emotional health of families in Montreal. Their most important finding was that children's emotional health is closely related to the emotional relationship between their parents. When this relationship is warm and constructive, such that the husband and wife feel loved, admired, and encouraged to act in ways that they themselves admire, the children are happy and healthy. Couples who are emotionally close, who meet each other's needs, and who encourage each other's positive self-image, become good parents....

Another study, by Lewis *et al.*, found that parental role modelling is a crucial factor in the development of qualities that ensure personal psychological health and growth in families. They also discovered that healthy families have a relationship of trust, shared power, and close communication.

When Dolores Curran interviewed 551 professionals, she asked them to list characteristics of healthy families. According to their lists, the healthy family:

- communicates and listens
- affirms and supports one another
- teaches respect for others
- develops a sense of trust
- has a sense of play and humour
- exhibits a sense of shared responsibility
- teaches a sense of right and wrong
- has a strong sense of family in which rituals and traditions abound
- has a balance of interaction among members
- has a shared religious core
- respects the privacy of one another
- values service to others
- fosters family table time and conversation
- shares leisure time
- admits to and seeks help with problems

Chapter Summary

Chapter Highlights

- There is no one family form. Instead, families take many different forms depending on social and cultural values.

- Families are dynamic. They continue to grow and change in predictable ways.

- The simplest view of how families change is the three-phase model, which includes the beginning family, the expanding family, and the contracting family.

- The expanding stage of the family is the most complex and stressful.

- Family life cycle theory provides another view of family development. The Carter McGoldrick model identifies six stages in the family life cycle: between families, a new couple, family with young children, family with adolescent children, launching, and family in later life.

- Individuals in each stage of the life cycle have their own needs that must be met.

- Each stage also points to issues that concern parents and require resolution.

- Family meetings, problem solving, and using available parenting resources can help parents learn ways to manage family life.

- Violence toward children and poverty are negative cycles that need to be broken in families, but it is also true that strong families produce strong families .

Review and Extend Your Learning

1. Find photos or magazine pictures to illustrate the various family forms. Mount and label for your notes. **K/U**

2. In a small group, discuss the factors that may influence when a couple decides to have children. **C**

3. Explain how there can be an overlap: (a) between the family of orientation and the family of procreation; and (b) between the expanding family and the contracting family. **K/U** **T/I**

4. Describe exceptions to the six-stage family life cycle, and explain why family life cycle theory cannot be applied to all families. **K/U** **C** **A**

5. What social changes would need to occur to break negative family cycles, such as those of violence and poverty? **K/U** **T/I**

6. Using the Internet, investigate the social supports that are available for children and their families in your community. **T/I**

7. Research child outcomes in terms of emotional health and future family stability for children growing up in different kinds of families, such as one-parent, two-parent, or recombined families. **T/I**

8. Role-play family interaction in an unhealthy family, one that does not reflect most of the fifteen characteristics of healthy families outlined in the Schlesinger article. **C**

Research Opportunities

9. Many factors have influenced family size in Canada over the past hundred years. Using statistical information from dependable sources, such as Statistics Canada, determine the trends in Canadian birth rates for the past ten decades. Using more in-depth research, determine the most important factors that influenced the birth rates in each decade. Ask people you know what factors they would consider when deciding on the size of their own family.

10. In light of Campaign 2000:
   a) Investigate the lastest research that shows levels of poverty in Canada.
   b) Speculate why Campaign 2000 did not achieve its goal "to end child poverty in Canada by the year 2000."
   c) Describe some of the strategies that you would propose to break the cycle of poverty.

Chapter

6

Relationships with Children

By the end of this chapter, you will be able to:

- identify the various ways in which people interact with children throughout their lives

- describe the role parents play in how children form relationships within and outside the family

- demonstrate the skills and strategies needed to communicate with and about children

- describe parents' responsibility for ensuring quality communication in their family

- recognize the impact of child abuse and family violence on families, caregivers, and those who work with children, and outline strategies to secure a safe, non-violent environment for all children

- summarize how communication and decision-making and problem-solving skills are essential to human development

- identify job opportunities that involve working with older children and families at different stages of the family life cycle

Important Terms

acquiescence
active listening
child abuse
communication blocker
compromise
consensus building
external conflict
family violence
internal conflict
mediation

metamessage
mixed message
negotiation
non-verbal
  communication
one-way communication
talk starters
transition
two-way communication
verbal communication

Chapter at a Glance

How Do Children Affect Relationships?

A new baby! A forthcoming birth or adoption in a family brings delighted anticipation. Will it be a boy or a girl? What will they name the baby? How will the baby look? Will we get to hold or play with the baby? Before the child arrives, we begin to think about our connection to the child and the relationship that we might have with the new little person in our lives. A new baby connects the past with the future and is a wonderful symbol of hope.

Figure 6.1
The arrival of a new baby changes and enhances family relationships.

Babies Bolster Relationships

Words such as mother, father, brother, sister, aunt, uncle, cousin, grandfather, grandmother, great-grandmother take on new meaning! All signify an important relationship with a child. It is difficult to describe or even imagine the depth of feeling, the love, and the total absorption that is often experienced with a new arrival.

A baby can enrich and more deeply define relationships that are already established. Children can strengthen the connections between spouses, partners, friends, family members, and family generations. Sharing the experience of new parenthood with family, friends, and partners who truly care for both the child and the relationship can be very rewarding.

Before a baby arrives, couples can focus on each other. As the first pregnancy progresses, however, a woman's thoughts tend to turn toward the new baby, and she becomes less focused on her husband. As the following article demonstrates, however, dads can become highly involved in the pregnancy, too.

Case Study: Becoming a dad is a life-altering experience

The Record, November 25, 2002
by Bruce Alexander

My life changed four months ago. It will never be the same.

My wife delivered a baby girl on July 17—Tanis Lindsay Marion. But to be honest, my life changed on Dec. 22 last year when we found out we were pregnant. I say "we" in a very poetic sense. I knew that it was my wife, Sherry, who was carrying the baby, but I wanted to support her as much as possible.

I soon realized that despite being a teacher and having a master's degree in education, I knew very little about newborns and even less about being pregnant. So I hit the books. I read and learned that being pregnant can be a very collective experience. Here are some tips for any expectant fathers out there.

- With your partner, research the cord blood program. This is a promising new field of research where umbilical cord blood can be removed at birth and preserved for stem cell research and to help possible future family ailments. You need to sign up for this program early, so watch your time.
- Become the cook. Prepare well-balanced meals. They are great for fetal development. Also, try to reduce caffeine and sugar from your diet.
- Be part of the birth team. If you have a midwife or obstetrician, attend all the prenatal meetings and, no matter how dumb, ask those questions that are nagging you the most. Make clear the role you want to play.
- Go on long and brisk walks with your partner. The exercise is critical for her long-term health as long as it is not a high-risk pregnancy. Check with the midwife or obstetrician.
- Attend prenatal fairs and classes. This is a good way to get more information about how your municipality can help, and it is also a great way to network with others who are sharing your experience.
- Transform the house. Set up the nursery and do any last-minute renovations before the baby arrives. Trust me, there will be no time after the fact.
- Test-drive the strollers. Check for good wheels and how your arms are positioned on the handles. (It can be very tiring if you have to hunch to push the stroller.)
- Have fun. Get into some romantic routines while your partner is pregnant. Take her out for supper or a movie. Take some "belly" photos as the baby grows. Better yet, buy some plaster at the hardware store and make a belly cast; this will be a life-long treasure for the family.
- Talk and sing to your baby. The baby may be in the womb but you can still crouch down and tell him or her about your day. You can also buy a "womb song" that projects the voice and music to the fetus. You want your baby to recognize your voice at birth. I would talk to our baby on long drives in the car with this device, and Sherry would play Mozart during breakfast.
- Have some things ready to distract you on delivery day. You are no good to your partner if you are wound up too tight. Stay calm, focused, and well hydrated. You don't want to be another statistic on the delivery room floor.
- Give your partner something special to remember the delivery day. She just went through a great deal for you and your child; show her how much that means to you.
- Batten down the hatches. Before delivery, make sure the fridge is well stocked. Have a list of people to call, and make sure the bags are packed for the hospital. When the baby comes, you are going to want to stay at home and be low-key for a while. Keep visitors to a minimum until you develop your daily routines with the baby.
- Prepare to call in reinforcements. In our case, grandma and grandpa stayed over the first couple of nights. They helped with the baby and ran errands, prepared food, and took our bundle of joy at 4:30 am so we could sleep an hour or two.
- Take some time off—at least a week if you can. Your partner needs you to provide support and give her breaks by taking the baby. This will also give you bonding time with your baby. I enjoyed it so much I am planning to take a few months off to be Mr. Mom.

There is so much to do and so little time when the baby arrives. But it is the best time of our lives together as Tanis' arrival has strengthened our love as a couple and a family. Enjoy the precious first days when the baby arrives and try to get many pictures and videos of the baby at such a young age. They will be treasured forever.

Bruce Alexander is vice-principal at Empire Public School in Waterloo and was a Waterloo city councillor until 2000.

Figure 6.2
The parent–child relationship is the most important relationship in a family with a new baby.

Protecting the Couple Relationship—Tips for New Parents

- Take time to be alone as a couple.
- Share the parenting role.
- Understand what the other is going through.
- Acknowledge your differences as parents and partners.
- Work on problem-solving together.
- Communicate.

❖ Checkpoints

1. What steps did Bruce take to become involved in their pregnancy?
2. Identify five tips from his list for expectant fathers that helped him form a strong relationship with his daughter long before she was born.
3. What evidence does he give that a baby can bolster a relationship?

Children Change Relationships

The relationship between parent and child is the most important relationship to develop when a baby arrives. The baby becomes the centre of attention. This can change existing relationships by shifting priorities and perspectives. Some people grow closer; however, the presence of children has also been known to alter friendships, destroy couple relationships, and put enormous strains on families.

Relationships with family members change with the presence of children. A child requires a lot of time and attention. Jealousy and competition may emerge among brothers and sisters of a new parent. The transition to grandparenting can be difficult as well. The question of which set of grandparents is most closely involved can cause hurt feelings. A stepfamily can become even more complicated, with half-siblings, stepsiblings, and stepgrandparents all competing for recognition. A strong family will find ways to resolve everyone's need to be connected to the baby.

Teen parents who accept the responsibility of raising their child may find their friends drifting away. Interests in school, parties, and friendships do not mesh with child care, domestic chores, and working to make ends meet. Teenage parents rarely have others in their peer group to serve as positive teen parent role models. They may find themselves torn between being involved with their children and wishing for the carefree lifestyle of their peers. Married couples, too, may find themselves spending more time with friends and family who already have children and seeing less of those who do not.

If a couple does not have a strong relationship, a baby will not make their problems go away. Even strong marriages and partnerships feel the stress of a new baby. The presence of the child redirects the focus of the relationship, and can weaken connections in the couple. In the **transition** to parenthood, a couple has to learn to become parents.

What the experts say

SUSAN MILLER

Susan Miller is a parent, nurse, perinatal educator, and certified breast-feeding counsellor. She teaches, coordinates, and develops prenatal, post-natal, and early parenting programs in the Greater Victoria area in British Columbia.

The following material is excerpted from Island Parent (online), part of the Island Parent Group Enterprises.

And Baby Makes Three

The first year after the birth of the first child is a significant time of reorganization and negotiation for most couples. Even though others talk of this time of adjustment, it is really hard to comprehend your new life as a parent before you experience it first hand. All new parents agree that their lives changed in many ways once a baby came along. Like other challenges of life, the dynamics of early parenthood affect parents in different ways. Some couples make the transition fairly smoothly. For others, the transition will require a lot of work on the part of both partners, to come to workable solutions, and to find peace and contentment as a new family.

A popular belief is that there is a decline in the couple relationship once the baby is born. This is true for some but certainly not for all. In their book *The Transition to Parenthood: How a First Child Changes Your Marriage* (1994), Jay Belsky and John Kelly explain that "the direction of change is determined by the couple's ability to overcome the polarizing effects of transition." After following 250 couples from the third trimester of pregnancy to their child's third birthday, the researchers found that couple relationships fell into one of four categories:

Severe Decliners (12%); Moderate Decliners (39%); No Change (30%); and Improvers (19%).

These figures indicate that more than half of all couples are headed for a rocky ride after the birth of their first child. The first one to two years after the birth of the first child is a critical time for the marital relationship. According to Belsky and Kelly's research, new parents disagree about many things, but when they fight, they usually fight about one of five things: division of labour, money, work, their relationship, and social life. A sixth issue that cannot be ignored is disputes about extended family. Struggles with the in-laws (or out-laws!) can take many forms, and previously unresolved issues with extended family can resurface with more intensity once there is a new grandchild.

What can you do to "baby-proof" your marriage? Couples who were very successful in strengthening their relationship followed the philosophy of surrendering individual goals and needs to work together as a team. These couples merged their individual selves into a larger "us" to manage the increased demands of parenthood in a manner that was mutually satisfactory. Here are some strategies and approaches that new parents have used to make their relationship even better after the arrival of the baby.

Survival Tips

- Lower your housekeeping standards. This includes everything from cooking and cleaning, to yard maintenance and entertaining. Learn not to worry and learn not to nag.
- Recognize that baby care and household chores can't always be divided 50-50. It is inevitable that one parent will be doing more in one area

while the other does more of something else. This is just common sense. Try not to keep score.

- Consider hiring someone to help out with chores and other necessary tasks when you are feeling overwhelmed. If paying for help is not an option, try using the barter system or trade favours with another new parent or friend. Never be too proud to ask for help from your family and close friends.
- Agree to fight constructively. This means setting out ground rules for fair fighting, such as taking turns to say what you want to say, agreeing to

follow up on issues raised, and finishing the fight so that bad feelings do not go on forever.

- Understand that however good a marriage becomes after you have the baby, it will not be good in the same way it was before baby. Many couples say it is better, but it is different.
- Honesty in communication is generally good, remember that you want to nurture the relationship and some things are better left unsaid. Sometimes, too much honesty can hurt your partner and damage the relationship. Pick your battles carefully.

Personal connections can suffer with the overwhelming work of caring for a baby, meeting its needs, surviving the fatigue of late-night feedings, and simply adjusting to having another person demanding attention. Couples like Bruce and Sherry on page 118 find ways to balance their couple relationship with their parent relationship, and discover that parenthood is a wonderful experience.

❖ Checkpoints

1. Explain how newborns can change relationships among family members.
2. How can having a baby change a teenager's relationships?
3. Using the results of the study by Jay Belsky and John Kelly on page 121, describe how the transition to parenthood changes a couple's relationship.

❖ Connections

Family relationships and the challenges they pose are often explored by the media in North America. Newspaper cartoons and television comedy shows make us laugh and look at the lighter side of family life.

1. Make a list of five comic strips or television comedies that show different family models, such as lone-parent families, nuclear families, or extended families.
2. Analyze and compare the primary relationships in these comic strips or television shows. How realistic are they? Explain.

The Role of Communication in Family Relationships

From their first breath until their last, human beings are engaged in relationships. Newborn babies are born ready to form their first relationship. Their very dependence and helplessness invite touching, cuddling, feeding, and nurturing. Newborns respond to a cuddle by nuzzling into the cuddler. They grasp your finger with a strong grasp that seems far too powerful for someone their size. With this grasp they are communicating a physical and emotional connection. From birth, human infants establish the most important relationship of their lives, the connection with their primary caregiver.

All human relationships depend on communication. Newborns learn to communicate long before they can talk. Tiny infants send their caregiver cues and clues about their needs, wants, and feelings. They voice their distress by fussing and crying and express their pleasure with smiles and cooing. A baby will make a sound and wait for a parent to repeat the sound. Parents communicate with a newborn through touch, tone of voice, and facial expression, as well as with words. The give and take of communication is learned early in life.

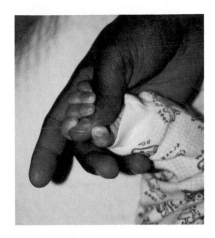

Figure 6.3
Newborns can grasp your fingers strongly.

> ■ *A touch is worth ten thousand words.*
> — Harold Bloomfield

Communicating Love

Love is communicated in many ways: giving a pat on the head or a smile, sharing the end of a fresh loaf of bread, going for nature walks, reading stories, playing games and sports. Children also feel they are loved when they learn more about their own family relationships—for example, when they look at family photos together or hear stories about when dad was their age. Teaching also communicates love: showing them how to make things or grow things, or having them set their place at the table. Through talking, answering questions, and listening, parents can communicate love and affection. Effective communication is essential to families, friendships, and the well-being of society. It is first learned in the family.

What Is Communication?

When people communicate, they exchange information verbally, non-verbally, or with both verbal and non-verbal symbols and signals. Communication can be one-way or two-way.

One-Way Communication

One-way communication occurs when one person is talking or sending out messages, but no one answers. Lectures, radio broadcasts, notes left

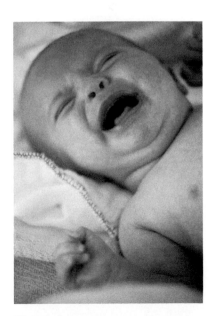

Figure 6.4
A crying baby could be communicating hunger.

We Communicate in Three Ways

- The words or symbols we choose
- The tone of voice we use
- The body language we exhibit

Sarcasm is one example of how we can give words an entirely different meaning by using tone of voice. "I just love your dress" can be said with such sarcasm that the listener understands the exact opposite. Someone could say "I'm listening," but their body language tells you they are not.

on the kitchen counter, or messages left on an answering machine are examples of one-way communication. Information is given out, but there is no immediate response. Like a child's cry, one-way communication gets information across quickly. The message in the child's cry is often "I'm hungry!"

Two-Way Communication

Two-way communication is communication with feedback. Two people are involved. The person who begins the communication will get a response from the person who receives the communication. The process begins with creating and sending messages and is completed by receiving and interpreting messages. This type of communication is most common between parents and children, and it is the quality and the tone of the back and forth interaction that defines their relationship. Effective listening is an essential part of two-way communication. Parents need to model good listening and feedback skills so that children can learn them by example.

Verbal and Non-Verbal Communication

Communication can be **verbal** or **non-verbal**. Verbal communication involves the use of words. Non-verbal communication uses body language or gestures, eye contact, facial expressions, and posture along with tone of voice to convey a message. People generally use both verbal and non-verbal communication at the same time. Mothers and fathers may smile and nod their heads when they are talking to their babies to reinforce the loving nature of their words. A child can receive **mixed messages** if the words in the verbal communication do not match the body language and tone of voice. If adults are trying to communicate a positive message to a child when they are stressed and angry, their negative feelings may still show on their face or in their voice. When talking with children, make sure that your face matches your words.

Figure 6.5
Non-verbal communication uses body language and gestures.

❖ Checkpoints

1. Compare the effectiveness of one-way and two-way communication.
2. Observe a baby interacting with a parent or caregiver. Record and describe the verbal and the non-verbal communication both use.

Figure 6.6
Examples of two types of conversations. How does body language contribute to communication?

The Need for Skillful Communication

Communication with small children is challenging, as children are in the process of learning language and the skills involved in communication. The goal of any communication is to have talking and listening happen effectively, without roadblocks or misunderstanding. Couple relationships, parent-child relationships, and even sibling relationships will be enhanced by skillful communication. Knowing how to communicate clearly is an essential parenting and child-care skill.

Differences in Male and Female Communication

In her book *You Just Don't Understand: Women and Men in Conversation*, Deborah Tannen (1990) explores the different "but equally valid styles" used by men and women in conversation. She notes that they each have different goals. For women it is intimacy; for men it is independence. This creates a problem when men and women communicate. Conversations that foster intimacy and connection are quite different from those that demonstrate independence. A woman may choose to do as she is asked to show she cares, while a man may avoid doing what he is asked to show his independence. Neither way is right or wrong, but recognizing and accepting these differences can lead to a better understanding of a spouse, partner, or co-worker.

■ *If you understand gender differences in what I call conversational style, you may not be able to prevent disagreements from arising, but you stand a better chance of preventing them from spiraling out of control. When sincere attempts to communicate end in a stalemate, and a beloved partner seems irrational and obstinate, the different languages men and women speak can shake the foundation of our lives. Understanding the other's ways of talking is a giant leap across the communication gap between women and men, and a giant step toward opening the lines of communication.*
— Tannen, 1990, p. 298

Deborah Tannen also examines male and female differences by looking at **metamessages**, which are an additional layer of meaning that we attribute to what we hear. Besides the words, what does the message represent? Asking for directions for a woman may represent a chance to engage in conversation and solve a problem. For a man, asking for directions may represent an admission of defeat.

Tannen's work in this book has generated an interest in gender differences and has been used to generate lists of differences between men and women. For example, women in conversation tend to face each other, while men tend to stand side by side. Tannen wants us to see it as a language difference rather than a personality difference.

❖ Connections

1. How might the different goals of male and female conversation affect communication between male and female adolescents in a dating or friendship relationship?

2. Listen to conversations between males and females in your school, in movies, or on television to identify examples of how "metamessages" (the meaning behind the message) are interpreted.

Communication with Children and Adolescents

Parents talk to their children long before children can talk. Playing Patty-Cake and rhyming are age-appropriate ways to communicate with babies. As children grow older, their abilities change. Baby talk and nursery rhymes give way to endless questions, then endless stories. Talking, talking, talking is an essential part of a child's day.

Children often interpret things in very concrete ways, and the meaning children give to words or expressions sometimes makes adults laugh. Chocolate mousse to a child might mean a large animal with antlers, made out of chocolate. Children invent words that have more meaning for them than the actual word. One child with a sore throat referred to a "horse" in his throat. Another called the "Heimlich manoeuvre" the "Heimlich remover." Children try to articulate based on what they hear. They try to make sense of their world.

Some parents record their children's special expressions in their baby books. Others have made childhood sayings into family legends. For example, one family still goes out to eat "ham-gur-bers" with their now 25-year-old son. If children are laughed at when they make mistakes, it can hurt their feelings, but if their sayings are enjoyed for their delight, it can enhance relationships.

Figure 6.7
Children try to say back what they hear. The results can be funny for both the child and the family.

What the experts say

KEVIN WICKHAM

Kevin Wickham is a speech-language pathologist. He explains the challenges for children who have difficulty with language.

Communication is an essential part of being human. If children have challenges communicating as a result of a language difficulty, their ability to relate to others can be problematic. Children who have problems communicating may also have difficulty making and maintaining family and social relationships.

As a speech therapist, I work with children who have a wide variety of difficulties. Some children have difficulty learning spoken language at the developmentally appropriate time. They are slow to develop their first words and do not start to combine words into two-word phrases between 18 and 24 months as most children do. Many of these slow-to-talk children will understand language at the expected level for their age; others will have trouble with both talking and understanding. The reason an individual child is having language difficulties is not always easy to determine, but early identification is important. Possible causes include hearing loss from middle ear infections; a language learning disability; developmental delay; more than one language spoken at home; or a motor-speech disorder. Early identification of a persistent speech problem is important in the treatment of stuttering, which can be difficult to treat later in life.

Children with preschool language learning difficulties are at risk for ongoing challenges in school. They will often have trouble learning both spoken and written language. Some children who have demonstrated hearing-related speech delays as preschoolers then struggle in the primary grades as they try to learn the associations between sounds and printed letters. Their lack of skill in this area of language makes learning to read and spell extremely difficult. Preschoolers who did not demonstrate any difficulty learning a spoken language may struggle with written language once they start school. Often, these are the children who are later identified as having learning disabilities.

Since school is a very language-based experience, it is important to help children as early in their development as possible. Age-appropriate speech and language skills are a critical factor in school success. When I work with children, there are often many others involved in the treatment plan. The parents and siblings can be very helpful in supporting language learning. Other medical professionals and specialists, such as doctors, dentists, audiologists, ear, throat, and nose doctors, and neurologists, may all be involved.

❖ Connections

1. Ask your parents and other family members for some examples of sayings or words that you used as a small child.
2. Volunteer to do yard duty at a local elementary school or child-care centre. Listen to children talking and report on the sayings or expressions that they use.

By the teen years, communication with friends becomes very important. In some instances, parents and their adolescent children argue more often than they talk. As adolescents strive for autonomy and independence, communication can become strained. Having a good relationship throughout childhood, and being available to teenagers when they are ready to talk, keeps the lines of communication open. Listening skills can be even more important at this stage. Many parents find that they reconnect after their children reach adulthood.

Communication Skills and Strategies

Effective communication skills and strategies are necessary for positive parenting, caregiving, and professional relationships involving children. After all, the ways in which adults communicate become the models that children follow. Children who are listened to and who are invited into conversation have stronger self-concepts. Some effective strategies to use when communicating with children of all ages include establishing eye contact, active listening, using "I" messages, and being attentive to body language. Some of the strategies require practice and patience to learn to do well.

Strategies for Effective Communication

1. Put on a **listening face**.

Barbara Coloroso, who is well known for her "Kids Are Worth It" lectures, uses the example of a third-grade boy who accused his teacher of not liking him. The teacher protested that she did like him. His response was, "Well, then, tell your face that!"

Children who want to be listened to often put their hands on a parent's face to turn it toward them while they talk. A listening face is attentive, shows warmth, and uses eye contact. By looking into the eyes of a child, you are making contact with the person inside, and the child will be able to make contact with you.

2. Try **active listening**.

Sometimes children cannot find the words to use when they are distressed, anxious, or out of sorts. A parent, caregiver, or professional working with children can use active listening to draw the child out. By identifying the emotion the child appears to be experiencing, the caregiver can invite the child into a conversation about the feeling. By saying, "You seem very angry (sad, worried, excited)…" or "You look

Figure 6.8
Making eye contact, nodding, and giving feedback encourages children to speak openly and engage in the communication process.

like you lost your best friend…," you give children the option to talk
about what is troubling them.

Active listening also involves concentrating on what you are
hearing instead of trying to figure out what you are going to say in
response. Focus on the speaker, not on your own thoughts. Then
give feedback to the other person to ensure that what you heard is
accurate. Nodding, smiling, paraphrasing what you heard to verify
its accuracy, and eye contact all let the speaker know you are listening actively.

3. Use **talk starters**.

After active listening, the child may need encouragement to continue.
Phrases that help keep the conversation going include

- Do you mean that…?
- Are you feeling…?
- Help me understand what you mean, tell me more.
- Tell me if I am wrong, but I think you are saying that…

These talk starters help a frightened or discouraged child to
keep talking.

4. Be aware of **communication blockers**, and avoid their use.

Communication blockers kill a conversation and weaken relationships.
They include the following:

Communication Blockers

Blocker	Example
Blaming	You are a lazy child; that is why you failed.
Sarcasm	All right, Mr. Genius, what happened this time?
Insulting	Only a baby would forget his backpack.
Name-calling	You loser!
Globalizing	You never, ever make your bed.
Changing the Subject	You are so cute when you are mad.
Not Acknowledging Feelings	Just relax.
Avoiding	Not now. I'm making supper.

Figure 6.9
Using communication blockers will defeat the purpose of the conversation.

Strategies for effective communication:
- listening face
- eye contact
- active listening
- talk starters
- encouragement
- positive feedback
- "I" messages
- attention paid to body language
- avoidance of communication blockers

5. Use **encouragement** and **positive feedback**.

Let children know when they are communicating effectively. For example:

- Where did you learn a great word like that?
- I understand exactly what you are feeling!
- You helped me understand that!
- That was careful listening!
- You described that so clearly I could see it in my mind!

6. Use **"I" messages**.

Children also need to know how adults feel. The "I" message lets the child know what the parent feels without putting the child down. Use phrases that communicate your feelings as a result of what has happened in this formula:

- I feel __(state how you feel about the behaviour)__,
- When you __(state the inappropriate behaviour)__,
- Because __(state the consequences)__.
- I need you to __(explain a more appropriate behaviour)__.
- **Example:** I feel anxious when you play near the road because a car could swerve and hit you. I need you to play closer to the house.

7. Attend to **body language** shown by the child.

Children often show their feelings more easily through their body language than through words. Frustration, boredom, discouragement, fear, and disgust all register in a child's face and body. In situations where a child is obviously in distress, it is important not to assume you know what the child is feeling. This may cause the child further difficulty as he or she may feel misunderstood. Helping children to "use their words" allows them to name their feelings rather than keep them inside. Giving voice to anger or frustration is much better than breaking something or hurting someone.

Effective and ongoing communication fosters mutual respect between parents and children because there is no screaming, yelling, or name-calling. It allows parents to retain their authority because they are not drawn into squabbles. Problems can be solved with input from both parents and children, and decisions can be made that are respectful of all family members. Conversations that engage children in talking and in listening help them develop and practise their communication skills.

❖ Checkpoints

1. Outline the strategies for effective communication with children.
2. Write an "I" message for each of the following behaviours:
   • pinching a sibling
   • talking back
   • helping set the table
   • cleaning up without being told

Conflict Management

Some conflict is a normal part of almost all relationships, especially those involving parents and their children, but breakdowns in communication can be the root cause. Since parents have the responsibility for dealing with the stresses of reaching family goals, making ends meet financially, keeping everybody healthy, and generally "keeping the family ship afloat," their opinions and values often come in conflict with other family members. Children, however, have strong opinions and many frustrations that can lead to conflict.

Conflict usually involves a struggle between two people or groups with different points of view in a situation. Even though conflict is almost always uncomfortable and is often painful, it should not be avoided in a family. Children need the opportunity to practise "using their words" as a way to handle conflict.

Sources of Conflict

Understanding the source of conflict helps in its management and resolution. **Internal conflict** arises within a person as he or she struggles with two sets of competing demands. For example, a mother may

Figure 6.10
Some conflict is a normal part of almost all relationships.

want to take her toddler to the park to relax and play after a busy day but feels tired and needs to rest. This is an internal conflict that pulls her in two directions and that will need to be resolved.

External conflict starts when the needs, wants, or values of one person conflict with those of another person. For example, a young teenager may want to have a curfew extended to 2:00 A.M. for the night of the Grade 8 graduation. He feels perfectly safe coming home at that time, but his father is apprehensive and wants him home immediately after the school ceremony. Such a situation requires effective communication and problem-solving skills to come up with a creative conflict-resolution strategy.

Conflict-Resolution Strategies

Conflict resolution is not so much a series of steps as a set of attitudes and behaviours. Resolving family conflict requires all members to

- approach conflict positively with the intention of reaching a successful outcome
- be honest and open, and use effective communication strategies
- avoid negative communication blockers such as name-calling, teasing, blaming, mind-reading, and the like
- use majority rule or a vote to resolve simple conflicts such as what movie to see (not a value-laden conflict in which feelings and self-esteem are likely to be affected). Parents need to structure decision-making so that, over time, the wishes of all family members are met equally.

Consensus-Building Strategies

Consensus building uses problem-solving strategies to accomplish a win-win solution where both parties feel somewhat successful. Consensus building involves the use of several techniques that can be used in solving more difficult family conflicts:

- **Acquiescence** means to change your behaviour because someone asks you. Acquiescence can strengthen a relationship and meet the other person's needs without necessarily sacrificing your own values and needs.

    Example: A parent uses acquiescence when allowing a child to paint the bedroom in a colour that is important to the child and which the parent does not like but is willing to paint over at a later date.

Figure 6.11
Allowing a child to paint her bedroom in a colour you do not like is an example of acquiescence.

- **Compromise:** If the two people in conflict are fairly close to agreement, they may agree to compromise or give up some of what each wants to settle the problem. Compromise protects the relationship and helps to maintain each person's self-esteem.

  Example: It is December, and Sally, age four, wants to wear her favourite summer dress to Grandma's for a holiday celebration. Mom knows it will be too cold and is also afraid that her sisters are going to look down on her because Sally is inappropriately dressed. Sally, however, is determined. In a compromise, Mom and Sally agree to the dress plus tights and a warm sweater. Mom plans to ignore her sisters' disapproval to let Sally express herself.

- **Negotiation:** This process involves sending and receiving messages in a face-to-face discussion with the goal of reaching a solution. Both parties must be very clear about their own position and listen carefully to the other for this to work. Negotiation works like a pendulum going back and forth with attempts to satisfy both parties until an agreement is reached.

  Example: Negotiation is often used when parents find they can no longer live together. Perhaps previous attempts at conflict resolution have failed. However, they have children and they must decide who will have custody and where the child will live, visit, and so on. They need to meet their children's needs first and foremost.

- **Mediation:** Sometimes people are unsuccessful in reaching a solution to a conflict. A deadlock occurs when the two parties cannot agree on a solution. In mediation, an unbiased third party is asked to help reach a solution that both parties can live with. Mediators ask questions and are careful listeners. They keep both parties calm and focused on reaching a solution. Often they can see a solution that both of the disputants are too upset to see.

  Example: Farid and Anna are first-time parents. Their baby, Josh, is six months old. He has developed a serious medical problem that could be corrected with surgery, but he risks death in surgery. Anna is terrified of the surgery and Farid wants to get it done as soon as possible. They cannot reach a decision. They are both so upset they have stopped speaking to each other. A school friend of both Anna and Farid, who is now a doctor, offers to help mediate their problem. They analyze medical risks and probable life chances if Josh does or does not get the surgery. Together, they make a decision to get the surgery done.

■ Consensus-building strategies:
- acquiescence
- compromise
- negotiation
- mediation

❖ Checkpoints

1. Describe the similarities and differences between internal and external conflict.
2. Give examples of each tool that can be used for consensus building.
3. Explain how each of the consensus-building strategies can result in a win-win outcome.
4. Describe how a win-win approach strengthens a relationship while win-lose weakens a relationship.

Interacting with Children

When Canada was still a rural society without automobiles, telephones, or televisions, children interacted with few people beyond their immediate family or their immediate community. Up until the 1950s, most Canadians grew up, married, raised their own family, and died all within a few kilometres from where they were born. Most communication took place between parents, children, and nearby neighbours. It is clear that our lives have changed immensely.

Today, children interact with a wide variety of people outside their immediate family. Besides their parents, they have relatives, neighbours, baby sitters, child-care workers, and teachers who guide, nurture, entertain, and watch over them. In the broader society, they meet people who clean their teeth, cut their hair, help them choose a library book, give them medical care, and even help them cross the street. There are also people they never see but who, through some form of communication, influence them in some way as well. Television programmers, clothing designers, producers of toys, games, and videos, food producers and packagers, and anyone else who makes a living from some aspect of children's lives have an impact on children.

Relating to Children

Adolescents relate to children in their many roles. An adolescent could be a sibling, an uncle, an aunt, or a volunteer in a child-centred program. Some adolescents coach children in sports, lead children in community activities, and baby-sit. Not all roles have the same responsibilities, but all involve relationships with children.

By observing parent and caregiver interactions with children, and by interacting with children themselves, adolescents learn some of the skills they will need in their future roles with children, particularly

Figure 6.12
Babysitting is one way you can get involved with children in the community.

their future role as a parent. There are many opportunities for getting involved with children beyond nieces, nephews, cousins, or younger brothers or sisters. Volunteers are needed in libraries, churches, preschools, and community clubs and organizations. Teachers, helpers, coaches, and leaders are required by many organizations.

Besides filling a community need, working with children enables adolescents to practise the skills they will need to work with children in the future. As a swimming coach, they learn to handle children's fears of water and experience the satisfaction of teaching a useful life skill. By coaching a team, assisting a teacher, or leading a special interest group in the community, adolescents can observe first-hand how children behave at different stages. They learn to recognize what children can do on their own or with help. Having fun, playing games, communicating, and getting down on the same level as children are excellent activities. They allow teens to develop an understanding of children that can be of benefit in the future, and may even heal previous hurts.

Roles and Relationships

Parents, caregivers, and people in occupations that involve working with children have different roles and relationships with them. All are concerned with the well-being of children and require the skills that define and advance their relationships.

Parents

The parental role is the most significant role in the lives of children. A parent not only provides the essentials of life such as food, clothing, shelter, and safety, but also has a nurturing role that meets the child's needs for love, belonging, and attachment, as well as self-esteem and self-actualization. Parents, as the child's first and most important teachers, shape the child's identity as they model many different roles: how to interact with adults; how to manage the economics of the family; how to communicate; how to show love and affection; or how to solve problems and manage everyday life situations.

The relationship between children and parents is complex and enduring. Many theorists have noted the importance of the parent-child relationship. Some of these theorists whose work is explored in later chapters include Sigmund Freud, Erik Erikson, Alfred Adler, Jean Piaget, Albert Bandura, Andrew Meltzoff, and Carol Gilligan. Parent-child relationships have been studied by sociologists, psychologists,

■ Comfort, play, and teaching are the three essential elements of the parenting and caregiving role you play with young children.

Figure 6.13
Grandparents can be non-parental caregivers.

and anthropologists, and continue to be the focus of research by both individuals and professionals.

"Invest in Kids" is a national organization devoted to ensuring that Canada's youngest citizens (ages 1 to 5) grow to their fullest potential. They help parents and caregivers develop positive relationships with children. Although research shows that there is no one single parenting or caregiving formula that will turn all children into happy, resilient adults, research has shown that comfort, play, and teaching are the three essentials of the parenting/caregiving role that will get young children off to a good start. These are ordinary, everyday activities that can be accomplished at home or in child care. Almost all adults are good at one of these essentials. Parents who understand how children grow and develop will be able to effectively comfort, play with, and teach their children at each stage of their life.

Non-Parental Caregivers

Non-parental caregivers take responsibility for children in place of the parent for a specified period of time. Grandparents, family members, family friends, neighbours, baby sitters, and child-care workers all take on the role of caregiver from time to time. It can be a difficult role since it may involve long days, and it requires great patience and understanding. Because many parents are employed at full-time or part-time jobs, the caregiver role is more important than ever today.

What is expected of caregivers? For the most part, they are expected to watch over the child, provide food when necessary, and provide activities and entertainment in a safe environment. They follow a schedule set out by the parent, or follow a routine that is acceptable to the parent. They are generally paid employees who must provide the quality of care that meets the approval of the parent.

Some caregivers have little or no formal training in child care. Being a parent oneself, or being fond of children, is sometimes the only qualification. Each province or territory has its own regulations regarding how many children can be in the care of one individual. Although specific ratios vary across Canada, all provinces provide guidelines. In Ontario, for instance, the Day Nurseries Act governs how many children can be in the care of one adult caregiver. A caregiver offering child care at home may care for up to five children without a licence. In licensed child-care facilities, the legal ratios of caregiver to children are as follows:

Legal Ratios of Caregiver to Children

Infants under the age of 18 months	3 caregivers to 10 children
Toddlers, 18 to 30 months	1 caregiver to 5 children
Preschoolers, 30 months to 5 years	1 caregiver to 8 children
Senior Kindergarten, over 5 to 6 years	1 caregiver to 12 children
School-Age Children, 6 to 12 years	1 caregiver to 15 children

Figure 6.14
Younger children require more caregivers to meet all their needs.

Caregivers who do have formal training in early childhood education are likely to care for more than one child in a child-care centre or home child-care setting. Nannies, who may have community college training, live with the family and care for children in their own home—a situation that is convenient but costly for the parents.

The regulations that exist in all provinces and territories govern formal or licensed child-care facilities. In reality, however, most children in Canada are in unlicensed care, such as home child care by a neighbour or family member. Parents cannot assume that conditions they might take for granted in a licensed setting will exist in unlicensed settings.

The relationship between caregiver and child is one that allows the caregiver authority but not control. Effective caregivers are kind and affectionate without replacing the parent's love and attachment. They act in place of the parent, but do not displace the parent. A caregiver must be skilled in handling children of various ages. A less than ideal relationship between the child and the caregiver is difficult both for children and for parents who have difficulty finding child care. To achieve quality care for all children in Canada, consideration must be given to shared values, affordability, quality, availability, accessibility, and accountability.

With these characteristics in mind, the Canadian Child Care Federation published the following guidelines in their online publication, *Child Care Canada*, in September 1996. The guidelines, developed at the National Forum on Child Care, represent principles for quality child care.

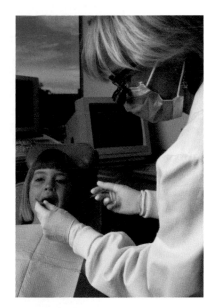

Figure 6.15
A trusting relationship between a child and a dentist requires humour and understanding.

Guiding Principles for Quality Child Care in Canada

Shared Values

- Children have first call on society's resources.
- Canadians have a collective responsibility for the care and development of all children.
- Every child has a right to quality child care.
- Quality child care is good for everyone—children, families, and communities. It is a social and economic investment for Canada.
- Parents have primary responsibility for their children. The child-care system has a responsibility to support parents.
- Early childhood care and education are valuable contributions to society.
- The child-care system has a responsibility to promote equality and diversity.
- A quality child-care system reflects the needs, interests, and cultures of communities.
- All levels of government have responsibility to ensure delivery of quality child-care services within a comprehensive and supportive family policy framework.

Affordability

We are committed to an **affordable** child-care system where:

- All children have access to high-quality child care regardless of family income, parental employment status, or geographical location.
- Appropriate services and funding are available so that cost is not a barrier to participation.
- Child-care programs are funded from government revenues and parent fees based on a sliding scale that realistically reflects family income.
- Affordability is not attained at the expense of quality.

Quality

We are committed to a high-**quality** child-care system where:

- Environments for children support optimal emotional, social, spiritual, intellectual, and physical development.
- The best current knowledge of ECE theory and practice is reflected.
- Inclusivity and diversity are honoured.

- Parent involvement is encouraged and respected.
- Education and specialized training in child development are essential.
- Caring for a living is recognized as a profession.
- Salaries, benefits, and working conditions reflect the responsibility of caring for a living.
- Ongoing research informs the child-care system.

Availability and Accessibility

We are committed to an **available and accessible** child-care system where:

- There is equitable access to a comprehensive range of high-quality child-care services that meets the needs of children, families, and communities in each province and territory and for Aboriginal peoples.
- A broader range of policies support families and allow parents to make choices that promote the harmonization of work and family responsibilities.
- National principles ensure equitable access to a range of high-quality child-care services and cost-sharing mechanisms that are sensitive to the provincial/territorial/Aboriginal/local governments' abilities to contribute.
- A broader range of child-care services is developed in partnership with parents, governments and community, education, child care, and social services.

Accountability

We are committed to an **accountable** child-care system where:

- Parents, families, communities, governments, training institutions, employers, unions, child-care associations, and child-care providers share responsibility for a quality child-care system.
- Federal/provincial/territorial/Aboriginal/local governments are accountable to the public for their decision-making and spending and for ensuring quality in child-care services.
- Provincial/territorial/Aboriginal governments ensure planning and coordination of a service-delivery system, which includes regulation, monitoring, and enforcement with community input.
- A coordinated federal legislative framework ensures comprehensive, high-quality services that are available, accessible, and affordable.

Occupations that Involve Children

Many people work in occupations that serve children in some capacity for example, a dentist, a hairdresser, or a store clerk. Their role is one that models what adults do in the world of work. It is not as intimate as that of a caregiver, yet it requires respect for the needs of the child in a given situation. Friendliness, demeanour, humour, and an understanding of what can be expected of children at different ages or stages are necessary.

The relationship with children in most occupations is usually not close, but it can be warm nevertheless. The child is expected to show respect and to follow the rules and instructions appropriate for the situation. Training in child development may or may not be required background for an occupation that serves children. When parents accompany their children to the child-care setting, they can monitor the behaviour of both the caregiver and the child and make suggestions to either one to strengthen the relationship and make it successful.

Working with Children

Many occupations provide opportunities to work with children. Two of the most obvious are teacher and child-care worker, but there are many others. The person who works with children requires special knowledge and skills. Knowledge of human development is very important. Knowing how children develop physically, socially, emotionally, and intellectually is essential for understanding their potential development in their knowledge, behaviour, and abilities. Skills in encouragement, listening, problem solving, decision-making, and leadership are necessary for working with children of all ages. The most important skill of all, the ability to make connections with children, will enhance any working relationship with them.

Throughout a child's life, many people are concerned with his or her welfare, so careers are many and varied. Many occupations require training at the community college or university level. By job shadowing, observing, and interviewing, you can learn a great deal about the actual job requirements. Researching and questioning can help you learn about required education and training and the salary you can expect throughout a career in that field.

Volunteer Work

Not all people who work with children are paid employees. Most communities have a wealth of volunteer positions that provide

Some Occupations to Consider

Here are some occupations that have contact with children. See the Career Capsules in this book for other career ideas.

Occupations Related to the Prenatal Period and Birth
- birthing coach
- designer of infant clothing
- designer of maternity wear
- dietitian
- interior designer of nurseries
- manufacturer of infant formula or diapers
- midwife
- obstetrician
- prenatal fitness instructor
- radiologist or ultrasound technician

Occupations Related to Infants and Toddlers
- baby clinic receptionist
- car seat manufacturer and installer
- child welfare support worker
- hairdresser
- infant swim and gym instructor
- kindergarten teacher
- librarian
- manufacturer and sales of clothing, furnishings
- toy designer
- pediatric nurse
- salesperson in baby department store

Occupations Related to the Early School Years
- athletic shoe designer
- audiologist
- camp counsellor
- home-care provider
- kids' help-line facilitator
- optometrist
- public health nurse
- theme-park manager
- toy designer
- social worker

Occupations Related to Adolescents
- basketball coach
- club organizer
- driving instructor
- fast-food restaurant owner
- physical therapist
- referee
- retail sales manager
- software developer
- teen magazine editor
- television writer or producer

opportunities to work with children. Community organizations and recreational programs require volunteers for leadership roles and coaching. Service organizations, youth clubs, and religious and cultural organizations all offer programs for children that require volunteers. Volunteers spend time with children in a variety of situations, such as reading stories, planning activities, demonstrating skills, and supervising children. Some high schools require students to complete a number of volunteer hours as part of their curriculum. Working with children can be a rewarding experience, and a very helpful one.

Working with Older Children

Opportunities for working with children do not stop when the child starts school. Many jobs, volunteer positions, work experience programs, and co-operative education experiences offer rewarding work with school-age children, adolescents, and families and individuals in all stages of the life cycle.

Work with older children often requires the ability to provide encouragement, offer understanding, and act on friendly terms. Coaching, instructing, training, supervising, assisting, and helping older children and adolescents can be very rewarding. It requires quick

What Do Parents Expect from Caregivers?

One of the key concerns for parents is that children will be safe while in the care of others. Parents expect a safe environment with safety and emergency procedures in place. They expect diligent supervision. They want to see concern for children's emotional well-being. Children's feelings cannot be ignored, shamed, or belittled.

Those who work with children must exercise authority appropriately but effectively. Children need authority figures in their lives to look up to, trust, and go to for help, but they are harmed by abusive power relationships. Any suspicion of abuse of power in an adult-child relationship should be followed up immediately. Most organizations that work with children, including the education system, are now requiring criminal record checks of people who work and volunteer with children. This is not meant to offend potential teachers and volunteers who sincerely want to help children, but to protect vulnerable children from the small minority of people who could hurt them.

Parents also expect that those who work with children will be prompt in communicating any concerns about their child. Whether it is a health concern, a behaviour concern, or an attitude concern, parents need to be informed. With very young children, details such as what a child ate, how long the child napped, or whether the child was fussy, in pain, angry, or fearful should be reported. Good communication between parents and those who work with their children is essential.

thinking, a sense of humour, and an understanding of what to expect from individuals and groups at that stage of development. Those who work with older children and adolescents are role models and should act accordingly. The working relationship they develop with older children and adolescents will benefit any future occupational role they may have with individuals at any stage of the life cycle.

❖ Checkpoints

1. Describe the roles that parents and caregivers have in their relationships with children.
2. What important skills are necessary to work effectively with children?
3. What expectations do parents have for those who work with and care for their children?

❖ Connections

1. Look through the classified ads in your community newspaper to find jobs that involve working with children.
2. Make a list of your own skills. How can you use these skills in occupations that involve working with children?
3. Look through the classified ads in a major newspaper or conduct an Internet search and summarize your findings concerning the job opportunities available for each stage of the life cycle.

4. Choose any child-related occupation that interests you. Investigate it using Internet career search sites or career studies materials in your school or local library. Prepare a poster with the relevant information for a secondary school student considering this occupation.

Healthy Lifelong Relationships with Children

How people relate to children throughout their life has a lot to do with their own experiences as children. If their own needs were met consistently in childhood, and they were able to form loving and trusting relationships in their family, chances are they will have no difficulty relating to children in a positive way. Positive, caring interactions with children by parents, siblings, teachers, neighbours, or caregivers are strong role models for interactions with children throughout life.

Healthy lifelong parenting relationships depend on many factors. Commitment, caring, and communication are essential. Empathy and flexibility allow relationships to grow and change over time.

Children begin life entirely dependent on their parents. At around eighteen months of age they begin to assert their independence, only to come back to the care and protection of their parents. Childhood is often characterized by an easy companionship between parents and children, and even though children are beginning to develop closer relationships with friends, they still look to their parents for advice and sharing. Adolescents are at a point in their development where they begin to push away from their parents toward greater independence. In adulthood, many parents regain a close relationship with their adult children, sharing their experiences and offering advice.

Relationships with Siblings

Children may also develop close relationships with brothers, sisters, and cousins. They imitate older ones and model behaviour for younger ones. These relationships depend a great deal on how the adults in the family encourage them. Differences in gender, age, and temperament can also affect these relationships.

Rivalry between children in the same family is common. Parents can diffuse some of the friction by encouraging self-esteem, spending time with each child individually, recognizing and appreciating individual qualities, and being careful not to compare children. Effective parenting can temper rivalry and promote strong relationships that last.

■ Adults whose needs were consistently met in childhood and who were able to form loving and trusting relationships will find it easier to relate to young children positively.

Unhealthy Relationships

A healthy relationship promotes healthy development, self-confidence, and a positive sense of self. Unhealthy relationships interfere with development and confidence, and diminish a child's self-esteem. Child abuse, neglect, and family violence are indicators of relationships that are not healthy.

Child Abuse

Child abuse involves non-accidental physical injuries, emotional abuse, and sexual molestation, and/or incest inflicted on a child by a parent or adult.

Sexual abuse involves an adult using a child for sexual pleasure. This form of child abuse is usually poorly understood by children and often requires therapeutic intervention by an experienced professional.

Emotional abuse involves placing demands on children that cannot be reasonably fulfilled at their stage of development. Adults whose expectations are excessive and unreasonable for their children often do not understand what should be expected at a certain age. Sometimes children do not possess the aptitudes to develop the skill the parent wants to see at school or in a certain sport. This can lead to harassment, nagging, or teasing, which undermines the child's self-esteem. Children who are not allowed to play with peers or develop friendships are also victims of abuse. Such children do not receive the love and affection they need to develop emotionally. This kind of abuse can create permanent emotional damage.

Figure 6.16
Adults in the family can help to encourage close sibling relationships.

■ Three forms of child abuse:
- sexual abuse
- emotional abuse
- physical abuse

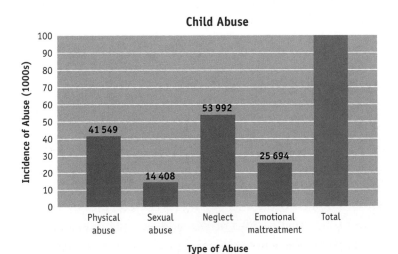

Child Abuse

(vertical axis) Incidence of Abuse (1000s): 0, 10, 20, 30, 40, 50, 60, 70, 80, 90, 100

Physical abuse: 41 549
Sexual abuse: 14 408
Neglect: 53 992
Emotional maltreatment: 25 694
Total

Type of Abuse

Adapted from Health Canada. (2001). "Canadian Incidence Study of Reported Child Abuse and Neglect." Ottawa, ON: © Minister of Public Works and Government Canada.

Figure 6.17
Of the 135 573 reported cases of child abuse, the largest number were cases of neglect.

Physical abuse is characterized by non-accidental physical injuries that may include bruising from broken bones, scalds, burns, bites, and beatings. Adults who abuse children often have short tempers and are easily provoked. Substance abuse may also be a factor. Hitting, slapping, and spanking are considered forms of physical abuse.

Child Neglect

Child neglect is the failure to provide the necessities of life to children. In the past, necessities included only food, shelter, clothing, and health care. Today's experts, however, include "failure to supervise" as the most common form of neglect. Therefore, parents who leave young children at home alone, or let them walk to school before they are really ready, or leave teenagers alone when they might have an opportunity to experiment with sex or drugs are now considered by experts to be neglectful. Neglect is a form of child abuse in which children are left on their own and not given the guidance or supervision necessary to be safe.

Family Violence

Family violence most often involves spousal abuse of the female. It ranges from physical abuse to emotional abuse, blackmail, threats, manipulation, and other controlling behaviours. Spousal abuse may also involve abuse of men by women who are controlling, manipulative, or who resort to emotional abuse.

Children who witness family violence often exhibit the same abusive behaviours as children who are themselves abused. Children who witness spousal abuse are more likely to repeat these patterns of behaviour in their own families. They may play the same role—abuser or abused—as they saw their own parents play.

Intervention

For children to survive abuse, neglect, or family violence, intervention is usually required. Social services may need to become involved. It is the responsibility of every citizen and every person who works with children to report suspected abuse. Law enforcement officers are receiving more training in handling domestic violence, abuse, and neglect.

Safe houses now exist in many communities where abused women and their children can go for assistance. Some communities have intervention teams that go into homes and provide intervention and assistance in situations where drugs, alcohol, or mental health issues are causing concern. Some provinces and territories in Canada have laws that require adults, such as teachers, who work with children to

■ **Family Violence—A Definition**
Family violence is abuse of power within relationships of family, trust, or dependency. It can include many forms of abusive behaviour: emotional abuse, psychological abuse, neglect, financial exploitation, destruction of property, injury to pets, physical assault, sexual assault, and homicide.
— *The National Clearinghouse on Family Violence*

report any suspected cases of child abuse to an authority such as the Children's Aid Society. Failure to do so carries a significant penalty.

Education and intervention are needed to develop the skills and attitudes that can ensure a safe and peaceful family for all children. Anger management training, special help-phone lines, identification of at-risk parents, intervention plans, support systems, parenting courses, and parenting drop-in community centres are providing many opportunities to teach ways to prevent abuse, neglect, and family violence. The more aware people are of the many options available, the easier it is to provide help for parents and children.

❖ Checkpoints

1. Explain the strategies and support needed for a child to survive abuse, neglect, or family violence.
2. Describe the settings that provide education and intervention to secure a safe environment for children.

Chapter Summary

Chapter Highlights

- Children strengthen some relationships and significantly change others.
- Communication strengthens all relationships.
- Effective communication is learned in families.
- Two-way communication is an ongoing exchange between two people, using words as well as gestures and tone of voice.
- Men and women communicate in different ways, and need to acknowledge and accept these differences for their relationships to grow.
- Communicating with children begins at birth with touch and face-to-face interaction.
- Listening and talking are the basis of communication with children, but several techniques can be used when you interact with children, such as putting on a listening face, active listening using nods and smiles, asking questions, and using "I" messages to respectfully let children know how you feel about their behaviour.
- Communication skills and conflict-resolution skills enhance relationships.
- Adolescents and adults relate to children in many ways. Adolescents interact with children in the community and family, while parents and caregivers have special roles and relationships with children.
- Many people have important relationships with children in their chosen occupations.
- What you learn about people from working with children and adolescents can enhance working relationships with families at all stages of the life cycle.

- Healthy families contribute to healthy life-long relationships with parents and with siblings.
- Unhealthy relationships within families do occur. Abuse, neglect, and family violence need to be resolved through intervention and education.

Review and Extend Your Learning

1. The birth of a child changes many relationships. Describe specific relationships that would change for a teenager who had a child. **K/U** **A**
2. Outline the ways in which parents can communicate love to their children at various stages in their childhood. **K/U**
3. Communication is a very complex process that is often subject to errors. Make a list of the common communication types of errors. With a partner, brainstorm as many examples as you can think of that relate to communication errors with children. Make a pamphlet or note-page poster that outlines ways of avoiding these communication errors. **K/U** **T/I** **C** **A**
4. Describe the differences in the communication styles of men and women. Explain how these differences might affect male-female parent relationships. **K/U** **A**

5. Using a conflict that is common in families as an example, role-play the various strategies that can be used to successfully resolve the conflict. **K/U** **C** **A**
6. Change five of the examples of Communication Blockers described in the chapter to "I" messages that would communicate information to the child in a more positive manner. **T/I** **C** **A**
7. Compare the relationship between children and their parents with that of children and their caregivers. **K/U**
8. List the skills and abilities needed to work successfully with infants, preschoolers, older children, and adolescents. **K/U** **C**
9. Identify careers that work with individuals at all stages of the life cycle. **K/U** **A**
10. Locate a recent article about child abuse. Identify the type of abuse in the case, and list some of the strategies that might be used to resolve the issue. **K/U** **T/I**

Research Opportunities

11. Investigate what quality child care means in your province or territory by conducting an Internet search using "Quality Child Care" plus your regional municipality, your province, or your territory. Write a report on how quality child care is defined and ensured in your context.

Unit 4 Children in Your Future

The decision to become a parent or to work with children has lifelong consequences. This unit informs you about the challenges of parenting, caring for, or working with children. You will learn steps you can take to ensure a healthy pregnancy and the best start for a child's life. You will examine the consequences of choices made by expecting parents and the impact these choices have on the lifelong well-being of children.

- Preparing for parenthood contributes to the health and well-being of children.
- Planning and training help prepare for future roles as parents, caregivers, and those who work with children.
- Many aspects of development in older children and adolescents depend on the prenatal start they were given.

KEY INSIGHTS:

- The decision to parent has lifelong implications.
- Those who care for and work with children share in the parenting challenge of raising children in Canada.
- Parents need to develop decision-making skills for raising children while participating in the workforce.
- Cultural and religious perceptions of parent roles and responsibilities influence the decision to parent.

Unit at a Glance

Chapter

7

Deciding to Parent

By the end of this chapter, you will be able to:

- recognize the need for planning and preparing to become a parent

- describe the responsibilities involved in parenting

- identify the critical nurturing and teaching roles of parents and caregivers

- assess the expectations of society for parents and caregivers, and identify the supports that society provides

- specify the issues and challenges for parents and caregivers as they interact with children

Important Terms

abstinence

biological clock

contraception

family home child care

infertility

informed decision-making

latchkey kids

lifestyle

parental leave

private child care

public child care

responsibility

Chapter at a Glance

How Important Is Parenthood in Canada?

For most Canadians, being a parent is a role that they either fulfill now or plan to take on in the future. The decision to nurture another generation is a deliberate choice for most people, and despite the challenges of being a parent, most would choose to do it all over again. Those who do not have children of their own may use parenting skills in other ways, such as supporting a needy child, becoming a foster parent, coaching children's teams, working with youth groups, or helping another adult raise children.

Figure 7.1
Parenting skills are important for anyone involved with children.

Still, some argue that parenthood is not that important to Canadians. As evidence, they point to the number of adults who never become parents either by choice or because they just never got around to it. They might point to the fact that people are having fewer children and that families are much smaller than they were 50 years ago. They suggest that parenting cannot be important if children are being left in the care of others while their parents go to work.

Nevertheless, in Canada, most adults choose to become parents biologically, through adoption, or through a combination of these. Children are both wonderful and challenging. They are expensive, they require round-the-clock supervision at first, and at times they can be very demanding. Yet despite the potential challenges, Canadian statistics indicate that most Canadian adults become parents.

Parental Leave

Having and raising children is important to both men and women in Canada. In 2001, the federal government changed its policy on parental leave to reflect the involvement of both parents in the care of young children. Research indicating the importance of the first five years of life for future success, such as that which contributed to the *Early Years Study* (McCain & Mustard, 1999), was another reason for the policy change. A father or a mother can now take **parental leave** from employment to care for a newborn child for a full year. They can also divide the leave between themselves. Of course, to qualify for these Employment Insurance parental benefits, they both must meet the Employment Insurance requirements.

Some family-friendly corporations and individual employers may add to the federal parental leave plan. For instance, some employers may allow parents to save up holiday time and extend their parental leave, while others may allow an employee to take a leave of absence

The Number of Families in Canada

For census purposes, Statistics Canada defines a family as "a married couple (with or without children of either or both spouses), a couple living common-law (with or without children of either or both partners), or a lone parent of any marital status, with at least one child living in the same dwelling. A couple living common-law may be of opposite or same sex. 'Children' in a census family include grandchildren living with their grandparent(s) but with no parents present."

Number of Families in Canada by Family Structure, 2001

Family Structure	Number of Families
Total number of all family types	8 371 020
Without children at home	3 059 225
With children at home	5 311 795
Families of married couples	5 901 425
Without children at home	2 431 725
With children at home	3 469 700
Common-law couples	1 158 410
Without children at home	627 505
With children at home	530 905
Lone-parent families	1 311 190
Male parent	245 825
Female parent	1 065 360

Adapted from the Statistics Canada Web site, 2001 Census, "2001 Census Data on Marital Status of Canadians, Families and Household Living Arrangements," Catalogue No. 97F0000 5XCB01006

Figure 7.2
According to Statistics Canada, what is the most common type of family structure?

when the partner's parental leave ends. Both of these plans extend family time with the new baby and recognize the critical role played by parents.

Parenting is a lifelong commitment for many people in our society, because parents continue to support their children financially and emotionally after they have left home. Adult children often rely on their parents to provide financial assistance for schooling, business and household start-up costs, or debt repayment. In Canada, parents and children usually maintain an emotional connection throughout their lives. Adult children sometimes return home to live with their parents. Unemployment, loss of income, divorce, physical or mental illness, and drug rehabilitation are just some of the reasons that grown children might return to the nest. Parenting is a responsibility that changes but does not end when children reach adulthood.

Relationships between parents and children continue to grow and change throughout life. The parent-child relationship usually improves as children become adults, and the conflict that parents and adolescent children experience diminishes. Having children of their own can draw adult children even closer to their own parents. Encouragement, offering advice, and being a good listener are skills that parents use with their children, no matter how old they are.

■ *Home is the place where, when you go there, they have to take you in.*
— Robert Frost

Exploring the Decision to Parent

Parenthood does not just happen. Whether you are 14 or 40 when you become a parent, parenthood results from choices that have been made. Partners may have planned to welcome a child into their lives. But even if a child was unplanned, his or her arrival is the result of choices. For example, the couple chose to have sexual relations. Every form of **contraception**, except for **abstinence** or refraining from having sexual intercourse, has a failure rate. When the woman discovered she was pregnant, she made the decision to keep the baby rather than terminate the pregnancy or give it up for adoption at birth. People who become parents because they are legal guardians of a child must also make decisions about their future role as parents. For some, these decisions are easy. For others, they are very difficult to make.

■ Children need and deserve the best parents they can get, so the decision to parent cannot be made lightly. Not only is this a lifetime decision that parents make for themselves and their future children, but it is also a decision that affects the social fabric or quality of life in our country. When parenting is done well, children reach adulthood with good physical and mental health, and society benefits as a result.

Informed Decision-Making

When you take the time to weigh the advantages, disadvantages, and consequences of becoming a parent, you are using **informed decision-making**. Every situation is different. Some people are ready and willing to become parents early in life. Others may wait to become parents later on in life, while still others may decide that parenting is not for them. If the decision is an informed decision, it is usually a good one.

Uninformed Decision-Making Techniques

Here are some ways to make an uninformed decision:

- Flip a coin.
- Make the same decision as your friends or others in your family.
- Choose not to decide and live with whatever happens.
- Decide based on how you feel at the moment.

Figure 7.3
What do I want to accomplish before I have children?

Uninformed decisions are appropriate when the consequences are not critical. However, the decisions you make about parenthood will affect you, your partner, and your children for the rest of your lives. As a result, the decision to parent must be made carefully.

Many factors may influence your decision to have children. You may not be ready to have children until you first do other things with your life. Do you want to travel, complete a certain amount of schooling, or pursue expensive hobbies that a parent might be unable to afford? Do you want to learn things, build things, save some money, or feel more like an adult before you choose to become a father or a mother?

The Decision Web

One way to make an informed decision is to create a decision web. In the centre of a page, identify the problem. Each time you think of something that would affect a decision, write it down and draw a line back to the problem. You can make an informed decision after you have listed all the factors and given thoughtful consideration to each.

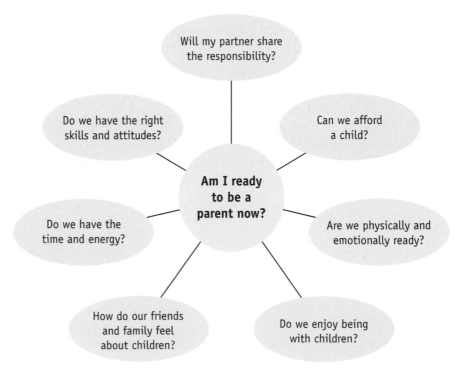

Figure 7.4
Try using a decision web for a decision you need to make this week.

The Five-Step Decision-Making Model

Using a five-step model lets you weigh two or more options and predict what would happen if you make the choice.

A Five-Step Decision-Making Model

Step 1	Define the problem. **Example:** Do we have children now or get a business started first?
Step 2	List the options that are available. **Example:** Have children now and work for someone else, or start your own business and wait to have children.
Step 3	For each option, determine the • advantages • disadvantages • consequences
Step 4	Make the best choice for you and your unborn children.
Step 5	Re-evaluate your decision if circumstances change before you have children.

Figure 7.5
Describe the differences between the decision web and the five-step decision-making model.

Case Study: Astrid and Emil's Decision

Astrid, 24, and Emil, 27, have both dated others casually in the past but are now quite serious about each other. They have been together for more than a year. Astrid has a high school diploma and is an assistant manager in a department store. Emil has worked in building construction since graduating from a community college. They have talked about opening their own contracting business. Astrid could manage the calls and record-keeping, and Emil could handle the building contracts.

They have a great time as a couple and have many interests in common. Both Astrid and Emil would like to travel more. They play co-ed slo-pitch and enjoy cycling. They love movies and enter-

taining their friends. They plan to get married within the next year and are talking about whether to have children right away. Astrid's parents are anxious to become grandparents, whereas Emil's parents already have several grandchildren and are not concerned about having any more at present. Astrid worries that she would be the last of their friends to have children. Emil is concerned about starting his own business.

Question
1. What do you think is the best solution to Astrid and Emil's dilemma? Apply either the decision web or the five-step decision-making model.

Factors Influencing the Decision to Parent

Many factors influence parenting decisions. These factors may affect the success of a pregnancy, the health of your child, the quality of parenting available for the child, or even the well-being of your future

■ What influences the decision to parent?
- social/cultural views
- education
- finances
- partnership
- maturity
- age
- health
- life experience

family. The decision to become a parent has long-term implications for you, your parenting partner, and the children in your future.

Social and Cultural Influences

The decision to parent is influenced more by culture than by any other single factor. From birth, children begin to absorb beliefs and values about parenting and about when to become a parent from their family, friends, community, and the media. Some of these messages may conflict with each other. Movies and television may celebrate the world of childless, unattached young adults, while your ethnic background may encourage early marriage and large families. The pressure to parent may come from friends who already have children or parents who long to have grandchildren. In general, our Canadian society pressures youth to stay in school, acquire a reliable income, and establish a strong relationship before committing to parenthood.

Education

Most young people hope to complete school before they have children. Some have successfully combined children and schooling, while others have had to drop out of school once children came along. Education does not necessarily make you a better parent, but it does provide greater learning opportunities in many areas, including par-

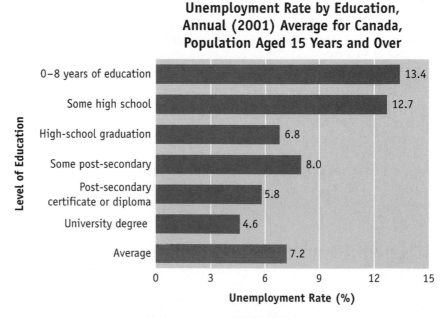

Figure 7.6
According to these statistics, what relationships can you see between level of education and unemployment rate?

Adapted from the Statistics Canada "Labour Force Historical Review," Catalogue No. 71F0004, 2001

enting. Higher education opens doors to better paying and more interesting jobs. In addition, the longer people stay in school, the less likely they are to be unemployed. Unemployment and the resulting financial problems increase the stress faced by parents.

Finances

Having money does not make you a better parent, but when finances are a problem, it can put a strain on a lone parent or a couple alike, and it can affect the parent-child relationship. Parenthood means more expenses and more time away from paid work, resulting in a significant drop in income. Couples and single parents need to think ahead and consider the costs before having a child.

Figure 7.7
Two parents can share the responsibilities of raising children.

Parenting Partnership

Although there are many examples of successful lone-parent families, there are advantages to raising children with two parents who can share the responsibilities. When one parent is tired or ill, the other can take over. Children have the advantage of seeing more then one perspective when there are two parents in the home. Also, children learn to communicate and negotiate by watching the successful communication between their parents. As a result, another factor in the decision to have children is whether the adults have been in a successful long-term relationship.

Personal Maturity

Successful parenting requires a certain level of emotional and intellectual maturity. Age does not determine maturity. Future parents who are emotionally and intellectually mature tend to be considerate, respectful, and responsible in their dealings with others. These personal qualities allow parents to establish a psychologically healthy family atmosphere in which children can thrive.

Age

Current wisdom indicates that, physically, a woman is best able to have a healthy baby from her early twenties to mid-thirties. Before age 19, a woman's body is still growing, so she competes with her baby for nutrients. Chances of pregnancy complications and birth defects are greater for mothers in their teen years and for mothers after the age of 35. In fathers, the production and quality of sperm deteriorates as a man gets older, which may affect the development of the child. Both men and women experience a decrease in fertility as they age. Waiting too long to become a parent may mean that you may not physically be able to do so.

Figure 7.8
A couple's lifestyle will change when they have children. They will not have the free time that they once enjoyed.

Health

The physical and mental health of both parents are important for surviving the stress of pregnancy and child rearing. Both parents should be healthy at the time of conception. Substance use and abuse prior to conception and during pregnancy can negatively affect the healthy development of children. In addition, potential parents should consider any inherited diseases or birth defects that may be passed on to their children. These include, but are not limited to, cystic fibrosis, Down syndrome, other developmental delays, Huntington's disease, sickle cell anemia, phenylketonuria, muscular dystrophy, thalassemia, Tay-Sach's disease, and glaucoma.

Life Experience

Some men and women have had difficult experiences in their lives that may require thoughtful processing as they plan to have children. In some cases, abuse, incest, or buried anger may need to be addressed. How you were raised has a lot to do with how you will raise your own children, because people tend to imitate their parents. What parenting model do you want to follow with your own children?

Lifestyle Changes Related to Parenting

The decision to parent may also depend on the **lifestyle** you have now or wish to have in the future. What is lifestyle? Your style of life includes your job, your income, where you live, your friendships, your leisure activities, as well as how you live—whether you sleep in every morning, dine out, enjoy hobbies, travel, go camping, spend time alone or with others. When a baby arrives, life changes completely, and as a result, so does an individual's lifestyle. In some cases, all disposable income is necessary for daily family expenses and to meet the child's needs. The lifestyle of the family will change as a result. Potential parents need to ask themselves, "How will life change if I become a parent?"

Talking Parenting

Michel, 33, is the father of Lara, 9, Tom, 6, and Tina, 5. He describes how his life changed when he became a parent.

Lara was born when I was 24. By then, I had been working for a few years as a commercial artist. We had been married only a year when we found out Mila, my wife, was pregnant. At first we were shocked and then delighted because we had planned to have children.

Nothing could have prepared me for being a dad and the main wage earner for our family. Mila and I had never planned anything. Before we married, we just did what we wanted and spent most of the money we both brought in having fun. Houses, even small ones, cost a lot. Babies cost even more. I worried. We had arguments. We missed going out with our friends. We eventually figured out what we could and could not afford, but we made a lot of mistakes in the process.

Mila took maternity leave from her job in a large department store, but the benefits did not equal what she had made. When Lara was a year old, Mila had to go back to her job because things were just too tight financially. Fortunately, we found good child care and everybody adjusted.

Lara was the first baby I had ever cared for. I was not prepared for sleepless nights. Mila had a bout of depression soon after Lara was born. It took a while for us to figure out what was wrong. The midwife was fantastic and got us the help we needed, and Mila got stronger. Meanwhile, I was looking after the baby every minute I was home, and this had an unexpected result. I bonded to Lara like superglue. I would never admit it to the others, but she is still "Daddy's girl." After Mila got better, we both took care of the baby and life went on, as a family. It was different from what we expected, but very satisfying.

By the time Tom and then Tina came along, we had a much better idea what parenthood was all about. We are coping, but it's busy and demanding, and we are giving advice to all our friends who are back in our lives with their babies. I don't think parenthood is a good choice for everybody but for most people I know, it is a good decision.

Sometimes I think of what life would be like if we didn't have our family…and… yes, I'd do it all over again in a minute.

Babies and children determine how life in a family is lived. They must eat when they are hungry. They awaken during the night when they are infants and must be fed or changed. As they get older and experience teething, bed-wetting, colds, fevers, and nightmares, children continue to keep parents up during the night. Baby things take over a home. Toys, diapers, bedding, clothing, and equipment spill over into every room.

■ *People who say they sleep like a baby usually don't have one.*
— Leo J. Burke

For Better or For Worse®   by Lynn Johnston

For Better or For Worse © UFS, Reprinted by permission.

Figure 7.9
Describe what you have learned so far about how parents can prepare for parenthood.

First-time parenthood can be a challenge and a turning point. Most married couples find that it is one of the most serious upheavals that they face. Time to be alone or to pursue personal interests all but disappears. They need to maintain a sense of humour and open communication as they find their time together altered by the demands of a child. Intimacy and privacy can become rare, and they will need to find ways to maintain their own relationship while learning their new roles as parents and parenting partners. Couples who have thought about and prepared for parenting are often able to face this stressful time more successfully than those who have not.

The Pleasures of Parenthood

As demanding as parenting is, parents can also expect wonderful new experiences with their children. Playing Peek-a-Boo with an infant, listening to their laughter, and watching their first steps are thrilling moments for parents. Long walks with a baby or toddler in a stroller are healthy and enjoyable for all members of the family. Stopping for ice cream is a big treat. A previously unnoticed falling leaf or dog passing by is of great interest. Most parents have not played mud pies or sand castles for a long time and can delight in rediscovering childhood pleasures. Reading to a freshly bathed child who then falls asleep in your arms is almost magical. Parenting may have its challenges, but it also provides intense pleasures.

Figure 7.10
Taking the baby for a hike is fun and good exercise.

On Changing Priorities—One Mother's Thoughts on How Parenthood Has Changed Her Life

After I had children I noticed a change in my priorities. You just change your activities and do different things, but parenting for me is not really work. I almost think parents need children more than the children need parents. My kids make me a better person. For example, a while ago Daniel looked out the window and said, "Look Mommy, big moon, big sky!" He was showing me the full moon that I would have missed before he was born. I would have probably been washing dishes or cleaning up. Children have a way of showing you the important things in life. They always live in the present moment. Don't ask them what they ate for breakfast or where they are going tonight. All that matters to them is now. My children have taught me to live in the moment.

As you have seen, there are many things to consider as you make a decision to start a family. If you have friends to share the experience with, a family that is supportive, and a culture that encourages children, it makes the decision to parent much easier. If you have matured, experienced some of life, grown together as a couple, and have a love and understanding of children, then parenthood can be a satisfying and rewarding journey.

When a couple takes the time to carefully consider the decision to parent, they are showing a love and understanding of children, because they are placing the interests of the children above personal interests. Planning for the future and consciously making a place in their life for children are the first steps in building a parent-child relationship. For the critical task of raising children, it is essential that thoughtful consideration comes before, rather than after, the fact.

Making the decision to have a child... is momentous. It is to have your heart go walking around outside your body.
— Elizabeth Stone

❖ Checkpoints

1. Describe the recent policy change that indicates that the government values children and parenting.

2. Outline the ways in which parenting can be a lifelong commitment.

3. List and describe the factors to take into consideration before deciding to parent.

4. Identify what parents bring to their role from their own family background and past experiences.

5. Would you say that the pleasures of parenthood outweigh the impact of a new baby on established relationships and pre-parenthood lifestyle? In what ways?

❖ Connections

1. Describe three goals or dreams that you want to accomplish before you have a child. Describe two life goals that you could accomplish after you have a child or children.
2. Talk to several parents that you know. Ask them about the misconceptions they had about parenting before they had children.

Delaying Parenthood

When is the right time to have children? In the past, young women, particularly in rural Canada, often married in their early twenties. Their husbands were usually in their mid-twenties. Because they did not have reliable and available birth control, they had children early in their marriage, and often. The spacing was approximately two to three years—long enough to breast-feed and wean the older child before the next one came along.

In today's society, natural and artificial methods of birth control are both reliable and available, though not completely failure-proof. Depending on their beliefs and values—many Canadians belong to religions that forbid artificial methods of birth control but do allow for the natural spacing of children—a woman or a couple can delay having children for years.

Those who delay parenthood for personal reasons often face pressures from others to change their minds. Once a couple is well-established or married, pressure to have children mounts from friends, family, and even mere acquaintances. Peer pressure is commonplace. If your friends are not having children yet, you might feel out of place if you have children already. If others within your peer group are starting families and getting excited about having babies, however, it is easy to get swept up by the enthusiasm.

The right time to have children can depend largely on one's cultural identity. Because of the variety of cultures that make up Canada, there are many variations in the timing of children. Some cultural groups in Canada value education and home ownership over early parenthood, while others value marriage and large families. If it is the tradition of your culture to have children early in a relationship, you may feel pressure if you are seen to be taking too much time.

Figure 7.11
Families sometimes put pressure on young couples to have children. What are good reasons for starting a family?

Advantages of Delaying Parenthood

Delaying parenthood allows individuals and couples time to build the knowledge, skills, and other resources needed for the parenting role.

They are able to complete their education, begin their careers, and get their relationship or marriage off to a good start, thus creating some stability in their lives.

Individuals who wait to have children are able to grow in experience and maturity while developing economic stability. Many couples today are, indeed, delaying parenthood while they study, travel, and buy a home or acquire other material goods.

Disadvantages of Delaying Parenthood

The ticking of the **biological clock** or the aging process may be a reminder not to delay parenthood too long. Women have only a limited number of years that are optimal for childbearing. Although men can father children well into their later years, they do experience a decline in testosterone in their late forties that reduces the number of sperm they can produce. Caring for children takes time and energy, and younger parents tend to be more energetic and resilient. **Infertility** is often a consequence of delayed parenthood. Even though medical intervention may be an option for couples experiencing difficulty conceiving, infertility treatment is stressful, costly, and has a very high failure rate. This combination of factors often encourages both men and women to choose to have children earlier rather than later.

The Choice to Remain Childless

Some people make a conscious choice to remain childless or child-free, while others may be childless because of circumstances in their lives. There are sometimes too many obstacles to overcome, including economic or social concerns, infertility, health problems, including the inability to sustain a pregnancy, or childhood experiences that prevent them from wanting to have children. Those without children often delight in caring for children of friends and relatives and contribute richly to the lives of others, or they focus their energy on work or other interests.

Adoption

Adoption is a social custom and now a legal process that has been used for centuries. It connects children without families to people who want to parent or to parents who want to add more children to their family. Historically, adding children to a family by adoption was fairly simple. There were many children and babies available.

Today, not as many children are available for adoption because many young single mothers keep their babies or terminate their

Figure 7.12
Some Canadians travel to other countries to adopt a child. Jessica went to China to adopt Simone.

pregnancy. This makes adopting a baby in Canada difficult and time-consuming, and many Canadian families who want to adopt an infant have turned to international adoptions. There are still many older toddlers, preschoolers, and school-age children available in Canada for parents who are willing to take on the challenge of raising a child who has often had an uncertain start in life.

Theresa Sansome describes her experience with infertility and her decision to adopt.

Case Study: The Journey to Adoption

by Theresa Sansome

Last year, after five years of infertility treatment, my husband and I adopted a beautiful 10-month-old baby girl from Russia. It was a long and sometimes tortuous journey to parenthood and today, when I look at my daughter, Julia, I can't for the life of me remember why we didn't just skip the infertility treatment and go straight to adoption. I'm so frustrated with my past self for taking so long. At times, I want to yell at the old me: "So you're infertile. Get over it!"

But, five years ago, when I began my battle with infertility, I remember receiving any suggestion to adopt like a slap in the face. This fight was personal. It was about ensuring our genes got added to the cosmic soup. If we failed, it was as if we would be shut out of eternity. The quest was noble and worthy of my martyrdom. I underwent surgical, naturopathic, and spiritual treatment. I was poked, prodded, anesthetized, opened up, stitched up, opened up, stitched up, scraped clean, flushed, pricked, bled, and inserted into.

The last straw was in vitro fertilization. Fifteen other poor souls and I convened at 6:30 AM twice a week to have blood tests and receive injections to promote egg production. We felt like cattle. As we waited, a collective sadness and quiet embarrassment settled over us like smog. Occasionally, we would smile sympathetically at each other as if to say, "It will all work out in the end—won't it?"

Things got better when my husband watched as the cream of the crop of embryos was injected into me. The hospital had produced these embryos in a petri dish by mixing my hormone-pumped super-eggs and my husband's sperm. This was the moment of conception.

Unfortunately, even though the eggs initially did their job and I got pregnant, I miscarried six weeks later. After yet another day-surgery procedure and a few months of recovery, we tried again. We had some embryos waiting for us in reserve—enough for one more try.... In a touching moment as these last embryos were inserted, a nurse handed the petri dish to my husband as a souvenir. It never made it to the mantelpiece, however, because the seed hit rocky ground, so to speak. It was then that we called it a day. We pulled the emergency handle and got off the train. It was time to talk about adoption.

And so here we are, on the opposite side of the fertility chasm, and all that battling with infertility seems like so much drama. While we were tying ourselves in knots, our little girl was patiently waiting for us in Russia—our beautiful, blue-eyed, joyful little girl who has a way of saying "bubbles" that will melt your heart.

Why did we take so long to get here? Well, because like so many others, I wanted to witness the miracle of a child born from two people who love each other. I wanted the honour of bringing a new life into this world. To me, then, it seemed like the only way. So really there is no point yelling at the woman I used to be. I could never have budged until I explored *all* the different avenues—natural, surgical, medicinal, homeopathic, and spiritual—to the very best of my ability, calling forth every ounce of physical and inner strength I could muster. Many people choose to go a lot further in their fertility journey than I did, but once I had reached my personal limit, I was ready to embrace what had hitherto been unthinkable—adoption. It was a decision that, once made, was mysteriously perfect. In that moment, the need to become pregnant evaporated and I realized all I had ever wanted to be was a mother.

And now I *am* a mother and what a great place to learn to give up the idea of controlling everything! A new journey has begun and, once again, I am picking it up as I go along. But, hey, that is just fine with me.

❖ Checkpoints

1. How does delaying parenthood influence the parenting process?
2. Why does the "biological clock" sometimes cause people to feel pressured to have children?
3. What are the advantages and disadvantages of delaying parenthood?

The Responsibilities of Parenthood

Parenting is a **responsibility** that does not end when your child goes to bed or when he or she starts kindergarten. It requires parental involvement 24 hours a day, 7 days a week, 365 days of the year, especially with young children. Strong parenting partnerships make the job of parenting more manageable. Lone parents may envy parenting couples who can share the parenting load.

Parenthood involves both legal and social responsibility. By law, parents are accountable or answerable for many things, including the provision of adequate food, shelter, care, and education. Unfortunately, many families in Canada may not be able to provide adequate food or shelter, and they may have difficulty providing care or getting children to school on a regular basis. Being aware of the responsibilities of parenthood and planning ahead to meet those responsibilities is taking a mature approach to the lifelong commitment to parenthood.

Socially, parents are expected to take responsibility for how their children behave in public, ensuring that they get along with and respect others, and ascertaining their children can be trusted. Parents are expected to teach children the accepted ways of society, and the difference between right and wrong. Children learn what they live. When parents model and explain the accepted ways of society and treat their child with respect and empathy, children generally learn to understand and comply with society's expectations.

Some parental responsibilities are constant while others change as children grow and develop. As a child matures, parents continue to provide the basics of feeding, clothing, and hygiene, and the essentials of love, comfort, and interaction, and they continue to meet the needs that the child cannot manage alone. By teaching everyday skills and providing love and security, parents promote the transformation from helpless infant to independent person at the end of the maturation process.

Figure 7.13
Parents are expected to teach their children what is acceptable in society.

Figure 7.14
Using an infant simulator makes a student aware of some of the challenges of parenting.

❖ Connections

1. Identify the specific ways in which your parents, other family members, or child-care providers met your needs as an infant, preschooler, school-age child, and adolescent. If you have family or child-care photographs, they may be helpful in completing this exercise.

2. Reflect on how the teaching and support changed as you got older. Explain the differences.

Practising Responsibility

There are many ways to practise some of the responsibilities of parenthood long before becoming a parent. Providing child care for younger family members, friends, or neighbours allows young people the opportunity to practise parenting skills without having the full-time responsibility. Couples who are thinking about having children should spend time together caring for children to learn how they relate to children individually and as a couple.

In many real-world situations, people who are planning to work in particular fields practise their skills on simulators before trying the real thing. Flight simulators, space shuttle simulators, race car simulators, and transport truck simulators are successfully used as preparation tools. In some schools across Canada, students in parenting education classes are encouraged to spend time with an infant simulator. These are life-like dolls that need to be tended for feeding, and in some cases changing, burping, and comforting.

The Infant Simulator Experience: A Parenting Student's Testimonial

To be honest, the prospect of having an adorable "baby" for the weekend excited me. After one sleepless night, however, my attitude completely changed, and after one very long weekend, my respect for parents worldwide dramatically increased. After years of baby-sitting infants, I was still shocked to discover how all encompassing the "baby's" presence was in my life. Regardless of what I was doing, or how tired I was, the "baby's" needs came first and foremost, and it was exhausting. Every teenager should have to care for an infant simulator for a weekend before graduating. I thought I knew what it was like to be a parent. Discovering how incorrect my beliefs were was immensely beneficial to me, and the lesson will stay with me for the rest of my life.

— *Sarah Taylor,* a Grade 11 student, Don Mills Collegiate Institute, Toronto, Ontario

Culture, Religion, and Parental Responsibility

It is advantageous to think about what parenting roles and responsibilities are expected within your own cultural or religious group before you have children. Here are some questions that every future parent should be able to answer from the context of their culture or religion:

1. Who is expected to take responsibility for caring for a newborn baby?
2. Is it acceptable for men to take time from work to care for children?
3. What role do women play in child rearing? Is it acceptable for women to continue working when children are young?
4. Who holds the power in the family? Is it shared or held almost exclusively by the father or mother?
5. What methods of discipline are permitted, recommended, or expected?
6. Does one parent play the role of disciplinarian, or is this role shared?
7. What is the role of grandparents and other relatives in the rearing of children?
8. Will marriages be arranged for your children? At birth? Later in life?
9. Who is responsible for meeting the needs of children when they are infants, of school age, or adolescents?
10. Do all family members share household chores?

When partners from different religious or cultural backgrounds become parents, they often must deal with differing parenting traditions. A great deal of communication, acceptance, and understanding will be necessary to resolve conflicting beliefs, values, and customs. Paying attention to the variations in both cultures long before children arrive helps to reduce the stress of surprises. Because it may not be possible to achieve balance in every instance, it is particularly important to plan how a parenting issue will be resolved.

❖ Connections

1. Take responsibility for a child you know (or an egg, a plant, or an electronic doll that represents a child) for a minimum of 24 hours. Record the details of how you cared for this "child." Reflect on what it means to be totally responsible for a child, and share your reflections with other students.
2. Conduct research into the parenting role and responsibility expectations of a particular religious or cultural group in Canada, and report your findings.

The Challenges of Parenthood

Because "parenthood" spans many years, it usually includes many ups and downs. Not every person or couple will experience parent-hood in the same way, but all will face challenges at some time. The challenges of parenting begin immediately with, for example, parental lack of sleep or a constantly crying, colicky infant. They continue and change with each stage of development. Parents are frequently challenged when trying to guide and discipline young children. Other challenges, such as divorce, poverty, or raising a child with special needs, are stressful for the family throughout the parenting process. Outside influences from the community, or job demands that compete with family life, also provide challenges for parents.

When potential parents inform themselves about parenting challenges, they are able to think more critically about what it means to be a parent. As they reflect, they can better understand their own parents and speculate about the possibility of their own future as a parent.

Balancing Work and Family

Balancing work and family is one challenge shared by most families in Canada today. Regardless of the type of family—a married or common-law couple, or a lone-parent family—all experience similar concerns as they balance employment with raising children.

There was a time in Canada when women worked from dawn until dusk while at the same time caring for their children. They did not leave the home for paid work, but they did their share to support the family business, which was often a family farm. If a husband became ill or if the family needed a second income to make ends meet, a wife would venture out into the paid work force to find a job, but often with the disapproval of other women.

During the First World War, many Canadian women contributed to the war effort by joining the paid labour force, but they returned home when the war ended. After the Second World War, however, many women who had been employed during the war stayed in the labour force, and by the late 1960s, many Canadian women had full-time jobs outside the home. Now Statistics Canada indicates that it is common for women to participate in the paid labour force on a full- or part-time basis.

Figure 7.15
There are many tasks to accomplish in the morning before parents can leave for work.

Participation, Unemployment and Employment Rates, by Sex and Age Group, 2002

Males

Age Range	Participation Rate (%)	Unemployment Rate (%)	Employment Rate (%)
15–24 yrs	67.7	15.3	57.3
25–44 yrs	92.4	7.3	85.7
45–64 yrs	79.4	6.1	74.6
65+	10.5	2.9	10.2

Females

Age Range	Participation Rate (%)	Unemployment Rate (%)	Employment Rate (%)
15–24 yrs	64.9	11.8	57.2
25–44 yrs	81.2	6.7	75.8
45–64 yrs	64.2	5.5	60.7
65+	3.7	3.6	3.7

Source: Statistics Canada, Table 282–0002

The participation rate for a particular group in the labour force is expressed as a percentage of the population for that group. Unemployed people in a particular group should be considered as wanting or needing to work.

Figure 7.16
While men still outnumber women in the workforce, the gap between the two groups has narrowed significantly during the past several decades.

Balancing paid work and family obligations is a major challenge, and both lone parents and couples face many issues if they work full-time while their children are young. To understand some of these concerns, it is necessary to examine a typical workday in a family with preschool and school-age children.

Case Study: A Day in the Life of Neil, a Working Parent

Another working day and it is 6:00 A.M. Jennifer, my wife, has just left for her twelve-hour shift at the hospital. I get up, have a fast shower, and get dressed. Wake the kids on the way downstairs. Quickly get three lunches ready, one for me, one for Devon in Grade One, and another one for Emma in Grade Three. Remember that Devon wants his dill pickle sliced while Emma wants hers whole. Devon's bread must be cut cross corners. Get three bottles of formula (the only thing the sitter does not provide)

(continued)

packed in the cooler for Jasmine, who is 14 months old. (I hope she will be off the bottle before she's five!) Put everything beside the door, and listen with one ear, hoping to hear some kind of "getting up" action upstairs.

Get cereal bowls out, and set the cereal on the table. They like to pour their own. Get out the milk and juice, and as the older kids eat their breakfast, get the baby changed and dressed, put her in the high chair with her cereal. Sit down with coffee that Jen left in the pot. Tie Devon's shoes. Eat cereal while helping Jasmine with hers. Cut up her banana, and give a few banana pieces to Devon, who is whining. Pour more juice for Emma, who hates banana.

Ask the older kids to carry dishes to the sink and put juice and milk in refrigerator without fighting, and go get their books and coats. I wipe up the spills, wipe down the baby, and get her coat on. Go back upstairs with her to get her "blankey." Remind Devon to flush and meet me at the car. Remember the lunches and formula. Put the baby in the car seat, and get the kids strapped in. Back out of the garage and suddenly remember it is recycling day. While getting the recycling, remember to get hamburger out of the freezer for supper. Check that the doors of the house are locked.

Drive to the baby sitter's house, and wake Jasmine up from her car nap. Calm her down enough to hand her over to the sitter with her cooler pack of formula and her blanket. Drive 30 minutes in the opposite direction and drop the children at the "before school program" at their elementary school. Drive another 25 minutes through rush hour traffic and get to work with 15 minutes to spare. Grab a quick coffee and get my mind in gear for my working day as an insurance broker.

I leave work early enough to pick up the baby from the sitter's house. She does not want to leave when it's time to go and starts to cry. Bribe her with a left-over piece of sandwich from my lunch. Get home in time to take in the empty recycling boxes, change the baby, change my own clothes, and watch at the window for the school bus. This is Jasmine's favorite

ritual. Pour milk and get out cheese and crackers for after-school snacks. Get down on the floor with the kids. Play silly games for half an hour. Send them all out to the backyard, reminding Emma to make sure Jasmine does not eat dirt. Quickly brown the hamburger and heat water to cook the noodles. Go to the door to get Jasmine. Blow her nose and wipe sand from her lips. Put her in the high chair with a toy. Add a can of tomato sauce to the meat. Call the kids in, as it is getting quite dark. Remind them to hang up coats, wash their hands, and come to the table. Supervise the eating of spaghetti, and then wipe everyone and everything down.

Put all three in the bathtub with promises that they can watch a children's video. Dry all three and supervise nightwear. Put in the video, put supper dishes into the dishwasher, and read some of the newspaper.

Turn off the television, turn on some children's music, and let Jasmine play with toys while getting the other two to do some schoolwork. Watch Devon colour some worksheets and help Emma with her arithmetic and spelling. Listen for Jennifer's car. Greet Mommy at the door. Sit around the table as she eats warmed-up spaghetti and the kids have a bedtime snack. Make up formula for tomorrow while she sits with the kids and watches a cartoon or reads a story. Put out the children's clothes for tomorrow. Then supervise tooth brushing, and help get the kids into bed. Throw a load of laundry in, spend some time with Jen, put the laundry in the dryer, and then fall exhausted into bed, so we can do it all again tomorrow.

Questions

1. How typical is Neil's story?
2. What are the effects of the parent's full-time employment on the children and on family life? How would part-time employment by one spouse affect family life?
3. How would having one parent at home and the other in paid employment affect this family?

❖ Connections

1. Parents can make some choices to balance the demands of paid work and family life. One parent could work full-time while the other stays at home. One parent could work full-time and the other part-time, or both parents could work at jobs with flexible schedules that allow one parent to remain at home with small children. Make a chart that shows the advantages and disadvantages of each general type of work arrangement.

2. The concept of a "family-friendly workplace" is gaining acceptance in our society. Brainstorm ideas that employers could use to make their employees better able to balance the needs of their families and their work. What possible advantages does a family friendly workplace have for the employer?

Challenges Facing Working Parents

Fathers and mothers who go out to paid work while raising children have many issues that affect their job as parents.

Meal Planning

Eating a healthy diet is a priority for most parents, but it takes time to shop and prepare healthy meals. Processed and packaged foods take less time to prepare in a busy day but are often poorer in nutrients and higher in calories and fat. Working parents find meal planning and preparation a daily challenge.

Time Management

Children do better if they have routine in their lives. If parents work, a routine can benefit them as well as their children. It enables everyone to know how long the morning activities will take each day, to schedule parent and child after-school activities on a weekly basis, and to plan for family time every weekend to help manage time problems.

Not all parents work from nine to five. In some two-income families with small children, the parents may arrange to work different shifts or at different times. Then, one parent can be home in the morning to see the children off to school, and the other parent can be home in the afternoon when the children arrive home. Or, one parent could stay home all day and work evenings while the other parent works days. In this way, one parent is always available to care for the children.

Figure 7.17
Meal preparation will go faster if children are encouraged to help.

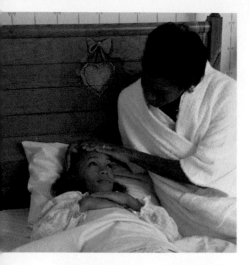

Figure 7.18
Parents need a backup plan in case a child becomes ill on a workday.

Care for a Sick Child

Another challenge that working parents face is finding care when a child is ill. Most child-care situations where more than one child is being cared for refuse to take children when they are ill. If parents are not able to take time from work when a child is ill, they will need to make other arrangements. Since illness is unpredictable, more than one backup plan will likely be needed.

Before and After School Child Care

Not all parents can be at home in the morning when children are waiting to go to school or in the afternoon when they arrive home. Parents need to make arrangements for children, particularly those under the age of 12, to receive proper care in their absence. Most parents do this for their own peace of mind; however, some parts of Canada have laws governing how old children must be before they can be left on their own or baby-sit younger children. Parents should become familiar with the laws in their province, territory, or municipality and ensure that their children are properly supervised. In many communities, baby-sitting courses are available to provide young caregivers with the appropriate training. The following material is excerpted from *Child and Family Services Act,* (2001), Government of Ontario, (p. 23).

Parental Responsibility for Care in Ontario

"Any person having charge of a child, less than 16 years of age, must make reasonable provision for the child's supervision and care, ensuring the child is free from physical and sexual harm. The person in charge must ensure supervision and care that is sufficient for the particular child, taking into account the child's age and developmental level. Other considerations are the time of day, the length of time the child is left, and the competency of the child and/or caregiver in meeting basic needs (e.g., eating, toileting, and obtaining help in emergencies).

"Caregivers must also ensure that alternate caregivers (e.g., baby sitters) are capable of providing adequate care for the child."

Child-Care Options

Child-care decisions can be stressful. Parents are concerned with many aspects of the care that they choose for their children. They will have many questions such as: Will my child be safe and happy? Will my child have the opportunity to develop his or her unique personality?

Will my child follow the same routine as at home? Will my child's needs be met with attention and care? Knowing others who have children in child care makes it easier to find suitable care and to evaluate before making a decision. In some cases, connections with community or religious and cultural groups are an excellent way to locate a caregiver or a facility that meets child-care needs. There are a number of types of child care available in most communities in Canada.

Parents may have a choice between **public child care** that is run by the municipality and open to all and **private child care** that is care provided by an individual or organization. Although both are governed by legislation, public child care may have long waiting lists, while private ventures may offer more services, but are more expensive. If parents want their children to be in a home setting, they may choose to place them in a **family home child care**. Another option may be to have a nanny live in; however, this is very expensive.

Figure 7.19
Finding suitable child care in a convenient location may be a challenge for parents.

1. Community Programs

Some communities have programs for after-school care in local schools, churches, or community centres that cost far less than full-time child care. Neighbours can share child care if one person is free in the morning and the other in the afternoon. Hiring a baby sitter or making arrangements with grandparents or other family members who live nearby fills in the child-care gap for many school-age children who should not be left alone.

2. School-Age Child-Care Programs

Child-care centres also provide before- and after-school care for students who can safely get there from their school. Some elementary schools have child-care centres close by or even right on the premises. For families who have preschoolers enrolled in the child care and school-age children enrolled in the elementary school, this means only one drop-off and one pick-up each day.

3. Family Home Child Care

Family home care is available in most communities. It is often offered by a stay-at-home parent who provides care for his or her own child or children and a few others. Often, the children being cared for are of a similar age. This creates advantages in meeting the children's needs, planning activities, and providing playmates. This type of care is usually not covered under provincial or territorial child-care legislation.

Parenting Skills

Children who spend part of the day at home alone before or after school have been called **latchkey kids**, after the locking mechanism on the doors of older houses. They carry a house key, let themselves into the house, and prepare their own after-school snack, and some even start preparing the evening meal for the family. Parents need to establish firm ground rules that may include not having friends over, not answering the phone, or calling a parent, neighbour, or relative to report that they are safely home. Children are often expected to begin homework or complete certain chores to ensure that they are behaving in a responsible manner. For many children, this is a step toward independence.

Career Capsule

NANNY

Tasks and Responsibilities

Nannies look after young children while their parents are at work or in other activities. A nanny may live with the family or commute to the family's home five days a week. Typically, the nanny gets the children up, washes and feeds them, supervises and organizes their play activities, and takes them for walks to the park or to community events. In other words, the nanny plays the parental role. A nanny may also be expected to do light housework, pick up groceries, or drive the children to community play groups.

Nannies are expected to discipline children effectively and calmly and are completely responsible for the children's welfare and safety when their parents are absent. The nanny is a very important person in a young child's life, and young children often bond to their nannies because of the love and attention they get from them.

Work Environment

The work environment for a nanny is a family home. The work is both physically and emotionally demanding, and the hours are long. Nannies are on their feet for much of the day with small children. Nannies often work evenings and weekends if the parents have activities that keep them away from home.

Since the nanny's job is to provide the same care as a parent would, they can become emotionally attached to the children. A positive bond with children can be rewarding.

Education and Training

Families usually require that their nanny have a minimum of high-school graduation. An ability to read in the children's language is also critical. Some of children's earliest experiences may be the stories that a nanny reads to them. A certificate in early childhood education is good preparation for a job as a nanny. Some nannies have college degrees, diplomas, or degrees in education.

❖ Connections

1. Investigate the types and costs of child care for children of different ages in your community. Work in groups to assemble the information. Prepare a poster that could be displayed at a community centre to inform parents about available child-care resources.

2. Sometimes, parents feel that they are working for very little when they return to paid work after parental leave. Investigate the financial and emotional costs and benefits of going back to paid work after parental leave, as opposed to staying home to continue to provide child care.

3. Prepare a report on the efforts of Canadians to obtain low-cost or subsidized child care for all children in Canada. Some topics to consider are groups involved in the action, advantages of subsidized child care for all children, opposition to subsidized child care, costs, and the future prospects of subsidized child care for all Canadian children.

Challenges Facing Caregivers and Those Who Work with Children

Those who care for or work with children often face the same challenges that parents face. Children who experience problems and stress in their family lives need careful attention. When parents work all day, the only family time available is at night. Irritability and fatigue may be signs to watch for if children are up late participating in family activities. If you work with children, being able to reassure parents of your expertise and commitment to their children is essential.

Divorce and family breakdown must be handled carefully when children come into your care. A child may be afraid of being left at child care if one parent has recently left the family. Tearful episodes, unaccustomed anger, and inappropriate behaviour may be some of the signs that the child is not happy with things at home. It may be necessary to recommend counselling for a child in your care or even to participate in counselling to learn how to be supportive of children who are experiencing distress.

Those who care for and work with children have an important role. They spend a large part of the day working with children. They need to be respectful, understanding, and supportive of children who are facing the same challenges that parents face from time to time. A caregiver is a substitute for the parent, and this person sometimes sees the child for more hours in the week than the child's parents do. Some of the qualities that caregivers need to bring to their interactions with children are patience and stamina. It takes a lot of energy and understanding to care for several unrelated children at once.

Surviving Challenges

The fact that parenthood comes with many challenges is no reason to avoid parenthood. As challenges arise, parents need to find ways to work through them. Sometimes a parent, a couple, or a family requires counselling or other types of support to help them find ways to resolve issues that are causing difficulty. There are a variety of private and public resources in most communities. These agencies can offer information and support to parents as they deal with issues and challenges in caring for their children.

Self-help books and "how-to" books offer suggestions and techniques. There are books written by experts on every topic. Bookstores have shelves of information aimed especially at parents. Newspapers, magazine articles, advice columns, and Internet articles also provide helpful information. Parents may find that defining the problem is more difficult than finding suggested solutions.

Many support groups and networks help parents and caregivers deal with their challenges. Whether there are problems with feeding, discipline, or communication, groups can help and support parents and caregivers in resolving their difficulties. Many groups are organized through local services such as community centres, hospitals, or places of worship. Parents and caregivers have a wide variety of resources they can access when facing the challenges of caring for children in today's society.

❖ Checkpoints

1. Outline the factors that make balancing work and family such a demanding challenge for many parents.
2. Why is finding suitable child care sometimes difficult?
3. Describe the difficulties that caregivers face in their daily work with children.

❖ Connections

1. Locate a parenting self-help book at the library, and write a book review.
2. Find two kinds of self-help resources that provide parents with advice on the same parenting issue. Compare the advice

given and the approach used by each. Select from a newspaper article, magazine article, advice column, pamphlet, and an Internet source.

3. If you were a caregiver, what kinds of information would you look for in how-to resources written for parents?

Chapter Summary

Chapter Highlights

- Parenting is a lifelong commitment that requires careful consideration.

- Many factors can influence the decision to become a parent including age, emotional and intellectual maturity, life experience, health, education, finances, and the partnership relationship itself.

- These factors also influence the health and well-being of children and the future family.

- Potential parents should consider the impact that children will have on their lifestyle.

- Couples often feel pressured to become parents as they move through the childbearing years, yet a careful decision must put the well-being of children first.

- Adoption as a method of creating or adding to a family is a decision that requires thoughtful consideration.

- Those who choose parenthood need to recognize the legal and social responsibilities of parenthood, including what it means to be a parent in the context of the individual's religion and culture.

- Becoming a parent has its challenges, but one of the biggest is balancing work and family.

- Working parents face many challenges from meal planning and time management to arranging appropriate child care.

- Caregivers and those who work with children face related challenges, and knowing where to turn for help can go a long way toward meeting them.

Review and Extend Your Learning

1. Describe three different scenarios in which new parents manage the financial challenges they face after the birth of their first child. **K/U** **C**

2. What does emotional and intellectual maturity have to do with eventual parenting success? **K/U**

3. Describe three to five life experiences you have had that will affect how you would parent in your future. **C** **A**

4. Describe three life experiences that might negatively affect a person's ability to parent. **K/U** **A**

5. Summarize health issues that can affect a person's ability to parent effectively. **K/U**

6. How much education should a future parent have? Explain your answer to a partner. **C**

7. Describe the ways in which a child can change a couple's lifestyle. **K/U**

8. Outline how parental responsibilities change as children get older. **K/U**

9. Why would a couple decide to adopt a child? **T/I**

10. Interview parents with children of various ages. Ask them about their most difficult challenges as a parent. Compare your results with your classmates. Create a list of challenges for each stage of the family life cycle. **T/I** **C** **A**

Research Opportunities

11. Interview a mother or father with several years of parenting experience. Ask the following questions:

    a) How old are your children?

    b) What do you consider are the advantages and disadvantages of being a parent?

    c) If you could start parenting all over again, what would you do differently?

    d) What personal qualities, skills, and experience do you feel are necessary for being a parent?

    Keep the names of all respondents confidential. Compare your responses with those collected by your classmates. Write a statement of generalization based on your analysis of the data.

12. Adoption is a complex issue that can be researched from a number of perspectives, such as those listed below. Share the responsibilities for researching some of these perspectives with others in your class. From your collective data, put together a comprehensive class presentation—it could be a video, a computer slide presentation, or a play.

    Topics of interest may include, but are not limited to

    • the adoption process for open versus closed adoptions

    • public, private, and international adoption

    • the role of medical histories in adoption

    • questions of cultural heritage in cross-cultural adoptions

    • giving a child up for adoption

    • personal experiences of being adopted

    • attachment issues for adoptive parents and children

13. Research one challenge of parenthood that interests you. Confirm your topic with your teacher before you start. Topic suggestions may include: unemployment, divorce, child custody, television violence, poverty, Internet safety, or affordable housing. Present the results of your research as a research paper or as a visual presentation to your class.

Preparing for Children in Your Future

By the end of this chapter, you will be able to:

- specify your current roles in relation to children and predict roles that you might have in the future

- describe the importance of planning for future parenthood

- explain the need for preparation to become a parent

- describe strategies for promoting healthy pregnancies and optimum birth weights

- identify how new parents can become capable and confident in making choices that are in the best interests of their children before and during birth, and in the first few months after birth

- identify and describe the training opportunities available for preparation for parenthood and for occupations involving children

Important Terms

birth defects

empathy belly

Fetal Alcohol Spectrum
  Disorder (FASD)

genetic loading

neurotoxin

prenatal health care

progenitor

spina bifida

Sudden Infant Death
  Syndrome (SIDS)

teratogen

Chapter at a Glance

Figure 8.1
What role will I have with children in the future?

Are There Children in Your Future?

There are many ways that you may be involved with children throughout your life. You could be an aunt or an uncle, you could be a brother or a sister, or have a foster child in your own family or in another country. You might be a neighbour, friend, baby sitter, or regular caregiver of children that you know well. Some people volunteer their time to teach or coach children at school or in the community.

In every relationship that you have with children, you play a role. It is much like a role in a play or a movie. You play a particular part that has clear expectations. Your role as an uncle or aunt will be different from your role as a volunteer in a community program. Throughout your life, you will continue to relate to children in many ways. You may become a parent, a sports coach, a teacher, a health-care worker, or even a grandparent some day. Imagine all the roles you could possibly have with children in your lifetime! Courses in parenting and human development help you to understand how to relate to children in any role, present or future.

Classes in parenting and human development are offered in elementary and secondary schools, colleges, universities, and various community settings. There are baby-sitting courses, credit courses, and general interest courses. Some students may plan to eventually work with children, many plan to become parents in the future, and others may never have children of their own, but all will encounter children in many aspects of their lives. Courses are designed to meet a variety of needs. In many communities, there are also courses for people who are already parenting babies, toddlers, preschoolers, school-aged children, and adolescents.

❖ Connections

1. Assess the current roles you have with children in terms of how important they are to you, and what you have learned from each role. How have these interactions shaped your thinking about parenting?

2. What roles involving children do you foresee for yourself in the immediate future and in the long term? Explain.

The Importance of Being Prepared for Parenthood

The success of every important undertaking or responsibility depends on the preparation that goes into it. To drive a car safely, you need to learn the rules of the road and practise your driving skills. Preparation is also required for higher education or job training. Those who are not prepared for the demands of driving, higher education, or job training are not ready for that next important step. Parenthood, too, is an important responsibility that requires preparation for success. In the case of parenting, success is measured in the lives of the children involved.

The dictionary provides us with a very limited definition of parenthood. In dictionary terms, a parent is defined as a father, mother, or **progenitor**—one who produces offspring. In human terms, a parent is the person who has full responsibility for a child. Parenthood takes into account all the things that parents do when they are responsible for a child.

Parenthood is the job of raising children. It involves meeting the needs of children before and after they are born. This includes nurturing, teaching, and guiding children throughout their lives. It requires a long-term commitment, a whole range of parenting skills, knowledge, patience, understanding, unconditional love, a sense of humour, and last but not least, money, time, and energy.

When parents are not prepared for parenthood, it can seriously affect their own lives and the lives of other family members. Hopes and dreams may take much longer to achieve. Education, career, and travel plans may be put on hold, and arrangements may be altered. Children who are born before parents are ready for them may be affected physically, emotionally, and intellectually. Child neglect and abuse may sometimes be the result.

WANTED: Full-Time Parent

Seeking an individual who is kind, caring, and patient. Must have good listening and conflict-resolution skills. Must be able to cook and clean and be flexible with hours of work. May be called upon for duty, day or night, up to 24 hours per day.

Skills and Training Preferred
- knowledge of human development—physical, emotional, social, intellectual
- knowledge of hygiene, basic first aid, and safety practices
- understanding of, and skills in, the planning and preparation of nutritious meals
- ability to manage time and money effectively
- knowledge of all family-related government and community services
- ability to read stories over and over again with enthusiasm
- the patience to answer questions such as "Why is the sky blue?"

Ability to sing, colour, dance, and play are assets. Preference will be given to applicants who have a supportive partner with the same or similar skills, and a network of supportive family and friends.

Figure 8.2
The job of raising children is demanding.

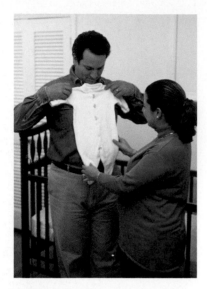

Figure 8.3
A couple prepares the nursery and completes the layette.

❖ Connections

1. Is the want ad asking for a "super parent" or a "good-enough parent," and what would be the difference?
2. What qualities of a full-time parent have been overlooked? Explain.

Human pregnancy is 40 weeks long. There should be plenty of time to prepare for a baby. But is it enough time to prepare for parenthood? What does it mean to be prepared for parenthood? Two different images come to mind. On the one hand, we can picture a happy couple delighted with the news of a first pregnancy, who are painting the nursery, choosing baby furniture, completing the layette by purchasing the proper number of diapers, undershirts, booties, sleepers, and bathing and feeding necessities. On the other hand, we might see a pregnant teenager who has no income, no education, no family support, who does not have any baby clothes, blankets, or diapers for a newborn. Who is more prepared? If we look more closely, we may find that the happy couple may be better prepared for the baby but may not be any more prepared for parenthood than the pregnant teen.

What to Consider When Preparing for Parenthood

Once the decision has been made to become a parent, there are many questions to answer about the nature and level of preparation that is required. The decision to parent requires the commitment to plan ahead and be prepared.

You will need to answer questions such as the following:

- What are the knowledge, skills, and attitudes needed for parenthood?
- Do I have the maturity necessary to be a parent?
- What strategies can we use to make sure we have the money, time, and energy for parenthood?
- What health and lifestyle issues do we need to deal with prior to parenthood?
- How do we get the support of family, friends, and community?

Potential parents who take the time to consider these questions and to use them to plan ahead for the responsibilities of parenthood can become more capable and confident in making choices that are in the best interests of their children.

Knowledge, Skills, and Attitudes

Parents need to know a great deal about children to nurture them well. This knowledge includes how they grow and develop beginning from conception and understanding what harms and what helps a developing child. Parents need to know how to handle the challenges of daily life with children, including the basics of feeding, clothing, hygiene, and health. They also need to know how to meet the changing needs of children without neglecting their own needs. There is so much to learn that bookstores and libraries devote entire sections to childhood and parenting.

Parents will need to learn a full range of skills, from the basics of comforting, holding, and bathing a baby, to the more complex skills of communication and problem solving. Many of these skills can be developed by spending time with children, watching other parents in action, and by asking questions before having a baby. Parents continue to practise and improve their skills "on the job" as their children grow and develop.

A positive attitude is essential for parenthood. Attitudes about children and parenting often result from an individual's experiences as a child. How your parents touched you, taught you, played with you, and trained you becomes the basis for your own feelings about children and how to parent children. Your thoughts, feelings, and emotions about children will influence your relationships with them.

Figure 8.4
One of the many things parents will have to learn is how to bathe the baby.

❖ Checkpoints

1. What is the meaning of the word "parenthood?" What does parenthood involve?
2. List and describe some of the knowledge and skills needed before becoming a parent.

Physical and Emotional Maturity

Maturity is necessary for every step in human development. It requires a certain level of physical maturation to walk, talk, climb, or run. It also requires a certain level of maturation to biologically produce children, and an even greater level of emotional maturity to be a parent.

A person needs to be physically ready to parent. Although males and females can biologically produce a child once they reach puberty, both continue to grow and develop throughout their adolescence. The energy required for adolescent growth is better directed at the individual than both the individual and a new life. Teenage women are still growing and would have to compete with a fetus for their nutritional needs. Adolescent fathers and mothers who choose to raise their children find it physically challenging to finish school, provide an income, care for a child, and meet their own needs as well. Making certain that they have reached physical maturity before becoming parents ensures a healthy outcome for themselves and their unborn children.

Emotional maturity is essential for parenting. A psychiatrist from a medical family, Dr. William C. Menninger outlined seven criteria of emotional maturity, which include a number of adaptive abilities and the capacity to love. Patience, understanding, and being able to put a child's needs ahead of your own indicate a level of maturity that contributes to the willingness and desire to parent. Self-centred, childish, uncaring individuals do not make very successful parents because they are still child-like in their behaviour, regardless of their chronological age.

Emotional Maturity Criteria

by William C. Menninger, M.D.

- The ability to deal constructively with reality
- The capacity to adapt to change
- A *relative* freedom from symptoms that are produced by tensions and anxieties
- The capacity to find more satisfaction in giving than receiving
- The capacity to relate to other people in a consistent manner with mutual satisfaction and helpfulness
- The capacity to sublimate, to redirect one's instinctive hostile energy into creative and constructive outlets
- The capacity to love

Emotional immaturity may seriously affect the mental health of the father or mother who has children before he or she is ready. Child neglect, physical and emotional abuse, and life-long mental and emotional difficulties could result for the child. In the long term, physical and emotional immaturity can take their toll on the health of the mother, the father, and the child.

Time, Energy, and Money

Children place huge demands on personal and family resources in terms of time, energy and money. The cost of raising a child from birth to age 18 in Canada is staggering. Being a parent requires a regular income, the means to provide child supervision twenty-four hours a day, seven days a week, and the energy for active parental involvement. Lone parents may find it difficult to provide adequate income and supervision for their children. They may also find it difficult to maintain the physical energy necessary to keep up with their children without the help of either a generous family member or a paid caregiver. It is much easier for two parents to provide both the income and the supervision needed for children's activities.

Time

Children require an ongoing investment of time. When very young, they require 24-hour supervision, which often leaves parents feeling as though they have no time to themselves. As children move out into the world of kindergarten and school, they continue to need parental time and attention to provide balance in their lives. Adolescents may be spending more time away from the family, but they still benefit from talks and shared activities with their parents. Children thrive on high-quality time spent with parents. You need to be prepared to give your time to a child and plan how you will spend it on supervision and on parent-child activities.

Figure 8.5
Parents must be prepared to spend time supervising their child's activities.

Energy

Children require a great deal of time and personal energy because they themselves are bundles of energy. Children are naturally active, curious, and busy. They need parents who can keep up with them. An active child is a learning child, and for much of their early childhood, children need parental involvement in their activities. Parents who are not ready to invest the energy needed to keep up with young children may find themselves neglecting some of the most important aspects of helping children to learn and develop. Children who are encouraged to be less active, to watch television, or sit quietly instead of playing actively may not do as well in school and may encounter life-long health problems such as obesity and diabetes.

■ *Insomnia: A contagious disease often transmitted from babies to parents.*
— Shannon Fife

Money

Financial changes often occur, not only after the baby is born, but sometimes before the baby is born. Some women may need complete bed rest in the final three months of pregnancy. This affects the family income and comes as a complete shock to a woman who had planned to work or go to school until her due date. Of course, there are ways to be frugal and economical, and children all over the world have survived in less than ideal circumstances.

Estimated Costs of Raising a Child to 18 Years, Canada, 2002

	$ Boy	$ Girl
Child care	54 397	54 397
Shelter, furnishings, household needs	38 621	38 621
Food	25 751	22 329
Clothing	14 783	15 819
Recreation, books, gifts, school	14 945	14 945
Health care	4 655	4 655
Personal care	2 686	3 659
Transportation	3 725	3 725
TOTAL	159 563	158 149

Adapted from "The Cost of Raising a Child," (2002), Manitoba Agriculture and Food [Online]. Website: http://www.gov.mb.ca/agriculture/homeec/cba28s02.html

NOTE: This chart is intended to provide an overview of costs involved in raising a child to the age of 18. These costs should not be used verbatim or in any legal proceedings. Depending on a family's income, values, goals and lifestyle, needs can be subjective. What one family considers essential may not be necessary for another. Family living costs must be adjusted according to each individual situation.

Figure 8.6
What information on this chart surprised you? Explain.

Deciding to parent includes planning for the financial responsibilities of parenting. Potential parents must plan to have a reliable source of income, so that they will be able to provide the necessities of life for their children. Living in poverty or having to give up their children to foster care until they can once again provide for them has long-term physical and emotional consequences for both children and families. Studies such as the one conducted by the Quebec government in 1998 show that the infant's health is negatively affected by poverty.

Poverty Affects Health of Children

The Record, November 7, 2001

Infants born to poor families are at higher risk of health problems than the children of higher income families, a study released yesterday suggests.

The study by a Quebec government statistics agency indicated that in 1998, 28 percent of Quebec families with children aged five months lived in difficult conditions.

In these families, the mothers of one in three children said their youngsters were in poor health. For families with sufficient income, the proportion was one in five.

The study indicated a link between social standing and babies' health and development.

Other contributing factors were the educational levels of the parents and whether or not the family exhibited signs of dysfunction.

Healthy Mind, Body, and Lifestyle

We often hear expecting parents say, "I do not care if it is a boy or a girl, as long as it is healthy!" The health of a parent has a direct bearing on the ability to parent and on the health of the child.

Mental health

Good mental health is very important for positive parenthood. Humour, resilience, and the ability to adapt to change help parents survive the challenges and enjoy the pleasures of parenthood. In fact, the Canadian Mental Health Association's "10 Tips for Mental Health," printed below, could also be considered 10 tips for successful parenthood.

10 Tips for Mental Health

Canadian Mental Health Association

Determine which of the following statements is fact and which is opinion:

1. **Build Confidence**
   Identify your abilities and weaknesses together, accept them, build on them, and do the best with what you have.
2. **Eat Right, Keep Fit**
   A balanced diet, exercise, and rest can help you to reduce stress and enjoy life.
3. **Make Time for Family and Friends**
   These relationships need to be nurtured; if taken for granted, they will not be there to share life's joys and sorrows.
4. **Give and Accept Support**
   Friends and family relationships thrive when they are "put to the test."
5. **Create a Meaningful Budget**
   Financial problems cause stress. Overspending on our "wants" instead of our "needs" is often the culprit.
6. **Volunteer**
   Being involved in community gives a sense of purpose and satisfaction that paid work cannot.
7. **Manage Stress**
   We all have stressors in our lives, but learning to deal with them when they threaten to overwhelm us will maintain our mental health.
8. **Find Strength in Numbers**
   Sharing a problem with others who have had similar experiences may help you find a solution and will make you feel less isolated.
9. **Identify and Deal with Moods**
   We all need to find safe and constructive ways to express our feelings of anger, sadness, joy, and fear.
10. **Learn to Be at Peace with Yourself**
    Get to know who you are and what makes you really happy, and learn to balance what you can and cannot change about yourself.

When parents suffer from a mental illness, a child can experience a great deal of anxiety, shame, and doubt, and because of genetic or hereditary factors, the child may be prone to the mental illness as well. Certain forms of depression, schizophrenia, psychoses, and other forms of mental illness can make caring for children very difficult. No one can predict their own long-term mental health, but prospective parents should be aware of some of the symptoms of mental illness and know where to turn for help for themselves and their children if problems arise.

Physical Health

Parenthood gets off to a much better start if both parents are in good physical health at the time of conception. The importance of maternal health before and during pregnancy has long been recognized as being critical for healthy fetal development. However, the health and age of the father is just as important for healthy sperm. If the sperm is not healthy, or comes from a father who is older, birth and developmental defects can result. In order to have the best chance to produce a healthy baby, both parents should be practising good nutrition, avoiding environmental risk factors, be physically fit, active, and free from active sexually transmitted infections (STIs).

Healthy Lifestyle

A healthy lifestyle has immediate and life-long implications for parents and children. Parents generally expect to live long enough to see not only their children grow up, but also their grandchildren, and maybe even some of their great-grandchildren. Smoking, alcohol abuse, abuse of prescription and illegal drugs, exposure to chemicals, inappropriate risk-taking, over- or-under eating, over-exercising, and lack of exercising are just some of the lifestyle choices that can have serious implications for the health and life expectancy of parents and their unborn children. All of these factors are choices, and future parents can make choices that will contribute to the optimal health and development of their children.

Supportive Family, Friends, and Community

In a country where parenthood is equated with adulthood, a good indicator you have reached adulthood is that friends, family, and members of the community are ready to accept you as a parent. An extensive support network from those around you can help you through many difficult times. When new parents have role models and supportive, experienced parents in their community, they can get advice or ideas that can make parenting much easier. Without these kinds of connections, parents may feel isolated and become overwhelmed with some of the problems of parenthood. Children may suffer neglect, or may be prevented from forming nurturing relationships with their extended family or others in the community. In addition, the social isolation of parents and children is considered a primary contributor to unreported child abuse.

Figure 8.7
A support network of family, friends, and community members can help parents get through the rough times.

Everyone is born into a cultural group that has social norms and personal and family values that guide behaviour. How people think about health, pregnancy, and parenting is definitely influenced by their cultural group. A future mother and father might share similar views about how to prepare for parenthood. They may be from cultural groups with very different ideas about pre-parental roles, health care during pregnancy, eating and drinking habits during pregnancy, child care while parents work, and connections to the extended family. Future parents need to discuss these issues, preferably before conceiving a child and make decisions about how they will do things in the new family they will be forming.

❖ Checkpoints

1. Explain how physical and emotional maturity, physical and mental health, and a healthy lifestyle affect children in the long run.
2. How can potential parents prepare ahead of time for the money, time, and energy it takes to raise children?
3. A supportive family may not be available in some cases because of recent immigration to Canada or a physical or emotional distance from one's family. How can potential parents create a substitute support network?

❖ Connections

1. Predict the long-term influence of achieving each of the Canadian Mental Health Association's 10 tips for Mental Health on a person's ability to parent.
2. Collect stories from your own family that illustrate particular cultural viewpoints related to prenatal health, pregnancy, and parenthood. Compare your stories with those of others in your class. Identify similarities and differences.

The Challenges of Adolescent Parenthood

Are teen parents prepared for parenthood? Many teens have had a lot of experience with children from their roles as older siblings, baby sitters, and caregivers. They may have the knowledge, skills, and attitudes necessary for parenthood, but may lack the maturity, support, and a healthy lifestyle that are required for the role.

Figure 8.8
What challenges do you think face teen parents?

Throughout history, there have always been young women who have become pregnant before marriage. Although things are changing now, historically, the male progenitor or father generally bore no responsibility for the pregnancy. Generally, the girl's family cared for the baby in some way until a marriage could be arranged. In some cases, the grandparents raised the child as their own, while the adolescent mother was treated as an older sister rather than a parent. Sometimes arrangements were made by the family for the baby to be given to another family to raise as their own.

Not until the 1950s and 1960s did homes for unwed mothers become common in Canada. In her book *Gone to an Aunt's: Remembering Canada's Homes for Unwed Mothers*, Anne Petrie (1998) recounts the experience of being treated as a problem that needed to be solved. Many of the homes were funded by religious institutions and were intended to save families from the embarrassment of having a pregnant daughter. A pregnant daughter was sent to the home until her baby was born and put up for adoption. Later, the mother of the child could return home, telling friends and neighbours that she had "gone to an aunt's" for a visit. Here is an excerpt from Petrie's book.

The question of what would happen to the child was settled for me very early. It would be put up for adoption. That was what I always told myself, as if it were the government's choice, not mine. I did not fight for or want anything else. Being a mother had never been a part of my fantasy life, so I did not feel a dream was being lost. And no one ever suggested that I might want to—or could—bring up a child on my own. Where was the necessary husband? What about my education? I would have asked the same questions myself. Career was not really a word in my vocabulary yet, but I had an idea I'd be doing something, whatever it might be. And I felt sure the child would go to a good home, that my preferences would be considered. When I talked to the social worker about the kind of family I would like, the values—religious, cultural, educational—that were important to me, I never doubted those arrangements would be made. In accepting adoption, I did not think I was doing anything noble or shameful. I was just doing what was done.

Today, most teen parents do not give up their babies for adoption. Teen parents and parents-to-be frequently describe troubling experiences, such as a lack of understanding and support, discrimination, judgmental comments, misconceptions, and negative attitudes toward them—even from those employed in the business of helping them. They also feel they do not fit in anywhere. The most overwhelming issue for most adolescent parents is the economic disadvantage they and their children experience. The pressing need for money leaves no room for going back to school or planning for their future. Although most want to break the cycle of poverty, they often do not have the skills, knowledge, and support network to do so.

The following quotes are taken from *Voices of Pregnant Teens. A Collection of Interventions* (1998) by K. McEwen Shadgett.

Teen parents talk about the challenges of parenthood.

"I worry a lot about finances, both our families are poor and we agreed we were going to be different...now what?" (Expectant father)

"I hope some day soon I can afford to pay the rent and buy food, not one or the other like it is now." (Mother of twins)

"When you're pregnant everything around you just vanishes, all the things you think you can count on disappear and suddenly you are in a huge mess and all alone." (Student parent of toddler)

"I wanted to stay in school but my daughter was born three weeks into the semester and I didn't know how to make up the work... but I went back the next semester because I had a ride, child care, and I knew who I could talk to." (Mother of 6-month-old baby)

"If you want help, it's usually there, you just have to know who to ask. It took me two years to figure it out! Some haven't been able to sort it out." (19-year-old mother of two)

Case Study: Jasmine, Age 16

I found out I was pregnant on my 15th birthday! I was blown away and in shock. I never thought this would happen to me. Chandra is a year old now and the light of my life, but it has been so hard. I was three months pregnant before I knew for sure. I was just so tired, and when I started throwing up in the mornings, my mother got suspicious and made me take a home test. Sure enough—there were the two blue lines. My boyfriend dumped me right away—he was into fun, not fatherhood. An abortion was not an option in my religion and by the time the baby was born there was no way I would have given her up for adoption. I thought and thought about this, but how could I give up something that had been part of me for all that time?

I was not welcomed at school when I started to show, but I was able to finish Grade Ten at a maternity home. Chandra was born in June. They showed me how to care for her, and I took a lot of life-skills classes. They helped me apply for student welfare and find a basement apartment, but it is not very nice. When Chandra was three months old, I went back to school, because I know I need an education. I was able to take Chandra to the high school child care, but it was so hard looking after the baby and everything.

My parents both work, but they did take Chandra some evenings so that I could do my homework, laundry, go shopping for the baby, and so on. She was my kid and I tried to be independent. I had no social life, my marks dropped, and then I dropped some courses second semester because I was so run down. I had to give up my part-time job because I had no time. It was hard to make ends meet.

It's summertime again. I am totally responsible for a one-year-old child. I am still on welfare, but I am doing everything possible to finish school. I sometimes feel like we will never get ahead. I love Chandra very much. I just hope she will be proud of my efforts some day.

Questions

1. What kinds of support is Jasmine able to access for herself and Chandra?
2. Why do Jasmine's friends seldom call or ask her to go out with them?
3. Discuss abortion and adoption options for teen pregnancy. Why were they not options for Jasmine?
4. How would an adolescent father's experience compare with Jasmine's in terms of acceptance at school and by friends, ability to complete school, and his role as a parent?

Teen Pregnancy and Infant Outcomes

Besides the obvious economic concerns related to teen pregnancy, the health of the infant must be considered. Teen pregnancy can contribute to problems such as spina bifida, low birth weight babies, and **Sudden Infant Death Syndrome (SIDS)**. Teenage women who become pregnant are still growing themselves. Getting pregnant before they have matured can negatively affect the birth weight and physical development of their baby. Most women do not reach their full physical maturation until their late teens or early twenties. Many adolescent females do not eat a nutritious diet. Their diets generally lack folic acid, the essential nutrient for preventing the birth defect **spina bifida**. An early pregnancy means that the growing mother is competing for the nutrients that the fetus needs, and her growth combined with fetal growth depletes calcium and iron reserves. This contributes to low birth weight, which is a factor in some physical and intellectual delays and in higher occurrences of Sudden Infant Death Syndrome.

❖ Checkpoints

1. How does a baby benefit when the mother has finished her own growth before she becomes pregnant?

2. Explain how it is possible to be an effective parent when facing the difficulties that are associated with adolescent parenthood.

❖ Connections

1. Reread the excerpt from Anne Petrie's book on page 188. How does her experience differ from many unmarried mothers today?

2. Teen fathers have the right to raise a child if their paternity can be established. In addition, teen fathers can be obliged to financially support children they father. How well prepared for parenthood are today's adolescent males?

3. Review the section called What to Consider When Preparing for Parenthood on page 180. How do the factors mentioned apply to what you consider a "typical" teenage parent in Canada today? Do you think your view represents reality or a stereotype? Explain your reasoning.

4. Conduct an informal survey of students in your school to determine the number of pregnant teens they know who were

forced to leave their parents home when they became pregnant, how many they know who are living with friends or relatives, how many are living alone, how many live with parents, and how many have the support of the teen father. How representative are these results of the pregnant teen population in your province or territory?

Choices Affecting the Future of Your Children

The goal of every pregnancy, whether the parent will be raising the child alone or with a partner, or giving up the child for adoption, should be a full-term baby with an optimum birth weight who is born healthy and without complications. Every baby should have the best chance possible for future health, growth, and development.

Lifestyle Choices

There are many ways that men and women can assure a positive future for their children. Future parents can avoid many of the problems that contribute to detrimental development before, during, and after the birth of a child. In men, poor nutrition, drug use, alcohol, and tobacco use can affect the quality of the sperm, while in women, the same things directly affect the development of the fetus. Although Figure 8.10 outlines some of the detrimental effects of various lifestyle choices, research continues to bring to light new understandings about the fragility of human life.

Men and women must avoid any substance that has detrimental effects on the fetus or newborn. This applies to the pre-conception period as well as to the pregnancy and breast-feeding period. Many substances such as alcohol, tobacco smoke, and Accutane (a medication prescribed for acne) have been conclusively shown to produce drastic negative effects on a developing fetus and should be completely avoided. However, there are a variety of other substances, such as over-the-counter stomach and cold medications, that should be avoided by pregnant women even though studies have yet to determine the potential nature and extent of their harmfulness. A pregnant woman should consult her pharmacist or doctor before consuming any medication. This also includes herbal preparations, some of which are known to produce harmful side effects on the fetus.

Figure 8.9
By selecting healthy lifestyle choices, parents can avoid many of the problems that contribute to detrimental development before, during, and after the birth of a child.

Thinking About Your Unborn Children

Detrimental Lifestyle Choice	Immediate Effects	Long-Term Effects
• Poor eating habits. Mothers-to-be should follow Canada's Food Guide to Healthy Eating. • Folic acid deficiency. Mothers-to-be need at least 0.4 mg of folic acid in their daily diet before conception and during pregnancy. • Excessive exercising. This increases body temperature.	• Affects sperm count • Contributes to low birth weight, premature birth, miscarriage, stillbirth, neural tube defects (NTDs) involving the spine and brain, spina bifida • Lowers sperm production • May result in miscarriage or premature birth, lower birth weights, brain or organ damage	• Delayed development • Possible health problems, death in early childhood, lifelong disabilities that may require daily care • Developmental delays
• Tobacco smoking	• Reduces quality of sperm • Low birth weight • Higher incidence of cleft palate • Immature lungs • Great chance of miscarriage • Higher incidence of Sudden Infant Death Syndrome (SIDS)	• Irritability • Attention deficits • Behaviour problems • Behind others in math and reading • Smaller in stature • Asthma and allergies • More ear infections
• Alcohol consumption	• Reduces quality of sperm • Causes a wide range of birth defects • Causes Fetal Alcohol Spectrum Disorder (FASD) • Contributes to low birth weight and premature birth, still birth and miscarriage, organ damage, skeletal damage	• Irreversible brain damage • Vision and hearing problems • Ongoing learning difficulties • Problems concentrating, following instructions, or sticking to a task • Delayed physical, social, emotional, and intellectual development • Lifelong mental illness • Unemployment • Criminal behaviour
• Drug and chemical use **Examples:** prescription drugs, illegal drugs, caffeine, aspartame, some food additives	• Defective sperm and ova • Still birth, miscarriage • Premature birth • Birth defects • Brain damage • Damage to heart and other organs • Newborn addiction to drugs	• Irreversible brain damage • Long-term care required • Lowered immune function • May lead to vision and hearing impairment • May be missing limbs • Learning and behavioural problems • Emotional problems

Figure 8.10

These lifestyle choices have detrimental effects on the present and future health of unborn children.

A Supportive Partner

Women who are pregnant need support from their partner throughout the pregnancy. Partners need to support women by taking a personal interest in their pregnancy. They can encourage them to eat nutritiously and to avoid alcohol, tobacco, drugs, chemicals, and excessive exercise, and, in many cases, stop smoking and drinking alcohol themselves. These changes in lifestyle can help a pregnant partner produce a healthy, full-term baby. Continuing this healthier lifestyle after the birth of the child, particularly with regard to avoiding tobacco and eliminating harmful second-hand smoke, creates a better environment in which to raise a healthy child.

Choosing Prenatal Health Care

Regular **prenatal health care** checkups are essential for a healthy pregnancy. A medical doctor or midwife is trained to pinpoint any problem and offer the necessary guidance for a healthy, full-term pregnancy. Healthy regular weight gain is monitored. Blood pressure and urine samples are analyzed to determine whether there are any complications. Pregnancy is not an illness, but women who do not have early and continuous monitoring of prenatal health care are putting their own and their baby's health at risk. Complications during pregnancy can happen to anyone. Ongoing prenatal care provides a safety net should they arise.

Choosing Healthy Workplace Environments

Hazards encountered in the workplace can affect the reproductive potential of both men and women. Toxic substances can affect the developing fetus. Since male sperm take three months to develop, workplace hazards also pose a definite risk for men. Hazards that are sometimes difficult to avoid include toxic chemicals, some biological substances, and radiation. Oil-based paints and tobacco smoke are another class of hazardous substances found in some workplaces.

Workplace hazards that particularly affect pregnant women and are easier to avoid include: heavy lifting, standing or sitting for long periods, working for over 40 hours per week, and getting too hot or too tired. The workplace is also the source of harmful infectious diseases. Diseases such as German measles, chicken pox, and mumps, for a woman who has never had these diseases or been vaccinated against them, can have devastating effects on the fetus. Future parents need to be aware of the potential harm their workplace holds. Damage to the fetus may occur before a woman even knows she is pregnant. Some family friendly workplaces have policies that allow pregnant women to alter their working conditions, but often their only choice is to seek other employment.

Figure 8.11
Part of prenatal health care is continuous monitoring of the mother and the unborn baby.

❖ Checkpoints

1. Outline a 10-step plan that includes important choices for promoting a healthy pregnancy.
2. Identify lifestyle and workplace problems that are detrimental to the health of an unborn child, and for each one, propose a realistic solution.
3. How do prenatal checkups contribute to healthy birth weights?

Hereditary and Genetic Factors to Consider

Before having children, people should know what health risks they might be passing on to their children, and make their choices accordingly. DNA testing and genetics research are identifying more inherited illnesses and genetic **birth defects** all the time. Some are strictly hereditary and usually consist of defective recessive genes present in both parents. Examples of these birth defects are cystic fibrosis and sickle cell anemia. When both parents pass on a recessive gene, **genetic loading** has occurred. Both parents carry the disease but do not show it themselves. Some traits that are not harmful, such as eye colour, are also passed on in this way. Chromosomal birth defects are different from genetic defects. In these cases, extra copies of chromosomes or the rearrangement of parts of chromosomes can produce a defect. Down syndrome is an example of an extra chromosome producing a serious birth defect.

The Role of Heredity

Chromosomes contain all your hereditary information. Human beings have 23 pairs of chromosomes (46 total) in every cell of their bodies except for the sperm and egg cells, which contain only 23. Each chromosome is made up of thousands of genes. The gene is the basic unit of heredity. Genes carry all the characteristics that will be transferred from parent to child. Genes occur in pairs, and every human has about 30 000 pairs. In each pair of genes, one gene is from the mother, and one gene is from the father.

If you are adopted, you may have limited knowledge of your genetic history, so when you have children of your own, you and they may face medical problems that were never expected. If you ever become the father or mother of a child that is given to another family through adoption, one thing you can do to contribute to that child's future is provide the adoptive family with a detailed medical and genetic history. It is important for the adoptive parents to know the drug, alcohol, and nicotine usage history as well, since both the child's biological parents contribute to the health of the child.

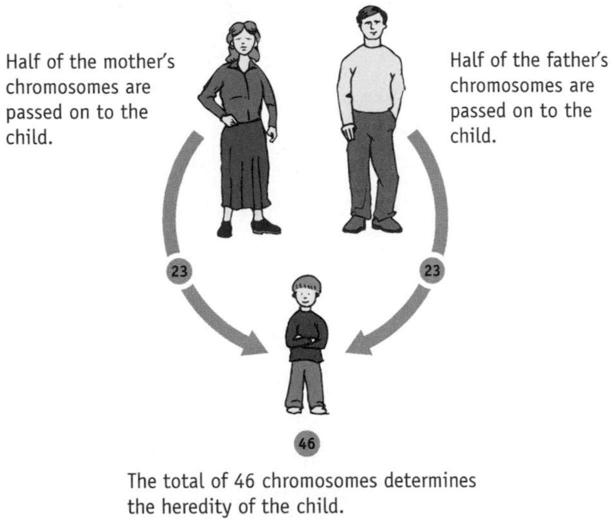

Half of the mother's chromosomes are passed on to the child.

Half of the father's chromosomes are passed on to the child.

The total of 46 chromosomes determines the heredity of the child.

Figure 8.12
A child's heredity is based on equal numbers of chromosomes from the mother and father.

ADAM@HOME © 1997 by Universal Press Syndicate. Reprinted with permission. All Rights Reserved.

Figure 8.13

Where to Find Information on Birth Defects

There are many places to find information about birth defects. Pharmacies, clinics, and medical offices often have pamphlets and videotapes that provide information. The Internet and the local library are also excellent sources of information, and in some cases, your own family members can tell you what kinds of problems run in the family. Most major cities in Canada have at least one hospital that offers genetics counselling services by referral from a family doctor to future parents who wish to know if they are likely to pass on a specific gene or chromosomal birth defect to their children.

What the experts say

JEANNE KENNEDY

Jeanne Kennedy is a genetics counsellor for the Regional Genetics Program at North York General Hospital in Toronto, Ontario. She answers the following question:

What should couples know about the risk of birth defects and the role of genetics counselling?

First of all, couples should realize that not everybody needs genetics counselling. Most babies will be born healthy. Only two or three percent of pregnancies carry a risk of birth defects. Some pregnancies are at an additional risk for chromosomal or genetic disorders. Any concerns you may have should be discussed with your family doctor or midwife who may refer you to a genetics clinic.

During genetics counselling, the aim is to provide women and their partners with the necessary information to enable them to make informed choices about prenatal testing. Some people do not wish to have any testing in pregnancy and others want to have as much testing as is available. Most couples that do receive genetics counselling feel very reassured after talking with a geneticist or genetics counsellor.

When I counsel couples, we discuss many factors to determine their risk for abnormalities in the pregnancy. Maternal age over 35, medical problems like diabetes, kidney disease, or heart problems, three or more miscarriages, already having a baby with a birth defect or a baby that was stillborn, and work environments with chemical or radiation exposure all may increase the risk of birth defects. Family history may

also be important in determining risk. Your ethnic group can play a role, too. For example, French Canadians and Ashkenazi Jews are at higher risk for Tay–Sach's disease.

Some abnormalities are caused by the interaction of susceptible genes with environmental factors, such as the food we eat, medicines we take, and exposure to toxins in the environment. Some of these abnormalities are passed down in families, and others occur as the result of a first-time mutation in a gene. The most important thing to remember, though, is that most babies are born without defects.

There are several tests available to determine if a pregnancy is at risk for abnormalities. Maternal serum screening is a blood test that can be routinely offered to every pregnant woman at 16 weeks of pregnancy. It will indicate a woman's risk for Down syndrome, neural tube defect, and trisomy (three chromosomes instead of a pair). It is recommended that women have an ultrasound test done 18 weeks into their pregnancy. Most ultrasound tests will reveal a normally developing fetus. Although ultrasound is a good tool in prenatal testing, it will not show all abnormalities. Amniocentesis is a test where a small sample of the amniotic fluid surrounding the baby is removed for analysis.

The cells in this fluid are from the baby and are tested for specific or suspected abnormalities. Chorionic Villi Sampling (CVS) is yet another test where cells are removed for testing. These last two tests carry some risk to the pregnancy; therefore, I always discuss both the benefits and the risks of the two tests with couples so their decision can be an informed one.

If problems concerning the expected baby are revealed, some choices may need to be made. The decision each couple will make depends on many factors such as their personal and religious beliefs, their current situation, and how serious the anticipated problem could be. As a genetics counsellor, I often discuss these issues with couples.

If tests reveal problems, a couple may wish to plan for special care for their baby, adoption, or foster care or, in some cases, to end the pregnancy. For many couples, terminating the pregnancy is not an option; thus they may elect not to take any of the tests that could reveal a serious problem. When serious birth defects are revealed in one of my patients, I face the most challenging part of my counselling job.

Fetal Alcohol Spectrum Disorder (FASD)

Imagine having or adopting a baby that you hoped was going to be perfect, only to find a growing list of problems. Low birth weight, tiny head, unusual facial features, irritability, difficulty nursing, delayed development, heart, vision, and/or hearing problems are just a few of the difficulties and behaviours linked to alcohol abuse in pregnancy.

Sometimes, you may get through infancy with relatively few problems only to find your toddler does not talk clearly or your preschool child fails to develop "on schedule." Then your child enters school, and it becomes obvious that there are serious difficulties learning. Rages and tantrums become common and there is little you can do to stop them. The worst, however, is yet to come.

When adolescence starts, life for most parents of FASD children disintegrates. Nothing works. Control is out of the question. School truancy, sexual promiscuity, and alcohol and drug abuse are common. Parents join self-help groups and marriages can fail. FASD adolescents frequently run away from home, and many end up in jail. Depression in these adolescents is common as is teen pregnancy. Some adolescents die as a result of their severe risk-taking behaviours.

As recently as 25 years ago, people had no idea why some children were born with these very unusual yet similar birth defects, or why seemingly normal children behaved in the bizarre but similar ways described above. Now we know these effects are caused when mothers drink alcohol during pregnancy. Research is now suggesting that alcohol use during the conception and breast-feeding periods is also dangerous.

People are becoming aware that any alcohol use during pregnancy is not an option. Advocacy groups such as FASworld Canada are developing to educate the public and deal with the thousands of people currently challenged by this disability.

■ There is no safe level for alcohol consumption during conception and pregnancy.

Figure 8.14
This four-year-old girl was diagnosed with ARND, Alcohol-Related Neurodevelopmental Disorder.

FASD Facts from *FASWorld Canada*

FASWorld Canada is an organization that is devoted to educating the public about the dangers associated with any amount of alcohol consumption while pregnant. The following material is taken from the organization's Web site at www.fasworld.com.

FASD stands for Fetal Alcohol Spectrum Disorder. The conditions it covers are all caused when alcohol is consumed during pregnancy. In this context, alcohol is a **teratogen**, a substance that causes birth defects. Alcohol damages the systems "under construction" when consumed. The heart, hearing, and skeletal systems are often mildly damaged. The brain sustains the most damage because alcohol is a **neurotoxin**. Since neurotoxins destroy brain cells, the damage is permanent.

At present, FASD includes the following conditions:

- FAS: Fetal Alcohol Syndrome
- pFAS: Partial Fetal Alcohol Syndrome
- ARND: Alcohol-Related Neurodevelopmental Disorder
- ARBD: Alcohol-Related Birth Defects

Many people consider FAS to be the most severe of these conditions because the physical and mental abnormalities are so obvious and because society considers people with FAS to be challenged. Although the physical symptoms of the other related FASD conditions are more subtle, the effects of these conditions related to the brain damage caused by alcohol are often just as severe. For example, individuals with these related disorders may frequently act out, fail at school, and find themselves repeatedly in trouble with the law. Society finds it difficult to understand why these seemingly "normal" people behave in such a bizarre fashion and, therefore, individuals with the related disorders are often misunderstood and punished.

In North America, it has been estimated that one percent of all live births are affected by FASD. This means, for example, that in the city of Toronto approximately 30 000 people have some kind of Fetal Alcohol Spectrum Disorder. Of this group, 5000 is under the age of 18. Nevertheless, there is ongoing research that indicates that the one percent incidence estimate for FASD is low.

Most people with Fetal Alcohol Spectrum Disorders have IQs within the normal range; however, FASD is still considered by experts to be the leading cause of mental retardation in North America.

Other expected symptoms and side effects can include, but are not limited to

- problems with anger management and impulse management
- difficulty with learning from consequences (related to poor impulse management)
- immature conscience development or "lack of conscience"
- learning disabilities, attention deficits, and memory deficits leading to
  - serious effects on schooling
  - inappropriate sexual behaviours
  - inappropriate displays of affection, especially in young children
  - poor judgement, resulting in mild to severe behavioural disorders
- heart, ear, skeletal, and facial abnormalities (most apparent in full FAS)
- growth deficiencies with respect to age

On average, individuals with a Fetal Alcohol Disorder will cost the public more than $1.5 million during their lifetime in welfare, housing, special education, medical services, and costs to the criminal justice system.

Fetal Alcohol Disorders are completely preventable if no alcohol is consumed during conception or pregnancy. There is no known safe level for alcohol consumption during conception or pregnancy.

Talking Parenting

Carol Ann and Will Allen, Sr. talk about their adopted children, who have conditions related to FASD.

Figure 8.15
All five of the Allen children have conditions related to FASD.

My husband Will and I both wanted to have a large family. We married and to our great shock never got pregnant. We discussed adoption but ruled out a FASD child because we might not live long enough to provide him or her with the support needed.

In September 1987, a baby became available for private adoption. We were told there had been no drugs or alcohol involved. Vincent was born and spent the first six weeks of his life in the newborn intensive care unit. His biomom came with us on the day we picked him up. She told us that he had been a preemie and had had seizures, meningitis, and a skull infection. The doctor was cautious in answering our questions but did say that Vincent had FAS and that if he lived he might be severely retarded.

It was too late; we were in love and could deal with retardation. I had been a special education teacher before I became a nurse. So home we went and the years went by. We worked hard with Vincent to develop his intelligence. He was lovable, charming, bright, a problem-solver, and very independent. There were puzzling things, though, that no doctor could explain for us. For instance, he was diagnosed with Attention Deficit Hyperactivity Disorder (ADHD), but the treatment for ADHD did not work. His behaviour worsened, we asked if prenatal drug and alcohol use could be causing neurological problems. He was fine we were told—improve your parenting skills!

Vincent was told from day one that he was adopted. This was fine but he wanted siblings and did not care how we got them. We thought and prayed and discussed fostering because we were told we were too old to adopt any more children. We took foster parenting classes and hoped for an eight-year-old boy, close in age to Vincent.

The day we were certified as foster parents, two children, aged 5 and 3, needed an emergency placement. Because 5+3=8, we took them. They were two children out of a family of six siblings. Two months later another sibling needed an emergency placement and a week after that the youngest became available. And so our new life began.

All five of our children were alcohol and drug exposed. We joined FASlink—an electronic bulletin board for individuals dealing with FASD. We found a geneticist to find out what we were dealing with. Coincidently it turned out to be the same doctor, unknown to us,

■ Parents of FASD children face very different challenges compared to those of other parents.

who diagnosed Vincent with the "unequivocal stigmata of FAS" as a baby. We were just never given any information!

On September 4, 1998, Paul, 10, Will Jr., 8, Carol Ann Marie, 5, and Anthony Paul, 4, were adopted forever into the Allen family. They all chose their own names. Vincent and Tony have Fetal Alcohol Syndrome (FAS), the other children all have Alcohol-Related Neurodevelopmental Disorders (ARND) (formerly known as FAE— Fetal Alcohol Effects). They are the sweetest, most lovable children on earth and have brought more joy to our lives than can be imagined.

It has not been easy. One of the children was so out of control, he had to be removed for a time. We have had battles with the system, the schools, and with those who cannot or will not understand our children. We are surrounded by a few very faithful friends, both online and offline. Most likely none of our children will ever be fully independent. We have a long, hard road ahead of us but we are stubborn, persevering, and determined.

People ask us "why" at our ages? It is very simple: vacations and cruises and all the other things that go with retirement last but a moment; children, however, are forever. They are our retirement. We have a full and happy life and the richest life possible.

❖ Connections

1. Create a Web site, poster, or three-fold pamphlet designed to provide future parents with the knowledge necessary to produce a healthy baby.
2. Create a plan to make the public aware of the necessity to avoid alcohol consumption during pregnancy.

Planning Ahead for a Future with Children

There are many things to consider when planning for a future with children. If you hope to become a father or a mother, you will need to plan ahead for the many changes that will take place. Lives change when babies are born. There will be physical, emotional, and financial changes. Parents who are adopting children also need to plan ahead for the arrival of the child. Generally, the first eighteen months after the birth or adoption represents the most difficult period of adjustment to parenthood.

Prenatal classes help couples and individuals plan for the many changes they will encounter and prepare them for the actual birth. Some classes provide an **empathy belly** for the father to try out. When a woman becomes "heavy with child," there are many things that she will need help with, including tying her shoes. The empathy belly is designed to simulate the size, weight, and discomfort of a pregnancy. Men are encouraged to tie their shoes, pick up toys, and climb stairs while wearing the device, which presses against their lungs and bladder. For many it gives a different appreciation for the discomforts that a pregnant woman experiences.

Training to Work with Children

Many women offer child care in their own homes without having formal training. They may be mothers of children themselves or they may have taken a St. John's Ambulance course in baby-sitting or first aid. Some may have taken parenting courses or cooperative education courses in high school, or gained their experience from volunteering in community settings.

However, if you are planning ahead to work with children in a formal child-care setting or a profession, you will require more extensive training. Courses in Early Childhood Education are available at community colleges. Universities also provide degree programs in child development, family studies, and human ecology. Graduates from university programs may go on to qualify as teachers, social workers, health-care professionals, child and family therapists, family law practitioners, or in other professions involving children and families.

Career Capsule

EARLY CHILDHOOD EDUCATOR

Tasks and Responsibilities

The tasks and responsibilities for an early childhood educator range from child-care needs in the areas of supervision, safety, feeding, and cleanliness to educational needs that are met by planning and implementing activities that help children develop physically, socially, emotionally, and intellectually. Children will learn important relationship skills in a good child-care setting, and the early childhood educator is responsible for ensuring a safe and enriching environment.

An early childhood educator provides substitute care for a young child's parent(s) for most of their early years. All early childhood educators must develop good relationships with the parents of the children they serve so that a smooth bridge between home and child care can be built.

Work Environment

Early childhood educators find jobs in nursery schools, a wide variety of public and private child-care facilities, community centres and recreation programs operating after school and on holidays, schools for special needs children, hospitals, and education centres. These environments are noisy and active with children learning and having fun.

Early childhood educators usually work eight hours a day, five days a week. Shift work is common, and most childcare facilities operate from at least 7:00 A.M. to 6:00 P.M. Some provide overnight care.

Directors and supervisors of child-care facilities may work longer hours but are less involved with the children and more active in administrative activities.

Education and Aptitudes

An ability to respect children is essential for an early childhood educator. Patience and understanding are two other required aptitudes, because every child needs encouragement and support. Enormous energy and a genuine liking for children and their play activities are also essential for success in this career.

A fully qualified early childhood educator has an Early Childhood Education (ECE) diploma. These are usually obtained after two years of full-time study at a community college. Supervisors may require a university degree in a program featuring child studies.

Whether you go on to an occupation that specifically relates to children or to any other job or profession, learning about children along the way will contribute to the overall knowledge that benefits anyone who also becomes a parent.

Chapter Summary

Chapter Highlights

- Experience with children, either through family or community contact, helps prepare you for the important job of parenthood.

- Preparation for parenthood is essential for the future of both parents and children. It involves acquiring the knowledge, skills, and attitudes for parenthood; becoming physically and emotionally ready for parenthood; planning for the money, time, and energy it takes to be a parent; having a healthy mind, body, and lifestyle; and knowing that you have the support of family, friends, and community.

- Lifestyle choices such as smoking, drinking, and drug and chemical use, have immediate and life-long detrimental effects on the health, development, and future of children.

- It is important to know your medical history and the possibility of passing on genetic illnesses or disorders to your children.

- Fetal Alcohol Spectrum Disorder (FASD) can be totally eliminated by avoiding all alcohol in pregnancy.

- Whether you plan to be a parent, or plan to work with children, or both, education in parenting and human development is an important part of preparing for the children in your future.

Review and Extend Your Learning

1. Describe the differences between a progenitor and a parent. **K/U**

2. Pretend that you think you are ready to become a parent. Make a list of all the knowledge, skills, and attitudes you possess that make you ready to be a parent. **K/U A**

3. Describe the ways in which a lack of financial resources can negatively affect parents and children. **K/U T/I**

4. Analyze the challenges of being a teen parent, and describe a teen parent's life 10 years in the future. **K/U T/I C**

5. Investigate a specific birth defect. Describe its causes, how it can be detected, and the options available to parents upon detection. **T/I C**

6. Review Figure 8.10 on page 192. Plan a week prior to conception during which a couple makes the healthy lifestyle choices they would need to follow during pregnancy to ensure the health of a future baby. **K/U A**

7. Design an "empathy belly" yourself using a large bag of cat litter or similar material as the weight. Have male and female friends try bending over to tie their shoes or pick up toys and envision carrying that weight around for three months. Record their reactions to share with your class. **K/U T/I C A**

8. Many jobs provide knowledge and skills that will help men and women become better parents. Select two such careers and analyze the skills that are used in the job that would help a person be a better parent. **T/I A**

9. For one of the following scenarios, describe the issues and suggest choices that would produce positive outcomes: **K/U T/I C A**
   a) The child you adopted four years ago has been diagnosed with Fetal Alcohol Spectrum Disorder (FASD).
   b) Your genetics counsellor informs you that you carry the gene for a particular birth defect.
   c) Both you and your partner are smokers and are planning to have your first child.
   d) You and your spouse are two months pregnant and have been invited to a party given by a close friend who has been a drinking partner in the past.

Research Opportunities

10. As a group research project, brainstorm a list of all the items necessary for a new baby. Include furniture, equipment, and clothing. Use catalogues, advertising flyers, or the Internet, or visit stores to determine

how much each of the items would cost new. Then using classified ads, local thrift stores, flea markets, or garage sales, determine how you could afford the same items on a restricted budget. Compare the findings of your group with other groups in the class.

11. Search the Internet for training or education programs across Canada related to childcare. Select three programs that interest you. On a large recipe card, write a brief description of the program including details such as who is eligible to take it, who offers the course, the province or territory and site where it is offered, cost or tuition, how long it takes, entrance requirements, name of graduating certificate, diploma, or degree. Collect the information gathered by the class, and create a visual presentation by linking a string from your write-ups to their locations on a map of Canada. Create a title banner: "Child-Care Education across Canada."

Issue Analysis

12. Preparation for parenthood contributes to healthy pregnancies and long-term healthful outcomes for children. Should those who are not prepared for parenthood be allowed to have children? Take a position and consider the implications for both parents and children. Write a five-paragraph essay to persuade others of your position.

Unit 5   The Nature of Children

This unit examines human growth and development and the essential foundation provided by early brain development. Ways to promote optimal growth and development from conception through adolescence are explained.

KEY INSIGHTS:

- Those who live and work with children contribute to human growth and development.
- Early brain development benefits intellectual development in older children and adolescents.
- Early brain development and beneficial environments contribute to the overall progress of human growth and development.
- Healthy development begins before conception and continues thereafter.
- The quality of lifelong development can be traced to pregnancy and infancy.
- Bonding and attachment at birth are essential for growth and development.
- The first year of life shapes later development.
- Early attachment shapes social and emotional development in older children and adolescents.
- Bonding and attachment theories point out the critical role of parents in overall human development.

- The early years experience is critical for human development.
- Early learning and brain development provide the foundation for learning in childhood and adolescence.
- Children learn rapidly in the first five years of life through human interaction and play.
- Parents of older children and adolescents face unique challenges as they continue their development.
- The goal of human growth and development from childhood to adulthood is physical, intellectual, psychological, social, and emotional maturity.

Unit at a Glance

Human Growth and Development: An Overview

By the end of this chapter, you will be able to:

- understand the multifaceted nature of and the various influences on child development

- identify environments provided by families, caregivers, and others that offer positive conditions for child development

- describe various child development theories and evaluate their relevance

- explain, using basic principles of brain science, the role that stimulation plays in the intellectual development of infants

- evaluate the significance of neuroscience and theories of brain development during critical periods in early childhood

- analyze changes in human development throughout the life cycle

Important Terms

aggressive
axon
brain wiring
cognitive science
conception
critical period
dendrite
developmental
    psychologist
fine-motor skills
gross-motor skills
interdisciplinary
    studies
neuron
nurturing relationship
overstimulation
placid child
pruning
resiliency
sensitive child
stimulation
stimuli
synapse

Chapter at a Glance

What Is Human Growth and Development?

Look at all the people you know. They come in all shapes, sizes, and ages, with different skills, abilities, interests, and temperaments. Some are happy, some are sad. Some are talkative, some are quiet. Some need lots of help with even the simplest tasks, while others are totally independent and able to help themselves and others.

Although every person is a unique individual, social science researchers have noted patterns of human growth and development from birth to adolescence all over the world. When parents and caregivers are aware of these broad patterns, they are able to play their role more effectively. The study of human growth and development helps to make sense of both the differences and the similarities.

The study of human growth and development is concerned with human change from conception to old age. Human beings grow and develop physically, socially, emotionally, morally, and intellectually. Technically, growth refers to a change in size, and development indicates a change in skill level, but in the study of children and adolescents, the terms are often used together, and interchangeably.

Why Study Human Growth and Development?

How many children do you interact with everyday? Have they ever left you feeling frustrated or thinking that you do not understand their behaviour? Have you ever thought their parents were ineffective, or believed a child just needed to be firmly disciplined by an adult? Being aware that temper tantrums and mood swings are common starting around 18 months makes this behaviour much easier to accept. Knowing that normal developmental changes bring on mood swings makes it easier to care for and nurture the young child who is working through them. Understanding human growth and development enables you to be more empathetic and a better caregiver. Fortified with knowledge, caregivers are less likely to abuse or neglect a child. You can continue to learn more about the stages of human development by paying attention to children around you and by finding out what others have already discovered.

Adolescents, who are still developing, may not always feel as happy as they want to be. It should be comforting for them to know that most of these feelings are normal and will pass as they move into adulthood. However, some feelings and moods are a cause for concern. Studying human growth and development will help you recognize what is normal and what situations may need professional

Figure 9.1
We come in all shapes and sizes, and have different abilities and temperaments.

■ Human beings grow and develop
• physically
• socially
• emotionally
• morally
• intellectually

attention. As you study, you will also remember or be told stories of developmental events from your own childhood. You may be able to reflect on them and as you do this, you will develop a better understanding of how you developed into the person you are today. As a possible future parent or caregiver, or as someone who interacts with children or adolescents, you will be more sensitive to when a child would benefit from professional attention.

Figure 9.2
Although all aspects of human growth and development are interrelated, they can be studied separately.

▪ Studying human growth and development will help you make thoughtful choices about your future.

When you bring the study of human development to your own memories of childhood, you will better understand why you are the person you are today with unique personality, intelligences, and skills. You are the person that you are for a reason.

A study of human growth and development will help you make thoughtful choices about your future. Will you want to become a parent when you find out what to expect of children and adolescents in all their ages and stages? Will the important role of parenting work well with the career choices you are considering? Can you see yourself in a career with children, perhaps as an orthodontist, an art therapist, a school-bus driver, or a teacher?

Human Development from Conception to Adolescence

Human development starts at the moment of **conception**, when the sperm unites with the egg and cell division begins. The union provides a full complement of chromosomes—23 from the father and 23 from the mother—with all the genetic material that will contribute to the development of the embryo from that moment on. Conception establishes human potential; however, the degree to which that potential is achieved depends on many things. The quality of the pregnancy and delivery, the nurturance and care provided, and the life experiences that follow all continue to influence and shape human potential.

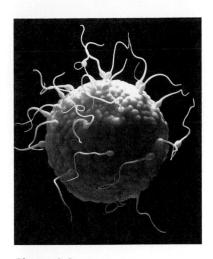

Figure 9.3
The moment before conception. One sperm will successfully enter the egg.

❖ Connections

1. Some parents keep baby books with pictures and developmental milestones. Find yours, or share someone else's baby book of memories, and observe the growth and development of a child. If possible, interview the person who made the baby book.

2. Reflect on the milestones that were included, and write a one-page summary of your observations. You may wish to reflect on information such as when the child began sleeping through the night or when the first steps were taken. For example: "My parents must have been really glad when I finally let them get a good night's sleep at 11 months." Or "Chasing me around when I started to walk at 9 months gave them a lot of exercise."

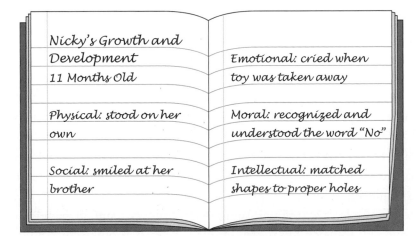

Nicky's Growth and Development
11 Months Old

Physical: stood on her own

Social: smiled at her brother

Emotional: cried when toy was taken away

Moral: recognized and understood the word "No"

Intellectual: matched shapes to proper holes

Figure 9.4
Parents sometimes document their children's growth and development.

The study of growth and development in infancy, childhood, and adolescence includes five distinct areas. All of the areas of development are interconnected and occur simultaneously. In fact, progress in one area often triggers progress in another area. However, **developmental psychologists**, who are the social scientists who study human development in detail, have divided human development into physical, social, emotional, moral, and intellectual (or cognitive) growth and development. Their research assists parents, caregivers, and those who work with children in understanding where most children are in their development at a particular age, as well as what to expect of them as infants, toddlers, preschoolers, school-age children, pre-adolescents, and adolescents.

■ Human development is
- similar in all humans
- sequential
- individualized
- interrelated
- continuous

Characteristics of Human Growth and Development

Although each person develops at an individual rate and in an individual way, all human growth and development follow similar patterns the world over. Development is sequential and builds on previous stages. It is individualized for each person, and all areas of development are interrelated. Human growth and development are continuous throughout life.

Development in human beings is similar all over the world. In all countries of the world, babies follow the same pattern of development. For example, all babies make the same babbling and cooing sounds, no matter what language is spoken in their home. Then, at about the same age, they start to make sounds that closely imitate the language they hear being spoken around them, whether it is Russian, Chinese, French, or English.

Development is sequential and builds on earlier development. Babies always lift their heads before they turn over. The ability to stand alone always precedes walking. Earlier development and learning is necessary before new development takes place. Physical growth is a critical factor in the sequence in which new skills appear. For example, the muscles controlling the bladder must develop before real toilet training is possible.

Development is individualized. Parents are always cautioned not to overreact if their child's development varies somewhat from that of other children. Every child proceeds at his or her own rate in all areas of development, even though progression follows a similar pattern for all children. Some children walk much earlier than other children do, perhaps because they are bigger and stronger. Other children will be talking fluently before they decide to walk.

A Sequence of Emily's Physical Development

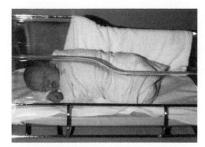

as a newborn

at two months, needs support
to sit, stares at hand

at three months, lifts head and
chest, reaches for objects

at six months, sits alone

at nine months, crawling on hands
and knees

at ten months, pulling to stand

at eleven months, climbing

by one year, standing

Figure 9.5
Development is sequential. To be able to run, a baby must gain control of the body
through the steps of lifting the head, crawling, standing, and walking.

Figure 9.6
Knowing the difference between right and wrong causes children to struggle with feelings of guilt.

■ Children exhibit different temperaments:
- sensitive
- placid
- aggressive

Development is interrelated. Physical, social, emotional, moral, and intellectual development are all interrelated. A child who is physically able to climb on a chair and sneak a cookie before supper is at the same time old enough to know that doing so is wrong. She may end up struggling with feelings of guilt before deciding whether to take the cookie. All five areas of development are interdependent and reinforce one another.

Development is continuous throughout life. Although human growth and development is most dramatic and rapid from conception to about three years of age, it continues throughout life. Children and adolescents have very little control over these changes and may find them confusing and disturbing. Individuals continue to grow and learn throughout life, but adult development is slower and more in their control. Most wellness experts today recommend that to be healthy, everyone needs to grow, learn, and change throughout the course of their entire life.

The Five Areas of Human Growth and Development

Physical growth and development involves the actual growth of all body tissues. It is the only area where actual growth, in addition to development, takes place. The four other areas of development depend on physical readiness, which is achieved as children grow. Bones, muscles, organs, and body systems generally become bigger and more able to perform complex actions. As children grow older, their **fine-motor** skills, based on the growth of small muscles, and their **gross-motor** skills, based on the growth of large muscles, become more sophisticated. Human contact, nutrition, hygiene, exercise, and rest contribute to healthy growth and development.

Social development progresses from being completely self-centred and dependent as an infant to becoming an independent adult, capable of behaving in socially acceptable ways. Mature social skills include being able to make and keep friends, form intimate relationships, get along with others, show leadership, and function as an individual as well as part of a team. These skills are built on self-confidence, co-operation, and a sense of trust, which starts with a secure and loving relationship with the child's primary caregivers beginning at birth.

Emotional development is the process of developing positive feelings about oneself, family, friends, other individuals, and the world at large. Every child seems to be born with a certain temperament. Some are **sensitive**, react intensely to their environment, and cry easily. **Placid** children are easygoing and more content. **Aggressive** children respond to and interact with their environment more vigorously and so are more wakeful as infants. Caregivers need to respond with warmth to the innate nature of a child and accept and support it, rather than trying to change it. Children need to develop a full range of feelings and learn to handle those feelings appropriately. Only then will they be resilient and able to handle the challenges that life offers.

Moral development is a relatively new area of study, which was considered part of social and emotional development in the past. Moral development refers to the development of a sense of right and wrong. This could be described as the conscience, which governs thoughts, feelings, and behaviours. Moral beliefs usually involve concepts of justice, rights and responsibilities, and fairness. Parents and caregivers influence early moral development through their own example, explanations of, and attitude toward ethical and unethical behaviour. For example, children will learn to tell the truth if they are certain that their parents are always truthful.

Intellectual growth and development has recently been the focus of worldwide attention in **cognitive science**, or the study of how we learn. Learning depends on brain growth as well as stimulation of the brain and central nervous system by the five senses. Humans learn to communicate, think, be creative, focus their attention, solve problems, and make judgements. Brain growth during the earliest years of life is critical to cognitive development and is related to every area of human development. Infants and children need supportive, warm, nurturing, and sensitive interactions for their brain to grow and their intellect to develop.

Figure 9.7
All areas of development work together to create a functional person. A child's ability to understand and express emotions is developing at the same time as the ability to take on new physical challenges.

❖ Checkpoints

1. What is human growth and development?
2. Describe and give examples of the five ways in which human beings grow and develop.
3. Explain why knowledge of human growth and development is valuable for all adults.

The Role of Nurture in Human Development

Healthy and positive human growth and development depend on nurturing relationships. The three key elements of a **nurturing relationship** as identified by early years experts for the Invest in Kids organization are the ability to comfort, play with, and teach children. As the child grows

Figure 9.8
Parents who play with their children contribute to their development.

older, the nature of comforting, playing, and teaching changes to remain appropriate for the child's needs.

Comfort: Children can become frustrated, anxious, or over-whelmed as they pass through the stages of development. Parents need to acknowledge the child's discomfort and offer an appropriate response. Gentle rocking and soothing are appropriate for infants, while calming words may be more appropriate for an older child.

Play: Play exercises a growing body and mind while providing a way to express emotions, develop social abilities, and explore moral thinking. Parents who engage in play with children contribute to the child's development while strengthening their parent-child relationship.

Teach: Teaching provides children with the "know-how" to accom-plish important tasks at each developmental stage. For example, a parent can show a toddler how to go up and down stairs safely, or teach an ado-lescent how to calmly restart a stalled car. Parental teaching of skills, knowledge, and attitudes moves children along in their development.

Sometimes, all three elements are included in one activity. A parent who takes a preschooler to a petting zoo may teach the names of the animals, play a game of imitating the geese stretching their long necks, and offer comfort when the goat frightens the child by butting its head against the wire fence.

Effective caregiving involves the three elements of nurturing and therefore, fosters healthy and normal development in children and adolescents and helps them move on to the next developmental stage.

From conception to adolescence, all areas of development work together to achieve a functional person who moves forward in recog-nizable stages. Child psychiatrists Dr. Stanley Greenspan and Dr. T. Berry Brazelton identified the functional milestones in development from birth to adolescence. They clearly identified the close connec-tions among physical, social, emotional, moral, and intellectual development at every stage. An overview of their findings appears on the chart on the next page.

❖ Connections

1. In your opinion, is one area of growth and development more important than the others? Explain.
2. Which area of development is easiest to identify in children? Explain your reasoning.
3. Describe a parent-child activity for any age level in which a parent uses all the comfort, play, and teach elements appropriately for the child's age level.

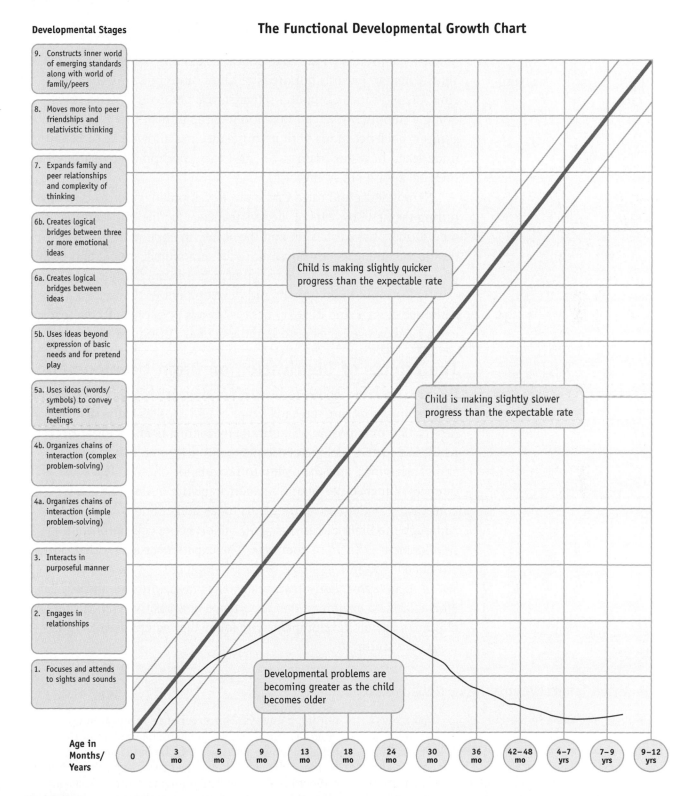

Developmental Stages

9. Constructs inner world of emerging standards along with world of family/peers

8. Moves more into peer friendships and relativistic thinking

7. Expands family and peer relationships and complexity of thinking

6b. Creates logical bridges between three or more emotional ideas

6a. Creates logical bridges between ideas

5b. Uses ideas beyond expression of basic needs and for pretend play

5a. Uses ideas (words/symbols) to convey intentions or feelings

4b. Organizes chains of interaction (complex problem-solving)

4a. Organizes chains of interaction (simple problem-solving)

3. Interacts in purposeful manner

2. Engages in relationships

1. Focuses and attends to sights and sounds

The Functional Developmental Growth Chart

Child is making slightly quicker progress than the expectable rate

Child is making slightly slower progress than the expectable rate

Developmental problems are becoming greater as the child becomes older

Age in Months/Years: 0 | 3 mo | 5 mo | 9 mo | 13 mo | 18 mo | 24 mo | 30 mo | 36 mo | 42–48 mo | 4–7 yrs | 7–9 yrs | 9–12 yrs

Figure 9.9
The middle line represents the age at which most babies achieve these milestones.

The Importance of Brain Development

Modern computers continue to amaze us daily by what they can do. Yet the human brain is hundreds of times more powerful than the computer you use. Computer scientists are not even close to developing a computer that can function like the human brain. However, computer science along with neuroscience has allowed us to better understand how our brains work and why good practices during the prenatal period are so important.

Neuroscience indicates that brain development prior to birth and during the first six years of life sets the stage for lifelong learning, mental and physical health, and the ability to cope with stress. Brain development affects our physical, social, emotional, moral, and cognitive development. Lifelong development is influenced by many factors during the rapid brain growth and development of the first six years. Although change and development is always possible, effective parenting and caregiving is critical and essential during that time period.

The Effects of Deprivation on Brain Development

What do we know about children who are deprived, neglected, poorly fed, or abused during the early years of life? Studies show that severe deprivation or exposure to harmful environments and substances can result in negative lifelong consequences to learning, health, relationships, behaviour, and the ability to provide for oneself. The consequences of ineffective parenting and caregiving in the early years contribute to many social problems today and cannot be ignored. Although the brain already has 100 billion nerve cells at birth, its development is far from complete. The experiences a child has during childhood continue to shape brain development.

In their report, *Early Years Study*, Dr. Fraser Mustard and Margaret Norrie McCain examined the importance of a positive environment on children's overall development. The following material is excerpted from their study.

Negative Environments Have Negative Impacts

A toddler sits alone in her crib, crying loudly. Her mother is depressed and alone too. She thinks it is better to let the child cry than spoil her by holding and comforting her. Her husband arrives and is abusive about her care of the child and starts shouting at the mother. The toddler's brain senses a highly stressful situation through her visual and auditory sensing pathways. This experience is repeated day after day. The arousal and emotional system of the child's brain becomes wired to be upset and disturbed by these stimuli. This can lead to an abnormal stress response that can persist throughout life and, among other things, influence mental health.

There are two hopeful signs in this bleak picture. First, people are now realizing the importance of parenting and are seeking to improve their parenting skills. Second, new research shows that exposure to even one caring, committed adult in early childhood and the adolescent years can produce **resiliency** or the ability to overcome childhood problems and manage life effectively as an adult.

■ Brain development combined with nurturing in the early years is the key to growth and development in subsequent years.

How Babies Learn

In the past century, researchers have held differing views on whether learning behaviour occurs in newborn babies. Some scientists have argued that babies' behaviour was not learned or thoughtful and operated as a spontaneous reflex. They did not think newborns got much information from any of their senses. In fact, until fairly recently, male babies were usually circumcised without painkillers because it was believed that infants did not feel pain.

When developmental psychologists began to study babies' reactions to stimuli, it became obvious that babies interacted with their caregivers. The most active senses, or at least the most researched, are those of sight and hearing. We do know, however, that all of an infant's senses are working and active. Any caregiver who has tried to feed a baby strained green peas will immediately recognize that as the baby's taste buds are stimulated, they react to the peas by spitting them out.

For Better or For Worse®   **by Lynn Johnston**

FOR BETTER OR FOR WORSE © UFS, Reprinted by permission.

Figure 9.10
It was once believed that babies received little information from their senses.

Babies are ready to learn from the moment they are born. They learn about the world through their five senses: sight, hearing, taste, smell, and touch. Information or **stimuli** from the outside world arrive at the baby's brain through the senses. The brain, operating like the most powerful computer imaginable, processes this information, and the baby reacts. The caregiver's reaction to the baby's behaviour produces more stimuli and more reactions. Through a series of actions and stimuli, baby and caregiver fine-tune or change how they react to each other.

■ Learning depends on at least one caring, committed caregiver who responds positively to a baby's behaviour.

When a change in behaviour takes place, **learning** has occurred. At least one caring, committed, and positive caregiver who responds to the baby's behaviour is essential for learning. Researchers have noticed an increase in brain development every time a caregiver responds to a baby by talking or touching. Talking, singing, playing, touching, and teaching continue to enhance brain development throughout childhood.

Researchers now recognize that in infancy, connections in the brain are rapidly being made. These connections are evidenced by identifiable leaps in the child's learning. Many researchers refer to this type of brain development as **brain wiring**.

How the Human Brain Works

The brain is the most complex organ in the human body. It is connected by the nervous system to every part of the body. Every appendage and every organ relies on different signals from the brain to function. Likewise, the brain relies on impulses from every part of the body to continue its function.

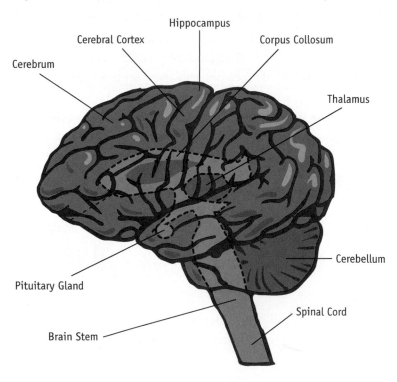

Figure 9.11
Parts of the human brain and their functions

How Does the Brain Get Wired?

Theories about learning are continuously evolving. Behavioural research that began in the 1970s has become the brain research of the 1990s. Brain wiring has been the subject of numerous books, theses, journal and newspaper articles, and media interviews. The new research has provided a new and exciting concept about how we should be nurturing our children. The story is quite simple:

- Because their brains are proportionally larger, human infants are born earlier in terms of their development than any other animal species, and they remain dependent on adults for a longer period.

- At birth, the human brain is one-quarter the size of an adult's. During the time from birth to age five, the brain grows from 300 cc to 1300 cc in size; it is during this time that learning is most natural and very rapid.

- At birth humans have almost all the **neurons** or nerve fibres they will ever have, but most are not yet connected.

- The brain stem, which controls vital functions such as breathing and heartbeat, is already connected or **hardwired**, but almost all other behaviours or reactions to stimuli need to be learned or "wired in."

- During infancy and the first six years of life, our brain is "wired" in a way similar to that of a new house. Once the wiring is "in," it is difficult but not impossible to change; therefore, getting it right the first time is very important as lifelong learning, self-confidence, and overall health depend on this brain wiring.

- "Wiring" connections, or **synapses**, between neurons allow electrical currents to flow. This electrical flow from the nerve endings makes the brain work and signals which behaviour or reactions to particular stimuli should occur.

- Connections are reinforced when a neural pathway is used over and over again by talking and physically responding to a baby. For example, if a baby gets positive emotional feedback, such as a big smile and excited talk from Dad when she babbles "da-da-da," she is going to try it over and over again to get the same positive reaction. This wires that circuit and the baby has learned a basic speech sound. On the other hand, if she is ignored, she does not get feedback and will lose interest. Her behaviour is not reinforced, and will likely not be repeated.

- Connections that are not reinforced are weakened. These connections to the neurons atrophy or die off in a normal process. Researchers call this **pruning**, because in the same way that a tree grows stronger when the weaker and unnecessary branches are removed, so too the existing brain connections can be strengthened if those that are not reinforced disappear.

Figure 9.12
This sensory activity aids in neuron connections.

- Caregiver reactions to the baby, which motivate the baby to make connections to the world through the senses, are called **stimulation**. The more stimulation a baby receives when awake, the more connections are made in the brain. Talking to a baby and young child is one of the most important forms of stimulation a parent or caregiver can provide, as are touching, smiling, singing, and gazing fondly into an infant's eyes.

- **Overstimulation** occurs when a baby's senses receive too much information. Infants may react by turning away, becoming fussy or irritable, or by falling asleep. Babies need to rest their senses from time to time for optimum development. Quiet play, time alone, and naps give them time to think, retrieve what they have learned, and provide rejuvenation.

Figure 9.13

In the embryonic stage, neurons and axons are formed. After birth, sensory experiences determine which corrections will be maintained or pruned.

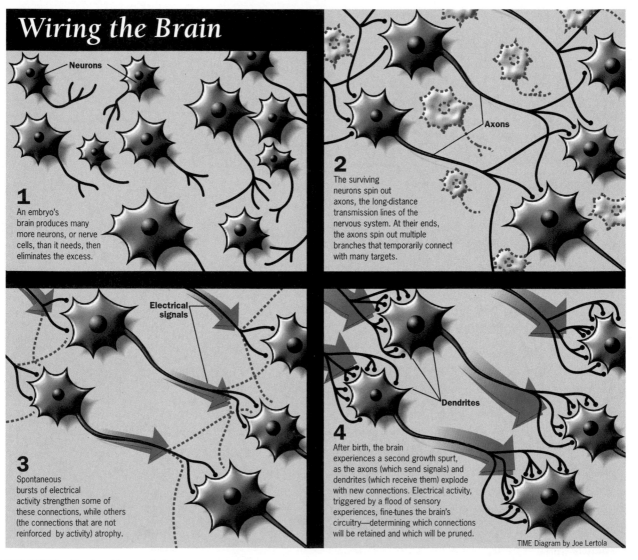

Wiring the Brain

Neurons

1
An embryo's brain produces many more neurons, or nerve cells, than it needs, then eliminates the excess.

Axons

2
The surviving neurons spin out axons, the long-distance transmission lines of the nervous system. At their ends, the axons spin out multiple branches that temporarily connect with many targets.

Electrical signals

3
Spontaneous bursts of electrical activity strengthen some of these connections, while others (the connections that are not reinforced by activity) atrophy.

Dendrites

4
After birth, the brain experiences a second growth spurt, as the axons (which send signals) and dendrites (which receive them) explode with new connections. Electrical activity, triggered by a flood of sensory experiences, fine-tunes the brain's circuitry—determining which connections will be retained and which will be pruned.

TIME Diagram by Joe Lertola

Some Definitions

Neurons are the nerve cells that make up the brain. Neurons are composed of a cell body, an axon, and dendrites. Humans are born with billions of neurons. When neurons are lost during normal brain development and aging, none are added.

Dendrites are the arms of a neuron. They resemble tree branches sprouting from the cell body. Dendrites receive messages from other neurons and pass them to the cell body to be processed. Stimulation during infancy and childhood dramatically increases the number of dendrites and "wires the brain." A baby has very few dendrites compared to an adolescent.

Axons resemble bead-like tails emerging from the cell body. At the end of the bead-like section, a simpler branched structure emerges to carry the neural message to the next neuron by passing the message across the synapse.

A **synapse** is the extremely small gap between neurons. The ends of the axon do not touch the next neuron. Instead they release a chemical neurotransmitter, called ethylcholine, to carry the message to the dendrites of the next neuron.

❖ Checkpoints

1. Each part of the brain has a specialized function. Explain which of the following parts of the brain would be needed for a child to learn how to hop on one foot: cerebellum, cortex, corpus collosum, spinal cord, and hippocampus.

2. Draw a flow chart to illustrate how the game of Peek-a-Boo would involve the following: neuron, axon, dendrite, and synapse.

3. Briefly summarize the meaning of "brain wiring" and how it relates to development.

4. The quote "use it or lose it " is used frequently. How does it apply to "brain wiring"?

Promoting Early Brain Development

The human brain cannot develop in isolation. Healthy lifestyle choices and good nutrition during pregnancy contribute to the health of the brain at birth. The human infant requires love, nurturance, and consistent and dependable interaction from at least one caring person to stimulate positive brain development.

Breast-feeding may be one way to promote brain development. Studies have indicated a connection between breast-feeding and higher intelligence scores in children and adults. To date, however, researchers have not determined whether the contributing factor is the breast milk itself, the close contact that is part of the breast-feeding experience, or the social and economic status of the women who took part in the studies that caused the higher intelligence effect.

Figure 9.14
There may be a link between breast-feeding and higher intelligence in children.

Critical Periods of Brain Development

Different parts of the brain develop at different times to prevent overload. For example, vision starts to develop immediately after birth, but vocabulary development starts in the third month of life. These are called **critical periods**, and if the brain circuits involved do not get stimulated or exercised during this time, they may not develop.

According to research included in the *Early Years Study* by Margaret Norrie McCain and Dr. Fraser Mustard, most critical periods occur in the first five years of life, as shown below. Different degrees of opportunity remain open, decreasing after age ten. Knowledge of human growth and development enables parents or caregivers to take advantage of these critical periods. They can teach, comfort, and play with their child in ways that encourage the best growth and development possible in that developmental period.

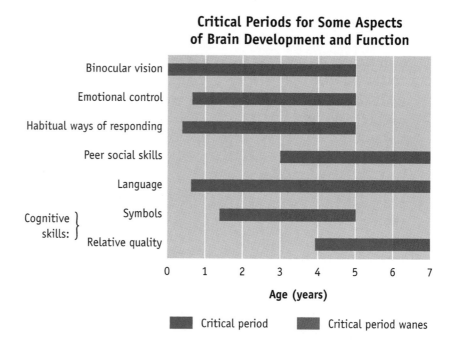

Figure 9.15
Research has shown that there seems to be critical periods for some components of brain development and function.

Stimulation and Brain Development

Parents and caregivers can provide infants with a variety of daily experiences as they care for and play with them. Different kinds of stimulation develop different neural paths. Words and sounds, especially baby talk and repetition, encourage development in the language centres of the brain. Counting, music, and repeated patterns of colour and sound build up the mathematical centres in the brain.

The taste, smell, and touch associated with the satisfaction of feeding can make comfort connections for infants that provide the security and contentment necessary for making human attachments.

Researchers continue to look for a connection between stimulation and enhanced cognitive functioning. One such study conducted by Frances Rauscher and Gordon Shaw (1995) concluded that listening to Mozart enhances spatial-temporal reasoning in preschool children. Their theory was dubbed The Mozart Effect and focused media attention on playing Mozart to babies before and after they were born to enhance their intellectual development. The Mozart Effect has been celebrated and refuted on many fronts. Rebecca Green (1999), in her article "An Ode to Joy: Listening to Music May Not Make Children Smarter But It Will Make Them Dance," notes that the increase in reasoning observed in the study was merely temporary and lasted for about ten minutes. She suggests that using music to enhance grades is misguided. She suggests that promoting music appreciation in young children simply for the very joy of it is much healthier.

❖ Checkpoints

1. What role do nutrition and nurturance play in early brain development?

2. How does play facilitate development when critical periods for such things as language development, fine-muscle development, and early social development overlap?

3. Explain why reading to children is an excellent form of brain stimulation.

❖ Connections

1. When "brain wiring" research was first in the media, many parents wanted to know how they could prevent neuron atrophy or "pruning." What advice would you give these parents?

2. Play with a number of different toys that appeal to children of different ages. While you are playing with each toy, think about which of your five senses it is stimulating. Imitate and repeat the actions a baby or child would make when playing with the toys to determine the kind of learning that is being reinforced. Compile a chart for your notes that records the kind of toy, the age of child it appeals to, the senses it stimulates, and what the child learns.

Figure 9.16
A guideline for parenting: Be warm, loving, and responsive.

3. Ask a student who speaks a foreign language to teach you how to count to ten in that language. What did you find most difficult about this exercise? Using the theory of brain wiring, explain why language acquisition is easier early in life.

4. Survey fellow students, teachers, or members of your community whose second language is the one they currently use. What is the correlation between the age at which they learned the second language and their fluency in it?

Parenting Skills

Promoting Young Children's Healthy Development and School Readiness: Ten Guidelines

- Be warm, loving, and responsive.
- Respond to the child's cues and clues.
- Talk, read, and sing to your child.
- Establish routines and rituals.
- Encourage safe exploration and play.
- Make TV watching selective.
- Use discipline as an opportunity to teach.
- Recognize that each child is unique.
- Choose quality child care and stay involved.
- Take care of yourself.

❖ Checkpoints

1. Describe how each of the ten guidelines promotes healthy growth and development, emphasizing brain growth.

Theories of Child and Adolescent Development from the Social Sciences

Childhood is a recent concept in western society. It was not all that long ago that children were viewed as "blank slates" that parents then inscribed. Children were to be seen not heard, they spoke when they were spoken to, and they followed the strict rules set out for them. By the time they were teenagers, they were considered adults and took their rightful place in society. Only recently in western cultures has it been customary to think of the period between childhood and adulthood as a distinct stage of development, now referred to as adolescence.

In the late 1800s, Sigmund Freud theorized that adult personality was very closely related to early life experiences. His theories were the beginning of a growing interest in human development, research into infants, children, and youth, and the beginning of a number of contemporary theories about children and childhood.

Theories must be able to offer a convincing explanation of reality and stand up to rigorous questioning. Theories inform practice on many levels. For example, parents often have theories about why their children behave in a certain way. They then take steps to reinforce or change their children's behaviour. Their theory may change as events unfold.

Theories affect the way in which people do their jobs and play their roles in life. The practice of teaching is based on learning theory; the practice of medicine is based on scientific theories. The practice of parenting, caregiving, or working with children is often based on theories about children.

There is a huge body of research into child and adolescent development because it has been actively studied for the last 125 years. The chart below describes some child development theorists. There are many more. No one researcher has ever provided a complete, undisputed theory of how humans develop or how to parent a child, but taken together, the theories have revealed a great deal about human development. In an effort to do the best job, parents, caregivers, and students in parenting courses must learn to think critically about theories and strategies, discuss them with other informed people, and decide what is best for themselves in their own interactions with children.

Theorists of Child Development from the Social Sciences

Theorist	Theory	Importance to Parenting
Sigmund Freud (1856–1939)	**Personality Development Theory**	
• Austrian psychiatrist and psychoanalyst. • Studied affluent, mainly female Austrians who came to him for treatment of psychological ailments. • Strongly affected by the times in which he worked with its stifling straight-laced Victorian morality and attitudes toward sexuality.	• The Id, Ego, and Superego are the basic parts of human personality and motivate our behaviour. • Personality develops from infancy to adolescence in five stages: Oral, Anal, Oedipal, Latency, and Genital. • Personality forms as a result of positive and negative emotional experiences with caregivers in infancy and early childhood. • These experiences are usually forgotten, and negative experiences cause adult pain.	• Freud is considered to be the "father of psychiatry." • Many theorists studied with Freud and changed his theories into new ones, e.g., Carl Jung, Alfred Adler, and Erik Erikson. • Freud's strong belief in the effect of the caregiver during infancy and early childhood is being reaffirmed today while discoveries related to "brain wiring" are being made, even though many of his other beliefs are questioned.

(continued)

Theorist	Theory	Importance to Parenting
Jean Piaget (1896–1980)	**Intellectual Development Theory**	
• Swiss biologist, psychologist, and educator. • Started out doing research in biology but became interested in the scientific study of intellect when his three children were born. • Piaget's wife worked with him as they observed and made elaborate scientific notes on the intellectual development of their three children.	• As children develop intellectually, they go through four stages: Sensorimotor, Preoperational, Concrete Operational, and Formal Operational. • Stages begin in infancy and are completed by adolescence. • Each stage of thinking causes the child to see the world in a different way. • Thinking becomes more and more complex as the child ages.	• This theory reinforces the idea that nurturance (comfort, teaching, and play) should be suitable for the developmental stage of the child or adolescent. • He provides a clear guide for what can be expected of children at each stage. • He overlooked stages of adult intellectual development.
Maria Montessori (1870–1952)	**Education and Learning Theory**	
• Italian physician and educator. • Became interested in and worked primarily with Italian children from poverty-stricken areas. • Realized these children needed a better start in life to promote success in the education system, and set out to test her ideas.	• Used Piaget's theories as a base for her teaching methods and theory. • Felt that children must use their senses to learn and that using motor skills (physical skills) was critical to learning. • Children learn best when they are pursuing an activity in which they are interested. • If age-appropriate learning materials are provided, children will take over their learning process.	• One of the first theorists to see the value of "hands-on" learning, which was described as a form of work. • Later, others interpreted her concept of work as play. • Her learning theory provides an explanation of why students learn best when they are self-motivated or in control of their learning.
Arnold Gesell (1880–1961)	**Growth and Development Theory**	
• American psychologist. • Founded the Gesell Institute of Human Behaviour in 1911. • The Institute is a leading centre for the study of child development.	• Pioneered in the organized study of child development. • Developed the first framework of child growth and development information. • Provided the basic data on the order and rate of child development.	• Parents and caregivers use his information to nurture children effectively at different stages of development. • Gesell mentored many prominent researchers, such as Louise Bates Ames, who have furthered his work.
Lev Vygotsky (1898–1934)	**Social Learning Theory**	
• Russian psychologist and lecturer. • Started to do laboratory research in his twenties. Died of tuberculosis in his thirties. • One year after his death, Stalin outlawed developmental psychology, and most of Vygotsky's students were imprisoned.	• Saw adults as a tool that children used to solve "knowledge problems," to learn how their culture worked and how they fit in. • Language is a unique, natural, and biological feature of humans. • Thinking skills and language skills reinforce each other. • Social contact is essential for learning.	• Makes us realize that social contacts are essential for children. • Caregivers who are able to provide plenty of opportunities for social contact for children will encourage good language and thinking skill development. • Some of Vygotsky's work has been supported by today's research and some of it has been refuted.

Theorist	Theory	Importance to Parenting
Erik H. Erikson (1902–1994)	**Theory of Personality Development**	
• German psychologist; later moved to America. • Studied under Freud and later refined Freud's theory. • Erikson's father abandoned his mother before his birth, causing identity problems for Erikson that he was able to resolve. • This adolescent turmoil was partly responsible for Erikson's theory.	• In refining Freud's theory, Erikson postulated that personality developed in eight stages starting in infancy and ending with old age. • Each stage had a unique psychological crisis whose outcome is dependent on how caregivers and significant others in a person's life respond to the needs at that stage. • Each stage could have a positive or negative outcome, and positive outcomes at one stage make the crisis at the next stage easier to solve.	• Erikson researched and wrote until he was over 90, which kept him in the public eye. • Today, his theory is still considered valid. • Caregivers can use this theory to effectively meet the different emotional needs of each age from infancy to adolescence. • Erikson is also one of the only theorists to tackle young, middle, and older adulthood. • Many parents are able to look at their own development and where they are today as a result.
B. F. Skinner (1904–1990)	**Behaviourism**	
• American psychologist and educator. • Most of Skinner's laboratory work was done with small rats in mazes. • No systematic research was done on children. • Research was done mainly in the first half of the 20th century. • This behaviourism became very "fashionable." • Cognitive theory was not in favour at this time.	• Skinner argued that children will repeat rewarded behaviour to get more rewards and that children will stop "bad" behaviour that gets repeatedly punished (this was a kind of conditioning). • He saw children as "blank slates" that could be shaped entirely by using rewards and punishments. • Children's environments are the chief influence on their behaviour.	• Skinner's theory does not have much support today. Many parents, however, still use rewards and punishments to get the behaviour they want from their children. • Many of today's experts support simple rewards such as positive support for children's emotional needs, but "punishment" as such is not supported.
Urie Bronfenbrenner (1917–)	**Human Development Theory**	
• American psychologist and lecturer. • Has studied children and their families in the light of the social changes that occurred in the 20th century.	• Theories concern the well-being of children in families today as a result of massive social changes. • Examples of these include two-income families and family breakdown that leads to fatherless or lone-parent families.	• Parents, caregivers, and politicians can use Bronfenbrenner's theories to support requests for more money and social support for families in general. • His theories and concerns for children give support to the real challenges of raising a family in the 21st century.
Albert Bandura (1925–)	**Social Learning Theory**	
• Canadian psychologist. • Has done a number of well-planned and highly controlled experiments in children's behaviour and the environments in which children's behaviour is shaped.	• Influenced by Skinner but does not agree with all of Skinner's theory. • Bandura argues that children's behaviour is shaped by the environment but that the behaviour also shapes and changes the environment in a back and forth way.	• The main influence is to support what most parents and caregivers know by intuition: good role models are essential to produce good behaviour.

(continued)

Theorist	Theory	Importance to Parenting
Albert Bandura (1925–)	**Social Learning Theory**	
	• Bandura believes that role modelling by adults and others, and observation of others' behaviour, is critical to how children learn behaviour. • Good role models will produce better behaviour than negative role models.	• This theory influences parents and caregivers to be the best role models they can be. • Many parents could use this theory to support their refusal to allow their children to associate with others they consider to be bad influences.
Lawrence Kohlberg (1927–1987)	**Theory of Moral Reasoning**	
• American psychologist, philosopher, and educator. • His work was influenced by Piaget's theories of cognitive development and done at a time when Skinner and the behaviourists were in fashion. • Studied male children in an attempt to chart moral development in children.	• Moral development in children happens in three stages with two parts. • As children gain social and intellectual skills, they are better able to understand the complexities of right and wrong. • This theory brought together science and moral reasoning for the first time and still inspires research today.	• Parents, especially of boys, should be able to identify parts of this theory that apply to their sons at particular ages. • The absence of female participants in Kohlberg's studies is a cause for concern for many parents and researchers.
Robert Coles (1929–)	**Theory of Moral Development**	
• American psychiatrist and professor of literature and social ethic. • Studied the moral development of children.	• Believes that the behaviour of parents shapes the moral character of their children from birth. • In addition, Coles's research indicates that when parents try to protect a child's self-esteem, moral development may suffer because children are unable to learn clear concepts of right and wrong.	• For children to achieve adulthood with good moral development, it is necessary for parents and caregivers to model good moral behaviour.
Carol Gilligan (1936–)	**Theory of Moral Development**	
• American psychologist and professor. • During the 1970s, Gilligan realized that most moral development theory was based on studies of "privileged white men." • Questioned the then-common belief that data derived from studies of men could be generalized to women without further research. • Revolutionized moral development thinking with research on men and women, which she reported in the popular book *In a Different Voice*.	• Outlines three stages of morality development: Selfish Stage, Belief in Conventional Morality, and Post-Conventional Morality. • The male approach to adult morality has a "justice orientation." Individuals have certain rights that need to be respected; therefore, the individual's behaviour is limited. • The female approach to adult morality has a "responsibility orientation." Being moral means that you have to care for others.	• Provides a perspective on male and female moral development differences that was missing from the work of previous theorists. • Some of her research has been criticized for not being replicable. • Says that men think in terms of rules and justice and women are more inclined to think in terms of caring and relationships. • Encourages parents and caregivers to approach the nurturance of moral development in male and female children differently.

Theorist	Theory	Importance to Parenting
Alison Gopnik (1955–) **Andrew Meltzoff (1950–)** **Patricia Kuhl (1946–)**	**Cognitive Science Theory**	
• American psychologists and co-authors of *The Scientist in the Crib* (1999). • Performed many experiments showing that babies use their senses from an early age to learn. • Revolutionized the fields of child psychology and language acquisition.	• These scientists in developmental psychology and speech acquisition have produced much of the data to support the theory that babies learn from an early age by using their five senses. • Their data also supports the "brain wiring" theories that show that learning results when brain circuits are used repeatedly. • In addition to research, these three scientists are skilled at presenting their findings to the public in an easily understandable format.	• The major importance of these three scientists is the support provided for "brain wiring" theory and the importance of effective caregiving, particularly in the period of infancy and early childhood. • These scientists are in the productive stages of their careers and more high-quality material can be expected from them.

Career Capsule

PSYCHOLOGIST

Tasks and Responsibilities

Psychologists investigate people's behaviours, thoughts, and feelings. They work directly with clients to help them function more effectively in their day-to-day lives. Psychologists work with clients who have emotional or mental disorders, or those who have problems with their spouses or families. They also deal with people who have psychological problems linked to illness or disease, and people who have trouble adapting to school, work, or other life events. Some also work with those who are well to enhance their development. Psychologists usually specialize in particular areas.

Clinical psychologists work in places such as hospitals and clinics to help patients with mental, emotional, or medical problems. Neuropsychologists study the relationship between the brain and behaviour and are often involved in research and teaching graduate students as well. School psychologists work in both elementary and secondary schools. They are concerned with how students learn and how well they interact with others at school. School psychologists sometimes assess other aspects of a student's functioning in school or at home.

Work Environment

Community institutions such as hospitals and schools often employ clinical and school psychologists, as well as neuropsychologists. Usually they work regular office hours, although they may be called upon to work or be "on call" during evenings and weekends. Frequently, psychologists work as part of a team and consult with other psychologists and professionals. Psychologists may also work in private practice. In this case, they have their own offices and can set their own hours.

Education and Aptitudes

Because most psychologists work with people with all kinds of behavioural, emotional, physical, and mental problems, they need skills that allow them to cope with difficult interactions. Dealing with people in these situations requires emotional maturity and stability. Psychologists also need to be patient and detail-oriented, since their jobs require them to gather evidence from their patients, to determine the best treatment for them.

In Canada, psychologists are licensed provincially, and the requirements to obtain a licence vary from province to province. In some provinces or territories, a doctoral (Ph.D.) degree is required while others accept a master's degree. After graduating with the appropriate degree, you must apply to the College or Association that regulates the practice of psychology in your province or territory. Once your application is accepted, you must pass an oral and a written exam and work for several months or years under the supervision of a licensed psychologist.

What the experts say

ANDREW MELTZOFF

Andrew Meltzoff, Ph.D., is a Professor of Psychology at the University of Washington in Seattle. He coauthored the best-selling book The Scientist in the Crib: What Early Learning Tells Us About the Mind *(1999). Dr. Meltzoff answers the following question:*

What role does your work as a developmental psychologist play in providing information about human growth and development?

My main responsibilities as a developmental psychologist are to conduct research on early childhood development; to write about my work for scientific journals; and to teach others about my research. My job requires in-depth understanding of child development, adult psychology, some statistical expertise, and, more and more, understanding neuroscience.

The greatest reward for me occurs when I discover something new about how children learn and

develop. For example, I found out that newborn babies only a few hours old are able to imitate an adult who makes faces at them or sticks out his tongue. This information made a difference in the way scientists and others thought about the minds of babies and how children learn. I have also researched how babies remember things. In the future, this information may be used to change the way we organize day care centres and preschools and how we teach infants and young children.

To be the first person in the world to know some new fact, to make a new discovery, is one of the most thrilling things about being a scientist. Every scientist loves the "ah-ha!" moment. When your discoveries influence others and have a practical and positive influence on children and teachers, it is doubly rewarding.

In this society, we underpay child-care providers and we have a sort of "physics envy" where we elevate hard scientists like physicists above scientists who work to discover truths about the human mind. But this is changing, and it should change. There is nothing more important than learning how the mind works. Eventually, our knowledge will help all children reach their full potential.

A challenge we face is in designing studies that "ask the babies the right questions." Babies cannot talk. Therefore, for hundreds of years they were not considered as sources of information about the mind. But studies can be designed to "talk with them" even before they can talk back. We have discovered that babies are like computers with the printers turned off. There's a lot of knowledge inside them, but they're not displaying it. What we developmental psychologists do is to peer inside the baby's mind even before the printer is turned on, before they can

speak. That way we can discover things about children and also about ourselves, because all of us are just big children.

I believe that developmental psychology, especially when coupled with neuroscience, will spark a great intellectual revolution with implications for education and policy-makers. Discovering the basis of our thoughts and emotions is the next frontier in science, and these discoveries will be as influential as those of the Genome project and the computer revolution. What could be more interesting than discovering who we are and how we get that way, or investigating personality development and why one person acts in a certain way and another acts in a completely different way? By studying babies and children, we can answer age-old philosophical questions about the human soul in a scientific way.

Many students who take parenting courses become interested in careers that involve the growth and development of children and adolescents. For students interested in these careers, the main post-secondary fields to investigate are psychology, sociology, and anthropology. Often these disciplines combine with other areas to investigate children and adolescents in interdisciplinary studies. Examples of **interdisciplinary studies** include social psychology (sociology/psychology), biopsychology (biology/psychology), or cognitive science, which is a complex union of psychology, computer science, philosophy, and linguistics.

❖ Checkpoints

1. List all the theorists who use a stage-by-stage approach to child development.
2. Describe a relationship between Freud and Erikson's theories.
3. Which theorists went against the current thoughts of the times and tended to revolutionize the way child development was studied? Explain.

❖ Connections

1. Outline three examples of how the child development theorists were affected by the times in which they lived? For example, the government banned Vygotsky's research.

2. You are in the bookstore with a new father who is buying a book on parenting. The number of resources available confuses him. Give him some advice.

3. Show how the older research seems to support the newer (1970s onward) cognitive science on "brain wiring" and the importance of nurturance during the first years of life.

Finding Information on Child Development Theories

After a social scientist forms, tests, and refines a theory, it is written up in scholarly journals, discussed, and then "translated" into everyday language for parents and caregivers to use in nurturing their children. Experts in the field of childhood and adolescence write most of this kind of material, designed for reading by the general public. It is based on applying the theories of actual scientists to the practice of parenting. These experts may be the researchers themselves, clinical psychologists, pediatricians, teachers of human development or parenting, or any member of the general public who sees an opportunity to help other parents and caregivers. They do not always agree on how a theory should be interpreted or applied, so their views should be given critical consideration.

Books that focus on human growth and development are published every day. There are many magazines devoted to the subject of parenting. Internet sites related to parenting and problems experienced by parents and children are numerous. Every subject imaginable related to children, parents, and caregiving has been explored. Some are short-lived fads, while others are worthwhile endeavours and have stood the test of time. Some ideas work for some parents, but not for others. Reading critically and with a good understanding of children and human development will let you determine which theories will benefit you as a future parent or caregiver.

■ Information on human growth and development and theories related to it are available to parents, students, and the general public. it is essential to study this material carefully so you can determine which theories and their applications will benefit you most as a future parent or caregiver. Parenting education will help you develop the knowledge, skills, and attitudes to be a wise consumer of parenting information.

Chapter Summary

Chapter Highlights

- All humans experience development in similar ways.

- Human development begins at conception and continues throughout life, but the most critical and most rapid period of development is from conception to age six.

- The five areas of growth and development that are commonly studied include physical, social, emotional, moral, and intellectual development.

- All areas of development are interconnected as a child achieves functional developmental growth, and all rely on a strong, nurturing relationship with a significant parent or caregiver.

- All human growth—physical, social, emotional, moral, and intellectual—relies on brain development.

- Interaction with parents, caregivers, and the environment forge pathways between existing neurons in the brain.

- Stimulation from all the senses contributes to learning and helps develop the very specialized centres in the brain for language, mathematics, and human relationships.

- Every day scientists are learning more about how important the years from birth to age six are for health, well-being, and learning throughout life.

- Developmental theorists, following the footsteps of Sigmund Freud and others before him, continue to present new theories about human growth and development that help parents, caregivers, and those who work professionally with children.

Review and Extend Your Learning

1. Explain how knowledge and understanding of human growth and development will help you relate to children. **K/U** **C**

2. Describe the steps you would take in a social science study to answer the research question, "Do parents with training in human growth and development teach their children differently from parents with little or no knowledge of human growth and development?" **K/U** **A**

3. How do comfort, play, and teaching relate to the stages identified by Stanley Greenspan's "functional development growth chart?" **K/U** **A**

4. Choose a particular theorist from this chapter, or other child development theorist you are interested in, and research his or her theory in detail. Develop a persona for a role-play for this theorist to show how this researcher's theory would be applied in a real-life situation. Based on your findings, which of the other theorists supports and opposes your theorist's point of view? **K/U** **T/I** **C** **A**

5. How does knowledge of "brain wiring" improve the way a parent or caregiver interacts with an infant or small child? **K/U**

6. Using information from the theorists profiled in this chapter, describe three ways in which parents and caregivers can support positive growth for each of the five areas of human growth and development. **K/U** **A**

7. Find a recent article in a parenting magazine that describes new child development research. How does the new research relate to any of the theories you have studied? Describe the connections. **T/I** **A**

8. Research brain development in adolescents. Compare the adolescent brain to that of children and adults. **T/I**

9. Locate actual toys or pictures of toys that appeal to infants and young children. While you play with the toys, or imagine yourself playing with them, determine how a child's brain would be stimulated. Demonstrate and explain to others in the class how playing with the toys would enhance brain development. **K/U** **T/I** **C** **A**

Research Opportunities

10. Conduct a search for information linking breast-feeding to intellectual development. Compare and briefly summarize two viewpoints, one based on research and one based on opinion. Which one do you find more convincing and why?

11. Write a book review similar to one published in a professional journal, based on a book written about childhood, human growth and development, or parenting children at a particular stage of development. What approach does the book take? What theories are the bases for the views taken? Describe what you learned about human growth and development from this book. Outline why you would or would not recommend it to others. You may do a review of a Web site instead.

Issue Analysis

12. There are two schools of thought on playing music or reading to a developing fetus. Gather research and opinions for and against this practice. Write a position paper based on your analysis of the issue.

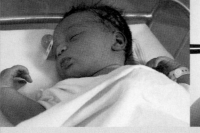

Chapter

10

Healthy Beginnings for Every Child

By the end of this chapter, you will be able to:

- describe the factors that contribute to the healthy development of children before, during, and after birth

- identify and describe environments provided by families, caregivers, and others that offer positive conditions for child development during pregnancy and childbirth

- demonstrate an understanding of the link between healthy prenatal and infant development and long-term growth and development

Important Terms

active labour
amniotic fluid
birth canal
birth plan
blastocyst
bonding
Braxton Hicks contractions

Caesarean delivery
capillaries
cell differentiation
chromosomes
conception
daughter nuclei
dilation

early labour
effacement
embryo
episiotomy
fetal blood
fetus
full term
maternal blood
mitosis

molecule
placenta
premature
quickening
rooming in
toxoplasmosis
transitional labour
trophoblast
umbilical cord

Chapter at a Glance

Why Is the Beginning So Important?

Healthy, full-term newborn babies are complete human beings. All of their internal organs, though immature, are formed and functioning. All of their senses—sight, hearing, smell, taste, and touch—are performing at various levels, and except for eyelashes and teeth, which grow in later, and tear ducts, which do not produce tears right away, they are complete in every way, right down to their tiny fingernails and toenails.

Parental health and lifestyle both before and after conception can have a profound effect on the health and quality of life of a child. Health before conception affects the quality of eggs and sperm. Lifestyle choices support the growth and development of the fetus and contribute to helping the child reach optimum potential.

Nine months of prenatal development enables the human infant to live outside the mother's body, but to survive, the newborn is totally dependent on others for food and personal care. The beginning of life provides the foundation for all the years that follow. What a parent does for a child before, during, and after the birth will affect that child forever. The human potential of a newborn is an enormous responsibility for parents.

Figure 10.1
Newborn babies are complete in every way.

Parents from Preconception to Birth

In China, a newborn child is considered to be a year old at birth. There, the prenatal period includes the three months before pregnancy when the mother's body is getting ready for the pregnancy and the egg is ripening, plus the nine months of actual prenatal development. The year before birth is recognized as essential.

The ABCs for Making the Most of the Year Before Birth

1. Act pregnant before you become pregnant
   - value and take steps to ensure preconception maternal and paternal health;
   - follow Canada's Food Guide for Healthy Eating for pregnant or nursing mothers;
   - stop smoking and taking non-prescription drugs or herbal remedies of any kind;
   - check with your pharmacist to learn how to avoid dangerous prescription drugs;
   - stop drinking alcohol, and avoid caffeine and artificial sweeteners in all beverages;
   - take a maternity vitamin that contains 400 micrograms of folic acid;
   - visit your dentist for a check-up—unresolved gum problems can lead to pre-term delivery;
   - read about pregnancy to learn about new research into having a healthy pregnancy.

2. Be environmentally sensitive
   - stop working if your workplace exposes you to chemicals or elements detrimental to infant development;
   - evaluate the safety of the community in which you live (e.g., birth defects have been associated with high levels of chemical pesticide use); and
   - check your home for lead-based paints, fumes, or chemicals that could be a problem.

3. Consider yourself a parent
   - spend time with other peoples' children;
   - pay attention to how others parent children; and
   - talk about what it means to be a parent with other parents.

What the experts say

LINDA SILVER

Linda Silver is a Project Manager for Better Beginnings—Community Action Program for Children (CAPC) in Toronto, Ontario. She answers the following question:

What does your organization do to promote infant health and development?

Better Beginnings—Community Action Program for Children (CAPC) serves children from birth to 6 years, their families, and pregnant women who live in "at risk" circumstances. The project that I manage serves families in one part of Toronto. However, this is part of a federally sponsored program with projects in many areas of Canada intended to give Canadian children the opportunity to start their lives in a healthy way. Families enter our programs through self-referral or on the recommendation of a social worker, public-health nurse, or other professional in the community.

Better Beginnings—CAPC believes that parents and families who live in "at risk" circumstances should have equal opportunities for the healthy development and achievement of potential of their children. A lot of research now shows that a healthy

pregnancy resulting in a healthy birth outcome together with the child being well-nurtured in the first six years of life will vastly improve the "life chances" of that child.

Canadian women and infants are privileged to have universal health care that contributes to one of the highest healthy birth outcome rates in the world. However, research indicates that we need to continue to monitor these outcomes. *The Canadian Perinatal Report*, 2000 indicates a number of areas that need to be addressed. These include preterm births and cigarette and alcohol use during pregnancy.

Preterm births (babies born before they are due) have increased risks, which bring a greater burden of illness for these infants. Although pregnant women are more likely to quit smoking and smoke fewer cigarettes than women who are not pregnant, smoking remains an important public-health problem. Prenatal alcohol consumption can result in alcohol-related birth defects on a continuum of severity from spontaneous abortion through Fetal Alcohol Syndrome (FAS) to the other Fetal Alcohol Spectrum Disorders (FASD). Since no safe level of alcohol consumption has been determined, Health Canada recommends that women abstain from alcohol consumption when pregnant or planning to become pregnant.

Parents can do many positive things to give their children a good start in life. During pregnancy, it is important to maintain a healthy lifestyle and to become as informed as possible about pregnancy. This means taking care of yourself by eating a nutritious diet that follows Canada's Food Guide to Healthy Eating, as well as seeing a doctor or midwife. It also means not smoking, drinking alcohol, or using drugs.

After the birth, parents are their babies' first teachers and protectors. Infants depend on their parents for comfort, food, and security. Babies learn that the world is a safe place in which to grow and learn when they are given a quick response each time they cry or when they are hungry. Mothers are encouraged to breast-feed because breast milk is the perfect food and provides an initial immunity to a number of health risks. Talking and singing to infants promotes their communication skills and a positive bond with their primary caregiver.

By helping parents understand how to have a healthy pregnancy and the importance of good nurturance, in tune with their child's development, Better Beginnings—CAPC is helping to ensure a better future for all of Canada's children.

Conception

About midway in a woman's menstrual cycle, a ripened ovum, or egg, is released from the ovary to begin its journey down the fallopian tube to the uterus. If it is not fertilized on the way, no pregnancy will result, and it will be eliminated with the lining of the uterus during the next menstrual period. However, if the egg is fertilized, **conception** (the beginning of human development) takes place.

Human conception is an elaborate process in which egg and sperm meet and form a new life. It takes millions of sperm to ensure that the egg is fertilized. Most sperm never make it to the egg, but those that do surround it and roll it over and over with the force of their movement. It was originally believed that the first sperm to reach the egg was the one to fertilize it, but now scientists, using state-of-the-art cameras, have determined that it is not necessarily the first one. They do not know why one particular sperm is successful, but finally, only one sperm penetrates the outer surface of the ovum (egg). Chemicals in the sperm covering enable it to penetrate this outer surface. The ovum immediately develops an outer coat that prevents all other sperm from entering. The tail the sperm needed to swim the distance falls off. The egg absorbs the head containing the nucleus and all the genetic material needed to create a new human being. When this occurs, **mitosis** (cell division) begins. **Chromosomes** in the nucleus of the sperm and egg carry the genetic material from the father and mother. This material will determine the genetic characteristics of the new baby.

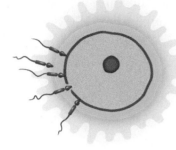
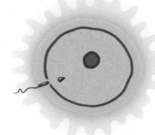

a Sperm cells try to enter the egg cell. A single sperm cell penetrates the cell membrane.

b The body and tail of the sperm cell are pinched off by the cell membrane of the egg cell.

c The nucleus of the sperm cell finds the nucleus of the egg cell, and the 23 chromosomes from the sperm cell combine with the 23 chromosomes from the egg cell.

Figure 10.2
An egg is fertilized when a sperm penetrates the egg.

When mitosis begins, the chromosomes in the nucleus of the ovum pair up with the chromosomes in the nucleus from the sperm cell. Then the chromosomes are duplicated exactly, and the two copies are distributed into what are called **daughter nuclei**. These two identical nuclei are for two completely new cells, each containing 46 chromosomes, 23 from the sperm and 23 from the ovum. The creation of the daughter nuclei is one of the most studied but least understood biological events.

Period of the Zygote

It takes about one week for the cells that continue to divide to move down the fallopian tube to the uterus. This is called the period of the zygote. Chromosomes are copied and divided into two more cells. Then those four cells divide into eight cells, and so on. Eventually enough cells (6×10^{13}) to make a whole human being are produced by mitotic division.

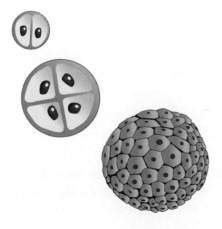

Figure 10.3
Chromosomes are copied and divided into two more cells. Cell division continues until there are enough cells to make a whole human being.

Ectopic pregnancy. A pregnancy that takes place in the fallopian tube. If the cluster of cells stops moving down the fallopian tube, the cells continue to divide inside the fallopian tube until it bursts. Severe pain and blood loss result, and some women have died without immediate treatment. Smoking, pregnancy late in life, and the prolonged use of some contraceptives are factors that increase the risk of an ectopic pregnancy.

Cell differentiation is one of the most puzzling questions confronting reproduction biologists. It allows approximately 100 different types of human cells to be made. Scientists are only beginning to understand what prompts a particular cell to become a brain cell or a toenail cell. Even though all cells have the same chromosomes, each cell prepares for its own specialized function.

By the time the ball of about 100 cells reaches the uterus, it has developed two layers of cells. The inner layer is known as a **blastocyst**, while the outer layer is called the **trophoblast**. Hormones released by the uterus allow the trophoblast layer to attach itself to the uterine lining. The two layers of cells, all containing the same genetic material, are all programmed for a particular function by cell differentiation. The outer layer of cells becomes the **placenta**, while the inner layer becomes the embryo containing all the cells that eventually become the fetus.

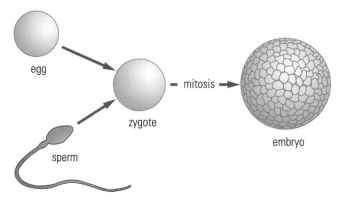

Figure 10.4
Through mitosis, the zygote becomes an embryo.

Period of the Embryo

The developing organism is known as an **embryo** from the time it is implanted in the uterus until it takes the basic human shape of a **fetus**, with arm and leg buds, a trunk, distinct head, and organs formed. It takes about eight weeks for the embryo to become a fetus. At the same time, the placenta is maturing so that it can support fetal development.

The period of the embryo is the most critical stage of prenatal development, because the brain, nervous system, heart, and other major organs are taking shape and beginning to function. Many women do not even realize they are pregnant until nearing the end of this stage, but their health, food intake, and lifestyle are already having significant positive or negative effects on the embryo's development.

The Period of the Fetus

The fetal period continues from around eight weeks until birth. The fetus is surrounded by **amniotic fluid** that cushions it and allows it to move freely within the uterus while it is connected to its life support, the placenta.

The **placenta** is an organ that grows in the uterus only during pregnancy. It functions to sustain life in the same way the heart, liver, and kidneys sustain human life. It is rich in blood vessels, which absorb nourishment from the mother's blood for the fetus. The placenta also transfers waste products, such as carbon dioxide, from the infant to the mother's blood stream. The **umbilical cord** is about 50 cm to 60 cm long and carries **fetal blood** from the fetus to the placenta. A vein in the umbilical cord carries the oxygen and nutrients from the mother to the fetus, while two large arteries carry the waste products back from the fetus to the placenta as part of the fetal circulatory system.

In the placenta, the fetal blood vessels become smaller and smaller leading into tiny **capillaries**, which line up beside capillaries filled with **maternal blood**. The blood of the mother and fetus do not mix; however, many different **molecules** do pass from the mother's blood to the fetal blood and from the fetal blood to the mother's blood through the membranes of the capillary walls.

Molecules like oxygen, vitamins, minerals, carbohydrates, protein, and fat are essential for fetal growth and development. But other molecules also cross the placenta. Alcohol, caffeine, nicotine, environmental chemicals, drugs, bacteria, and viruses will be absorbed into the fetal blood stream where they can cause birth defects, slow prenatal growth, and disturb essential fetal functions.

Figure 10.5
The umbilical cord carries oxygen and nutrients from the mother to the fetus, as well as carries waste products from the fetus to the placenta.

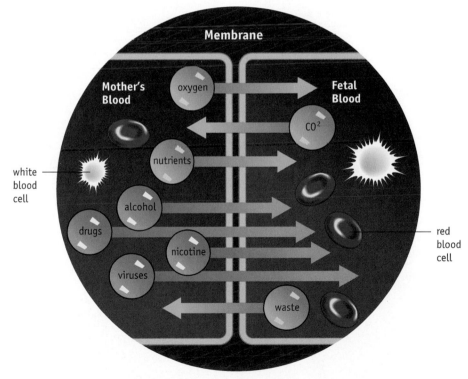

Figure 10.6
Oxygen, nutrients as well as alcohol, drugs, nicotine, and viruses are small enough to pass through the membranes separating the fetal blood from the maternal blood. Blood cells are too large to cross the barrier.

Fetal Development

The first three months

0 weeks	1 week	2 weeks	3 weeks	4 weeks	5 weeks
First day of last period.		Egg is fertilized.	Egg implants in lining of uterus.	Missed period.	Embryo just big enough to be visible.

6 weeks

The beginnings of a backbone and brain forming. The heart starts to beat. A pregnancy test will show that the mother is pregnant.

7 weeks

Four tiny swellings have developed. These are the beginnings of hands and feet.

8 weeks

The embryo has eyes but no eyelids. It starts making its first tiny movements but its mother cannot feel them yet.

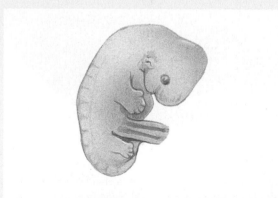

12 weeks

The features of a human being are now recognizable in the fetus, although its head is still very large in proportion to the rest of its body. Girls and boys start to look distinctly different from each other at about this stage.

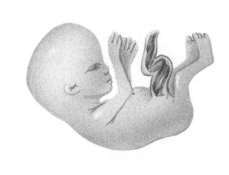

16 weeks (4 months)*

The uterus is now entirely filled by the fetus, placenta, and waters, and gradually stretches from now on as the fetus continues to grow. The fetus begins to swallow and to pass urine. It has fingers and toenails. At this stage, its skin is bright red and transparent.

Actual length = approx. 13 cm

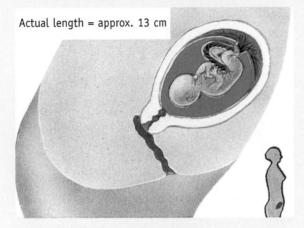

The mother's bulge is just beginning to show and her clothes are getting tight. Any sickness she was feeling earlier has usually gone by this time.

20 weeks (5 months)

The hair is starting to appear, and the fetus now has eyebrows and eyelashes. Its eyes are still tightly closed and the whole surface of its body is covered with a fine, downy hair called lanugo. Its skin is now less transparent but very wrinkled.

Actual length = approx. 20 cm

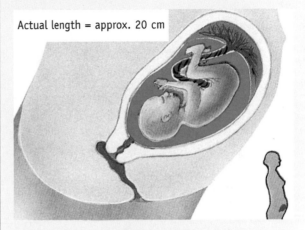

Sometime between about 18 and 22 weeks, the mother usually begins to feel the fetus moving when it wriggles about and exercises its arms and legs.

24 weeks (6 months)

The fetus now has distinct periods of sleep and wakefulness. It can probably hear voices, music, and other sounds from outside its mother above the continuous noise of her heartbeat and blood circulating. At this stage, it is still very thin and wrinkled.

Actual length = approx. 28 cm

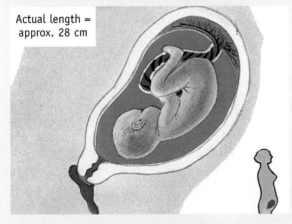

The mother is obviously pregnant now. The heartbeat can be heard through a special listening device called a fetal stethoscope.

*Dated from the first day of the mother's last period

28 weeks (7 months)

If born now, the fetus would have a good chance of surviving, but it would have to be put in an incubator because its lungs are still not well developed. It is now covered with thick, white grease called vernix, which helps to stop its skin from becoming waterlogged.

Actual length = approx. 33 cm

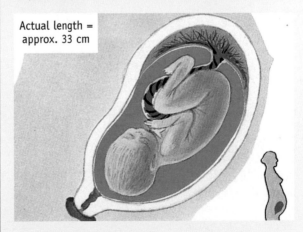

The kicks are quite strong now and can be felt by putting a hand on the mother's abdomen. Sometimes she can feel her baby have hiccups.

(continued)

32 weeks (8 months)

The fetus starts to put on some fat and become less wrinkled. Its lungs are starting to mature and getting ready to take their first breath. It may begin to practise sucking—some suck their thumbs before they are born.

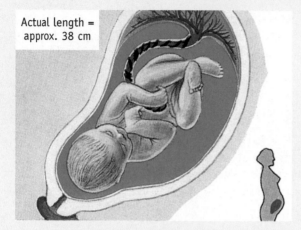

Actual length = approx. 38 cm

The mother may lean back noticeably by now to counteract the weight and walk with her legs slightly apart to help her balance.

36 weeks (9 months)

By now, the fetus has usually taken up its final position in the uterus—usually head down. From now on, it has no room to somersault about because it fills the uterus, which cannot expand anymore. The fetus continues to get fatter.

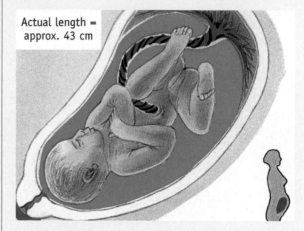

Actual length = approx. 43 cm

You may be able to see the mother's abdomen moving when the baby moves its limbs. Often you can guess whether the bump is a hand or a foot.

40 weeks (10 months)

Some time from 36 weeks onward, the baby's head drops down into its mother's pelvis (engages). The baby is ready for birth.

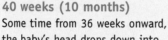

Actual length = approx. 50 cm

Pelvis

When the baby's head engages, the mother may notice a slight sensation of relief as the rest of her insides have been getting very squashed and this allows them a little more room.

The time when the baby is fully ready to be born is referred to as "full term" or "term." Forty weeks is only an average length of pregnancy and it is perfectly normal for a baby to arrive anytime between the 38th and 42nd week.

By this time, the lanugo has usually disappeared from everywhere, except perhaps the shoulders, but the baby's body may still be covered with vernix.

During the fetal stage, overall physical growth continues, facial features become fully formed and refined, and organ development is completed. Fetal growth and development corresponds to changes taking place in the pregnant woman's body.

❖ Checkpoints

1. List and describe some of the things parents can do before conception to foster a healthy pregnancy and a healthy child at birth.
2. Why is the period of the embryo the most critical stage of prenatal development?
3. What role does the placenta play in the prenatal process?

The Three Trimesters of Pregnancy

The nine months of pregnancy can be divided into three distinct periods, called trimesters. Each trimester is three months long. Often a woman is already part way through the first trimester of pregnancy before she realizes she is pregnant. Her due date is calculated as 40 weeks, from the start of the last menstrual period she had, before she became pregnant. This calculation is used because doctors cannot determine exactly when conception took place. However, some women may continue to have a menstrual flow at the beginning of their pregnancy. In this case, ultrasound images may provide a better indication of her due date.

The last trimester varies in length depending on when the baby is born:

- **Premature:** born six or more weeks early or weighing less than five pounds
- **Early:** born a week or more before the due date, but weighing more than five pounds
- **Full term:** born on or near the due date
- **Overdue:** born a week or more after the due date

Did You Know ...

Because umbilical cord blood is especially rich in stem cells (cells that give rise to red blood cells and lymphocytes), some parents choose to save it in special cord blood banks in case of future need as a transplant alternative to bone marrow. Studies have shown that even people not related to the donor (genetically mismatched) can benefit from transplants of umbilical cord blood in combating leukemia and other cancers.
— *infoplease.com*

At this time in Canada, facilities to store cord blood are quite limited. If a couple is thinking about saving cord blood, plans need to be made early in the pregnancy.

First Trimester

Changes in the Mother

- She feels tired.
- She begins to notice some of the signs and symptoms of pregnancy such as fatigue, frequent urination, a late menstrual period, breast swelling, and nipple soreness.
- She may experience morning sickness or feelings of nausea throughout the day and have an increased sensitivity to smells.
- She will gain a small amount of weight and notice that it is difficult to do up some of her clothing.
- She may feel she is on an emotional roller coaster.

Changes in the Fetus

- The embryo takes on human shape.
- Major organs (such as brain, central nervous system, heart, liver, kidneys) form and begin to function.
- At eight weeks, fetal development begins.
- The face acquires a human look and features become more refined.
- Nails and bones form.
- The sex of the fetus can be determined.

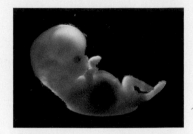

Figure 10.7
A fetus early in the first trimester.

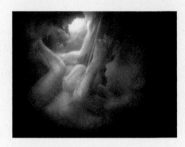

Figure 10.8
A fetus later in the first trimester. Describe the differences between this photograph and Figure 10.7.

Second Trimester

Changes in the Mother

- Morning sickness usually ends and appetite returns because her body has adjusted to the change in hormones.
- Stretch marks and a dark, vertical pigmentation line may appear on her abdomen (*Line of Negra*).
- She develops the rosy glow of pregnancy.
- She starts to "show" and may begin wearing maternity clothes midway through this trimester.
- Around her fifth month, she will experience fetal movement known as **quickening**.
- Fetal heart sounds can be heard through a stethoscope.
- She continues to gain weight.

Changes in the Fetus

- The fetus grows rapidly.
- Distinctive facial features develop, and the eyes open and shut.
- The fetus may suck its thumb and swallows amniotic fluid.
- It moves freely in the amniotic fluid and moves into a head-down position.
- Its heart beats strongly, and blood circulation is well developed.
- Lanugo (soft downy hair) grows all over its body.
- The body grows larger, and the protruding tail-like tailbone is less obvious.
- It has periods of quiet sleep and periods of active movement.
- It grows to 32 cm in length and weighs about 500 g to 1 kg.
- It responds to sound and pressure.

Figure 10.9
A fetus in the second trimester.

Third Trimester

Changes in the Mother	Changes in the Fetus
• She feels awkward, uncomfortable, and may retain fluid in hands, feet, and face. • The uterus has grown so large, she has trouble bending over. • Sharp jabs result from fetal movement. • She becomes short of breath as the growing uterus presses on her lungs. • Heartburn, leg cramps, backache, more frequent urination, hemorrhoids, and varicose veins are common. • Sleep is disrupted and uncomfortable. • "Lightening" is a feeling of room at the top of the uterus as the fetus drops into the pelvis, pushing against the cervix. • The uterus tightens from time to time with **Braxton Hicks contractions**. • The total weight gain over the entire pregnancy could be 13.6 kg or more.	• The fetus can survive if born in the last trimester, but a full-term pregnancy is always better. • The fetus usually remains in the head-down position. • There is less room in the uterus for movement as the growing fetus fills the uterus. • The fetus grows quickly, acquiring an essential layer of fat in the last month. • Lanugo hair disappears, and the body is covered with vernix, (a cheesy wax-like coating). • Brain development is rapid. • The fetus can detect light and sound (e.g., music). • "Practice" breathing movements become stronger to prepare for life outside the womb. • The average full-term baby will grow to 50 cm in length and have a mass of 3.4 kg.

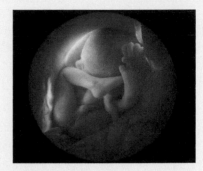

Figure 10.10
A fetus in the third trimester.

Entire books have been written about the nine months of pregnancy and can be found in school libraries, parenting classrooms, local libraries, bookstores, and community parenting centres. Midwives, public-health nurses, doctors, and other maternity practitioners can answer questions and provide reading materials about pregnancy.

What Fathers or Partners Can Do During Pregnancy

Some fathers start to feel left out when their partners are pregnant. Mothers naturally turn inward and pay close attention to the growing new life inside them, and focus less on the couple relationship. However, there are many things a couple can do to make the pregnancy meaningful for both of them. Expectant mothers need their partners to be involved in the process that will change their family forever. During pregnancy, an expectant father can

• take an interest in the pregnancy by reading, attending medical appointments, or talking to other new fathers
• understand that while his partner will be very centred on all the physical and emotional changes that take place almost daily, she does not mean to leave him out
• discuss any feelings of being left out or fears he may have related to the pregnancy, for example,

(continued)

losing the baby, the sight of blood in the delivery room, preparedness for fatherhood
- follow a healthy lifestyle himself and encourage his partner to quit smoking, completely avoid alcohol and non-prescription drugs, eat properly, take pre-natal vitamins, drink milk or take a calcium supplement, and drink plenty of water
- stop drinking and smoking himself to support his partner and to prepare for the baby
- accompany his partner on regular leisurely walks
- go to prenatal check-ups with her whenever possible
- help out as much as possible with meal preparation and housework

- encourage rest
- give his partner back rubs and leg and foot massages
- monitor the environment and eliminate anything that can be harmful, such as fumes, chemicals, lawn and garden sprays, and toxic paints or cleaners
- change the kitty litter so she is not exposed to **toxoplasmosis**, the parasite often found in cat feces that causes major congenital deformities in infants
- attend prenatal classes and participate in learning the comforting and breathing techniques and exercises

FOR BETTER OR FOR WORSE © UFS, Reprinted by permission.

Figure 10.11
What other ways can you think of for fathers to help their partners during pregnancy?

❖ Checkpoints

1. What do the terms premature, early, full term, and overdue mean? How do they relate to the length of the third trimester of pregnancy?
2. What are the most significant changes in the fetus during each trimester?
3. Highlight the changes in the mother within each trimester of pregnancy.

❖ Connections

1. Think about an expectant couple you have seen on television or know personally. How does the description of a father's role in supporting a wife's pregnancy on page 247 fit in with what you have observed? Talk to a parent to determine how the description fits with his or her experience of pregnancy.

The Four Stages of Childbirth

It is very reassuring to know that giving birth is a normal function of human reproduction. Just the same, both new and experienced parents have many options to consider when managing the birth of a child. A **birth plan** gives parents some control over the event.

Thinking about the options ahead of time helps to ensure that both the parents and the practitioners are aware of each other's wishes and preferences. There are many questions to be answered.

Figure 10.12
The birth plan is an outline of preferences that parents and practitioners have for the birth.

- Home birth or hospital birth?
- Midwife or obstetrician?
- Birthing chair or bed?
- Induce labour or wait for labour to start naturally?
- Pain medication?
- Routine episiotomy?
- Forceps or vacuum extraction?
- Family members present?
- Home movies or photography?
- Emergency options?
- Caesarean delivery with anesthetic or with epidural?
- Birthing coach?
- Breast-feeding coach?
- Circumcision or no circumcision?

Although every birth is unique, childbirth does follow a pattern of labour, delivery, afterbirth, and recovery. These are the four stages of childbirth. The length and intensity of labour, the speed of delivery, and the time needed to deliver the afterbirth will be different for every pregnancy.

Case Study: Miscarriage—Marg and Adam

Marg and Adam were high-school teachers. They had both been only children and wanted to make sure that their toddler, Jack, had at least one brother or sister. Marg, in particular, felt strongly about having another child because she had missed the companionship of siblings herself and grew up surrounded by adults. While this had been wonderful because she always had someone to read to her and pay attention to her, she had longed for older brothers like the children in the stories she read. Therefore, after an easy and uneventful pregnancy with Jack, she and Adam became pregnant again when Jack was about 15 months old. They were thrilled and shared the news.

Three months into the pregnancy, Marg miscarried. She received excellent obstetrical care and underwent a procedure called a dilation and curettage or a "D and C" to make sure that her uterus was clean. "Wait three months and try again. One in five pregnancies end in miscarriage. These things happen," she was told. Afterward, Marg felt guilty and went over everything she had done that could have caused a birth defect.

Having told their friends and relations that they were expecting, now Marg and Adam had the terrible task of "untelling" everybody. "It's nature's way and all for the best," said her friends and relations. The trouble was it did not feel that way particularly to Marg and she fell into a deep state of grief. Nobody understood, not little Jack who could not understand why Mommy was so sad, not Adam who had not had that baby inside him, only Marg who felt terrible and noticed every pregnant woman on the street.

Everybody was pregnant, she thought, everybody but me. "What is the matter with me?"

She found that her friends and relations stopped being supportive after a few weeks and she had little or no support while she finished grieving. Marg did not realize until years later that she could have looked around for a support group during this painful time. Eventually she recovered and life went on.

Unfortunately, Marg developed a physical problem that meant that further pregnancies would be risky. So, determined to have at least two children, they entered the adoption process. Luck was with them. When Jack was almost four, Marg and Adam were thrilled to be able to adopt a baby girl. Now everybody teased them that they had the "millionaire's family" of a boy and girl. They did not care that they did not have a million dollars; they were just glad that they had been able to have the family that they had always wanted.

Many years later, Marg was helping her students do some research and came upon several studies on miscarriage. The process she had gone through was typical, she found. All those strong emotions she had felt were common for many women. Lack of support from family and friends was also common. Now, Marg is especially supportive to anyone who has had a miscarriage.

Questions
1. What are the emotional effects of a miscarriage on the family?
2. Investigate the causes of miscarriage. Can it be prevented? Explain why or why not.

Labour: The First Stage of Childbirth

The purpose of labour is **effacement** and **dilation**, which is the thinning and opening of the cervix. Labour begins with the first real contraction and ends when the cervix has dilated enough to allow the baby's head to pass into the birth canal. Labour has three phases and takes an average of 12 hours.

Signs That Labour Has Started

- **Bloody show:** a blood-tinged discharge is noticed when the mucous plug is released from the cervix
- **Cramping:** the low backache or menstrual-like cramps are felt, sometimes with diarrhea or indigestion
- **Ruptured membranes:** the amniotic sac breaks, releasing amniotic fluid. This is known as "the water breaking" and is an unmistakable sign of labour.
- **Regular contractions:** the uterus tightens and hardens briefly at regular intervals

Phases of Labour

Early labour, the first phase, begins with very mild contractions and continues until the cervix has opened to three centimetres. Some women continue with their daily activities and may find out that they are already dilated at a weekly medical appointment. As contractions become distinct, they also come closer together. When they are five minutes apart, it is time to go to the hospital or birthing room to prepare for the next phase of labour and delivery. If a midwife is delivering the baby, this person should be with the mother by this time.

Active labour then follows with noticeable contractions lasting for a full minute, every two or three minutes. This phase involves three to four hours of labour on average, until the cervix dilates to seven centimetres. The work of labour becomes more intense and demanding. Breathing, relaxation, and comfort techniques are crucial.

Transitional labour is the final phase in which the cervix dilates to ten centimetres. Contractions last longer, are much stronger, and happen one right after another. The urge to push the baby out sometimes happens before the cervix is fully open, so panting exercises help the mother make it through transition. Transitional labour lasts an hour or less, but is very exhausting, and can be emotionally distressing. Pain medication may be used during this stage.

The three phases of labour:
- early labour
- active labour
- transitional labour

Delivery: The Second Stage of Childbirth

After the cervix has dilated to ten centimetres, it is time to push the baby through the vagina or **birth canal**. Contractions are still strong, but further apart, allowing mom to rest between pushes. The vagina is very elastic and stretches to accommodate the baby's head, which makes way for the rest of the baby. In some cases, to prevent tearing, an incision or **episiotomy** is made to allow the baby's head to exit the mother's body. Delivery usually takes one and a half to two hours, or less, depending on the size of the baby, and the energy of the mother.

■ The four stages of childbirth:
1. Labour
2. Delivery
3. Afterbirth
4. Recovery

In normal, uncomplicated childbirth, the head is born first, and mucus is suctioned from the baby's nose and mouth so that the baby's first breath is clear of fluid. Then one shoulder is released, followed by the other, and the rest of the baby slips out easily. The umbilical cord is clamped, cutting off the oxygen supply from the mother, and the baby inhales its first breath. Some babies cry lustily, while others make a brief sound.

Once the baby is born, the time of birth is noted. The baby is usually placed on the mother's abdomen while the cord is cut, and a quick neonatal assessment is made. If there are no concerns, the baby is wrapped in a prewarmed blanket and placed on the mother's chest. Then the parents can become acquainted with the new little person they have brought into the world.

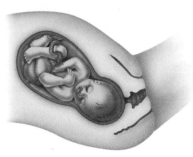

a   cervical opening starts to enlarge

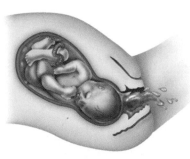

b   amniotic sac breaks and fluid flows out

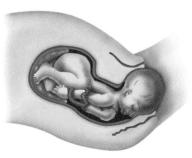

c   uterine muscles contract to push the baby out

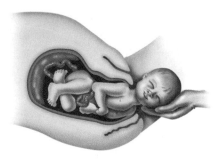

d   baby emerges from the birth canal

Figure 10.13
Stages of the birth process

Afterbirth: The Third Stage of Childbirth

While the parents are examining the newborn, there is still work to do. One or two more pushes are needed to deliver the placenta. This stage of childbirth may last anywhere from five minutes to half an hour.

A Cultural Viewpoint

Many aspects of pregnancy and childbirth are deeply rooted in culture and tradition. Linda Tuhiwai Smith (2000) in *Decolonizing Methodologies: Research and Indigenous Peoples* published by University of Otago Press in Dunedin, New Zealand writes:

> Most indigenous peoples regard blood, the placenta, and afterbirth as something "special." For Maori people it is regarded as "still active" and highly *tapu*. The afterbirth used to be buried in the land. The Maori term for land and afterbirth are the same word, *whenua*. Hospitals until very recently refused to recognize Maori requests to take the afterbirth away and have it buried. Now that the blood from the cord and the afterbirth have been shown to be useful for treating certain sorts of diseases, there has been a request from some medical professionals in New Zealand to "farm" (their word) the cord blood from aborted fetuses. While non-indigenous people will also find that difficult, they are more likely to be persuaded by arguments that the cord blood is useful, and that "farming" it will not harm anyone as long as the mother gives consent, because they have no other cultural grounds on which to object. Maori do object culturally.

❖ Connections

1. Investigate a variety of pregnancy and childbirth practices in different cultures. Report your findings in the form of a storyboard.
2. Describe some of the conventional wisdom that is still shared about pregnancy and childbirth. How did these stories originate?

Recovery: The Fourth Stage of Childbirth

The first two or three hours after birth is sometimes referred to as "the fourth stage of childbirth." During this stage, the mother and child receive extra attention and care as they recover from the hard work of labour and delivery. Mothers may feel chilly and have trouble passing urine. A prewarmed blanket is often provided after the mother is cleaned up. Stitches may be necessary to repair the episiotomy or a small tear. Mothers are encouraged to drink fluids and eat a light meal if they are hungry.

The baby will be cleaned up, weighed, measured, given a vitamin K injection to promote blood clotting at the site of the umbilical cord, and diapered for the first time. Since babies may cool off quickly at this time, a little hat is provided to keep body heat in. Babies also receive an "on-the-spot" health assessment using the APGAR scale during recovery, and necessary medical interventions are completed if the baby is at risk. Newborn screening tests for inherited diseases will be done. These diseases can have serious, lifelong consequences such as mental retardation if not detected at birth. Following these procedures, the baby goes back to mother's arms and may be nursed. At this point, the new family can rest from the tiring journey. Mothers will often find it necessary to sleep during some part of the recovery period.

Parenting Skills

What Fathers or Partners Can Do During Labour and Delivery

Fathers or partners can

- be in the birthing suite or labour and delivery rooms
- keep track of the length of contractions
- practise comforting and breathing techniques learned in prenatal classes
- get ice chips and water if his partner is allowed to have them
- adjust the bed, the bedding, the light, the music
- take his partner for walks if she is allowed to walk
- rock, massage, and humour his partner
- give encouragement and cheer her on
- cut the umbilical cord after the baby is delivered
- hold the baby soon and often

Quick Quiz: True or False

1. A pregnancy test will not come back "positive" until after the period of the embryo.
2. Light social drinking is not harmful during the period of the embryo.
3. All women of childbearing age should take a folic acid supplement.
4. Pregnant women should not drink diet soft drinks or use artificially sweetened products.
5. Herbal weight loss tonics are safe during the period of the embryo.
6. When starting an exercise program, a pregnant woman should consult her doctor.
7. Women should quit smoking before they get pregnant.
8. Prescription drugs can harm a developing embryo and fetus.
9. Some women will continue to have a "period" during the beginning of a pregnancy.
10. Women should start eating for two as soon as they learn they are pregnant.

Answers: 1. (F) 2. (F) 3. (T) 4. (T) 5. (F) 6. (T) 7. (T) 8. (T) 9. (T) 10. (F)

Promoting Bonding at Birth

The beginning of life in the animal kingdom centres on the mother and newborn child. **Bonding**, which is a strong connection between parent and child, is a fact of nature. Animal mothers instinctively nurse and protect their young. Human mothers and babies must be given the same opportunity, but as Michele Landsberg relates in the following passage, from *Women and Children First* (1985) the sterile, medical intervention in childbirth sometimes interferes with that essential connection between mother and child.

Figure 10.14
The strong connection between mother and baby is part of the animal world, too.

Birth and New Life

Remember one of the most sacred tenets of child-hood wisdom? Never touch baby birds you may find in the nest, or the mother bird will abandon them. In fact, it was almost instinctive whenever a child encountered a newborn animal of any kind: hands off, because you might interfere with something delicate and mysterious happening between mother and babies.

We were right. Scientists have long known that all mammals experience a "sensitive period" immediately after giving birth, when a deep bond is formed between mother and offspring. Violate that, and something can go haywire: the mother may reject the infant, leave it to die, or even attack it herself. Why did it take so long to apply the same simple, obvious wisdom to human mothers and babies?

Maybe we've all been so hocus-pocussed by medical wizardry that we didn't stop to think... or dare to question. What brand-new mother dares to rear up on the delivery table and demand, "Hey, where are you going with my baby?" But scientists in England and the U.S. have been proving for a decade that the "nestling" principle applies just as firmly to human beings. If you don't separate a mother and her baby in that incredible hour after birth—that shaky, exhausted, triumphant, overwhelmingly emotional hour—something terrific happens. Months and even years later those babies are still benefiting from that crucial hour of "mother-infant bonding." They cry less, smile and vocalize more, are healthier, score higher on IQ tests, and are breast-fed longer and more success-fully. Rarely are they battered or neglected. All through infancy, they get more cuddling and maternal attention than other babies do. (pp. 169–170)

Research findings on mother-infant bonding have led to improvements in childbirth practices in hospitals. At one time, labour took place in one room, while delivery took place in another. Today, most hospitals have birthing rooms that are cheerful and inviting, where both labour and delivery occur. Babies are being handed over to their mothers right at birth whenever possible. If the birth is a **Caesarean delivery** (the surgical removal of the baby through an incision in the abdomen), a mother can be awake for the surgery by having an epidural that freezes her from the waist down. This allows her to see and touch the newborn right away, rather than waking up hours later to a newborn stranger.

Career Capsule

MIDWIFE

Tasks and Responsibilities

The role of midwife has existed for centuries as women have always assisted each other in the process of childbirth. Midwives are professionals who help mothers with normal, uncomplicated pregnancies, labours, and deliveries. Midwives view pregnancy and childbirth as a normal, natural process. They are specially trained to recognize complications that require medical intervention and have the mother-to-be access other medical resources all through the pregnancy and birthing process if complications arise.

Midwives deal with all aspects of pregnancy and childbirth. They examine pregnant women, do lab tests and give diet, exercise, and lifestyle advice to ensure the healthiest pregnancy possible for the mother and baby. After the birth, midwives assess the baby's health and dietary needs. They give advice to the mother on caring for herself and the baby. Many women today are finding that primary care by a midwife is safe, natural, convenient, and personal.

Work Environment

Midwives provide care in private practices, community clinics, hospitals, and educational facilities. Many midwives run their practice with a partner. Other midwives combine caring for their mothers with teaching prenatal courses in hospitals or doing research. Midwifery involves long hours and irregular schedules—babies do not usually make appointments to be born. Being called out to a person's home or the hospital to deliver a baby in the middle of the night is quite common. However, prenatal and postnatal care can be delivered on an appointment basis.

Canada has only recently recognized midwifery as a profession. All provinces recognize the designation of midwife and several have moved to regulate midwifery. With regulation comes professional recognition and the need to be accountable. This increases the stature of the profession.

Education and Aptitudes

Caring and concern for the welfare of others on a personal basis are good aptitudes for this career. Midwives need to have a calm and reassuring personality. Good communication skills are absolutely essential for success in midwifery. Since midwifery has been practised for centuries in many parts of the world, a familiarity with and respect for the values and traditions of other cultures would be helpful for a successful midwife.

A four-year university degree is required to become a registered midwife in most Canadian provinces. A Bachelor of Health Sciences in Midwifery or an equivalent degree prepares a graduate to practice midwifery. This is an interdisciplinary program that features courses in health, social sciences, and women's studies. At present, entrance to these courses is highly competitive.

Many other changes have taken place to improve chances for bonding. In the past, fathers were sent to the waiting room until it was all over and only then told whether they had a boy or a girl.

Today, they routinely stay with the mother throughout labour and delivery. While infants were once whisked away from their mothers to a sterile nursery and kept apart from them by glass walls, **rooming in** (staying with the mother in the same room day and night) is now the norm. Home births and midwife-assisted births are also on the increase in Canada. All of these practices are improving the possibilities for bonding and attachment. Besides spending the first hour face-to-face after birth, the single most important factor is breast-feeding.

Breast-Feeding Encourages Bonding

Breast-feeding has many advantages for both the mother and the infant and is now encouraged and promoted widely by many health-care professionals. Plans to breast-feed should be made before the baby is born. The mother will need to toughen her nipples by rubbing them with a towel so that she is physically ready. She can prepare emotionally by discussing her feelings and concerns with her health practitioner. Making the decision to breast-feed before the baby arrives allows the father and other family members to become supportive right from the beginning.

Breast-feeding has to be learned by both mother and baby. Together they become a breast-feeding team. The mother learns how to hold the baby and direct the infant to the nipple. She has to learn how to get the nipple into the baby's mouth, and the baby has to learn how to latch on properly. Breast-feeding confidence increases if breast-feeding begins shortly after the baby is born. Some hospitals and midwives provide breast-feeding coaching and follow-up to prevent breast-feeding failure. Like any new learning, it takes time, but after about three weeks, it becomes very natural. Mothers who cannot breast-feed should not feel guilty or incompetent, however. Infants thrive on formula when breast milk is unavailable.

In Canada and North America, breast-feeding was not the first choice of mothers for a time. The 1930s brought canned milk, infant formula, and Pablum, and women chose what was considered a more nutritious and sterile alternative. A combination of factors, including the back-to-nature movement in the late 1960s and early 1970s and research into the long-term advantages of breast-feeding, changed the trend back to breast-feeding. In recent years, mothers who breast-feed their children have outnumbered those who do not.

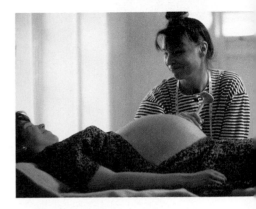

Figure 10.15
Plans to breast-feed should be made before the baby is born.

■ Seven women founded the La Leche League in 1956. This organization has branches across Canada and throughout the world that provide hospitals and libraries with resource materials that not only promote breast-feeding, but also answer all the questions new parents might have about breast-feeding.

❖ Checkpoints

1. What are the indicators that labour has started?
2. What can a father do at each stage of labour and delivery?
3. How are breast-feeding and bonding related?
4. Why is breast-feeding promoted by health professionals today?

Father Bonding

Fathers today are seen everywhere with their babies and children. They have a key role in pregnancy and delivery, which leads them to a closer bond with their children. When both parents are present throughout the pregnancy and at the birth of their child, it is a shared experience that cements their parenting relationship with their newborn baby. The experience promotes the bonding necessary to establish the love between parent and child that lasts a lifetime. The birth of a child is a rare miracle that is witnessed only a few times in life.

Talking Parenting

Talking Parenting with Anil, 30 (First-Time Father)

My wife, Mansa, and I have been married for two years and we have a brand-new six-month-old baby boy named Philip. Mansa and I went to university together and married soon after we graduated. She teaches and I do corporate law. We both work very hard at our jobs and consider ourselves successful, but nothing could have prepared us for getting used to being new parents. This is something you have to experience to understand. I do not understand it yet, but I am getting used to the increased responsibility of being a father, sharing my wife with a very demanding son, making do with less money and less sleep, and not being able to do things on the spur of the moment anymore.

Things have sure changed around the house since Mansa and I found out we were going to be parents. There were really strange things like Mansa bursting into tears when she was pregnant for what seemed like no reason at all, then she would worry about the baby and I would calm her down and then lie awake worrying about the same thing myself. One night when we were falling asleep, Philip moved inside Mansa and "kicked" my back. I did not sleep much that night thinking about this first real contact with my baby-to-be.

Once Philip came home, life was never the same. Baby equipment took over the house and our home now revolves around his needs; naps, feedings, diaper changes, laundry, burping up the gas bubbles, and sometimes just keeping him amused when he is not doing any of the above. Now at least I feel useful because I can do everything but breast-feed him. I am not anxious about impending fatherhood anymore, only tired and happy.

Fortunately, Mansa could take time off from teaching to stay home with the baby for a year. I took advantage of the new paternity leave legislation that allowed me to stay home with Mansa and the baby during the first two weeks, but that was all the time I could afford to stay away from my practice.

I come from a culture where men have little to do with baby care so my parents' eyebrows really went up, but they got over it. Now, they are over all the time doting on their first grandchild. My dad never used to do that with me. In fact, we had nannies to do most of the child care back home. I rarely saw my parents during the day or evening when I was a child, and became very attached to my nanny. Although this is a lot harder work for parents, the attachment I feel to my son is so special and wondrous, I would not want to share it with anyone but Mansa. I can't explain this attachment, I just feel it. It is like being in love all over again, but a different kind of love.

Bonding with Premature Babies

In spite of parents' best efforts to promote a healthy pregnancy and birth, some babies may still be born premature. A premature infant will require special efforts by medical professionals to ensure that development continues in an environment that is as close to the womb as possible. Premature infants may spend weeks in an incubator, with the right mix of warmth, oxygen, and feeding tubes if needed.

They look frail because they were born before they could lay down the layer of body fat that gives newborns their cuddly appearance. The entire experience may be intimidating for parents, yet the best thing parents can do for themselves and their baby is to bond with the child as soon as possible. Human touch is critical for infant survival. Stroking the infant through special port holes in the incubator, talking, singing, and watching baby sleep helps parents form a connection that can only be strengthened when the day comes that they can take their baby home.

Chapter Summary

Chapter Highlights

- The beginning of life provides the foundation for the rest of life.

- What a parent does for a child before, during, and after the birth will affect that child forever.

- The human potential that is represented in every child born is an enormous responsibility for parents.

- Both parents need to contribute to a healthy pregnancy for the sake of their unborn children.

- From conception to birth, prenatal development is like a miracle, as the embryo becomes a fetus, which continues to grow until it is completely formed and ready for birth.

- The birth process involves four stages—labour, delivery, afterbirth, and recovery.

- Fathers or partners can play an important role throughout the pregnancy and as birthing coaches.

- Being present at the birth of a child contributes to bonding, the basis for the life-long love connection and attachment between parents and child.

Review and Extend Your Learning

1. Describe the reasons that the period before conception and birth is so critical to the child. **K/U**

2. Given that the period of the embryo is the most critical phase of pregnancy, outline specific do's and don'ts for women in this phase of pregnancy. **K/U** **A**

3. Describe a day in the life of a woman who is
   - 8 weeks pregnant
   - 24 weeks pregnant
   - 39 weeks pregnant **K/U** **C**

4. Take a tour of a hospital delivery room. Find out about the options available for parents and birthing professionals. **T/I**

5. Locate and evaluate prenatal and post-natal care/support programs available for parents in your community (e.g., prenatal classes, breast-feeding clinics, Healthy Babies, Healthy Children Program). Prepare an information pamphlet that would be useful to expectant couples that outlines the programs and services available to them. **T/I** **C** **A**

6. Interview three "willing" moms about their labour. How long did it last? What challenges did they face? What were the memorable moments? Compare and contrast the experiences and write a report about your findings. **T/I** **A**

7. Analyze why early bonding between mother and child is so important in the life of a child. **K/U** **T/I**

8. Assess the importance of the father-child relationship in the birthing process for both father and child. **K/U** **T/I** **C** **A**

Research Opportunities

9. Review a book or video about pregnancy and childbirth available at a local library, bookstore, health unit, or parenting centre. Design a pamphlet that reviews the resource and could be printed for distribution to expectant parents in doctors' offices or by midwives.

10. From the options that need to be considered in a birth plan (see page 249), select three terms that you are not completely familiar with. Research the terms, and, based on the definition, explain which you would choose if you and a partner were preparing a birth plan.

11. Choose one of the congenital diseases that newborns are screened for at birth such as fragile congenital hypothyroidism, sickle cell anemia, phenylketonuria (PKU), or galactosemia. Describe the test that is used. Note the incidence or frequency of the disease, symptoms, and long-term implications for the child who is diagnosed with this condition at birth.

Issue Analysis

12. Conduct interviews or an Internet search to determine the advantages and disadvantages of home births and hospital births. Based on your findings, explain which you would choose for the birth of your children and why.

13. Our Canadian teenage mothers lag behind the older population of mothers in choosing to breast-feed their babies.
    a) Explore the reasons that teen mothers often do not breast-feed.
    b) How might the media be used to encourage breast-feeding for all mothers, but especially teen mothers?

Chapter
11

The Important
First Year of Life

By the end of this chapter, you will be able to:

- outline the link between healthy infant development and long-term growth and development

- describe the factors that contribute to the healthy development of children in the first few months after birth

- identify and describe environments provided by families, caregivers, and others that offer positive conditions for child development during infancy

- understand theories of bonding and attachment and describe their effects on the social and emotional development in children and adolescents

- demonstrate an understanding of the consequences of environmental deprivation in infancy

- explain, using basic principles of brain science, the role that stimulation plays in the intellectual development of the infant

Important Terms

anxious ambivalent infants
anxious avoidant infants
APGAR scale
attachment
childproofing
failure to thrive
fontanels
infant reflexes

motor development
neonate
regression
secure infants
sense of trust
separation behaviour
stranger anxiety

Chapter at a Glance

How Does Infancy Affect Later Life?

The first year of life. It is the time in our lives when we grow the fastest, sleep the longest, and learn the most. Infants arrive into the world totally dependent but by the end of that first year are able to stand upright, handle a spoon, and let others know exactly what they want. In that year, they become a person in their own right, and all the opportunities they are given for growth and development will provide the foundation for the rest of their lives.

Because most people have little or no memory of the first years of their life, they have limited sense of their importance. However, research indicates that the beginning of life affects all areas of subsequent human development. Research in infant development continues to provide evidence that the beginning of life is critical to long-term health, growth, and development. Both Dr. R.A. Casl in the *Global Forum for Health Research* and Dr. Fraser Mustard and Margaret Norrie McCain in their *Early Years Study* cite a number of studies indicating that health and progress throughout life is related to prenatal and infant environment and experiences.

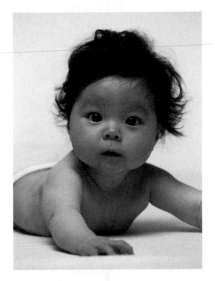

Figure 11.1
Infants become persons in their own right within the first year of development.

Infant Well-Being and Later Life: Research Connections

- Overall fetal and infant health is related to health in the long term.
- Nutrient intake during infancy plays a role in blood pressure and cholesterol levels later in life.
- The quality of care an infant receives affects the stress response and production of the correct level of cortisol (a stress hormone) in adults.
- The quality of early stimulation of the infant's senses influences the brain's ability to think and regulate body functions.

- Breast-fed infants may score higher intellectually later in life and achieve better overall health later in life.
- A rich language environment in infancy contributes to intelligence, language acquisition, and early literacy.
- A sense of trust achieved early in life contributes to self-confidence.
- Lack of attachment with a significant caregiver in infancy is a factor in some criminal behaviour.

Human infants need total care at birth to continue their development. The quality of that care will influence every aspect of their future growth, their health throughout life, and their ability to form and maintain relationships. It will also affect their intelligence, how well they will do in school, and even their eventual success in the world of work. The role that parents play, particularly the parent who is the child's primary caregiver, is a significant factor in how the child turns out.

The Healthy Newborn

Have you ever seen a newborn or pictures of a newly born infant? They do not resemble the babies used to depict newborns in most television shows or movies. Most media babies are already a few weeks old and have lost their neonatal or newborn look. If a birth is depicted, an older baby may be slathered in cream cheese and grape jelly and held up on camera to represent a live birth. However, if you have seen an actual newborn infant you know that they might only be beautiful in the eyes of their parents.

Newborn Appearance

If you are unfamiliar with **neonates**, another name for newborn babies, their appearance may be a surprise.

- Their skin feels soft but dry and is wrinkled.
- They usually have a mass of between 2.7 kg and 4.0 kg.
- They average 50 cm in length.
- Their head accounts for one-quarter of their body length and seems huge.
- The foreheads of newborns are high and their noses are flat, and they seem chinless.
- They often do not look like anybody else in the family, which might be disappointing.
- Their eyes are steely blue in colour although they may eventually be dark brown, light brown, green, clear blue, or grey.

Since the birth process can be quite forceful, a newborn's head may seem lopsided, cone-shaped, or otherwise misshapen. There may also be bruises or marks on the baby from the force of being born. Though they may not look like the babies you have seen in pictures, to new parents their newborn will look like the most beautiful baby in the world.

Neonatal Assessment Scale (APGAR)

Whether a baby is delivered in a hospital or at home, midwives, doctors, and maternity nurses will quickly determine the baby's condition by making a note of various details.

The **APGAR scale**, developed in 1952 by Virginia Apgar, is still used today to assess the condition of a newborn. A score is given for

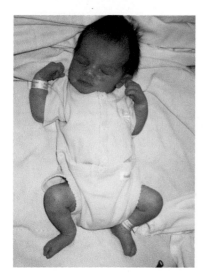

Figure 11.2
This baby is three days old. Her head is still cone-shaped, and she has marks from the force of being born.

different signs of appearance and response at one minute and five minutes after the birth. A score of 7-10 is normal; a score of 4-7 may require some resuscitative measures; while a baby with a score of 3 and below will need immediate resuscitation.

The APGAR Scale

Sign to Look For	0 Points	1 Point	2 Points
Activity (muscle tone)	Absent	Arms and legs flexed	Active movement
Pulse (beats per minute)	Absent	Below 100 bpm	Above 100 bpm
Grimace (reflex irritability when nose is stimulated)	No response	Grimace	Sneeze, cough, pulls away
Appearance (skin colour)	Blue-grey, pale all over	Normal, except for extremities	Normal over entire body
Respiration	Absent	Slow, irregular	Good, crying

Figure 11.3
The APGAR scale assesses the condition of the newborn. A healthy baby has a score of 7-10.

Generally babies who are born premature or who have low birth weight score lower on the scale. A low score may also signal complications that were not detected during pregnancy but which need immediate intervention.

Premature Birth

According to the *Encyclopedia Britannica*, a premature birth is

Birth less than 37 weeks after conception. Infants born as early as 23–24 weeks may survive but many face lifelong disabilities (e.g., cerebral palsy, blindness, deafness). Premature infants account for 8–9 percent of live births but two-thirds of infant deaths. Forty to fifty percent of cases have no explanation; other cases can be attributed to such causes as maternal hypertension or diabetes, multiple pregnancy, or placental separation. With good care, about 85 percent of live-born premature infants should survive. Infants born very early (before 32–34 weeks) lack fully developed lungs and often develop respiratory distress syndrome. They also have problems maintaining body temperature and fighting infection. Most deaths result from breathing problems, infections, and brain or lung hemorrhages. Premature infants are characterized by low birth weight, small size, irregular breathing, absence of subcutaneous fat, and thin skin.

❖ Checkpoints

1. List five ways in which infant well-being influences adult well-being.
2. Describe the characteristics of a healthy neonate.
3. Babies with low APGAR scores may not be placed on the mother's abdomen at birth. Why not?
4. What are the risks associated with a premature infant or an infant with low birth weight?

The Amazing Newborn

Newborns are ready to learn, grow, and form close attachments from the moment of birth. Though they appear helpless, they have many built-in responses and capabilities that ensure their survival.

Infant Reflexes

Because a newborn brain is so much larger than that of other animals, the newborn is actually born before the cortex of the brain "wakes up." The pelvis of most women is not large enough for a baby with a fully developed brain to pass through. Therefore, the brain needs three more months of development after birth before it can meet the baby's needs properly. Until then, the brain stem uses built-in **infant reflexes** or instinctive automatic reactions to stimuli to meet physical needs. All healthy infants display up to eleven neonatal reflexes.

Most infant reflexes disappear after the first three months of life. Some reflexes however, such as blinking, coughing, sneezing, and yawning, last for all of a person's life. Reflexes are necessary for the helpless infant to survive and have its six basic needs—food, safety, warmth, sleep, exercise, and cleanliness—met. Infant reflexes appear to be most closely connected to meeting the first three critical needs. Five reflexes that ensure the baby's survival through the first three months are the rooting and sucking reflexes, the grasping reflex, the startle reflex, and the rage reflex.

Rooting and sucking reflexes: Infants turn toward a touch on their cheek or lips and open their mouths. When a nipple or even a finger touches their tongue, they begin to suck. This ensures that newborns will "hunt" for a nipple, open their mouths, and start to suck, making sure they are fed. When they begin using their eyes to find the nipple, at about four months of age, this reflex will stop. These two reflexes work together.

■ Infants have six basic needs:
- food
- sleep
- safety
- exercise
- warmth
- cleanliness

■ Reflexes ensure that a baby's basic needs are met.

Grasping reflex: Infants automatically grasp anything that touches the palm of their hand. Caregivers with long hair quickly learn to keep it away from babies. Even infants who appear to be asleep sometimes exhibit this reflex. The grip is often so tight that it can be used to lift the infants, but because they can let go without warning, this is definitely not recommended. When they start to reach for objects at about three months of age, this reflex starts to weaken and subsequently disappears.

Startle reflex: Infants generally respond to a loud noise or a sudden change in position with the startle reflex. The arms and fingers extend and spread out. Legs are thrown up in the air, the arms are drawn back to the body, and the fingers grasp the air. They may start to wail when disturbed like this. A parent's immediate response is to hold and comfort the child. Also known as the Moro reflex, the startle reflex usually disappears around six months of age.

Rage reflex: Infants who are restrained from turning their heads or who have their mouths covered for 10 seconds will cry and struggle to get free from the restraint. This reflex, which disappears in two to four months, helps protect the infant from smothering.

Sensory Capabilities

Neonates are capable of using all their senses right from birth. Studies of newborn infants have shown that they prefer the taste of mildly sweet flavours to very sweet, salty, or bitter flavours. They also recognize their mother's voice, by turning toward it more frequently than to a stranger's voice. In studies where breast pads soaked with mother's milk and a stranger's milk were placed in the bassinette, newborns turned more often toward the mother's milk, indicating a highly developed sense of smell. Even though their vision will not fully develop for several weeks, newborns tend to focus best at the distance from mother's face to mother's breast, gazing longer at images of the human face than at random patterns or printed words.

With all of their senses and reflexes functioning, newborn babies are ready to absorb all of the love and nurturing needed for the bonding and attachment that will secure their future development. Until the 1970s, developmental scientists did not believe that babies were capable of much learning for several months. They were viewed as "animate vegetables." We now know that this belief was far from the truth. The human brain is like a computer and when we are born, "it is booted up" and ready to process data immediately.

Figure 11.4
The grasping reflex allows infants to hold on tightly.

Infant Reflexes Encourage Bonding

A mother of twins was asked whether she found it difficult to bond with her baby boy who had to stay in the hospital several days after his sister already came home. His mother noted that she was worried about that very thing; however, on the trip home from the hospital, he somehow managed to get his little hand out of the mitten, and grasp tightly onto her finger. That was the moment she fell in love with him, and from then on there was no problem.

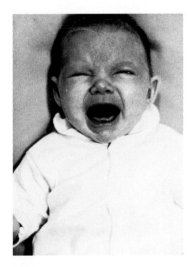

Figure 11.5
The rage reflex helps to protect the infant from smothering.

"The basic idea of cognitive science is that we think and reason and know because our brains run very powerful programs. Our brain is like a supercomputer with far better software than developed to date" (Gopnick, Kuhl & Meltzoff, 2000, p. 139). Adults take advantage of the natural learning tendencies of children. "What we do know for sure, or as sure as anything can be in science, is that babies are brilliantly intelligent learners and that grown-ups are devoted to helping them (p. 9)."

According to Alison Gopnik, Andew Meltzoff, and Patricia Kuhl (2000) in *The Scientist in the Crib*, the human brain is like a powerful computer that is programmed to function immediately upon birth. Their research demonstrates that children are amazing learners and that parents and other adults almost instinctively cater to these natural learning tendencies in infants and children.

Attachment Theory

Another element that contributes to newborn survival is their ability to form an attachment to another human being. **Attachment** is an especially close and affectionate bond between the infant and caregiver. For a variety of reasons, the primary caregiver for the infant is most often the baby's mother. Infants usually form just as strong an attachment in a different way to fathers who are highly involved with them. Human infants need to form a strong connection with at least one other person early in life to ensure their survival, growth, and social and emotional development.

The importance of infant attachment has been studied for some time. During the Second World War, orphaned babies in hospitals turned their faces to the wall and died in spite of being fed and changed. In cases where a nurse or caretaker actually lifted children out of their cribs and held them even if it was for short periods of time, the infants did much better. This phenomenon came to be known as a **failure to thrive** and caregivers began to realize that even small amounts of attention and holding improved the outcome for these infants. They gained weight and reached developmental milestones.

Attachment theory indicates that all humans need to form close bonds of affection, and that a connected, reciprocal (mutual) relationship early in life is necessary for normal human development. Three people who contributed to the development of the attachment theory were Harry Harlow, John Bowlby, and Mary Ainsworth.

Harry Harlow's Monkey Research

In 1966, Harry Harlow studied rhesus monkeys to see what would happen if they were separated from their mothers at an early age. He provided the young monkeys with a wire frame shaped like a mother monkey, which held the bottle. He also had a second wire frame "mother" covered with cloth and no bottle. He found that the young

Figure 11.6
Infants need to form a strong bond with at least one person.

monkeys would feed from the bottle when hungry, but cuddled up with the fabric one for comfort, or clung to the cloth mother when frightened. Monkeys who did not have the cloth-covered mother failed to grow, even though food was available. Harlow's studies showed the importance of touch and contact for the survival and growth of infants.

John Bowlby

In the 1960s and 1970s, John Bowlby studied actual children, and identified that human infants exhibit what he called "attachment behaviours" that elicit responses from adults, which in turn encourage these behaviours in the child. A feedback circuit is established. Proximity seeking, smiling, and clinging are examples of attachment behaviours, which in turn get an adult response such as touching, holding, or soothing. This interplay of attachment provides the security infants need to move forward in their development.

Figure 11.7
Infants use attachment behaviours to get responses from adults. An infant may smile so that a caregiver will hold him or her. In return, the infant is encouraged to keep smiling.

Bowlby also studied separation, and, in particular, separations in hospitals. He discovered that when children between eight months and three years are first left, they go through three stages of **separation behaviour** following the separation:

1. **Protest:** crying, protesting, and searching for mother
2. **Despair:** the child becomes very quiet
3. **Detachment:** the child withdraws as though cut off from the world

Children who are secure in their attachment are able to move beyond the detachment stage and become more active and interactive. Less secure children may go so far as to withdraw by crawling under a table.

When children go home after a separation, they may be angry and resist the parent, or they may become whiny and clingy. They need to re-establish a sense of security through their attachment to the parent. **Regression** (returning to a level of behaviour that is more common to an earlier stage of development) is another way they reclaim their attachment. Therefore, bed-wetting, thumb-sucking, or wanting a bottle may return them to a relationship that felt more secure. Regression allows them to refuel before moving forward again in their development. Children who were rebuffed or punished by a parent for showing such behaviour only intensified their attachment behaviours. Recovery is faster if the child is touched, held, or kept close after the separation.

❖ Connections

1. Suggest ways that parents can reconnect with their children after they pick them up from child care, nursery school, play school, or even a weekend visit to a relative.
2. Bowlby's work has received criticism. Conduct a Web search to find out who has criticized his work, and why.

Mary Ainsworth

Mary Ainsworth, a graduate of the University of Toronto, is known for her study of mother-infant attachment in Uganda in the 1940s. Upon her return to the University of Toronto, she continued this research with Canadian children at The Institute of Child Study. Later, she joined John Bowlby in his work on attachment theory. Her research showed that infants needed a "secure base" from which to begin their exploration, especially once they began to crawl. She noted that infants will give a signal such as a cry, a wail, a glance, or some other type of behaviour directed at the caregiver. The caregiver provides a secure base for the infant if he or she is able to:

- detect the infant's signal
- correctly interpret the signal
- make an appropriate and timely response

Caregivers who had a strong attachment to their children were better able to perform these functions than those who were indifferent to their children.

Ainsworth also noted different degrees of attachment among children. Not all children behaved in the same manner when their parent returned after being away. **Secure infants** were comfortable with the parent and sometimes sought contact, stood near the parent, or smiled at him or her from across the room. **Anxious avoidant infants** turned away from the parent, or avoided touch. **Anxious ambivalent infants** showed resistance, anger, or hostility when the parent returned. Secure attachment is essential for healthy development.

The best way for parents to foster attachment with infants is to respond consistently to their needs. Infants communicate mostly through crying. When newborns cry and a caregiver responds, they learn that the world is a good place and that someone is there who can be trusted to care for their needs. They then develop what Erik Erikson called a **sense of trust**. This strong sense of trust grows out of their early attachment, and is the foundation for lifelong social and emotional development.

Figure 11.8
Secure attachment results in a positive response by the infant.

❖ Checkpoints

1. Describe the purpose of infant reflexes. What might happen if infants did not have these reflexes?
2. What causes "failure to thrive?"
3. Describe parental behaviours that would promote mistrust instead of trust in an infant?

❖ Connections

1. Observe infants who have not yet developed language skills in a real-life setting (or on video). What cues do they use to let an adult know what they need and want? How do they behave when their cues are ignored or misinterpreted?
2. Observe children up to the age of three as their parents leave them at a play school, child care, or nursery school setting. What "separation behaviours" can you identify?

The Importance of a Secure Parent-Child Attachment

With a strong parent-child attachment:

- Infants move forward more quickly in all areas of development, but especially in verbal development and learning.
- Sleeping and eating disorders are less common.
- Children can handle their emotions better.
- Parents rarely abuse children with whom they have formed a close attachment.
- The map or template for other intimate relationships throughout life is created.
- A basis for good mental health is established.

Talking Parenting

The following magazine article discusses father-child attachment.

Falling in Love: The Father-Baby Bond

by John Hoffman, *Transition*

I remember very clearly falling in love with my first baby. Every time I went to visit my wife and new son in the hospital, I picked up Riley and held him for the entire visit. As I cuddled him, it felt as if that warm little bundle was burrowing his way straight into my heart. I knew that this was my kid and that I loved him.

Mothers do have a head start in the attachment process through pregnancy, birthing, and breast-feeding. Men can't do any of these things, yet we can still form a strong attachment with our children. It doesn't always happen right in the birthing room. Often a father's love grows gradually, as he spends time getting to know this new little being.

But starting early seems to be the key. A number of studies in the past 20 years have shown that men who have early contact with their infants spend more time with them when they are three to six months old.

When Chris Risley's second baby was born, this full-time dad knew from experience how their bonding would happen. "For me, the bond is directly related to the number of hours I spend in charge of

Figure 11.9
Fathers can form a strong attachment with a newborn by looking after it.

the baby," says Chris. Being "in charge" of an infant means holding, rocking, soothing, changing diapers. The message here is that you need to know somebody in order to love him. And the way to get to know a baby is to take care of him.

Meeting the Needs of Infants

Newborns have a way of taking over the household. Because they depend on adults to meet all their needs, they are very demanding. The first child is the one that causes the greatest concern for parents, because they have yet to experience what it is like to care for an infant. They will face many parenting hurdles in the first year. The parents' first concern is meeting the infant's physiological needs. Safety and security needs are equally important. A baby also needs love and affection from birth. By responding to all of the infant's needs in a consistent and loving manner, parents cannot help but contribute to their child's optimal development.

Food, clothing, shelter, physical safety, and sleep are the physiological needs that every parent needs to consider. Most parents in Canada have a place to live before the baby is born. Those who do not have a home of their own may find shelter with family members, or rely on social services to help them find shelter.

Figure 11.10
Infants need clothing that is appropriate for their environment.

Clothing for Infants

Infants need clothing to keep them warm and comfortable. They do not require extensive wardrobes, but they need indoor, outdoor, daytime, and nighttime clothing. Babies grow very quickly. Second-hand baby clothes from friends or family have lots of wear left in them. Some babies have an elaborate layette prepared for them long before they are born, which includes the prescribed number of undershirts, sleepers, socks, bibs, and diapers. Diapers are the primary item that babies will require every day for as many as three years. Parents may choose to use cloth diapers, disposable diapers, or a combination of both.

Feeding Infants

The two main options for feeding infants are breast-feeding and bottle-feeding. Both breast milk and infant formula can be fed by bottle. As mammals, humans are designed to nurse their young, who thrive on human milk. Research has demonstrated that breast-feeding has advantages.

For most babies, breast-feeding completely meets their nutritional needs for the first four to six months of life and is the only food they need. Some experts are now recommending breast-feeding for the first twelve months of life. During the second half of the first year, infant cereals, strained vegetables, fruits, and then meats complete the baby's diet, along with breast milk. Parents and caregivers need to know that eating habits that last a lifetime are started in infancy.

Advantages of Breast-Feeding, for the Baby

There are many immediate benefits of breast-feeding. Breast milk is always clean and is normally readily available. The milk contains antibodies from the mother that protect the infant from allergies and illness, and even help reduce the incidence of ear infections. Breast milk is easily digested, which reduces gas and constipation, and diapers are less smelly. Infants who are fed formula or cow's milk in the first year may develop diarrhea, which is not usually experienced by those who are breast-fed. Breast-feeding promotes visual development because the focus of the infant's eyes changes as he or she is nursed first on one side and then on the other. There is less chance of overfeeding an infant, because the child stops nursing when satiety is reached.

There are also long-term benefits. Breast-fed babies are healthier, are less likely to become overweight later in life, and may score higher on intelligence tests.

Advantages of Breast-Feeding, for the Mother

Breast-feeding promotes strong bonds between the mother and her child and provides a psychological benefit to both mother and infant. It helps shrink the uterus after birth and helps the mother return to her pre-pregnancy weight faster. It requires no mixing, sterilizing, or refrigeration, and it is readily available at home or away from home. Mothers do need to avoid alcohol and caffeine while nursing and should also check with their health practitioner about medications and food additives that can accumulate in breast milk. Breast-feeding provides nurture and comfort for the baby at any time of the day or night. It may also provide women with long-term benefits. Studies reported in the *American Journal of Epidemiology* in December 1997 and July 1999 indicated a correlation between breast-feeding and a reduced risk of breast cancer. Fathers can also be involved when a couple chooses breast-feeding. They can burp the baby after a feeding, or use a bottle to feed breast milk that has been pumped and refrigerated or frozen for later use.

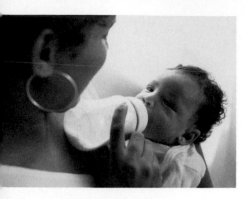

Figure 11.11
Successful bottle feeding requires close contact.

Formula Feeding

Not every mother can breast-feed, especially those who have HIV (human immunodeficiency virus), who smoke, or who are taking certain prescription drugs that can pass on through to the breast milk. Adoptive mothers and women who return to paid employment also need to use infant formula. Infant formula is harder to digest then breast milk and does not contain the quality of nutrients or the antibodies of breast milk, but it has been scientifically designed to come as close to breast milk as possible. To create a close bond through bottle-feeding, the parent or caregiver must hold the infant closely during the entire feeding, as a mother would do if breast-feeding.

Preparing Formula

Infant formula comes in three different forms. Powdered formula is prepared by mixing it with boiled, cooled water. A blender is useful for thorough mixing. The preparation of a liquid concentrated formula also requires the addition of boiled, cooled water. Ready-to-feed formula does not require preparation but costs significantly more. It can be poured directly into clean, sterile bottles, and immediately warmed and fed to the infant.

When using formula,

1. Bottles and preparation equipment must be sterilized for the first six months while the infant's immune system is developing.
2. Use exact measurements to ensure the correct proportion of formula to water.
3. Only prepare what you need for a 24-hour period and refrigerate completely, because formula spoils easily.
4. Warm formula to room temperature by placing the bottle in hot water. Shake gently before using to distribute the warmth evenly. Do not overheat.
5. Never reheat formula. Always discard any that is left over at the end of a feeding.
6. Do not overfeed an infant just to use up what is left in the bottle. Infants will signal when they have had enough.

Burping a Baby

Both breast-fed and formula-fed infants need to be "burped" after a feeding, because air trapped in the stomach can be painful. Even if babies have fallen asleep during feeding, they still need to be burped. It may take a minute or two of gentle patting or rubbing their back to produce a burp, but sometimes just lifting them to your shoulder will do it. A receiving blanket draped over the shoulder will protect your clothing from spit-ups.

Meeting an Infant's Need for Safety and Security

Babies need care and supervision around the clock. Although it will be months before they start getting into things, newborns can propel themselves with arm and leg movements, getting caught in bedding, or falling off change tables. Their grasp may result in pulling things over that can hurt them in some way. Infants should never be left unattended or unsupervised. If a parent is careless even for a moment, a tragedy could result.

Childproofing

Because infants are able to move around long before they can walk, it is important to consider their safety. Once they become more mobile through rolling, crawling, or reaching, parents not only need to continue to watch them, but may need to take extra steps in childproofing their homes. **Childproofing** the home by making it safe for a curious child is essential. Products developed for use with infants have strict safety standards and should be used only as intended. Parents should ensure that all sleepwear is flameproof and that there are no loose or dangling ribbons or ties that the baby could get caught in or choke on. Only cribs and playpens that meet the most recent safety standards should be used. Children sometimes get into things that parents may not consider harmful. Antiques, although lovely to look at, could pose toxic or other hazards to small infants because of lead paint or loose parts. A child could ingest a poisonous plant or a chemical that could be harmful. A phone call to the Poison Control Centre could save a life or put a parent's mind at ease.

Figure 11.12
When children become more mobile, parents need to take extra steps to childproof their home.

Ottawa sends out warning over playpen risk to kids

From *Toronto Star*, December 5, 1998

More than a week after an American recall of 9.6 million playpens, Health Canada issued its warning that some models of the playpens pose a risk to children in this country.

The federal agency said yesterday it had determined some of the playpens recalled Nov. 24 in the United States may have been sold here.

Its release said most are older models no longer on the market. Consumers are asked to check the upper edge of any playpen's top rail for protrusions such as metal rivets, plastic knobs, bolts or small components that extend more than 0.6 centimetres. If protrusions are found, the playpen should not be used.

Unlike the United States, there is no Canadian law forcing manufacturers to recall products. But Health Canada's "warning" can prompt voluntary recalls.

The U.S. announced the recall because children whose pacifier strings or loose clothing hook on protruding parts have strangled or could strangle. Eight children hooked on rivets in the States have died since 1982. No Canadian deaths have been attributed to the playpens.

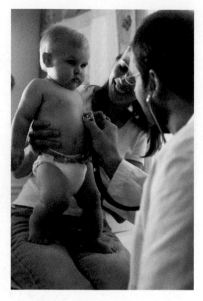

Figure 11.13
Caregivers must schedule regular medical check-ups and arrange immunizations for their child.

◼ It is now known that it is impossible to spoil a newborn. They signal their needs by crying, and it is a parent's job to meet their needs.

Health and Hygiene

Another aspect of safety and security is infant hygiene and health. From the day they are born, infants need to be bathed and kept clean, dry, and comfortably warm. Until their immune systems develop, objects that go into their mouths should be sanitized or sterilized. Parents or caregivers must schedule regular medical check-ups and discuss and arrange immunization with a health-care provider. During infancy, many common illnesses occur. Croup, ear infection, diarrhea, impetigo, and thrush are just a few that may need medical attention. Parents can tell if a child is ill by an increase in body temperature, a loss of appetite, a runny nose, listlessness, crying, or other signs of discomfort. The first time a child becomes ill can be frightening, but illness is a normal aspect of infancy.

All children need sleep, rest, and exercise for good health. Helping children establish a routine for sleeping and napping also gives them a sense of security. Play is the way infants exercise. New parents are advised to spend some time together every day playing with their baby. Gentle massage, manipulating arms and legs, and communication all help provide a healthy start in life. Developing infants are naturally active, and being able to kick their arms and legs, reach, stretch, and move is all part of their daily activity. As they become older, they should be able to climb, dance, push, pull, tumble, and roll in a safe environment.

Meeting an Infant's Need for Love and Affection

Infants respond to touch, smile, and voice in a way that invites a response from others. All babies need love and affection, and we know from the early attachment studies that infants who did not receive human contact were delayed in their development, and some turned their faces to the wall and died. In convincing studies performed by Dr. Berry Brazelton, newborn infants have shown an inborn capacity to attach to their parents.

There was a time when parents were discouraged from picking up their infants too readily when they cried, or too often, for fear of spoiling them. It is now known that it is impossible to spoil a newborn. They signal their needs by crying, and it is the parent's job to meet their needs. We now know that young infants are not able to comfort themselves and will learn how to quiet down from having their needs met appropriately when they cry. In fact, studies show that infants whose needs are met promptly cry for shorter periods of time.

Career Capsule

PUBLIC-HEALTH NURSE

Tasks and Responsibilities

Public-health nurses work with the general public to improve health. They share knowledge about disease and injury prevention and are often involved in providing information about healthy practices related to pregnancy, contagious disease, inoculation, and sexual health. Key focus areas include the very young, the elderly, neglect and abuse of children, substance abuse, and individuals and families receiving social assistance, who often do not have private health-care funding.

Work done by public-health nurses includes education and counselling to prevent disease, prenatal education, working with new mothers and babies, giving medication, observing, and assessing rehabilitation and recovery in individual cases. It is the focus of their work that makes the public-health nurse different from nurses working in hospitals and clinics. They focus on the social and economic factors affecting the health of people in the community instead of individual patients in recovery settings.

Work Environment

Public-health nurses may be found working in schools, nursing homes, community centres, and private homes. They are often required to travel from place to place in the course of their workday. Overtime and weekend work is sometimes expected.

Education and Aptitudes

Since a public-health nurse works with the public, good communication and interpersonal skills are required. This is a tiring job so you should be energetic and fit. Empathy, compassion, and a real enjoyment of helping others are essential qualities. In a multicultural country like Canada, knowledge and understanding of a wide variety of ethnic or cultural traditions is critical for success in this field. Experience in child care is also an asset.

Nurses in Canada will soon all require a four-year university degree. It is now preferred over the shorter community college diploma. After graduation, the candidate must pass the national nursing licensing examination and complete provincial certifications, which confer the title of Registered Nurse (RN).

When a baby is comforted quickly, a parent or caregiver is making an investment in the emotional stability of the child.

Children who are loved will form a strong bond and will develop an essential sense of trust. They are babies for such a very small part of their lives, and during that time, holding them, kissing them, rocking them, smiling and talking to them, and carrying them close to the body helps to fuel their growth and development.

In *Get Set for Life: Your Child's First Five Years*, the topic of reading and addressing babies' and children's cues is covered in some detail.

Reading Your Baby's Cues

Long before children can talk, they try to communicate by sending cues and clues about what they need, want, and feel. They learn about themselves through responses to what they are "saying."

According to *Growing with Your Child* (Ballantine Books of Canada, 1998), *Canadian Living's* parenting book, edited by Family Health and Family Matters director Christine Langlois, babies begin to develop the ability to respond to tone of voice and facial expressions even in the first few days. By two months, they begin to use sounds and to link them to the ways their parents respond to them.

To begin with, infants are totally dependent on adults or caregivers to meet their basic needs and for protection. They send signals to trigger responses to these needs, and they count on a consistent and healthy response. They begin to trust that when they are hungry, they will be fed; when they are upset, they will be comforted; when they are happy, adults and others in their lives will share their happiness.

Some children's clues are quite subtle, which means that parents or caregivers have to pay attention. But they soon understand what's being communicated when babies hold eye contact or turn away, how and when they move their arms and legs or arch their back, the type of cry or gurgle they make in different situations, and what they do when they are introduced to new people or new surroundings.

Learning to "read" babies is often fun and can seem easy. You smile, they smile. They reach out, you take their hand. But it can also be hard: if babies turn their head away when you speak, it feels awful. You want to speak louder and make them listen. But because they are overtired or overstimulated, or perhaps because they are particularly sensitive to noise, they may be telling you that they need your voice to be softer, not louder—or just to leave them be for the moment.

As you respond to children's needs and care for them, they are forming a "secure attachment" to you. According to Dr. Freda Martin, Director of The Hincks-Dellcrest Institute in Toronto, the pattern of this attachment becomes part of the brain's wiring and sets the basic model for future close relationships. It also influences a child's ability to actively explore and learn. Fundamentally, children need three things from a parent or caregiver:

1. **Responsive love and devotion.** Since babies experience relationships through their senses, lots of warm parental behaviour, cuddling, and eye contact are the ways to tell children that you love them. You cannot always be there when they need a hug, but do notice when they "ask" for one, and do your best to deliver.

2. **Safety and protection.** Naturally, you want to look after children's health and keep them from harm. At the same time, you want them to feel safe to explore and move around their world, testing and learning how it works. It is impossible to avoid occasional bumps and bruises, but when children feel loved and secure, they seem to stop hurting much more quickly.

3. **Attachment and security.** Children learn to count on predictable and reliable care from you for meeting their needs. This helps them feel confident and trusting enough to begin discovering the world around them—which gives them opportunities for new experiences and thus new connections in their busy brains. They know that you will be there when they come to show you something or to get a hug before they venture off again. They know that when you leave to go to work, you will return. They know that they can try new things because you will praise the progress they make, however small. When they do accomplish something, they will be so proud of their achievements. And those circuits will really light up when your cues and clues—or those of your partner, the children's grandparents, the day care worker, or another caring adult in their lives—make it plain that your pride matches theirs.

❖ Checkpoints

1. Compare breast-feeding to formula feeding in terms of convenience, benefits for mother and child, and long-term advantages.

2. List and describe specifically what needs to be childproofed in most kitchens, living rooms, and bedrooms?
3. How can you help infants to get adequate exercise?

Infant Development

Columbia Encyclopedia defines infancy as a "stage of human development lasting from birth to approximately two years of age. The hallmarks of infancy are physical growth, motor development, vocal development, and cognitive and social development."

Physical Growth

Rapid physical growth occurs in the first year. A normal baby doubles its birth weight in six months and triples it in a year. During that time, the organs (the brain, heart, and lungs) continue to develop. The bones begin to harden, and the **fontanels** (soft parts of the newborn skull) begin to close. Brain mass also increases rapidly during infancy. By the end of the second year, the brain has already reached 75 percent of its adult mass.

The newborn infant sleeps almost constantly, awakening only for feedings. The number and length of waking periods gradually increases, and by three months, some infants have a fairly regular schedule for sleeping, feeding, and bowel movements. By the end of the first year, sleeping and waking hours are divided about equally.

Breast milk or formula is the only food that most infants need for the first four to six months of life. Once they can digest solid food, they can be given cereal. Rice cereal is offered first because it is easiest to digest and is less likely to trigger allergic reactions. Cereal is followed by strained vegetables, strained fruits, and strained meats. By the end of the first year, children are using their fingers and a spoon for pieces of solid food. Breast milk, formula, or whole cow's milk is still required for a large part of their food intake until they are two. There is no room for empty calories in an infant's diet. Everything they eat should provide nourishment for their rapidly growing brain and body.

Motor development depends on muscle development and progresses from head to toe, and from large muscles to small muscles. The infant generally lifts its head, rolls over, discovers its hands and visually directs its movements, is able to sit, crawl, stand, and walk in that order. Motor development proceeds more rapidly than actual physical growth by the beginning of the second year.

Figure 11.14
Physical growth is rapid during the first year. Infants progress from sleeping almost constantly to long periods of wakefulness where they can control their body movements and begin to learn through play.

How Infants Grow and Develop

From head to toe. They can control their head and shoulders before they learn to walk.
From inside to outward. Their organs mature and function before they can control their arms and legs.
From large muscle to small muscle. They can run and jump before they can colour or use scissors.

Figure 11.15
Cereal and other solids can gradually be added to the infant diet.

Figure 11.16
Toys with dials and knobs encourage small motor development.

To encourage large or gross motor muscle development, children need room to move around and should be given opportunities to use their arms, legs, and torsos. Climbers, tunnels, and ride-on-toys are good choices. To encourage small motor muscle development, they need to be able to manipulate things with their hands. Shape sorters and toys that have buttons to push and knobs to turn promote small motor development.

Normal, healthy infants may be delayed in one or more developmental activities, or may apparently skip a stage altogether. Infants tend to focus on one particular area of development. For that reason, they may be more interested in talking than in walking, or vice versa.

Bowel and bladder control are related to physical maturity, and become possible after 18 to 24 months. Many parents, however, wisely delay toilet training until after age two.

Cognitive Development and Language Acquisition

In infancy, huge strides in language development occur. Infants have a sense of language and even grammar long before they can talk in complete sentences. They begin to vocalize by crying, and then add what are called frontal vowel sounds such as "da da" or "ba ba" at about three months of age. This is known as the "babbling milestone." Somewhere between 12 and 18 months, babies start to use these earliest sounds or phonemes to duplicate the sounds they hear around them. Local dialects and accents are reflected in this earliest speech.

Soon, the remaining vowel and consonant sounds gradually begin to appear. First babies babble, then repeat sounds. By about 12 to 18 months of age, the first recognizable single words appear and should sound like the language the baby is hearing. By the end of the second year, the infant's active vocabulary may reach 250 words. Fascinating research reported in *The Scientist in the Crib* indicates that if an infant does not hear a sound spoken, he will not be able to say it as an adult. Languages such as Chinese, Korean, and Japanese, for example, do not contain the sound "rrr" as in "rice." As a result, adult speakers have a difficult time saying "rice." Scientists theorize that neural connections that were not developed in infancy will not be regained in adulthood. This supports the view that the time to learn a second language is early in life.

Lev Vygotsky, a Russian doctor who studied children's cognitive development and language acquisition, determined that grown-ups have a great deal to do with what children know. He suggested that children, especially in the development of language, use parents and other adults

■ Cognitive scientists who study how humans learn are just beginning to understand how babies develop speech or cognition. Electronic scans such as CAT, MRI, and PET allow scientists to observe the brain at work, and this has greatly advanced what is known about learning. However, this science is in its early stages, and it could take years to find out exactly what infants know.

as learning tools. Through social interaction, parents naturally encourage language development by repeating sounds, playing rhyming and word games, modelling correct usage, using point-and-say activities and singsongs, and reading aloud to their children. The human voice not only provides infants with a model for the language they will need to learn, but it continues to forge the bond that began with the very first words spoken to the child during pregnancy and after birth.

Mem Fox, the internationally recognized Australian literacy expert, hypothesizes that children who are read three stories a day will learn to read sooner and more easily than children who do not have this advantage.

❖ Connections

1. Listen to how early childhood educators, kindergarten teachers, or parents encourage children to use and develop their language skills. Demonstrate these techniques for the class.
2. Share the nursery rhymes, songs, and games you learned as a child.
3. Bring in one of your favourite short stories or children's book, or select one from your local library, and read it to the class.

Emotional Development

Infants show their emotions mainly by crying. They have at least three different types of cries, which caregivers learn to distinguish. The most common cry signals hunger, while the other two cries signal anger and pain. They can also show distress, disgust, and surprise. Infants soon develop a wider range of emotions. Pleasure, happiness, fear, and frustration are shown through gurgles, coos, wails, and cries. They are also shown through physical movements such as, kicking, arm waving, rocking, and smiling.

Sometime around 8 to10 months, infants become shy or fearful around strangers. This has been called **stranger anxiety**. Infants at this age will sometimes cling to their mother or father and will not want to be held or even touched by an unfamiliar person. Stranger anxiety can last well into the toddler years, but usually disappears by age two. Stranger anxiety is very common, and it is a sign that your child has formed a strong attachment.

By 18 months, infants develop a sense of self, recognize their image in a mirror, and begin to become independent from their parents and caregivers. At this age, they often have a broad range of emotional states. One minute they may be happy and playing, and the next they may be lying on the floor crying. They continue to need their parents' love and support during these difficult months.

Social Development

All areas of children's development are interrelated. Physical maturity contributes significantly to social development. Around three months of age, the reflexes start to disappear and the cortex of the brain awakens, as evidenced by the infant's ability to smile deliberately, or repeat an action or sound. Growing awareness of people and objects leads to increased interaction with the world. Interaction with loving others, improved control over muscles, and the development of language all help the infant form concepts and understand the world.

The first two years of life offer an amazing beginning for human development. Whether you are a first-time parent or a parent of several children, infant development is a fascinating experience. Infancy is but a brief time in a human life, but it requires the nurture and attentive response of at least one adult who is absolutely in love with that little person. This devoted response and interaction develops a blueprint for forming positive relationships for the rest of one's lives.

Just as a healthy attachment to a loving, nurturing parent has profound importance for lifelong development, unhealthy relationships between parents and children also have long-term implications. Sigmund Freud, considered the "father of psychology," was the first to point out that our personality is affected to a large extent by our earliest relationship with our parents. In his psychoanalysis, he studied adults who had problems later in life and was able to trace their problems to early parental behaviour. Freud's work from the late 19th and early 20th century has influenced the research of many psychologists and sociologists. Although many do not agree completely with his theories, there is common agreement on one central theme. Children who are neglected, abused, or treated with indifference often have problems with anger and interpersonal behaviour later in life. Alcoholism, drug abuse, and even suicide have been attributed to unhealthy relationships early in life. Most of the research into deviant and pathological personality disorders in our society illustrates that many people with these disorders did not have a good relationship with a significant person early in life.

Some children can recover if their circumstances change for the better, or if they get extensive counselling, but many will be lost to society forever. This provides a strong case for parents who are able to establish and maintain a loving, healthy, and vital interaction with their children from the beginning.

■ Infancy is a brief time in a human life. It requires the nurture and attentive responses of at least one adult who is absolutely in love with that child.

Figure 11.17
A healthy attachment to a loving, nurturing parent has a profound influence on lifelong development.

❖ Checkpoints

1. Describe the three ways that infants grow and develop physically.
2. What kinds of parent-child activities contribute to small and large muscle development?
3. How will a caregiver know what response to give to the different cries an infant makes?

Chapter Summary

Chapter Highlights

- The quality of life in infancy has long-term implications for the rest of a person's life. It is essential to understand the critical nature of the first year of life.

- Healthy newborns may look helpless, wrinkled, and misshapen, but they have many reflexes and sensory capabilities that ensure their survival.

- Bonding and attachment with at least one significant loving adult ensures survival and promotes growth and development.

- Parents have an important role in infant bonding and infant separation.

- Attachment theorists Harry Harlow, John Bowlby, and Mary Ainsworth state that attachment provides the grounding for life-long progress.

- A strong attachment encourages parents to respond positively to the needs of infants early in life, which contributes to healthy growth, motor development, cognitive and vocal development, emotional development, and social development.

- Healthy parent-child relationships early in life are necessary for positive lifelong development.

- Parenting in the first year of life is concerned in large part with meeting the infant's basic needs of food, safety, warmth, sleep, exercise, and cleanliness.

- Physical growth and intellectual, social, and emotional development in the first year occur in clearly identifiable stages.

Review and Extend Your Learning

1. Explain, using examples, how an infant's early development relates to later life. **K/U**

2. Speculate on why most infant reflexes do not last for very long. **K/U**

3. Compare and contrast the attachment theories of Harlow, Bowlby, and Ainsworth. **K/U** **T/I**

4. Some infants experience "regression" after a separation from their parents. What purpose does regression serve in this case? What other childhood experiences could trigger regressive behaviour? **K/U** **A**

5. List and describe the basic physical needs of infants. Describe how a parent could meet those needs effectively. **K/U** **A**

6. Write a short "advice" column for mothers who are unable to breast-feed. **C** **A**

7. Analyze the infant's language acquisition process, and suggest ways that parents can enhance language learning. **K/U** **T/I**

8. Alcoholism, drug abuse, and even suicide have been attributed to unhealthy relationships early in life. Investigate one of these negative behaviours to discover the frequency and extent of these connections. **T/I**

Research Opportunities

9. Using Internet sources, professional journals, or other resources, locate a study that relates some aspect of "early development" to "later life." Write an annotated bibliography entry for the study, which includes all the following elements:
   • a complete reference of the source (author, date, title of publication, where published and by whom or where available online, number of pages)
   • a brief summary of the article or study including who did it, when, and where. How many people were studied? What were the findings?
   • an outline of the implications of the study for parents and caregivers

10. The diaper debate revolves around which kind of diaper is the best choice for the environment and the baby. Using interviews and library research, separate the facts from the opinions regarding which kind of diaper to use. Based on your research, determine which kind you would choose.

11. Examine the literature on toilet training or potty teaching to determine which techniques are recommended and which techniques are discouraged. Interview a grandparent or older community member to compare toilet training techniques recommended in the past with those recommended now.

Issue Analysis

12. John Bowlby's work on attachment theory has raised concerns about how soon women should return to work after the baby is born. Develop arguments for and against a mother's return to work before the child's first birthday.

Growth and Development in Early Childhood

By the end of this chapter, you will be able to:

- appreciate the multifaceted nature of and the various influences on child development

- identify the role parents play in how children form relationships within and outside the family

- describe environments provided by families, caregivers, and others that offer positive conditions for child development

- explain the patterns in the social, emotional, intellectual, moral, and physical development of children

- evaluate your own practical experiences involving children

- identify and describe the challenges facing parents throughout the early childhood years

- evaluate the significance of neuroscience and theories of brain development during critical periods in early childhood

Important Terms

age-appropriate

emotional intelligence

environmental deprivation

growth spurt

learning environment

left-brain dominant

manipulation

numeracy skills

nurturance

problem solving

right-brain dominate

sense of autonomy

Chapter at a Glance

Figure 12.1
How much have these children changed from when they were babies?

What Distinguishes the Early Years?

Consider how much children change from birth to age five. They develop from infant, to toddler, to preschool child. The totally dependent newborn, curled up in the fetal position, grows into an upright, well-developed child who can walk, talk, run, climb, read some words, cut with scissors, print letters, eat, bathe, and dress without help, who can also make a bed, feed the cat, carry on a conversation, and who may even ride a two-wheeler. What an incredible change! Everything the child has learned, mastered, and experienced in the first five years has already shaped a unique individual.

Assuming that the prenatal period has been healthy in all respects, how a person faces the world, gets along with others, and continues to learn and grow is determined largely by what happens in the first five years of life. This time is marked by rapid growth and development of the human brain. Incredible leaps in learning result from this brain development. Parenting in the early years is more important than at any other time of a child's life. "The years before five last the rest of their lives" (Invest In Kids Foundation, 2001).

During the first five years of life, parents influence the long-term emotional and physical well-being of their children. They provide the foundation for their children's intellectual growth and learning. They furnish the framework for their children's selfhood. Parenting shapes the person a child will become. In fact, a quote from the Canadian Institute of Child Health echoes that of the Invest in Kids Foundation: "The early years last forever!"

What the experts say

DR. CAROL CRILL RUSSELL

Dr. Carol Crill Russell is the Vice-President of Research and Programs for the Invest in Kids Foundation. She answers the following question:

Why do the "years before five last the rest of a person's life?"

Research such as the Canadian National Longitudinal Survey of Children and Youth (NLSCY) shows that the first five years are pivotal in a child's ability to learn and create, to love, to trust and to develop a strong and positive sense of themselves. This is because most of the brain development in humans takes place after birth, much of it in the first five years of life. If this opportunity is taken, the positive consequences are lifelong. Conversely, if this opportunity is misused or lost, the negative effects are long lasting. How we care for our young children in their earliest years has a major impact on how productive, resilient, compassionate, and confident they will be as adults.

The NLSCY shows the importance of effective parenting. For instance, children of a lone but effective parent are five times *less* likely to have major behavioural problems than children of two parents who are hostile or ineffective. Sometimes we call effective parenting positive parenting. Positive parenting of young children can be simply described as comforting, playing with, and teaching a child in a way that is consistent with his or her developmental stage and temperament. Positive parenting has been shown to reduce the odds of a child developing a conduct disorder by 25 percent, developing an emotional disorder by 40 percent, and repeating a grade at school by 50 percent. These outcomes are certainly worth working hard to achieve.

It is myth that humans instinctively know how to parent or provide child care effectively. This is a set of skills that must be learned. But it is not difficult to learn parenting skills. First, parents must become aware of the temperament of their child, and how it matches with their own preferred styles of relating to people. Then parents need to know about the stage of development that goes along with the age of their child. Then parents or caregivers can find out which comfort, play, and teach techniques will work best at that stage to help the child reach the critical milestones in development common to that stage.

Our research at Invest in Kids has shown us that 92 percent of all Canadians with children under six think that being a parent is their most important activity. This is the good news. However, a big concern is that most parents have very limited knowledge about how children grow and develop and are very anxious and concerned that their parenting skills are not good enough.

As important and serious as the role of being an effective parent or caregiver is, we have to remember that young children are basically delightful, and most parent-child interaction can be fun. In fact, it should be fun! Children are only young once. Any seasoned parent will say that the miraculous first five years pass by in a flash. Enjoy them while you can.

❖ Connections

1. The Invest in Kids Foundation and The Canadian Institute of Child Health are organizations both devoted to promoting the best in the development, health, and well-being of children. Visit the Web sites of both organizations. Prepare a brief review of each Web site describing the mission of the organization, basic beliefs, and materials available for professionals and parents.

Age-Related Stages of Child Development

During the early years, parenting and development go hand in hand. Parents and caregivers need to know what they can reasonably expect of children of all ages and stages of development. They need to understand what children can and cannot do, what milestones to look for in

Long-Term Benefits

According to Clyde Hertzman, M.D., at the University of British Columbia, the period from preconception to age five can be referred to as the "investment phase" for child development. Research shows that this period is much more important than was previously realized. Failure to provide optimum conditions for a child's development during this time makes the developing brain physically different from the brain of children who have been well-nurtured, and these differences can have lifelong consequences.
— *Early Years Last Forever*

their development, and how to contribute to their learning at every stage. Even the kind of comfort they offer when children are upset will encourage learning and reinforce the attachment needed for continued development. The main activity of parenting or caregiving during the years from 0 to 5 is **nurturance**.

Nurturing young children effectively involves teaching, comforting, and playing with the young child in keeping with the child's levels of development. As pointed out by Carol Crill Russell in What the Experts Say on page 286, parents and caregivers need to be aware of the typical developmental achievements related to different ages and then tailor their nurturing efforts to these milestones. No one parent or caregiver needs to be good at all three areas of nurturance, but somewhere in the immediate circle of significant other people (parents, grandparents, caregivers, a neighbour, any caring adult), the child should be able find someone who can teach, comfort, and play appropriately, given the typical developmental milestones that the child should be reaching.

Although progress continues in all areas of development, including social, cognitive, language, emotional, and gross- and fine-motor skills, there will be times when parents notice a child making more progress in one area than in another. Sometimes, children put more effort into one area of development, and when that is mastered, they can work on another area. Some children may be more interested in learning words, or stacking blocks, while others the same age are more interested in running and climbing. As long as there is a general progression, parents should not worry.

Almost every parent will question whether his or her child is making normal progress along the developmental continuum. A medical practitioner or pediatrician can answer any parental concerns. In regular check-ups, these professionals will be able to determine if your child is developing normally. Generally, most concerns do not turn out to be serious, and a child who lags in some areas will catch up to peers in time.

The Invest in Kids Foundation provides an overview of child development from birth to the sixth year of life. They provide details of the developmental stages and offer guidance to parents, caregivers, and early childhood educators to contribute in a positive way to a child's development. We have reproduced pages from the foundation's booklet, *What a child will be depends on you and me: A resource kit for a child's first five years*, in the Appendix on page 463 of this book. This Appendix outlines developmental information for the following age categories:

The three areas of nurturance are:
- teaching
- comforting
- playing

Caregiving activities in each area must be appropriate to the child's level of development.

Career Capsule

PEDIATRICIAN

Tasks and Responsibilities

Pediatricians are doctors who specialize in the care of children of all ages. They diagnose and treat injuries, infections, and diseases. They also counsel their patients who have family problems or problems relating to puberty.

To treat patients, the pediatrician uses physical exams and information obtained from patients' medical histories, and examines the results of special tests, such as X-rays and blood tests. After diagnosis, treatment programs may involve medication, surgery, rehabilitation, or counselling. To complete the diagnosis and decide upon treatment, a pediatrician often communicates with social workers, family members, and health-care professionals (such as nurses and specialists). The role of pediatricians is becoming more important as psychological and social conditions worsen for many children.

Work Environment

Pediatricians treat patients from infancy through adolescence, and can often be found working in community offices and clinics. Pediatricians may also get involved in teaching and research, or become involved in the community to promote children's interests (for example, through organizations against child abuse).

Like other doctors, pediatricians work very long hours, especially at the beginning of their careers. Most average between 9 and 12 hours a day, 45 to 65 hours a week. They may have very irregular work schedules and may often work evenings and Saturdays to accommodate patients.

Education and Aptitudes

To be a pediatrician, compassion, patience, and a love of children are essential. It may be a good idea to do volunteer work with children to see if working with them suits you.

Most medical schools require applicants to have a minimum of two to three years of university education, including the successful completion of several key science courses. A medical degree takes four years, and that is followed by three to four years of residency in pediatrics. Successful completion of medical licensing exams provides certification by the Royal College of Physicians and Surgeons of Canada.

- birth to 6 months
- 6 months to 18 months
- 1 ½ to 2 ½ years
- 2 ½ to 3 ½ years
- 3 ½ to 4 ½ years
- 4 ½ to 5 ½ years

Following each of these pages is a summary of games and activities that foster child development in the areas of social, cognitive, language, emotional, gross motor, and fine motor.

❖ Checkpoints

1. Using the Appendix material from Invest in Kids, summarize in your own words where an 18-month-old, a 3-year-old, and a 5-year-old are in their emotional, social, and cognitive development.

2. How should parental or caregiver behaviour change in terms of comforting, playing with, and teaching children throughout the first six years of life?

3. Identify what you feel are the five most important achievements in language development from birth to 5 ½ years. Support your view with references to Invest in Kids: The Essentials of Development.

❖ Connections

Based on the Invest in Kids description of development, design an observation checklist that identifies developmental accomplishments for a given year of life between birth and age six. Compare your checklist with those designed for other age-related stages by other students, and make adjustments if necessary.

1. Use your checklist while observing children of that age category in either a classroom or community setting.

2. Compare your observations with those of students who observed children of other age categories, and identify the variations in development from birth to age six.

Growth in the First Five Years

Have you ever noticed how quickly children grow in the early years? For example, in the first six months, children grow so quickly that they may outgrow a sleeper or an undershirt within a week or two. However, no two children are alike, and their growth depends on both the adequacy of their nutrition and their inherited body type. Some children are dainty, and some are stocky. Nutritious food, exercise from active play, nature walks, or outdoor activities, and adequate rest are important for a growing child.

Children grow faster in the spring and slower in the winter. A parent can tell if a child is experiencing a **growth spurt** by the child's increased hunger. Likewise, growth slows from time to time, especially after the first birthday, when a child may suddenly not be eating as much. Children are the ones who know when they are hungry. Forcing them to eat when their growth has slowed may result in unnecessary struggles and promote unnecessary weight gain.

Figure 12.2
No two children are alike when it comes to physical growth.

Mealtimes

Mealtimes bring together many areas of development for young children. Food is essential for physical growth as well as brain growth, and it plays a role in effective learning. Social development is encouraged when families share a meal, as parents, siblings, and extended family members interact and teach acceptable manners. Language is practised when different foods and utensils are named. Mealtimes contribute to emotional development, since food represents "caring for" and love and belonging in many families. Fine-motor development is especially important as children learn to chew, hold a cup or spoon, manage to pick up small pieces of food with their fingers, and eventually learn to feed themselves without any help.

Not all children in Canada get adequate food. Some do not have the privilege of sitting down to a family meal. A hungry child may signify poverty, but it may also signify inadequate nurturing. Parental depression, alcoholism, or drug dependency may contribute to neglect that results in both immediate and long-term negative effects on a child's growth and development and ability to learn.

Figure 12.3
Most children want to feed themselves and learn from the experience.

❖ Connections

1. Children under the age of four can easily be overwhelmed with the amount of food parents give them. They need food that counts for its nutrient content without contributing empty calories. A serving size for a child is the size of his or her hand. Be creative and prepare a nutritious snack or lunch that includes appropriate serving sizes of healthy foods that would appeal to a child younger than age four.

2. Research a food-related problem that parents of young children may have. Write a report that names and describes the problem, outlines the symptoms and issues that need to be resolved, and makes recommendations for parents or caregivers. Choose from topics such as lactose intolerance, peanut, gluten, or other food allergies, celiac disease, picky eaters, PKU (a specific vitamin or mineral absorption problem), or juvenile diabetes.

Leaps in Learning

If teenagers or adults need to learn the things that children learn in the first five years of life (for example, after an accident that results in a brain injury, or after a stroke), they have difficulty doing so. In the first five years of life, children learn an entire language, including its vocabulary and grammatical structure. They learn the name and function of every object in their environment, from toys to toilets and everything in between, and they also learn how to use and manipulate most of them. Preschoolers learn concepts like hot and cold, before and after, today and tomorrow, boy and girl. In fact, they learn so much that researchers continue to study how children's brains really work.

Brain researchers have known for some time that different areas of the brain control different skills. There is a centre in the brain where language development takes place, and another centre in the brain for mathematics or **numeracy skills** such as number recognition and number concepts.

It is commonly understood that the right side of the brain is the centre for creativity and language, while the left side of the brain is the centre for logic and mathematics. Women are considered more **right-brain dominant**, while men are considered more **left-brain dominant**. It is important to note that men and women use both sides of their brain, even though there may be a gender-related dominance. As people learn, they perceive and process information differently depending on the side of the brain that dominates the process. Another significant characteristic of the brain is that it can sometimes be retrained if it has been damaged.

Cognitive scientists who study the brain have learned that different neural paths are formed in the brain early in life. By using the pathways over and over again, a person can make better use of the information stored in the brain. The way the pathways develop in young children is through the very things they love to do. Repetition, rhymes, songs, and games help build those pathways. Shared conversation that involves both talking and listening is essential from the moment of birth.

Reading to a child is also critical for developing the neural connections that lead to literacy. Mem Fox (2000) urges parents and caregivers to read three stories a day to all young children, starting in infancy. Children love to have the same stories read to them over and over again. This repetition helps them learn how language works, while attachments are strengthened through the proximity of reader and child. These factors help ensure that the child will be "ready to learn" when he or she enters the formal school system. Fox emphasizes that parents need no special talents to read to their children and should not attempt to teach their child to read. Just having fun reading together is all that is needed.

Figure 12.4
Reading to a child consistently and frequently helps to enhance the child's readiness for school.

Career Capsule

CHILDREN'S WRITER

Tasks and Responsibilities

Children's writers have the task of writing material for children that will "turn them on" to reading and literacy. Authors hold the key to the door of a special place—the world of being able to read for fun. Children's writers put together stories that will engage the imaginations of children and start them down the road to being lifelong readers.

Children's writers need to be aware of the ages and stages of children's development so that they can focus in on the actual issues and concerns of children at different ages. For example, dealing with bullies or getting along with others are concerns for school-age children, whereas going to the hospital or getting a new sibling will be of more interest to younger children. Fiction writers need to be able to create characters and situations that either reflect children's worlds and help them learn about it or give them a glimpse of real or imaginary places that they might not otherwise visit. Writers of children's books need to value and respect their audience.

Work Environment

Most children's writers work on a freelance (contract) basis. They can arrange their own hours and usually work at home. Some have other jobs and write as a hobby. If they are successful, the hobby may turn into a job. This is the dream of many part-time writers.

Children's literature often is illustrated. For many children, the visual element is almost more important than the words. Children's writers or their publishers work closely with the artists who illustrate their work. They need to communicate effectively with each other so the art conveys what the author wants.

Education and Aptitudes

Children's writers are well read. Demonstrated language skills and an active imagination are essential. Computer literacy and ability to manage desktop publishing are also an advantage. Writers must also have self-discipline and be able to meet deadlines. Editors and publishers require written work on time.

No formal post-secondary education is required to be a children's writer. Writing comes naturally to most good writers. However, most high-school graduates can benefit from further training to help their talents blossom. Some avenues of post-secondary education to consider include a degree in English literature, creative writing, or journalism. In a salaried position, say for a children's magazine, a degree would likely be required.

Children need activities, games, and toys that stimulate their senses. From the time they are born, they look intently at their parent's face and stare at people, animals, objects, and pictures. They listen with delight to songs, rhymes, and nonsense sounds, and follow their parent's hands in clapping games. They reach out and touch things to find out how they feel, from the softness of a puppy's fur, to the hardness of car keys. They enjoy smell, but none so much as the

Figure 12.5
A child learns from repeated actions and sensory stimulation.

smell of their own father or mother. They recognize what tastes good to them and make faces at what tastes bad. With every experience from their five senses, they learn something new.

❖ Checkpoints

1. What indicators show that a child may be going through a growth spurt?
2. How do the left and right hemispheres of the brain operate differently?
3. Describe some of the benefits of reading to children.

Environments for Learning

A positive **learning environment** is one that allows infants, toddlers, and preschoolers to safely explore using all of their senses. Physical safety is very important. Getting down to a child's level in a play area to look for choking hazards, sharp edges, breakable items, and other objects that are often taken for granted is critical to prevent injuries. The play area does not have to be elaborate or costly because children learn from everyday things. They need visual stimulation, the opportunity to hear language and music, and, above all, physical contact. A child's favourite toy is a parent as they gaze at each other, face to face, making noises, silly faces, and silly sounds.

What looks like play to an adult is a serious learning activity for a child. If you observe children at play, you see that they prefer different activities, games, and toys at different ages. If an activity is not **age-appropriate**—that is, if it is too difficult or too easy for the child—then the child becomes frustrated or bored. Learning occurs when the child is fully engaged in the activity for a period of time. Boredom and frustration do not promote learning.

Children also learn by solving problems on their own. Very young children begin to figure out how things work. They may try several different options before they find out how to do something effectively. By providing children with toys and objects that require **manipulation**, every time they figure out how to turn, push, slide, open, or close, parents are encouraging the beginning of problem-solving skills. Each success or failure registers in the brain. **Problem solving** stimulates thinking and reasoning skills and enables the child to store and retrieve information. As children reach school age, they need more challenging problems and activities to continue their learning process.

❖ Connections

1. Plan and evaluate an activity that would engage a pre-schooler socially, cognitively, and emotionally while encouraging language and motor skills. What modifications would be needed to make the activity developmentally appropriate for toddlers?

2. Plan an indoor learning centre that would encourage learning in children ages two to four years. Explain what a two-year-old, three-year-old, and four-year-old would be learning as they play at the centre you designed.

Environmental Deprivation

Researchers have found that if children are not exposed to language early in life but are taught to speak later on, they will never fully master it. If children do not learn to make certain sounds because they do not exist in the language patterns they hear, they will have difficulty making those sounds later in life. For neural pathways to develop fully, they need to be used. Other parts of the brain can take over if some functions are lost, but not to the extent that the original learning experience offers. Think of the saying "use it or lose it": it applies perfectly to the first five years of life.

The same holds true for all learning. If you were deprived of the use of any of your senses in infancy, you would find it very difficult to learn later in life. Some children will not have the same opportunity as others to learn because of this type of **environmental deprivation**. In fact, many scientists believe in "windows of opportunity" in the first years of life. These are critical or sensitive periods of time when the brain requires certain types of stimuli to create the brain structures that will last throughout the rest of life. These critical periods are explained in detail in the Windows of Opportunity feature on page 296. Parents need to be aware of this research to provide appropriate experiences for children as their brains develop. If children live in an environment with a lack of visual stimulation, limited exposure to language and books, or even minimal physical contact, they will be significantly disadvantaged. Deprivation may result from poverty, parental indifference, or lack of understanding. What a child does not learn in the first five years of life will be that much harder to learn later on in life.

Figure 12.6
What senses are these children developing with this activity?

Windows of Opportunity

Wiring Vision

WHAT'S GOING ON Babies can see at birth but not in fine-grained detail. They have not yet acquired the knack of focusing both eyes on a single object or developed more sophisticated visual skills like depth perception. They also lack hand-eye coordination.

WHAT PARENTS CAN DO There is no need to buy high-contrast black-and-white toys to stimulate vision. Regular eye exams, starting as early as two weeks of age, can detect problems that, if left uncorrected, can cause a weak or unused eye to lose its functional connections to the brain.

WINDOW OF LEARNING Unless it is exercised early on, the visual system will not develop.

	Age (in years)										
	Birth	1	2	3	4	5	6	7	8	9	10
Visual acuity											
Binocular vision											

Wiring Feelings

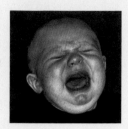

WHAT'S GOING ON Among the first circuits the brain constructs are those that govern the emotions. Beginning around two months of age, the distress and contentment experienced by newborns start to evolve into more complex feelings: joy and sadness, envy and empathy, pride and shame.

WHAT PARENTS CAN DO Loving care provides a baby's brain with the right kind of emotional support. Neglecting a baby can produce brain-wave patterns that dampen happy feelings. Abuse can produce heightened anxiety and abnormal stress responses.

WINDOW OF LEARNING Emotions develop in layers, each more complex than the last.

	Age (in years)										
	Birth	1	2	3	4	5	6	7	8	9	10
Stress response											
Empathy, envy											

Wiring Language

WHAT'S GOING ON Even before birth, an infant is tuning in to the melody of its mother's voice. Over the next six years, its brain sets up the circuitry needed to decipher—and reproduce—the lyrics. A six-month-old can recognize the vowel sounds that are the basic building blocks of speech.

WHAT PARENTS CAN DO Talking to a baby a lot, researchers have found, significantly speeds up the process of learning new words. The high-pitched, singsong speech style known as Parentese helps babies connect objects with words.

WINDOW OF LEARNING Language skills are sharpest early on but grow throughout life.

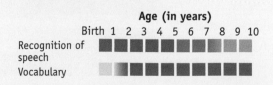

	Age (in years)										
	Birth	1	2	3	4	5	6	7	8	9	10
Recognition of speech											
Vocabulary											

Wiring Movement

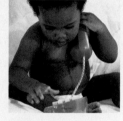

WHAT'S GOING ON At birth, babies can move their limbs, but in a jerky, uncontrolled fashion. Over the next four years, the brain progressively refines the circuits for reaching, grabbing, sitting, crawling, walking, and running.

WHAT PARENTS CAN DO Give babies as much freedom to explore as safety permits. Just reaching for an object helps the brain develop hand-eye coordination. As soon as children are ready for them, activities like drawing and playing a violin or piano encourage the development of fine-motor skills.

WINDOW OF LEARNING Motor skill development moves from gross to increasingly fine.

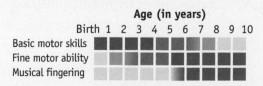

	Age (in years)										
	Birth	1	2	3	4	5	6	7	8	9	10
Basic motor skills											
Fine motor ability											
Musical fingering											

Becoming a Person

In the transition from infant, to toddler, to preschooler, a personality within the child is taking shape. Infants do not distinguish themselves from their primary caregiver in the first weeks of life, but as they become more aware of their surroundings and begin to deliberately interact with their environment, they begin to behave in ways that show and invite interaction.

The first social interaction that thrills parents is a baby's smile at around six weeks. Then there are sounds and cries that bring a response. This early social interaction between parents and infants forges the strong connection of attachment. Parents who respond appropriately and consistently to a child's attachment behaviour, which may include crying, clinging, or wanting to be close to the parent, provide the security infants need to interact with the world. Parents communicate their love and reassurance to their children in both verbal and non-verbal ways.

It is not always easy to know exactly what a child's signals mean. Sometimes parents are unable to respond appropriately. Sometimes they expect the same behaviour from a second child who is a totally different individual and may, therefore, miss the baby's cues. If the baby does not get the response that is needed, problems may eventually develop. Child psychologists have traced sleep disorders, eating disorders, and behaviour problems in some children to an insecure attachment to a primary caregiver. Counselling can help parents learn how to recognize and respond to a child's cues for cuddling, holding, conversation, and interaction. When a child regains the security that was missing, the troublesome behaviours often disappear.

Becoming Social

Around eighteen months, children begin to develop what Erik Erikson called a **sense of autonomy**, a period when they begin to form a sense of self. Words like "me" and "mine" become important. They insist on doing many things by themselves, and they begin to copy the actions of others. Often, older children at home or in playgroups are imitated and admired. Children who still have a secure attachment to a parent or caregiver will venture away from them to try out their new skills, but will come back for a hug or a cuddle, or will look back for reassurance.

Figure 12.7
At 18 months, children start imitating and admiring older children.

Erikson's Developmental Theory

The psychologist Erik H. Erikson (1902–1994) proposed a theory of the social aspects of psychological development. His theory showed a progression through eight stages from infancy to old age. The theory states that humans face a basic psychosocial conflict at each stage of life, which must be resolved before one can move on positively to the next stage. Erikson argued that failure to complete the task effectively leads to unhealthy development. Since parents have an active role in their children's development through most of these stages, they can assist with each developmental task.

Stage	Age	Developmental Conflict and Task
Infancy	0–1 year	**Trust vs. Mistrust** Children learn to trust others and feel secure in the world when parents are able to maintain a supportive, nurturing, and loving environment.
Toddler	1–3 Years	**Autonomy vs. Doubt** Children learn to develop a healthy attitude toward independence and partial self-sufficiency. If children are made to feel that their independent efforts are wrong, then shame and doubt are likely to develop.
Preschool Child	3–5 1/2 Years	**Initiative vs. Guilt** Children learn to act with a sense of purpose and to initiate actions on their own. If these initiatives are mostly successful, a sense of guilt will be avoided.
School-Age Child	5 1/2–12 Years	**Industry vs. Inferiority** Children learn to work hard to develop their skills and talents. This produces a feeling of competence, especially when dealing with their peers. Failure can result in a sense of inferiority.
Adolescence		**Identity vs. Role Confusion** Adolescents develop a sense of who they are, what they can do, and where they are going in life. Selecting a future career direction is an important activity during this period.
Early Adulthood		**Intimacy vs. Isolation** Young adults learn to integrate their life with the lives of others. The formation of close friendships and adult sexual relationships is vital to healthy development.
Middle Adulthood		**Generativity vs. Stagnation** Adults develop useful lives at this stage by helping and guiding others. The person at this stage provides an example to the next generation. Adults without children of their own can develop generativity in other close relationships with children.
Later Adulthood		**Ego Integrity vs. Despair** Adults review their life in this stage. Persons need to accept their life as it has been with all its joys and disappointments. A life well spent will result in a feeling of well-being and integrity.

The strong bond of attachment that was so important for infant development also provides a secure base for three- and four-year-olds, who begin to form attachments with other children and adults outside their family. Being able to come back to a strong connection with their own parents after being with others allows the child to regain a sense of security. As a child becomes older, parents can maintain a warm attachment by talking, reading, singing, and paying special attention.

Communication is the foundation of social development. Before children can speak fluently, they communicate their feelings and desires with cues that parents need to interpret. Some parents are teaching children to use sign language before they can talk. As language develops, children are able to connect with children their own age as well as other adults. Children, who have learned to communicate with their parents and who know how to take turns talking and listening find it easier to form relationships with others.

Changing Emotions

The charts in the Appendix on page 463 from *Invest in Kids: What a child will be depends on you and me: A resource kit for a child's first five years* indicate that infants in the first six months exhibit a range of emotions, including sadness, anger, happiness, and excitement. Parents help children express and control emotions. Touch and a soothing voice help to calm a crying infant. Comforting teaches babies how to quiet down until they learn how to calm themselves after being upset. Sometimes children quiet down more easily for one parent than the other. For example, they may respond more quickly to the low deep tones of a male voice. Having more than one person in the family, or having support in the community, helps when some emotions overwhelm one parent. Parents need to understand that children may be frightened when they feel strong emotions that they do not understand, and that they will need to be comforted.

The brain actually produces different chemicals when emotions are aroused. As children respond to their emotions, the brain develops response patterns. Having a good cry is sometimes all a child needs to release emotions, regain control, and move on.

Children who learn to express emotions in an appropriate way, who learn to use words instead of tantrums, and who are allowed to express negative emotions in the safety of their family will be able to face stressful situations in a healthier way. Being able to say "This is frust-er-ating!" may help a five-year-old persist at difficult tasks like riding a two-wheeler or tying shoelaces. Otherwise, discouragement may set in, preventing a child from attempting new learning. Children

Figure 12.8
Sometimes children quiet down more easily for one parent than another.

Emotional Intelligence

John Mayer and Peter Salovey, two American university professors, first published journal articles in 1990 that described **emotional intelligence** (EI). They also developed a test to measure emotional intelligence based on such things as the ability of individuals to

- recognize and identify their own emotions
- recognize and identify the feelings of others
- solve emotional problems

Identifying with the feelings of others is called **empathy** and is learned from parents as they demonstrate empathy toward their children.

Daniel Golemen used the term for the title of his 1995 book *Emotional Intelligence*, which made EI a popular concept. The idea that some people have a higher emotional intelligence—that is, are able to handle their emotions effectively, feel empathy for others, and handle emotional situations better than others—made it a popular notion for the business world. Having a high emotional intelligence quotient became a marker for a person's success in business and industry.

need to be able to feel and express emotions before they can control them. Punishing children for feeling emotions can lead to lower self-esteem and behaviour problems.

Culture may influence how children learn to express emotions. Some cultures are considered more emotional than others. What is acceptable in terms of expressing anger, pleasure, fear, or excitement may vary from one family to the next. Boys and girls may also be expected to handle emotions in different ways. In western societies, men and boys are discouraged from crying, while girls and women are allowed to cry. Concealing emotions may lead to social, emotional, and mental health problems later in life.

❖ Checkpoints

1. What happens when parents consistently misread their children's cues?
2. What role does communication play in social development?
3. How can parents encourage the qualities of emotional intelligence in very young children?
4. How can parents make use of Erikson's theory to help them parent effectively?

Promoting Healthy Development and School Readiness

Parenting during the early years is a huge responsibility and requires commitment and dedication. The first five years of life provide the foundation for future development, success in school, forming friendships

Figure 12.9
Culture influences how children learn to express emotions.

outside the family, and becoming a competent person in the world. Parents may find themselves turning to other parents, self-help books, parenting magazines, and parenting programs for answers and support.

Most societies are concerned about the education of their young people. If school success drives employment success, then it also contributes to the economic prosperity of the country. A child's success in school depends on many things, including fluency in the language of instruction, IQ, and a readiness to learn. Effective parenting in the first five years is directly related to eventual school success because the child is ready to learn. In the *Early Years Study, 1999*, Megan Gunner reported that "infants and toddlers who have experienced consistent, responsive, and sensitive care from secure attachments with their parents, tend to develop into socially competent preschoolers" (McCain & Mustard, 1999, p. 33). She noted that this social competence is closely related to readiness to learn.

Children must be equipped with knowledge, skills, and attitudes to proceed with learning in a formal educational setting. They need parents to foster their intellectual potential so that they have the foundations for acquiring literacy and numeracy skills. They need parents to support their emotional development so that they can behave and react appropriately in situations involving other children, as well as their teachers and other community members. They need parents to ensure proper nutrition, exercise, and rest to ensure optimal physical development. Most of all, they need parents to foster their sense of themselves and to help them develop positive self-esteem. Feeling that they are competent, capable, and worthwhile human beings will be the most important tool they have to work with in their future learning process.

What Is Readiness to Learn?

The child has:

- a healthy body and a good state of nutrition and rest
- no neurodevelopmental damage from alcohol, drug, or substance use by parent(s)
- excellent "brain wiring" with neurodevelopment consistent with age
- been read to and stimulated linguistically and is ready to learn to read
- good social development— able to get along with and cooperate with teachers and classmates
- the ability to control impulses, and the ability do what is expected and asked of them

Parenting Skills

The B.C. Council of Families, in cooperation with the Ministry of Health and Ministry for Children and Families, Province of British Columbia, has published a series of brochures for parents and educators that deals with children's development. The material below is reprinted from a brochure entitled "Your Child's Feelings."

Encouraging Self-Esteem

The definition of self-esteem is "belief in oneself." We know that children's ability to handle themselves and their world hinges on their sense of self-esteem. It is very important for parents to create an environment in which children's self-esteem can grow. How do we do this?

Figure 12.10
Give children the time they need to do things themselves.

Set the Stage for Success

The list of things children cannot do is so much longer than what they can do. Parents need to create an environment that makes success more possible. For example, they can place a sturdy stool in front of the sink so that children can wash their own hands. They can buy dishes that don't break when they're dropped on the way to setting the table, ride-on toys that don't easily tip, boots that are easy for a two-year-old to put on, and so on.

Let Them Do It Themselves

Parents should never do for children what they can do for themselves. Children may not do something as well or as quickly as a parent would, but they will get no sense of accomplishment if, for example, a parent puts on their shoes for them. Parents need to plan their activities with enough lead time for children to do everything they want to do for themselves. They should provide help if children request it but avoid giving unasked-for help or taking over.

Choice Is Power

Every person, including children, needs to feel some control over his or her own life. Children need to make age-appropriate decisions.
    For example:

- if a 6-month-old is refusing strained beans, he doesn't want them
- an 18-month-old can choose which chair she will sit on
- a 2-year-old can decide which shirt to wear today
- a 3-year-old will know which cereal she wants for breakfast

    Whenever possible, parents must allow their children to exercise some control over their own lives. They will make some mistakes, but this is how most of us learn to do or not do something. The sense of accomplishment they receive from making good decisions is worth it. Making good decisions is a skill, and children can get good at it only if they practise. Many adults have never mastered this skill because someone always made their decisions for them.

Show Some Respect

When children speak up and give their points of view, parents have to receive and consider the opinions. Children can be amazingly creative problem solvers! They may not always get their way, but parents need to provide an environment that makes them feel that they will always have their say.

Parents need to treat children with the same courtesy they expect in return. By modelling good manners, parents make their children feel respected and set a standard for behaviour in the home that applies to every member of the family.

❖ Checkpoints

1. What might happen if a child's toys are not "age-appropriate"?
2. Describe the effects of environmental deprivation.
3. In what ways can children express their "sense of autonomy"?

Chapter Summary

Chapter Highlights

- The first five years last forever.

- Physical growth, brain development, language development, social and emotional maturation, and large- and small-motor skills development all reach certain milestones at particular ages.

- Age and stage charts help parents recognize what they can and cannot expect from their children, how to stimulate learning and brain development, and how to foster and maintain attachment through comforting their children.

- Physical growth is rapid in the first five years and requires healthy food, exercise, and rest.

- As the brain grows and develops, children learn rapidly. Parents need to provide a safe and stimulating environment to encourage problem solving and learning. Mistakes are part of the growth process.

- The child also becomes a person during the first five years and needs a strong sense of attachment to venture into new learning and new relationships.

- There are many emotional ups and downs in the early years as children learn to identify and handle their emotions.

- Although it may seem daunting to be a parent during the important early years, being knowledgeable, responsive, loving, and respectful will provide the optimal conditions for child development.

Review and Extend Your Learning

1. You will be the guest speaker for a parenting class. Write a short speech, outlining the behaviours, conditions, and environments that influence positive and negative development in the first five years of life. **K/U** **C**

2. Produce a one-page poster that offers concrete examples of how to comfort, teach, and play with infants up to 18 months, or children between 2 and 4 years of age, or children 4 to 5 years of age. **K/U** **C**

3. Research the topic of reading to young children. Create a pamphlet explaining the benefits of reading to children in the early years. Suggest how to read to children so it is fun and enjoyable, and find, read, and list several books for each year (or half-year) from birth to five years. Distribute your pamphlet to class members. **K/U** **T/I** **C** **A**

4. Practise the nursery rhymes, games, and songs for each age stage, and demonstrate some of them for the class. Try them with young children in the classroom or community. **C**

5. Design two play-based problem-solving activities, one for a toddler and one for a preschooler. Evaluate their effectiveness by trying them in a real-life setting such as play school or while babysitting. Which children's responses to the activities suggest that they facilitate brain development? **K/U** **T/I** **C** **A**

6. Investigate recent research on brain hemisphere dominance. Find out the implications of brain-hemisphere dominance with respect to learning. Report your findings to the class. **T/I** **C**

7. Analyze a specific toy. Determine its function and the area of development it will enhance. According to manufacturers' age suggestions, do you find it age-appropriate? Write a short advertising feature about the developmental benefits of the toy. **K/U** **T/I** **C** **A**

8. Provide detailed descriptions of strategies parents can use to help their children learn to express and deal with their emotions. **K/U**

9. Create a pamphlet for parents describing what they can do to help their children prepare for learning when they enter the school system. **K/U** **C** **A**

10. Evaluate how your own interaction with children under the age of six in community-based settings or in your extended family has changed since learning about age-appropriate play, comfort, and teach techniques. **T/I**

Issue Analysis

11. Will children ever recover from missed opportunities early in life? Research and write a paper that investigates the long-term effects of inadequate nurturing and/or environmental deprivation of children in the early years (0–5).

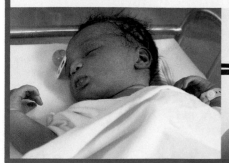

Chapter

13

Middle Childhood and Adolescence

By the end of this chapter, you will be able to:

- outline how the parental responsibility for the nutritional well-being of children and adolescents is best fulfilled

- describe the effects of attachment on social and emotional development in children and adolescents

- identify and describe the stages of moral development

- analyze the characteristics of the expanding family

- demonstrate an understanding of the ways in which communication and problem-solving skills are essential to human development

- analyze changes in human development throughout the life cycle, including early childhood and adolescence

Important Terms

adolescence
cognitive intelligence

concrete operations
emotional intelligence

emotional literacy
formal operations
internalization
moral dilemma
multiple intelligences (MI)
peer group

peer helpers
preoperational period
puberty
sensorimotor period
Shaken Baby Syndrome
sibling rivalry

Chapter at a Glance

Figure 13.1
Older children are more independent and autonomous.

What Is It Like to Parent Older Children?

Do you remember your earliest years? What did you like best about your childhood years? What did you do with your time? Where did you go? Who did you play with? How did you interact with your family? What activities did you enjoy? How did you get along with your family members? Childhood is frequently described in glowing terms—a happy time with carefree days and images of children laughing, playing, learning, and discovering. For many families, it is a peaceful time—a lull between the overwhelming days of early childhood and the turmoil of adolescence. Yet, for some, childhood is a difficult time. Parents may be weighed down with personal concerns and relationship problems and need to reflect on how that affects the quality of their parenting.

What is it like to have older children? It can mean having a little help around the house, or not always having to find a baby sitter if one of the children is old enough to look after the others. The routine of school, homework, and after-school activities shapes the pattern of the days. Life can be fairly predictable and manageable at this stage because the children are becoming independent and autonomous.

As the family expands and children grow older, however, there may be new challenges to face. By the time all the children are in school, the home may feel too small. Children take up a lot of room, and each child often wants his or her own room. If that means moving, it can be both exciting and stressful. According to figures released in 2001 by the Manitoba Department of Agriculture, the cost of raising one child to the age of 18 in Canada was $155 000. The costs of housing, feeding, and caring for a growing family can put a strain on the family budget, even if there are two parents earning an income.

A family can experience a lot of emotional ups and downs as children grow older. Living with others means that adjustments have to be made. Sharing space, juggling activities, and sharing chores at home can cause both friction and fun. In most families with more than one child, siblings often argue and fight, making **sibling rivalry** a fact of life that parents have to deal with. Knowing about child development in older children can help parents with the challenges of a growing family.

Growth and Development in Middle Childhood and Adolescence

Remember how exciting it was as a child to find out how tall you were? Physical growth is an important part of middle childhood and adolescence. Growth is continuous throughout childhood, but increases significantly at puberty. **Puberty** is the time in life when secondary sex changes occur in humans, marked by the beginning of menstruation in females and sperm production in males. Because girls generally reach puberty earlier in life than boys, they often have a growth spurt accompanied by the development of breasts and hips before entering high school. Boys reach puberty later, experiencing a significant growth spurt and change in physical appearance toward the end of their first year in high school. Boys continue to grow in height until their twenties, while girls generally stop growing by 18 years of age.

■ It is normal for girls to reach puberty earlier than boys. Boys then finish growing later than girls.

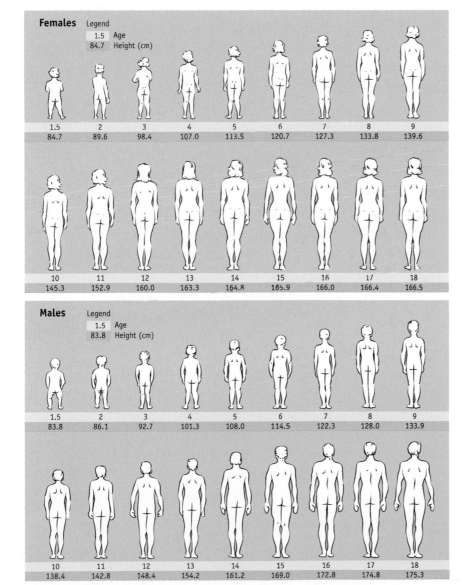

Figure 13.2
Notice the differences in the typical growth patterns of males and females.

Nutrition and Physical Growth

Children need to be well nourished to grow up strong and healthy. Movies or television programs set in the 1950s show families eating three wholesome meals a day, prepared by mothers who spent their days at home. Families sat down to meals that included meat, potatoes, and vegetables, some of which came fresh from the garden. Compare that picture with the reality of today, and you see why food and nutrition are a major concern for growing families.

Today, families run on a hectic schedule, often with little time for meal preparation. Food comes in a wide array of prepared, preserved, and pre-packaged variations. Children have become the direct targets of advertising for popular empty calorie foods that contain lots of calories but few nutrients. Fast food that is prepared and ready to eat becomes very tempting in such a rushed world. Parents may find it difficult to provide their children with adequate nutrition, even in families where there is an abundance of food.

Figure 13.3
Children and adolescents need a variety of nutrient-rich foods.

Childhood Obesity

Research indicates that childhood obesity in Canada has increased significantly. A study conducted at the University of New Brunswick by Mark S. Tremblay and J. Douglas Willms (2000), published in the *Canadian Medical Association Journal*, revealed that obesity and overweight in children have increased at an alarming rate in children aged 7 to 13. The data shows that the number of obese children between 10 and 12 has tripled since the early 1980s. Today, an alarming 61 percent of children between the ages of 5 and 17 are dangerously inactive, which leads to overweight. Overweight children face an enormous risk of diabetes and severe cardiovascular disease in early adulthood.

According to Dr. Lance Levy, director of the Nutritional and Eating Disorders Clinic in Toronto, there are a variety of reasons for these dramatic observations. Dr. Levy cites mood changes and sedentary activities, such as playing computer games instead of active sports, as primary causes of overweight and obesity in children. He notes that family dynamics have changed and food has often become a source of comfort for children, especially when parents are not available to talk to them.

Healthy Eating

What nutrients do children and adolescents require? How do parents determine which kinds of foods their children need to be healthy, and the quantities that will not contribute to overweight? Parents can use guides such as Canada's Food Guide to Healthy Eating or the Native Food Guide, which both offer sound advice for meeting the daily nutritional needs of all age groups. When children or adolescents eat the number of servings recommended for each food group, their nutritional needs are met, and their parents do not need to keep track of every nutrient their child consumes each day. Of course, parents of children with food allergies or absorption problems will need to find creative alternatives for foods that cannot be tolerated.

The servings recommended in a food guide provide energy and nutrients for growth and health. A serving size is a reasonable amount of food. Younger and less active children need fewer servings, while older and more active children and adolescents, especially males, need to eat more servings. Because they are growing, adolescents may need more foods containing calcium.

As parents plan the daily food intake for their children, they need to ensure that the food guide requirements are met before empty calorie choices are added. Desserts of fruit or milk-based puddings are better choices than foods that are high in fat or sugar. A snack could be a bowl of cereal with milk instead of potato chips. If children occasionally enjoy fast food, then they should drink milk at the same time. Children who have milk allergies could choose calcium fortified fruit juice or soy milk. Following the official food guide each day ensures that children and adolescents are well nourished.

Eating the right kinds and amounts of foods does not itself guarantee good health. Canada's Food Guide to Healthy Eating assumes that adults and children lead active lives. Exercise and healthy eating go together. If parents are active, then there is a much greater likelihood that their children or child will also be active.

Figure 13.4
Obesity in children has increased substantially in Canada today.

■ Exercise is essential for good health during childhood and adolescence.

❖ Connections

Locate the most recent online versions of Canada's Food Guide for Healthy Eating and either the Native Food Guide or the Aboriginal Food Guide.

1. Compare the two food guides and make a list of the differences.
2. Explain why the kinds of recommended foods are different in the two food guides.
3. Based on where you live in Canada, explain which food guide would be easier for a family with one adult, one teenager, and two preteen children to follow?

Case Study: Walk and Talk with Kids

The following material is excerpted from *Prevention* (March 2002) by M. Hewko:

I'm a 39-year-old mother with an 11-year-old daughter and a 10-year-old son. My husband and I work full-time, and I'm working part-time on my MBA. My daughter started going through puberty at age 10, and we take every mood swing with a grain of salt. It's especially tough to deal with uneven tempers at home when my husband and I have had rough days at work.

We have a solution to this problem: Every night I get my kids out for a 5 km walk. They usually resist, but when we're a couple of kilometres into it, they really start to open up about what happened at school, who said what to whom, and how they feel about certain situations. By the end of the fifth kilometre, we've caught up with each other's news and are at peace with the day.

Most parents don't find time to talk with their kids, but a walk forces you to ignore distractions and deal head-on with problems. Another benefit is that my daughter lost 12 kg, looks better than ever, and has found new self-confidence.

Questions

1. What are the physical and interpersonal benefits of walking with your children?
2. Besides walking, what other activities would provide health benefits and an opportunity to connect with children at the end of a busy day?

Picky Eaters

Sometimes, children who enjoyed a wide variety of foods as infants and toddlers stop liking certain foods. Picky eaters might be missing one or more food groups, which means they are also missing some of the nutrients they need for growth and good health. Forcing children to eat is not the answer. Food struggles can become no-win power struggles that have nothing to do with eating. They are emotionally upsetting and can lead to eating disorders.

Strategies for Picky Eaters

- Substitute equivalent foods such as crackers for bread, pasta for potatoes, peaches for carrots, or cheese or yogurt for milk.
- Allow children and adolescents to express their creativity with food by trying new combinations or creating interesting presentations.
- Give them meaningful tasks such as making their own lunch, chopping the vegetables, or stirring the soup.
- "Hide" nutrients by adding grated vegetables or powdered milk to soups or casseroles.
- If traditional breakfast foods are not appealing, allow an older child or adolescent to eat other favourite foods, such as leftovers from the previous night's dinner.
- Hold family meetings that allow children to influence some meal-planning decisions.

Nutrition and Learning

Studies show that children who go to school without breakfast do not do as well in school as their peers who have had breakfast. Food is the fuel they need for thinking, working, and concentrating. Have you ever heard your stomach growl in the middle of class? It becomes hard to hear anything else. Without food, your body tries to conserve energy. It slows down and you feel tired. It is difficult to learn when you are tired and hungry.

There are many reasons that children go to school without breakfast. One is economics. Not every family can afford to provide children with three meals a day every day. Breakfast programs, where students eat breakfast at school or in a nearby facility before going to class, are available in many communities. Where food is available at home, children sometimes skip breakfast for other reasons such as not feeling hungry or being rushed for time. There are many different ways to solve the problem.

Youth workers who are involved in coaching and leading community activities for children and adolescents may often encourage healthful eating more effectively than parents. They can set examples and involve young people in activities that encourage them to learn about the nutritional value of food. At home, children and adolescents can help with grocery shopping for the family, read labels, and plan and prepare meals. Children and teenagers can also be role models for others by making healthy food choices a regular part of their day.

❖ Checkpoints

1. What are some of the pros and cons of having older children in the family?
2. Describe some of the causes of sibling rivalry.
3. Outline how parents can ensure that their children are well nourished.
4. Explain the effects of inadequate nutrition on student learning, growth, and development.

Development in Middle Childhood

Great strides in development occur in the years between ages six and twelve. This period is the transition from early childhood to adolescence and is marked by many physical, intellectual, emotional, and social milestones. All areas of development are interdependent. A change in

Quick and Easy Breakfast Suggestions

- Get breakfast ready the night before.
- Eat hot or cold leftovers from supper.
- Whip up frozen fruit with milk in the blender.
- Grab cheese and a low-fat muffin to eat on the go.
- Have someone toast that bagel for you while you shower.
- Eat whole grain bread products to keep you feeling "full" longer.
- Include a protein, fruit or vegetable, and grain product in breakfast.

Figure 13.5
Children can influence each other to make healthy food choices.

intellectual ability accompanied by an increase in physical size may alter a child's social network and emotional outlook. The "What to Expect during Middle Childhood" chart separates the areas of development for clarity, but it also includes suggestions for how parents can support their children in their total growth and development throughout these years.

What to Expect during Middle Childhood: Ages 6–12

Age	Physical Development	Intellectual Development	Emotional and Social Development	What Parents Can Do
6 Years	• Becomes slimmer, losing baby fat. • Loses baby teeth as adult teeth grow in. • Wants to be physically active and not sit still; active games are popular, especially with boys.	• Pre-operational thinking: asks many questions. • More curious about sex. • Attention span is longer. • Begins to read. • Likes fantasy. • Entertains self.	• Relationships at school become important and change daily. • Sibling rivalry increases. • Begins to learn to take turns and work in groups. • Begins to separate right and wrong; tattling is an expression of this.	• Encourage active play and play board games. • Stay even-tempered. • Keep answers simple and honest. • Have realistic expectations. • Offer choices. • Read to them.
7–8 Years	• Gets taller and more lanky. • Balance and co-ordination improve as small and large muscles develop. • Team sports, skiing, swimming, biking, and racket sports are possible; naturally competitive.	• Concrete operations: understands time and money. • Attention span improves. • Thinks things over and loves silly jokes. • Self-criticism may emerge. • Enjoys reading. • Acquires academic skills. • Needs praise.	• Calmer but will have moods. • Forming a sense of values. • Fairness is important. • Same-sex, same-age friends. • Idolizes teachers and coaches but not parents. • Wants to fit in. • Wants to please. • More able to get along, take turns, and share.	• Spend time talking and listening to them every day. • Give genuine praise. • Encourage skills and assign responsibilities. • Encourage peer relationships. • Discuss ideas and events. • Be aware of bullying.
9–10 Years	• Coordination, timing, and balance have improved. • Physical and intellectual talents may emerge. • Enjoys organized games and sports. • Drawing may emerge as a skill. • Improved small motor skills allow him or her to build models, use tools, and do crafts. • Clubs, sports, and groups are of benefit.	• Often loves school and teachers. • Can work for hours at a task. • Makes connections and solves problems. • Understands truth, honesty. • Enjoys secrets, mysteries, and mental contests. • Likes to talk to adults and impress parents with knowledge.	• Self-motivated, business-like. • Needs things to be "fair." • Independence increases at 9. • Boys show disdain for girls. • Accepts blame more. • More interest in friends than family. • Happier with life by 10 years. • Girls are loyal to a best friend.	• Accept independence, but provide security and family activities. • Respect children's growing need for privacy. • Give warning of expected task transitions, such as bedtime. • Avoid petty instructions. • Try not to interrupt fun activities.

Age	Physical Development	Intellectual Development	Emotional and Social Development	What Parents Can Do
11–12 years	• Growth slows in males. • Females have a growth spurt. • Girls may start to menstruate. • Boys may show their strength in daring activities. • Girls, especially, start to become very aware of and concerned with their appearance. • Same-sex activities and team sports are still the most important.	• Able to solve daily problems. • Likes to read aloud and do cooperative projects. • Projects in science capture interest. • Mystery, adventure, and biography are preferred reading material. • Math concepts are grasped and applied. • The Formal operations stage begins.	• Less egocentric or self-centred. • Shows improved social skills. • More patient and friendly with younger children. • Likes to plan group activities. • Strong need to conform to peer group. • Both males and females experience mood swings related to hormones. • Begins to prefer friends to family.	• Enjoy the good days with your children and get past the difficult ones. • Support children in making decisions and accepting consequences. • Realize that children of this age still need limits and rules; too much freedom is very confusing. • Understand your pre-teen's need for more independence.

The Link between Schooling and Development

As we talk about school-age children or high school students, we immediately form a picture in our minds of how they look and behave. School becomes the focus of their daily lives. In infancy and early childhood, a strong attachment allows children to take steps toward independence with the assurance that they can return to the comfort of their parents. As they venture out into the culture of school rules, routines, and activities, they need the assurance of the parental connection as a kind of backup. Parents provide the emotional support that children need for their growing interaction with the world outside the family.

School is a cultural framework that provides opportunities for children and adolescents to make social connections and experience emotions. As they develop intellectually, new challenges become available. As teachers plan learning activities, they need to take into consideration where students are in their overall development. Behaviour problems and loss of confidence may result if parent and teacher expectations do not match a student's level of intellectual, social, emotional, or physical development.

Figure 13.6
School is the cultural framework for social, emotional, intellectual, and moral development.

Career Capsule

SPECIAL EDUCATION TEACHER

Tasks and Responsibilities

Some students learn more slowly and differently from the average. Others learn much more quickly and require continuous challenge to stay interested in school. Some students exhibit delays and extraordinary talents at the same time. The special education teacher is trained to work with students with special needs and put together programs that will allow each one of them to succeed and be the best they can be.

Special education may include any of the following categories: learning disabilities, hearing, visual, speech or language disorders, physical challenges, behavioural disorders, multiple challenges, or "gifted." Each student must be assessed and have a personalized learning plan formulated and implemented.

Teachers may concentrate on academic skills with some students or personal life management skills with others. In addition to teaching, the special education teacher is expected to assess, evaluate, and report on student progress, as well as work with the other professionals and the parents involved in the life of the student.

Work Environment

Special education teachers often work with individuals or small groups that are withdrawn from their regular classes for specialized instruction. Classes may be reduced in size to allow for more individualized instruction, or there may be an educational assistant. Special education teachers work closely with the principal, parents, social workers, school psychologists, physiotherapists, and the students' other teachers to plan and implement programs for individual students.

Education and Aptitudes

Special education teachers must have patience and a genuine desire to help students. Even though class sizes tend to be smaller for special education teachers, the job is very demanding. Special education teachers need to have a lot of physical, emotional, and mental energy to be successful. An open-minded and empathetic attitude is also a requirement for this career.

The province or territory in which you teach determines teaching qualifications for special education. It usually takes four years to complete an undergraduate bachelor degree before completing teacher training. Any undergraduate degree that gives the student "teachable subjects" in elementary or secondary school is acceptable at most faculties of education.

A Theory of Intellectual Development

By the time a child finishes kindergarten at around six years of age, his or her brain has already developed 75 percent of its capacity. The neural pathways and different centres in the brain are already well developed. Intellectual development continues throughout middle childhood and adolescence.

Jean Piaget, a Swiss biologist who studied infants and children many years ago, developed a theory about intellectual development that is still used today. Piaget separated intellectual development into four stages: **sensorimotor**, **preoperational**, concrete operational, and formal operational.

Piaget called the stage between age seven and twelve the period of **concrete operations**. Children at this age begin to see relationships among things. They know that a tall, skinny glass holds the same amount of water as a short, fat glass, even though the level appears higher. They know that ten pennies is the same as a dime. They can do math problems that compare several components. But they also see the world in concrete ways and may think that when someone uses an expression like "he got it for peanuts," actual peanuts were exchanged.

Around twelve to fourteen years, Piaget proposed that a person enters the stage of **formal operations** and becomes capable of logic, deductive reasoning, and abstract thinking. Mathematical theorems can be understood, and more complicated reasoning about the world and life can become important. At this age, questions representing abstract thinking become important. It becomes interesting to debate questions such as "If a tree falls in the forest and no one is there to hear it, does it make a sound?" or "What is infinity?" This type of thinking opens the door to more sophisticated learning, as reflected in more difficult school subjects.

Not everyone agrees with Piaget, because intellectual development is much more complex than the tidy stages he described. His stages do not account for children who are able to think abstractly long before they reach the stage of formal operations, or adults who are still concrete thinkers. However, his theory does provide an important framework for helping teachers, caregivers, and parents recognize what can be expected of most children at different stages of development.

A Theory of Multiple Intelligences

Many parents believe that if their children do well in mathematics and language activities at school, everything is fine and they are smart or intelligent. However, theorists such as the psychologist Howard Gardner have expanded the idea of intelligence to include **multiple intelligences (MI)**. Gardner theorizes that every human being possesses nine intelligences in varying amounts. Children are, therefore, good at a variety of tasks that parents and teachers need to identify. Learning in an area of strength can promote learning in another area. For example, children who learn best by doing have a kinesthetic intelligence and may do better at mathematics if they can move objects around instead of writing down numbers.

Figure 13.7
During the stage of concrete operations, children begin to see and understand the nuances of language, relationships, and various categories within science and nature.

■ **Piaget's Stages of Intellectual Development:**
- sensorimotor: birth to 2 years
- preoperational: ages 2–7
- concrete operations: ages 7–12
- formal operations: ages 12 to adult

Gardner's Multiple Intelligences

Howard Gardner and other scientists have identified the following nine intelligences that are common in humans in varying degrees:

Logical/Mathematical **Body/Kinesthetic** **Verbal/Linguistic** **Interpersonal** **Intrapersonal**

Visual/Spatial **Existential** **Naturalist** **Musical/Rhythmic**

I think, therefore I am.

Figure 13.8

In middle childhood, children begin to follow their interests and strengths, in preparation for their future goals. Allowing children to follow their interests provides great benefits to self-esteem.

This approach provides enormous benefits to self-confidence. It is important for parents, caregivers, and teachers to recognize that every person can be "smart" in more than one way. As children reach adolescence, their abilities in language and math may be challenged, but if they have been encouraged to develop strengths in a number of areas, they will be better prepared to make decisions about their future goals. Everyone is good at something. Attempting to make children or adolescents into something that they are not lowers their self-confidence and can have negative long-term consequences.

❖ Connections

Intelligence solidifies in adulthood. A person often develops his or her strengths after completing formal schooling. Interview an adult and identify the multiple intelligences identified by Howard Gardner in which this person excels. Report orally to the class on the following points:

1. In which area of intelligence does the person you interviewed excel?

2. How does this person demonstrate to others that he or she is skilled in that area?

3. When did this person first know he or she was skilled in that area?

4. What area of intelligence does this person think is his or her weakest, and why?

5. What advice can this person give about following and building on strengths?

Social Development

During childhood and adolescence, friendships become very important. It is in school where most social interaction takes place. The **peer group**, made up of others of the same age, influences friendships, behaviour, and how other choices are made. Children who develop a strong attachment to a parent early in life will have a strong reference point for making friends and withstanding peer pressure.

Making friends is an important social task. During the elementary school years, friendships are formed and abandoned on a regular basis. There are also gender differences. Boys tend to make friends and form groups around sports and active play, and they settle their differences with a scuffle or show of strength. Girls, on the other hand, form groups and friendships through conversation and shared interests, and they may suffer hurt feelings if their differences are not resolved through discussion. Both boys and girls at this stage are learning important skills for getting along with others.

Like parents, teachers, coaches, and youth workers are powerful role models for how to get along with others or resolve conflicts in appropriate ways. They help children form friendships, they control and manage interpersonal behaviours, and they can boost the social skills and self-confidence of the young people in their care. However, when a child's feelings are hurt, it is always good to have a parent who understands and is willing to listen, no matter how old you are. Being a good, active listener is a critical skill for any parent or caregiver.

❖ Checkpoints

1. What is the cultural role of school in middle childhood and adolescent development?

2. Describe how a parent with a seven-year-old and a twelve-year-old can encourage the development of both children.

3. Explain how concrete thinking differs from abstract thinking.

4. Explain how teachers, coaches, and youth workers influence social development.

Figure 13.9
Activities of a peer group may have a strong influence in social development. Positive environments, where good behaviour is modelled, provide a place to learn and practise social and interpersonal skills.

Emotional Development

Children experience a wide range of emotions—happiness, sadness, anger, frustration, anxiety, and delight, to name a few. As they mature, children learn how to handle their emotions. It is usually safer to show emotions within the security of their own families. A really good cry is less embarrassing at home than it is at school. Home is also where children learn to balance how Canadian society expects them to handle their emotions with what is acceptable in their own culture.

Schools influence emotional development because they have rules about behaviour. They expect students to handle their emotions in ways that are neither excessively negative nor overly positive. Traditionally, male and female children were expected to express their emotions in different ways. It was considered unmanly for boys to cry and unlady-like for girls to vent their anger. These perspectives are changing, but children continue to hear messages about which emotions are accept-able and which are not.

Adolescence can be a very emotional time. Relationships are formed and dissolve as quickly. Friends continue to be important, but the emphasis shifts to feelings associated with sexuality, passion, and longing, which is very confusing. Mood swings related to hormonal changes may give rise to all kinds of emotions. Sometimes, adolescents take their frustrations out on family members. When these strong emo-tions arise, adolescents often find it helpful to explore their emotions and learn to handle them in acceptable ways. As they mature, their moods become more stable and their emotions become easier to handle.

Figure 13.10
Parents and teenagers may find communication difficult.

Parenting Skills

As children reach puberty, the hormonal changes that signal the development of secondary sex characteristics also spark mood swings and intense emotions. At times, these new feelings trigger conflict with parents or siblings. A raging child can be difficult to ignore, but the techniques that worked with toddlers can be modified and put to use with older children and adolescents:

- Give them permission to express their emotions.
- Count to 10 or move away physically to keep from engaging in battle.
- Use active listening to help them identify and acknowledge their feelings.
- Provide the option to talk when they feel ready to talk.
- When they are calm, use "I" messages to indicate how their behaviour affects you and others.
- Acknowledge any evidence of a growing ability to manage their emotional ups and downs.
- Seek professional help if you detect signs of depression or self-destructive behaviour.

Emotional Literacy

Children and adolescents who have been treated with empathy by their own parents have good models for showing respect and care about the feelings of others. Some students are good at helping other students handle emotions and may become **peer helpers**. It is often easier to talk to someone your own age about a problem than it is to talk to an adult.

Recent studies have pointed out that children and adolescents can improve their **emotional intelligence**, or their ability to handle their feelings and to respond to the feelings of others, just as they can improve their **cognitive intelligence**, which is the knowledge they have learned. Those with a higher emotional intelligence are more successful at forming relationships, getting along with others, or holding down a job, and they even make better parents later on. Projects like the Roots of Empathy are designed to give children the tools to care for others. The project helps them develop **emotional literacy** or fluency in identifying, expressing, and talking about feelings.

Figure 13.11
Some students with good emotional literacy may become peer helpers.

Program prepares students for parenting

By John Earle, *Western Star*, June 13, 2001

Stephenville has been selected as the first place in Newfoundland to become a training base for Roots of Empathy, a parenting program for children.

Empathy is defined as the ability to identify with another person's feelings. According to the group's mission statement, the ability to see and feel as others do is central to competent parenting and successful social relationships in all stages of life, said founder/director Mary Gordon.

Based on that belief, when children are able to understand another person's point of view and respect their feelings, aggressive behaviour is less likely to occur.

Thirteen people attended the first training session, hosted by Gordon, at the L.S. Eddy Complex recently. The program was piloted in Toronto schools in 1996. More than 50 classrooms in Toronto, ranging from Junior Kindergarten to Grade 8, had a Roots of Empathy program in 1999-2000.

British Columbia, Prince Edward Island, and other locations in Ontario are currently offering the program with other provinces, including Newfoundland, and are now getting exposed to the innovative idea.

The initiative is a classroom-parenting program that teaches infant development, emotional literacy, and inclusion, and fosters the development of empathy.

The specific goals of the program are to develop empathy, prepare students for responsible and responsive parenting, reduce levels of bullying, aggression, and violence in children's lives, build peaceful societies, and increase knowledge of human development and learning, and infant safety.

Children share in monthly visits with a parent, infant, and a trained Roots of Empathy instructor. During the school year, 27 sessions are conducted, nine of which are family visits.

Those who attend reflect the cultural, ethnic, and cultural diversity of their neighbourhood. Parents are coached by Roots of Empathy instructors to become experts on infant development and serve as powerful role models for competent parenting to children.

The emotional literacy that the program teaches builds more caring classrooms. When children learn how others feel, they are less likely to victimize by bullying. Through Roots of Empathy's messages of respect and perspective taking, children learn the impact of their actions on others. This can have a profound effect in preventing domestic violence in the future, according to Gordon.

Roots of Empathy hopes to reduce child abuse in the next generation by teaching infant development and safety to students and by raising levels of empathy. Specifically, information on **Shaken Baby Syndrome** helps children understand the vulnerability of infants and the importance of handling babies with care and attention. Ultimately, children who learn from an example of competent parenting will be less likely to abuse or neglect their children in their future roles as parents.

■ *Giving a child a literacy of feelings gives them the vocabulary and the freedom to identify what they are feeling, and what they are thinking. It is giving children a licence to talk about their feelings, and know that they are being respected. It validates them as individuals. It also requires them to validate others as individuals, by identifying with another person's feelings and thoughts.*
— Mary Gordon

❖ Checkpoints

1. What might be the consequences if a child is not allowed to express emotions?
2. How are adolescent emotions related to family conflict?
3. The Roots of Empathy program is designed to teach empathy. What aspects of the program accomplish this?

Character Building in Older Children

Childhood and adolescence are important years for building character. Honesty, integrity, courage, caring, strong morals, and values are qualities that begin to develop in these years and are admired in adulthood. Children and adolescents need to learn these qualities and develop a strong character for adulthood.

Learning Right from Wrong

School age or middle childhood is a time when children develop a much stronger sense of right and wrong. Around seven years of age, rules become very important. If children are not playing games that already have rules, they will make them up to suit their play. Rules help children establish an acute sense of right and wrong. Tattling (telling a parent or a teacher when another child has broken a rule) is common in the early years of elementary school. It gives children great satisfaction when they can point out that someone else is wrong.

Early thoughts about right and wrong often have to do with following the rules to avoid punishment. In games, a wrong move may mean missing a turn. In real life, it may mean some kind of punishment if someone is wrong, and a reward if he or she is right. Parents and teachers may use stickers and stars for what is considered the right or good behaviour. This, however, does not continue to work, because it is external motivation. Eventually, everyone has to choose for himself or herself. **Internalization** is the goal so that, by adulthood, inner satisfaction, rather than an external reward, is what motivates people to choose right over wrong.

Figure 13.12
Children in the early years of elementary school tattle on each other because they are beginning to develop a sense of right and wrong.

Moral Dilemmas

The following definition of a moral dilemma is taken from the *Internet Encyclopedia of Philosophy* (2001).

A moral dilemma involves a situation in which the agent has only two courses of action available, and each requires performing a morally impermissible action. Plato presents the classic example of a moral dilemma. A man borrows a weapon from his neighbour promising to return it at his neighbour's request. One day, the neigh-bour, in a fit of rage, asks for the weapon back, apparently with the intention to kill someone. The man is faced with a dilemma: if he keeps his promise, then he will be an accessory to a murder; if he refuses to hand over the weapon, then he violates his promise. A moral dilemma, then, is a situation involving a choice between two opposing courses of action, where there are moral considerations in support of each course of action.

Adolescents may not see right and wrong quite as clearly as do school-age children. This is a good example of what Piaget meant by formal operational thinking. By Grade 9, as many as half of those who thought smoking was wrong in Grade 5 or 6 may have actually chosen to become smokers. What may have seemed very wrong at one time may not seem as wrong at another time. Teenagers may feel that a choice that wins them favour with their peers feels less wrong than a choice that would lose peer approval. Adults, who have a more highly developed sense of right and wrong may think that teenagers are immoral, but many teenagers are also capable of taking a stand showing empathy, recognizing injustice, and demonstrating tolerance.

Theories of Moral Development

Two researchers who have helped to clarify the development of moral thinking are Lawrence Kohlberg, and Carol Gilligan. Lawrence Kohlberg was a developmental psychologist and a professor at Harvard. In the 1970s, he developed a theory that came to be known as Kohlberg's Stages of Moral Development. Carol Gilligan was one of Kohlberg's students and questioned why he researched only male subjects. Gilligan set out to study female moral development and published a critique of Kohlberg's theory in 1982. Both theories can help us understand the differences in moral development between men and women and between children and adults.

Kohlberg's Theory of Moral Development

Lawrence Kohlberg believed that people move through stages of moral reasoning, each more sophisticated than the one before, and that once you leave a stage, you do not return to that kind of moral reasoning. Stages 1 and 2 he felt are typical of children in elementary school. Stages 3 and 4 are common among most adolescents and adults, and Stages 5 and 6 are achieved mostly by adults who have a highly developed sense of moral reasoning.

Kohlberg's Stages of Moral Development

Stage 1: Obedience and Punishment
You behave the way you are told to by an authority figure, such as a parent or teacher, or to avoid punishment. For example: "I am not allowed to have a cookie right before dinner."

Stage 2: Individualism
You behave the right way because it means you are acting in your own best interests. For example: "I will get my chores done right away so I have more time to play outside."

Stage 3: Approval
At this stage, you choose to act in a way that will gain the approval of others. For example: "Everyone at the club will be pleased if I help out with the annual food drive."

Stage 4: Law and Order
You choose to abide by the law and respond to the obligations of duty. For example: "I'll have to report my neighbour for receiving stolen property because it is against the law."

Stage 5: Social Contract
You choose for the common good because you have a genuine interest in the welfare of others. For example: "I recycle because I have to do my part to make this a cleaner world for everyone."

Stage 6: Principled Conscience
Your choice is based on your principles and the demands of your own conscience. For example: "I would not be able to live with myself if I did anything to hurt a child."

Gilligan's Theory of Moral Reasoning

Carol Gilligan thought that Kohlberg's theory did not value women's ways of moral reasoning. She noted that men and women have different responses to right and wrong. Women view morality from an "ethic of caring" rather than a "justice" perspective. When faced with moral dilemmas, women are more concerned about caring for others than for fairness or rules. They resolve moral issues in the best interest of others rather than in the best interest of a preconceived code of conduct.

The following chart offers a comparison between how men and women respond to moral dilemmas, according to Gilligan's research:

Comparison: How Men and Women View Moral Dilemmas

How Men View Moral Dilemmas	How Women View Moral Dilemmas
You have to be fair.	You need to care.
Everyone has rights.	Everyone has a responsibility for others.
Everyone should be treated fairly.	Everyone who suffers should be cared for.
Rules must be followed.	Feelings must be considered.
We are responsible for sticking to a code of conduct.	We are responsible for actual individuals.

For Gilligan, these views are distinct yet connected. Neither men nor women would treat someone unfairly, and neither men nor women would turn away from someone in need of care. Even though both males and females reason on a basis of justice and care, their initial orientation may be more one way than the other may. Neither view is better; they just show a difference in reasoning.

Although the comparisons are based on mature adults, some similarities are seen in how children respond. Girls on the playground look for connections (care), while boys on the playground are concerned with fairness (justice). However, both boys and girls behave in ways that will earn them approval. Perhaps boys are given more approval for fairness, while girls are given more approval for connections.

The Transition to Adulthood

Adolescence, the stage between childhood and adulthood, has become longer over the years. In pioneer times, it was not unusual for some women to marry as young as sixteen, even though most married in their early twenties, and men married as young as eighteen. Today, young people extend their education and often remain dependent on their parents well into their mid-twenties. There is no exact day when adulthood is reached. It is more a transition because growth and development continue in different ways into adulthood. See the chart on page 324.

Comparison of Adolescence and Adulthood

Adolescence	Early Adulthood to Midlife	Later Adulthood
Physical Development • Characterized by rapid growth in height and weight. • Sexual reproductive organs take on maturity. • Male and female sex hormones are in a state of flux.	• Final adult height achieved. • Optimal bone density and muscle mass are achieved. • Weight may fluctuate. • Reproduction characterizes this period.	• Height begins to decrease. • Weight loss results from loss of bone density and muscle mass. • Reproduction ceases. • Physical deterioration.
Intellectual Development • Abstract thinking develops. • Learning increases. • Neuropathways are solidified. • Intelligences are clarified. • Attention span lengthens.	• Higher-order thinking solidifies. • New languages and new learning may become more difficult. • Lifelong learning continues.	• Some loss of brain cells. • Continued mental stimulation maintains memory. • Dementia may occur. • Long-term memory may outlast short-term memory.
Social Development • Develops identity in context with others. • Begins to develop lasting relationships. • Establishes professional, career, and work relationships.	• Develops long-term relationships/partnerships. • Develops a sense of generativity through parenting/coaching/teaching. • Increases community and social interaction.	• May lose a lifelong partner. • Forms grandparent and intergenerational relationships. • Forms and reforms social relationships. • Adjusts to aging.
Emotional Development • Emotions and moods fluctuate. • Self-control develops over time. • Growing sense of other's needs/feelings.	• Develops emotional attachments with partners and children. • Caring and connectedness with others. • May face depression.	• Experiences grief and loss with the death of older friends and relatives. • May become more emotional and aware of aging.
Personality Development • In a state of flux and developing.	• Achieves consistency.	• Impacted by life events.

The chart demonstrates that most developmental milestones have been reached by late adolescence or early adulthood. Parents continue to play an important role in the lives of their children, but by early adulthood, most people will be in the position to direct their own lives. Some may even become parents at this stage. If this is the case, then parents will have the new role of supporting their children in their role as grandparents.

❖ Checkpoints

1. Why might adolescents not see right and wrong quite as clearly as school-age children do?
2. In your own words, describe Kohlberg's theory of the stages of moral development.
3. When does adolescence end? Explain your answer.

The Challenge of Parenting Teens

Being a parent of teenagers involves challenges. Parents may be experiencing their own mid-life problems. Both teens and their parents face identity problems, employment issues, and concerns for the future. Parents may feel they are losing control of many aspects of their lives. Teenagers are taking steps toward independence before parents are entirely ready. Conflict may arise that requires some of the best problem-solving and communication skills a parent has to offer. Here is an article published by Health Canada that provides some direction for parents of teens.

Talking Parenting

Parenting Teens: The Reward and the Challenge

Health Canada publishes an online magazine, *Health! Canada Magazine* (2). The material that follows is from an article "Parenting teens: The reward and the challenge" posted in February 2001.

"If you think you've got it tough now, just wait until they become teenagers!"

How many parents have heard that warning as their kids approached the teen years? Raising teenagers is often a challenge, but most parents find the rewards are more than worth it.

Adolescence is a time when kids must deal not only with changes to their bodies (known as puberty), but also with changes in their sexual, emotional, intellectual, and social identities. Put all these changes together, and parents may find themselves dealing with a person quite different from the child they are used to.

Teens are concerned with building their identity and individuality. They do this building in many ways: trying out "radical" ideas, driving themselves to excel in sports or artistic pursuits, wearing "different" clothes, paying more attention to the advice of their peers than their parents. In most cases, you needn't worry about your kids: they'll come through adolescence with flying colours.

How to relate to your teen

- Testing the limits is part of an adolescent's growing-up process. Although they may complain about rules and limits, teens need the security of knowing what is acceptable and unacceptable to their parents. The best thing to do is work with them to set rules,

Figure 13.13
Teens pay more attention to the advice of their peers than their parents.

including a mutual agreement on what will happen if the rules are broken.

- Remember that rules can change as your teens mature and assume more personal responsibility.

- If bad behavioural patterns persist or worsen, they may be signs of more serious problems such as depression. Keeping the lines of communication open will help you deal with many problems, but don't hesitate to obtain more information or seek professional help.

- Let your teens know you respect them as individuals with their own take on life. Trying to make them extensions of yourself can lead to trouble.

- The intellectual development of teens can be rapid, and they will want to test their ideas, values, and convictions. You may think their ideas are immature or outlandish, but it is important to listen to what they have to say.

- Be as consistent as you can be in your own behaviour. A good example is an excellent teacher.

If you need help

If you feel your family life is always in turmoil, or if you are worried about your teens, you have many options.

- Contact other parents for ideas and support.

- Join family life education groups.

- Consult family life education material. Your local public library will have resources available in audio, video, and printed form.

- Talk to your school or spiritual counsellor, doctor, or public-health nurse.

- Contact agencies where you can get professional counselling and parenting advice. Many are listed in the yellow pages of the telephone book.

- For serious problems—drug use, running away from home, suicide threats, unwanted pregnancy, breaking the law—contact the child-welfare agency, provincial or territorial social services department, or police force in your community.

Figure 13.14
It is fairly common to seek professional help when parenting teens. Many communities have a variety of options for helping parents and teens resolve conflicts and solve problems.

Chapter Summary

Chapter Highlights

- Families that include school-age children and adolescents experience many challenges.

- Children continue to grow throughout their childhood and adolescence, so it becomes important to provide them with adequate nourishment.

- The most recent Food Guide for your region and wise alternative choices for children with allergies and intolerances can ensure that children's nutritional requirements are met.

- Nourishment affects growth as well as intellectual development.

- Eating breakfast improves learning.

- School provides the cultural framework for intellectual, social, and emotional development throughout middle childhood and the teen years.

- Learning, making friends, and handling emotions are key to development at this stage. Building character goes hand in hand with moral development.

- Theories of moral development show how moral thinking is different according to gender and changes with age.

- As their children move out of adolescence and into adulthood, parents have completed a large part of the parenting journey.

Review and Extend Your Learning

1. Plan nutritious snacks, suitable for the following:
   - an inactive 6-year-old
   - an 8-year-old who practises gymnastics every day after school
   - a 10-year-old who has an evening paper route
   - a 14-year-old girl who is a star basketball player
   - a 16-year-old computer whiz who is allergic to milk products (K/U) (A)

2. Determine how many times in a day you are bombarded with messages that urge you to choose high-calorie, low-nutrient food. Devise a plan to help children resist these messages. (T/I) (A)

3. Design a pamphlet for parents of 9- and 10-year-olds that provides strategies to help support their children's overall development. (K/U) (T/I) (C) (A)

4. Boys and girls differ in many ways. Outline differences in how boys and girls make and maintain friendships. Interview some 10-year-olds to verify whether these differences are apparent in your sample group. (K/U) (T/I)

5. Describe emotional literacy and discuss how it can help improve a child's emotional intelligence. (K/U) (A)

6. Explain why internalization is the goal for children in learning the difference between right from wrong. **K/U**

7. Describe a common moral dilemma with which an adolescent may have to deal. Analyze how a male and female may deal with it in different ways. **K/U** **T/I**

8. Based on the physical, emotional, and social characteristics of a person who has reached adulthood, determine what you need to achieve before you reach this milestone. **K/U** **A**

9. Which aspects of parenting a teenager are rewarding and which are challenging? **K/U**

Research Opportunities

10. Besides parents, who influences your food choices? Observe, interview, or read about someone in the following occupations. Report on how they influence the food habits of school-age children and adolescents:
    - school cafeteria workers
    - restaurant wait staff
    - fitness instructor
    - food advertisers
    - family studies, physical education, or other subject teachers
    - professional athletes
    - grocery store employees
    - teen actors, movie stars, models
    - health-care workers such as dentists or doctors

11. Develop a questionnaire to test Gilligan's theory of moral reasoning amongst your peers. Create two or three scenarios and ask male and female peers how they would handle these situations.

Issue Analysis

12. With a partner, examine one of the following issues. Present your findings from two points of view, that of the parent(s), and that of the child or adolescent:
    - adolescent peer pressure
    - adolescent independence
    - setting rules and limits for adolescents
    - part-time jobs

Unit 6   Nurturing Children

This unit explores how children learn what is expected of them so that they can behave appropriately within society. Techniques for modelling and teaching behaviour throughout infancy, childhood, and adolescence are examined. You will learn a number of child-rearing theories, positive parenting skills, and discipline techniques for parenting and working with children of all ages.

- The goal of parenting older children and adolescents is to help them develop self-discipline and achieve independence.
- Nurturing, teaching, and positive parenting practices through all stages of parenthood are important for raising healthy, secure, and confident children.

KEY INSIGHTS:

- Children of all ages learn socially acceptable behaviour from a community of parents, caregivers, and workers.
- Human development through middle childhood and adolescence is shaped by positive and negative socialization experiences within society. Some child-rearing practices are more effective than others.
- Parents, caregivers, and those who work with children need a repertoire of successful strategies for encouraging positive behaviour and self-esteem.

Unit at a Glance

Socialization of Children

By the end of this chapter, you will be able to:

- identify a variety of social and cultural differences in child behaviour

- recognize the family's critical role in the socialization of its members

- describe the importance of the nurturing and teaching roles of parents and caregivers

- specify strategies that encourage age-appropriate behaviour

- analyze a variety of social and cultural differences in child behaviour

- define child abuse and family violence, and outline strategies to secure a safe, non-violent environment for all children

Important Terms

agent of socialization

anarchy

child abuse

criminal behaviour

emotional abuse

empathy

encouragement

family violence

malnutrition

negative socialization patterns

neglect

norm

parenting philosophy

physical abuse

positive feedback

positive learning experience

reinforcement

role model

sexual abuse

socialization

socially acceptable behaviour

thwarting authority

Chapter at a Glance

What Is Socially Acceptable Behaviour?

There are many unwritten rules for behaviour in our society, such as no butting into line, no picking your nose in public, and no spitting. Be polite, especially to elders, take turns, watch your language, keep your voice down. These are all **socially acceptable behaviours** that every child must learn. You might think of it as good manners, common courtesy, or showing respect to others. Children and adults both continue to learn what is acceptable and what is unacceptable behaviour in various circumstances. This is the process of **socialization**, which teaches children how to get along in the world.

The process of socialization is often difficult to understand for children. This difficulty occurs when what is acceptable in one situation may be unacceptable in another. A loud voice used on the playground may not be acceptable indoors, especially in a place such as a library. Some behaviour that is acceptable at home may not be appropriate in public. Some regressive behaviours in young children, such as clinging or thumb sucking, might be allowed at home, but not in the grocery store. You may be allowed to drink the last bit of soup from the soup bowl at home, but this is inappropriate when there is company, or when you are eating in a restaurant.

You soon know if you have behaved incorrectly by other people's reactions or cues. A frown, a raised eyebrow, or a cleared throat may be subtle signs that you have made a mistake. An angry look, a sudden silence, an "excuse me?," or a loud protest lets you know that your behaviour is inappropriate. The embarrassed or uncomfortable feeling you get may be enough to let you know that you have done something wrong.

❖ Connections

Think of something that is socially unacceptable, but not illegal, such as forgetting to turn around to face the doors when using an elevator, blowing your nose loudly in class, or taking your own tablecloth and silverware into a fast-food restaurant. Perform this activity and report to the class (a) what you did, (b) how you felt doing it, and (c) the reaction you got from others.

Encouraging Socially Acceptable Behaviour

Children are born without knowing how to behave. They need to learn the difference between acceptable and unacceptable behaviours.

■ The Ontario Ministry of Education defines socialization as "the process of passing on to new members the society's beliefs and ways of thinking and acting."

Figure 14.1
What types of behaviour were unacceptable when you were a child?

As new experiences arise, parents, caregivers, teachers, and anyone who works with children in any way can encourage appropriate behaviour. **Encouragement**—favourable comments that affirm behaviour—gives the child the *courage* to act in the preferred way in social situations. **Reinforcement** occurs when the child's preferred behaviour is acknowledged and encouraged repeatedly until it becomes second nature. Encouragement and reinforcement are part of the everyday interaction between parent and child.

Parental Strategies for Teaching Socially Acceptable Behaviour

Here are three effective teaching strategies: show them how, tell them how, and acknowledge when they do it.

Modelling: Parents, caregivers, and other adults set an example of expected behaviour when following accepted social practices. This gives the child an opportunity to imitate the appropriate behaviour. Effective attachment leads to identification with the parent, which encourages the child to imitate parental behaviour.

Stating Expectations: The child is told exactly what is expected in social situations such as visiting the library, being a guest in someone's home, and going to a wedding or a funeral. If a child has never experienced the social situation before, they need clear instructions to know how to behave. They must feel secure enough in new situations to observe and imitate adult behaviour and attitudes.

Giving Positive Feedback: When a child is polite, helpful, respectful of others, or follows the customary rules of good social behaviour, a smile, a word of praise, a small reward or privilege, and especially a thank-you reinforces the appropriate behaviour.

Figure 14.2
While playing in the kitchen cupboard may be an acceptable activity for two- and three-year-old children, it is not acceptable for eight- or ten-year-olds.

❖ Connections

1. Role-play one of the strategies parents use to encourage and reinforce appropriate behaviour.

Age-Appropriate Behaviour

Different behaviours are expected from children of different ages. It might be acceptable for a four-year-old to use his or her fingers when eating, but it is not usually acceptable for an eight-year-old or a teenager to do so. Adults may smile if a child stares at a stranger, but an adult who stares is considered rude and may even provoke an angry reaction in some situations. Older children are expected to be polite and helpful, while adolescents are supposed to take on more responsibility in the home and in the community as well. It is not acceptable for children to work, but older adolescents can have part-time jobs, unless they are devoting all their time to their studies and volunteer activities.

The behaviour that is expected from people of different ages relates to where they are in their development. The younger the children, the fewer things they are expected to remember. The following list presents some of the many "do's and don'ts" that children encounter and need to know about at different stages.

Learning Age-Appropriate Behaviour

Infants
- don't put that in your mouth, it's dirty
- don't hurt the cat/dog
- don't bite, grab, or pull hair

Toddlers
- don't hit, bite, or pinch
- be gentle with a baby
- don't throw things
- say please and thank-you
- use your words
- share your toys
- keep your clothes on in public

Preschoolers
- no kicking, yelling, or screaming in public
- no pinching or hitting
- say please, thank-you, and excuse me
- use your indoor voice
- eat properly

- don't fight with your brother/sister
- don't forget to flush

Older Children
- follow the rules
- be polite and helpful
- watch your language
- no showing off
- wait your turn
- mind your manners

Adolescents
- behave in a mature manner
- control your anger
- take responsibility
- help out at home
- think about what you are doing
- practise proper etiquette
- care for and respect others

How a parent, sibling, or adult responds to a child's unacceptable behaviour can turn the situation into a **positive learning experience**. Ridiculing, spanking, threatening, and shouting are negative or reactive responses that shame a child and damage his or her self-esteem. Gentle reminders, redirecting the child to more acceptable behaviour, and taking time to show the child exactly how to behave are proactive responses that encourage positive learning experiences. Children also learn from their mistakes and from the reaction to their behaviour. For example, when they butt into the line at the movies or the school cafeteria, they soon find out whether their behaviour is acceptable.

Mistakes, perhaps, are life's greatest learning experiences.
— Anonymous

❖ Checkpoints

1. Which of the three parental strategies for teaching socially acceptable behaviour is used to encourage or discourage the behaviours mentioned in the age-appropriate list?

2. Identify behaviours on the age-appropriate list that are considered misbehaviour:
   a) in a family
   b) in a caregiving or school setting
   c) in a public place or community situation
3. Make a list of behaviours that are socially unacceptable for children of a particular age group. For each one, suggest a way to encourage more desirable behaviour without damaging the child's self-esteem.

The Role of Family and Significant Others in Socializing Children

Parents are a child's first and foremost coaches and instructors. They stand between the child and the world, making the way easier for the child. A parent becomes a **role model** who shows the child how to act. Children learn skills for managing in the world long before they need to use them outside of the family. The family introduces children to interpersonal relationships. Oldest and only children must rely on their parents to show them the appropriate way to behave, while children with siblings often learn how to act from an older brother or sister.

Children learn acceptable behaviour more easily if they have their family's social support. Family members play an active role in all areas of child development. Playing games makes babies smile and respond, and at the same time encourages a give-and-take relationship. Peek-a-Boo is fun, but it also teaches the child to trust that a parent can be relied upon to be there every time. Parents' outstretched hands encourage children to take their first steps and also show them that their parents have confidence in them. Talking, smiling, cajoling, or encouraging are all second nature to parents, brothers, and sisters when there is a baby in the house. The family is the most important factor in early childhood learning and development. It is particularly important in helping children learn the ways of society.

Reading to Children

Reading stories and books to children is one of the best ways family members can contribute to a child's social development. Books are an effective resource that parents can use to teach children about the world and how people behave in it. Pictures of objects and human interaction prepare children for what to expect when they encounter

What Do Children Learn from Family Interaction?

Children learn how to:
- love and be loved
- interact with others
- share family resources such as space, furnishings, time, and parental attention
- co-operate and compete with siblings
- evaluate their own behaviour using family members as models
- establish ties with others outside the family

these circumstances themselves. Books can help to introduce many routines, manners, and new situations, such as a trip to the dentist.

It takes time to read to children, but by spending the time, parents show their children just how important they are. The ritual also enhances early learning. Reading the same book over and over may seem boring to an adult, but children revel in the repetition. It allows them to anticipate when a particular word will occur and to recognize what it looks like. Reading the same story over and over lets children predict the outcome and reduces their anxiety about the way events may unfold.

Reading to children means far more to them than just hearing words and seeing pictures. It provides a warm and caring environment in which children learn language and make connections between language and behaviour, as well as language and objects. As children learn concepts and become familiar with how people act and interact in the stories they hear, they develop the confidence needed to face the world. Children who are read to are more competent as learners and as social beings.

Since we know that the repeated reading of a book is an important factor in literacy development, it's a huge bonus when children demand the same story again and again. And they'll make that demand if they like the characters, empathize with the characters, or see themselves in the characters.
— Mem Fox

Play and Socialization

Children also practise their social skills through play. Pretend or imaginary play allows them the opportunity to imitate a role played out in society. Playing house, school, restaurant, king of the mountain, or follow the leader all bring in the rules of society through the eyes of a child. Play gives children a safe place in which to practise acceptable behaviour, as well as to try out unacceptable behaviour and imagine the consequences. The bank robber, the rude customer, or the uncooperative child can be played out with imagined appropriate responses.

❖ Connections

1. Review a number of children's books. Identify the morals and values that are being taught through the stories. Identify the specific socially acceptable behaviours in the story.

2. Write and illustrate a book for four-year-olds that teaches them how to act in a situation they may not have already experienced.

3. Observe children at play. How do they demonstrate and reinforce socially acceptable behaviour? How do they handle unacceptable behaviour?

Figure 14.3
Through pretend or imaginary play, children imitate roles and acceptable behaviour. Play gives them a safe environment in which to practise.

■ Agents of socialization are
- family
- caregivers
- peers
- school
- religion
- culture
- community
- mass media

Agents of Socialization

Individuals and groups that teach children the **norms** or accepted ways of society are called **agents of socialization**. Human beings are shaped by many agents of socialization in their lifetime. The following agents play a significant role in the socialization of children: family, caregivers, peers, school, religion, culture, community, and mass media. The agents of socialization, however, may have conflicting views about what is acceptable behaviour. For example, it may be the norm of a peer group to wear a hat at all times, but the norm at the group's school or local court house might be "no hats allowed, except where required for religious purposes."

Figure 14.4
The agents of socialization

❖ Connection

1. Draw a web diagram with a stick figure of yourself in the centre, with lines radiating out to descriptions of how each of the various agents of socialization influence your behaviour or way of thinking. For example, instead of using the word "family," identify each family member and how they influence you.

Roles Related to Socialization

Although parents are the initial and primary social agents, caregivers as well as others in the community influence children. Teachers, coaches, neighbours, members of community organizations, and those whose occupations touch the lives of children also play a significant role in the socialization of children.

The role of parents is to provide their children with a secure base for socialization through the love and nurturing they provide them from birth. Parents may need to rely on caregivers when they are working or away from home for various reasons. The role of the caregiver is to reflect the parents' values and attitudes regarding socialization. Parents must make it clear to the caregiver what they will and will not accept from their children, as well as how they want their preferences to be reinforced in the caregiving situation.

A **parenting philosophy** clearly and accurately explains what parents feel is the best approach to use with their children. Parenting partners must have ongoing and frank discussions about what they generally expect from their children to ensure that they both require the same behaviour and are not confusing their child. Parents should also have a framework for how to deal with misbehaviour so that they are prepared to respond to a stressful situation. Their philosophy also needs to be communicated to a caregiver. Most licensed child-care situations have published expectations of the behaviour that is expected and the consequences for misbehaviour. Their policy should be a good fit if it is consistent with the parents' own parenting philosophy. However, parents do not always have the luxury of choice and may have to deal with child-care providers whose philosophy does not match their own. If this is the case, they must emphasize to children that these are the rules, behaviours, and practices expected in "our" home.

As children engage in the process of learning what is acceptable in society, they may experience many different emotions. The job of growing up can be very difficult for young children, resulting in tears, tantrums, and frustration. After an outburst, a child often feels very unsettled and possibly frightened by his or her own reaction. Parents and caregivers must demonstrate **empathy** by understanding what the child is feeling, and by responding with the comfort the child needs to deal with the ups and downs of growing up. Seeing the world from the child's point of view can help a parent or caregiver respond in a way that helps the child through the situation while maintaining his or her dignity.

Caregivers who have a positive attitude toward learning and development help the children in their care to learn about what is acceptable in other families, or what is acceptable in a child-care situation. They, too, should model acceptable behaviour, state clear expectations, and give **positive feedback**.

See everything; overlook a great deal; correct a little.
— Pope John XXIII

Parenting Wisdom: A child who is losing control in the grocery store may benefit more from a warm embrace and a sympathetic response than from an impatient and angry reaction.

Figure 14.5
Many members of the community play roles in how children learn acceptable behaviour.

■ Life would be simple if children did everything we asked, but that is not reality. Parenting is often hard work.

   The community also plays a role in how children learn acceptable behaviour. As children become involved in the community informally through play groups and neighbourhood activities, and more formally through organized clubs and activities, religious organizations, and school, they learn how to get along with others in larger groups. Generally, schools, clubs, and social groups reflect the values of society as a whole. However, in some cases, parents may feel they are losing some control of their children's behaviour. Parenting approaches such as the Three-Stage Discipline Plan recommended by Elaine M. Gibson in her on-line publication *The Challenge of Difficult Children: Elaine M. Gibson's Insights on Parenting* (2002) can help parents regain control through encouragement, explaining what is required of the child, and having a backup plan that spells out the consequences of non-compliance. Gibson notes: "Life would be simple if children did everything we asked, but that is not reality. Parenting is often hard work. With a difficult child, it is ALWAYS hard work. With the techniques in Stage I, II, or III of this discipline plan, it may be a bit easier." (p. 4)

Parenting Skills

Three-Stage Discipline Plan

The following material is from Gibson's Three-Stage Discipline Plan (2002).

Stage I: Encourage the right response.

1. We can see what needs to be done and we want the child to tell himself what to do.

   We describe the situation or problem as we see it. The next step is to back off and let the child decide what needs to be done. "It is bedtime," not "Go brush your teeth and get ready for bed." Children blossom when they are allowed to tell themselves what needs to be done.

2. Sometimes we need to clarify the information if the situation is not obvious to the child. "Your wet towel is on the carpet. Wet towels can cause the carpet to mildew," instead of "Can't you ever remember to hang up your towel!"

CHAPTER 14 SOCIALIZATION OF CHILDREN

3. Children need reminders but the reminders need to be kind. Children do forget, and it takes years to develop the habits we take for granted. One word is often enough. "Bedtime." "Towel." Written notes are also useful, especially with children who are visual learners and do not remember what they hear.

Stage II: The parents must give an order, but first, they must know what they will do if the kids don't respond.

Stage II is for children who are beyond encouragement, who don't respond to the opportunity to tell themselves. In Stage II, parents must think first about the consequences for non-compliance and then give the order.

1. Explain exactly what we want the child to do. "I want you to or I need you to ...."
2. The second step is to back off and give the child a chance to comply. If we stand over the child, we are inviting a contest of wills.
3. The third step is to recognize compliance. "Thank you for doing that." We can thank a child for being responsible, for being respectful, for cooperating. A child's obedience should not be taken for granted.

Stage III: For children who choose to defy their parents.

The parents must take over. All children try it at least sometimes. Some children seem to spend their entire childhood testing all the boundaries. Stage III may be a constant state for parents of such a child.

1. **Give the child who fails to respond to a Stage I or Stage II request two choices: compliance or consequences.**
   - First, parents specify exactly what will happen for non-compliance.
   - Then the child is given a last opportunity to act.
   - If the child finally decides to comply, the child is told, "You made a good choice."

2. **If the child fails to do what is expected, enforce the consequences.**
   Don't allow a child to manipulate the situation at this point. The consequences have been set and should be carried out. If the child argues or begs and pleads, don't listen. This is not the time to feel sorry for your child.

Figure 14.6
Children can be expected to do only what they are developmentally capable of.

3. **Children must experience the consequences of their actions, of their choices.**

   Consequences should be reasonable and related to the incident. If a child doesn't like the consequences, the parent has found the right one.

Mistakes to Avoid

1. **Expectations that are too high.**

   One mistake is setting expectations that are too high or unrealistic. Children can only be expected to do what they are capable of doing. Books on child development can help parents figure out if their expectations are in line with the child's capabilities.

2. **Beginning at Stage III.**

   Jumping to a Stage III response immediately every time something needs to be done—big mistake. We want to foster respect, responsibility, co-operation, and self-esteem in our children. Perpetual Stage III parenting undermines those attributes and leads to very defiant children.

3. **Verbal abuse.**

   The greatest mistake is using methods that cause permanent damage to our children. Emotional abuse may be even more disastrous than physical abuse. Nagging, threatening, pleading, screaming demean the parent. Humiliation, name-calling, and inducing guilt demean the child. Neither are necessary.

❖ Connection

1. As a child, did you learn behaviours outside the family that were opposite to what your family valued? Where did you encounter these opposing expectations? What did your parents do?

■ When expected behaviour outside the home differs from expectations in the home, parents should clearly emphasize the rules, behaviours, and practices that are expected in "our home."

Social and Cultural Aspects of Socialization

Since societies change and evolve over time, behaviour that may have been unacceptable years ago may be acceptable now. For example, children in pioneer Canada were expected "to be seen and not heard." Today, children are encouraged to speak up and not to be shy. Some rules or ways of society have even become law. In the past, Canadian children worked for low wages in mines, factories, and on farms. Today, child labour is illegal. Male and female role expectations have changed over the years: fathers are far more involved in parenting and homemaking, while women participate in all levels of the paid labour force. Changes in society become part of the socialization process. Children—especially young children—imitate the behaviour they see modelled by adults in the family and in the community.

Within Canada, there are many different cultures. Every family has its own unique culture that it transmits to children. How adults live, work, communicate, and behave in one family may be just a little different from the next family. Acceptable table manners in one household may be considered unacceptable in another. In one family, being polite, respectful, and distant from elders may be common practice, while in another family, being familiar and affectionate with elders is preferred. Individual differences make the world an interesting place.

FOR BETTER OR FOR WORSE © UFS. Reprinted by permission.

Figure 14.7
Lynn Johnston's ability to capture life as it happens has made her one of the world's leading cartoonists.

Becoming a Good Citizen

For the most part, learning acceptable behaviour encourages individuals to function in society as a whole. The goal of socialization is not just to have well-behaved children, but also to produce individuals who are good citizens. A good citizen strengthens the social fabric of a country and makes it a better place for everyone.

Society as a whole is concerned with socially unacceptable behaviour that may threaten its very existence. Society depends on parents and those in authority to discourage unacceptable behaviour by responding to it. In responding to unacceptable behaviour, however, there must be a balance. Children must know their own rights so that they are not disadvantaged by those in authority. If, however, they are allowed to **thwart authority**, or defeat those with power, they may grow up to threaten the existing social order that exists in government and law enforcement. While the devastating effects of **criminal behaviour** on victims and society as a whole is understood, the federal Youth Criminal Justice Act (2002) is based on the belief that young people make mistakes, and first time offenders can be rehabilitated. Children and young people are expected to question the rules, but this questioning must not lead to **anarchy** or complete lawlessness. Since the family is the foundation for how people behave in society, parents have a major responsibility both to their children and to the society in which they live.

❖ Checkpoints

1. Describe how reading contributes to social development.
2. Which agents of socialization have the most influence on infants? Toddlers? Preschoolers? Adolescents? Account for the difference.
3. Explain the role of parents and caregivers in ensuring that children are healthy, secure, and confident.
4. Using examples, describe the short- and long-term effects on society of criminal behaviour, thwarting authority, and anarchy.

Issues and Challenges Affecting Socialization

Children need a caring parent or role model to teach them the ways of society. In some cases, however, children do not have a positive experience. There are many instances in which **negative socialization patterns** have more influence. Instead of being taught acceptable behaviour through positive techniques, there are situations in which unacceptable behaviour is modelled and expected, and negative feedback is given. When this happens, socialization is negatively affected, and as Dorothy Law Nolte's poem indicates, a child's growth and development may be compromised.

Children Learn What They Live

If children live with criticism,
they learn to condemn.

If children live with hostility,
they learn to fight.

If children live with fear,
they learn to be apprehensive.

If children live with pity,
they learn to feel sorry for
themselves.

If children live with ridicule,
they learn to feel shy.

If children live with jealousy,
they learn to feel envy.

If children live with shame,
they learn to feel guilty.

If children live with
encouragement, they learn
confidence.

If children live with tolerance,
they learn patience.

If children live with praise,
they learn appreciation

If children live with acceptance,
they learn to love.

If children live with approval,
they learn to like themselves.

If children live with recognition,
they learn it is good to have a
goal.

If children live with sharing,
they learn generosity.

If children live with honesty,
they learn truthfulness.

If children live with fairness,
they learn justice.

If children live with kindness and
consideration, they learn respect.

If children live with security, they
learn to have faith in themselves
and in those about them.

If children live with friendliness,
they learn the world is a nice
place in which to live.

Dorothy Law Nolte

Figure 14.8
This poem, which has appeared in countless journals, books, and magazines, was written in 1954.

Many family situations can have a negative effect on the socialization of family members. A variety of stresses influence how children are socialized within families. These include divorce, substance abuse, mental illness, addictions, unemployment, poverty, and parents having difficulty coping with a variety of challenges. Child abuse, neglect, and family violence have an extremely negative impact on the growth, development, and socialization of children.

Child Abuse, Neglect, and Family Violence

All children have physical and emotional needs that must be met if they are to develop to their full potential. Consistent loving care helps meet these needs, whereas child abuse, neglect, and family violence create disadvantages that can last a lifetime. Child abuse, neglect, and domestic violence are a misuse of power, violating a child's basic sense of trust in the very person responsible for their care. Signs of abuse may not always be visible, but knowing the indicators can alert neighbours, caregivers, and those who work with children to the possibility of abuse.

Child Abuse

When **child abuse** occurs, a child experiences either physical, emotional, or sexual harm. **Physical abuse** is the easiest type to detect, because there may be unexplained or repeated welts, bruises, burns, fractures, or cuts on the child. **Sexual abuse** is more difficult to detect. If a child has abdominal pain or pain when sitting down, displays unusual interest in sexual behaviour, or shows unexplained fear, it can be an indicator of sexual abuse. **Emotional abuse** involves not responding to a child's emotional needs for love and belonging. It can take the form of name-calling, putting the child down, not comforting the child when comfort is needed, belittling the child, or keeping the child in a state of fear and anxiety through mental cruelty, or physical or sexual abuse. Emotional abuse is difficult to detect and, therefore, is difficult to overcome.

Neglect

Neglect involves depriving a child of the basic necessities of life, such as love and affection, food, shelter, clothing, medical care, or rest. One of the most obvious signs of neglect is **malnutrition** (not having enough nutrients from food to grow or thrive). Signs of malnutrition include weight loss, paleness, fatigue, or illness related to

■ All children have physical and emotional needs that must be met if they are to develop to their full potential.

nutrient deficiencies. Neglect can also take the form of failing to supervise children in a manner consistent with their development. It also includes not seeking medical care when warranted, or not attending to tooth decay or childhood injuries. Poor health and poor hygiene can also be indicators of neglect.

What the experts say

NICO TROCME

Nico Trocme is a Professor of Social Work at the University of Toronto. He answers the following question:

What were the findings of your latest study for Health Canada, comparing 1993 and 1998 reports of child abuse?

The 1993 Ontario Incidence Study of Reported Child Abuse and Neglect (OIS 1993) was the first survey conducted in Canada to examine the characteristics of children and families investigated by child-welfare authorities. The OIS 1993 collected information on a sample of 2447 child maltreatment investigations conducted by a random sample of 15 child-welfare agencies. The OIS 1998, a similar study, was conducted as part of a national study of reported maltreatment called The Canadian Incidence Study of Reported Child Abuse and Neglect (CIS). The OIS 1998 was based on a second sample of 3053 child maltreatment investigations conducted in 1998. Comparison of the two studies reveals that rates of substantiated maltreatment have doubled in five years. Exposure to spousal violence has increased nine-fold, the number of neglect cases has more than doubled, while cases of sexual abuse are decreasing.

Three factors have generally contributed to the overall increase in reported child maltreatment and subsequent case openings by child-welfare agencies. They are mandatory reporting laws, growing public awareness, and training for professionals who come into contact with children. Reporting by family members, neighbours, and acquaintances has not particularly changed; however, professionals who work with children are making far more reports to child-welfare agencies since reporting child maltreatment became mandatory in the CFSA (Child and Family Services Act) in 1998. Now all professionals who work with children must properly report suspected cases of child maltreatment or face legal consequences.

The increase in reports from professionals is largely driven by investigations of neglect and exposure to domestic violence, two types of maltreatment that have drawn attention in the latter half of the decade. As with the recognition of sexual abuse in the 1980s, there is growing awareness of the harmful effects on children of exposure to domestic violence. Although this form of maltreatment is not specifically addressed in the CFSA, a number of organizations have adopted policies of systematically reporting these cases to the Children's Aid Society. It is noteworthy that nearly all the investigations involving domestic violence tracked in the OIS 1998 were reported by professionals.

Beyond increasing public awareness, several factors also support the argument that part of the increase can be attributed to more children being victimized, in particular in cases of neglect. Low income, poor housing, and lack of social supports are three of the key factors that have been shown to be associated with higher rates of neglect. The changes in the income-support programs and decreased availability of social housing in Ontario between 1993 and 1998 lend some support to the argument that poor families are under more stress than ever before and may be experiencing more parenting difficulties.

Ontario Incidence Study of Reported Child Abuse and Neglect

Type of Abuse	1993	1998
Neglect	4400	8900
Emotional Maltreatment	1000	8700
Physical Abuse	4200	8000
Sexual Abuse	3400	1900

Family Violence

Family violence is characterized by spousal assault. Spousal assault can take the form of physical violence, emotional abuse, sexual assault, threats, or simply putting down individuals or controlling them in ways that keep them in fear. Most often, family violence takes the form of assault against women (woman abuse). Children who witness family violence, or who are involved in some way in the power dynamics, display a variety of reactions. They may show a lack of trust of adults, demonstrate insecurity, or handle anger in inappropriate ways. They may also develop eating disorders, cry for no apparent reason, or may not want to go home at the end of a school day.

Surviving Abuse, Neglect, or Family Violence

To survive abuse, the abuse must first end. For many people, this is impossible without help. How can an infant end neglect? How can a child change how a parent behaves? How can a woman escape an abusive relationship?

Years ago, the treatment of women and children inside the family was considered a private matter. Society has gradually introduced policies and laws that now make the welfare of every person their business. Today, society realizes that child abuse is often a product of stress, parental isolation, and ignorance of the normal patterns of human development. Community programs and parenting centres attempt to provide support and education for improving the lives of children who are at risk.

■ Today, society realizes that child abuse is often a product of stress, parental isolation, and ignorance of the normal patterns of human development.

Education and Reporting Abuse

In recent years, education has helped many people by increasing awareness and by teaching that abuse and violence are everyone's concern. Victims of abuse feel powerless and often do not have the courage to report the abuse. Many cases of abuse go unreported for years. Education in schools and communities helps children learn to identify abuse, neglect, and family violence, and gives them information about how to get help. Education for professionals and others who work with children is even more important. It is very often someone outside of the family, such as a professional, who reports the suspected abuse and begins the process to get the required help.

Reporting laws make it an offence not to report suspected abuse. Abuse, neglect, and family violence are the responsibility of the entire community.

■ Reporting abuse, neglect, and family violence is the responsiblilty of the entire community.

Child Welfare Laws

Any person who knows about, sees evidence of, suspects, or is told about child abuse in confidence or not in confidence must report it immediately to a Children's Aid Society or equivalent agency in their community.

It is everyone's social responsibility to keep children as safe as possible. Child abuse reporting laws vary somewhat across Canada. In Ontario, for example, many professional people in positions of responsibility, such as police officers, school teachers, and school administrators, must, by law, report witnessed or suspected abuse of a child under 16 years of age to the Children's Aid Society. If these professionals do not report witnessed or suspected abuse, they are liable to be prosecuted to the full extent of the law.

Abuse, neglect, and family violence are criminal offences. Legal intervention brings these problems to court. Children are generally removed from the abusive family and placed in foster care or in the care of a guardian until it is safe to return to their own family. Individual and family counselling and therapy can help return a family to a stable situation.

■ Abuse, neglect, and family violence are criminal offences.

Community Support

Many community programs and agencies have been established in response to a growing awareness of the problems of abuse, neglect, and violence. Courses in parenting and anger management, and continuing education are available for parents who recognize that they need help with their behaviour or their parenting skills. Child help-lines, such as "Kids' Help-Line," are available for children to call for help or to talk over problems. "Crime Stoppers" allows people to report abuse or assault without identifying themselves. There are

The cycle of abuse can be broken. Last year, thousands of abused women and their children sought refuge through United Way agencies. Please call 1 800 267-8221 or visit our website at www.unitedway.ca to give. Without you, there would be no way.

United Way

Figure 14.9

This United Way poster raises public awareness about the abuse of women and children.

parent support groups, drop-in centres for parents and their children, and programs for mothers only, fathers only, or both, that explore the problems and frustrations of parenting in a group setting, and provide realistic alternatives to abuse and violence.

Barriers to Access

The problem with some programs is that sometimes the very people who need the services have difficulty accessing them. Access is a problem for people who do not speak the language that is spoken by the agency or used in the program. The way women and children are treated is not open for examination in some cultures in Canada. It is considered a breach of cultural values to go for help. Getting help may also mean a series of other challenges. Filling out paperwork, going to court, consulting a lawyer, and seeing a social worker can be seen as huge obstacles when education levels, low literacy skills, or command of the English or French language make those tasks seem impossible. Abuse, neglect, and family violence are problems for all sectors of society, and access to help and support must be made available to everyone.

Preventing Child Abuse, Neglect, and Family Violence

Child abuse, neglect, and family violence may be the symptoms of much deeper problems in the family. Men and women often parent children based on how their own parents raised them. If spanking was practised in their family of orientation, they are more likely to repeat that technique with their own children. Other factors such as stress, alcoholism, substance abuse, low self-esteem, depression, and frustration may contribute to and perpetuate the problems. Living in a safe and peaceful family, community, and social environment is the right of every child. All citizens must identify harmful situations, take a stand against abuse and violence, and take steps to prevent all forms of abuse, neglect, and violence.

Child abuse can also stem from being unprepared for the responsibility of parenthood. It might result from expecting far too much from an infant or child. It can be frustrating to hear a baby cry and not know how to respond, or have no understanding of what to expect of children at different ages, and not know effective methods of control. Friends, relatives, or partners who share the overwhelming job of parenting help reduce the risk of abuse.

Recognizing the intent to abuse before it happens can stop a parent or caregiver from acting against the child. Critical skills for preventing violence include having a plan for removing oneself from a potentially explosive situation, and learning what to do instead of hitting a child. Some individuals, however, have much deeper problems with power and control over children. They may not stop the negative behaviour unless they receive medical, psychiatric, or psychological intervention. Sometimes, they may need to be kept away from children altogether. Unfortunately, they are often the ones who will not seek help before there is a significant problem.

Neglect may happen for many reasons. Mental illness, depression, drug or alcohol addiction, and psychological problems of a deeper nature frequently lead to cases of neglect. A positive outlook plus a close bond and deep attachment to a child provide insurance against neglect. Parenting means putting a child's needs ahead of anything else, but parents may not be able to care for a child if they do not take care of themselves first. This is a very difficult concept for parents in stressful parenting situations. Good physical health and mental health go hand in hand in the prevention of child neglect.

Figure 14.10
Severe depression in caregivers can result in child neglect. Medical intervention and family support are necessary to help alleviate this situation.

❖ Checkpoints

1. Design a pamphlet that describes physical, sexual, and emotional abuse, and explains how parents can get help if they are having a problem.
2. Describe neglect and give five examples of neglectful parenting.
3. Create a one-page poster suitable to post in your community, with the title "Ways to Prevent Child Abuse and Neglect Before They Happen."

Career Capsule

SOCIAL WORKER

Tasks and Responsibilities

Social workers attempt to identify why an individual is having problems functioning effectively in society, and then help that individual make the changes needed to resolve the problems. They interact with individuals, families, and groups of people in the community in an attempt to make sure that their clients are socially as fully integrated and functional as possible.

Social workers assist those with problems such as substance abuse, unemployment and poverty, child neglect and abuse, family violence, criminal behaviour, and mental illnesses. These problems may have complicated physical, psychological, social, legal, and economic causes. A social worker helps the individual or family sort out the causes and get access to support or help in the community. Often the social worker can get individuals or families back on their feet so they can independently solve the rest of the problem. When this happens, the clients' self-esteem and social integration improve. Instead of being a drain on society, the people with the problems become functional and contributing members of society.

Work Environment

Most social workers are employed by government or community agencies. The record-keeping and administrative part of their job is done in an office. However, a large part of the day involves travel to meet with clients, attend community meetings, or interact with service providers bringing assistance to the community. Since the problems that a social worker deals with are often complicated and involve human suffering, emotional burnout is an issue in this line of work. Understaffing and large caseloads can add to this emotional drain.

Education and Aptitudes

Because this career deals with helping people with their problems, key components in the make-up of a successful social worker are emotional maturity and strength. A successful social worker must be keenly aware that a full-life career with strong relationship and community roles outside of the workplace is essential to maintain his or her health and wellness. Proficiency in other languages other than that spoken in the province or community is a definite asset for social workers whose clients come from a variety of backgrounds.

A four-year Bachelor of Social Work degree is the minimum educational requirement, although many employers prefer graduates of Masters of Social Work degree programs. A master's degree is essential for advancement or therapeutic positions, while research positions at universities require candidates who have a Ph.D. in social work. Some provinces require social workers to be certified.

Taking action against abuse, neglect, and violence is important. Recognizing what constitutes abuse and speaking out against it is important for both men and women in society. High-school students of both sexes have joined in the nation-wide March Against Male Violence. Men as well as women offer support to family members, neighbours, and friends who have experienced abuse or violence. Each individual can make a difference by taking steps towards the prevention of abuse, neglect, and family violence through self-awareness, education, and reporting.

Taking Action Against Child Abuse, Neglect, and Violence

- Wait until you are ready to parent before having children.
- Learn about child development before becoming a parent.
- Learn techniques to encourage children instead of hitting or yelling.
- Be sure you can count on friends or family for support.

- Put personal and family safety first.
- Know where to turn to for help.
- Make personal and child safety a priority.
- Report any suspected abuse or family violence.
- Support community programs that protect and support families.
- Speak out against violence portrayed in the media.

Chapter Summary

Chapter Highlights

- Socialization is a process that teaches individuals socially acceptable behaviour or society's expectations for how to behave.

- Socialization begins at birth.

- Modelling the preferred behaviour, stating clearly what the desired behaviour is, and giving positive feedback when the accepted behaviour has been noted encourages socially acceptable behaviour.

- Different behaviours are accepted from children of different age groups.

- Children begin by learning simple things, such as not pulling hair or biting.

- As a child matures, the rules for behaviour become more complex.

- Parents, caregivers, and others who interact with children in society help teach appropriate behaviour.

- Reading to children is an effective way to teach them about the world before they need to face it.

- Children practise appropriate behaviour through play, when they imitate adults, or make up imaginary situations.

- Because families have their own values and ways of behaving, there are social and cultural differences in what is considered acceptable.

- Some families face critical issues and challenges such as addictions, depression, alcoholism, and other factors that may interfere with the ability to model or teach appropriate behaviour.

- Child abuse, neglect, and family violence also disrupt socialization and can have lifelong negative consequences for children.

Review and Extend Your Learning

1. Define "socialization" and describe why it is an important part of the parenting process. **K/U**

2. Describe how misbehaviour can be turned into a positive learning experience. Support your answer with a specific example. **K/U** **A**

3. How important is it that caregivers know and agree with parents' parenting philosophy? Explain your answer with examples. **K/U** **T/I** **C** **A**

4. How do you know if a child is being abused? Write a short information pamphlet for community distribution that outlines the signs of abuse. **K/U** **C**

5. Why does most family violence take the form of assault against women? Investigate the issue and outline some of the strategies that can be used to combat this form of abuse. **K/U** **T/I** **C**

6. Investigate the opportunities for help and support that are available in your community. List the agency or community service, the type of support it provides, and how it can be accessed by individuals and families. **K/U** **T/I** **C** **A**

7. Investigate the relationship between low self-esteem and family violence. Make some recommendations as to how this problem can be resolved in families. **T/I**

8. Role play a situation that depicts the barriers to access that some individuals and families experience when seeking community or social support. Offer solutions for overcoming these barriers. **K/U C A**

9. Investigate and report on the relationship between life-long psychological adjustment and a childhood experience of family violence. **T/I C**

Research Opportunities

10. Find a novel, biography, or autobiography that recounts negative parental reinforcement, such as spanking or excessive force, in the early childhood experiences of the main character. Write a book report and discuss the effects this negative reinforcement had on the life of the character.

11. Investigate some North American practices that might be considered strange or rude in other societies. Report your findings to the class.

12. Find out what the child abuse reporting laws are in your province or territory. In groups, use the Internet to locate the reporting laws in the rest of Canada's provinces or territo-ries. Use chart paper to collect all the information and to form a national comparison.

13. Select one of the following social concerns:
   - divorce
   - alcoholism
   - drug addictions
   - unemployment
   - poverty
   - dual/single income
   - stress
   - lack of parenting support from friends or family
   - depression
   - mental illness

Conduct an inquiry to answer the question, "How does the problem affect children in the long term?" Report your findings.

Issue Analysis

14. Families often find that mental illness is the most difficult problem for which to find solutions.
   a) Where in your community can families turn to get help when one of the family members has a mental illness?
   b) The demand for mental health support is growing faster then the number of young people entering the profession. Analyze the reasons for and against a career in mental health.

15. Select one of the following and argue for and against:
   - Is parental smoking a form of child abuse?
   - Is not setting limits for behaviour a form of child abuse?

Parenting Practices

How Do Child-Rearing Practices Differ?

Children are raised in different ways in different places and at different stages of their lives. A stereotypical North American view of child rearing is of a nuclear family in which two parents share the responsibility for their children's upbringing. Modern families now take many forms. Parents do not always live with their own children. Because of divorce, separation, lone-parent households, or stepfamilies, children may not live in the same household as both their parents, and this can affect how they are raised.

In Canada, child rearing differs from one family to the next because no two families are alike. Every family has its own composition, history, and culture. Culture plays an important role in child-rearing and parenting practices. Beliefs and traditions influence care, nurture, parent-child interaction, and teaching and discipline practices. Vicki Ritts (1999), in the online publication *Infusing Culture into Parenting Issues*, states that:

> Parents' cultural belief systems (i.e., ethnotheories) and emotions underlie the customs of child rearing and validate the organization of physical and social settings of life for children. For example, the most important ethnotheories revolve around the beliefs concerning the nature and needs of children, parental and community goals for child rearing, and caretaker beliefs about effective parenting practices. These three components influence each other and cannot be examined in complete isolation (p. 2).

Child-rearing practices may differ between parents in the same family and will vary depending on the child, the moment, or the situation. Every parent will have a personal parenting style. How parents were raised has a strong influence on how they raise their own children. Often, parents who vowed they would never raise their children "like that," use the same techniques or hear the same words their parents used coming from their own mouths. Parenting is an ongoing challenge as parents try to provide the best for their children without resorting to some of the expressions or behaviours of their parents that they now recognize as negative.

Stages of Parenthood

Parenting practices change as children move from infancy, through childhood, to adolescence, and into their teenage years. Parenting an

Figure 15.1
Modern Canadian families now come in many forms.

infant or toddler is different from parenting an adolescent. As children grow and change, parenting changes as well. What worked with a two-year-old will not work with a twelve-year-old. Parents' expectations for themselves change as well. Psychologist Ellen Galinsky (1981) described differences in the stages of parenthood based on interviews with more than 200 parents. She documented her research in her book *Between Generations: The Six Stages of Parenthood*. Her framework is summarized in the section titled "Developmental Stages of Parenthood."

Developmental Stages of Parenthood

In her book, Ellen Galinsky (1981) describes how adults develop through the interaction with their children.

Husband and wife become father and mother at the birth of their first baby. This is the beginning of the first stage, the *parental image stage*, during which the mother and father form their image of themselves as parents. They have a desire to be perfect but often experience heavy demands that were unexpected.

The *nurturing stage* occurs during infancy, when attachment occurs and relationships with spouse, infant, and other people are challenged and determined. Heavy demands are often made upon parents at this time as they establish their roles.

During the *authority stage*, when the child is between two and four years of age, adults question their effectiveness as parents. The young child is beginning to develop independence, and more demands are made on a parent's time. Often, a second child is born, adding to the stress of the family.

The *integrative stage* extends from preschool through middle childhood. As children develop more autonomy and social skills, parents must set realistic goals, motivate their children, develop effective communication skills, and establish authority.

The fifth stage, the *independent teenage stage*, is the time that adolescents wrestle with identification, responsibility, and maturity. Parents must provide support for their adolescents, while maintaining authority and responsibility.

Finally, the *departure stage* occurs when the adolescent leaves home. At this time, parents evaluate their parenting performance and prepare for the future relationship with their offspring.

The important point of Galinsky's theory is that parenthood develops as the children grow and that the adult's self-concepts are shaped through interactions with children at each stage. When parents are aware of and can achieve their goals, they will be happy and satisfied. If not, they will be frustrated, stressed, and depressed. Therefore, it is important for people to increase their awareness and understanding of the developmental stages of parenthood.

Parenting Theories

Around the early 1900s, parents were advised to not spoil their children. John B. Watson, a leading authority in the United States at the time, warned parents not to kiss, cuddle, or rock their children and to put them on strict schedules for feeding, sleeping, and even toilet training. Physical punishment for children by parents as well as teachers was condoned. The strap was given to children who misbehaved in school. Children were seen as impulsive beings who required a strict regimen and physical punishment to train them to be responsible citizens and good workers.

Sigmund Freud's work relating early life experience to adult mental health led to a renewed interest in child and human development and the effects of parenting on children. Theories about the best ways to parent have come and gone, but recent evidence shows that certain parenting techniques are definitely better than others.

Key to theories of parenting styles is the distinction between **discipline** and **punishment**. The word discipline is derived from the Latin word meaning to learn (discere). Discipline involves providing examples, guidance, encouragement, and rules so that children eventually learn acceptable behaviours and the ways of society. Discipline is associated with authoritative or democratic parenting.

Punishment, on the other hand, is reactive, because it is a penalty imposed for wrongdoing. When parents impose their will on children, it is a type of punishment. This is most commonly associated with authoritarian parenting.

Dr. Benjamin Spock

Approaches to child rearing changed dramatically in 1946 when Dr. Benjamin Spock, a noted pediatrician, published the first edition of *Baby and child care*. His commonsense theories of child care helped guide parents around the world for the rest of the century. His opening line was "Trust yourself." He felt parents knew more about parenting than they thought. He deliberately set out to support parents and to counteract the rigid traditions of feeding schedules and concerns about spoiling children. His thinking influenced the movement to abolish physical punishment of children.

Over time, Dr. Spock became less popular because some people found his advice too permissive, but he continued to publish parenting guide books making changes along the way. In later editions, he included information about single parents, stepparents, and divorce. In response to the feminist critique, he stopped referring to the child as "he" and the parent as "she." As well, he emphasized that parents should teach morals and values and expect respect from their children.

Benjamin Spock not only guided countless parents with advice addressing the everyday concerns of parents hoping to raise healthy, happy children, but he also influenced others to continue to research parenting and develop other theories. His underlying belief, that caring parents who are not afraid of firmness will obtain good results without being either overly strict or overly permissive, is still found in the latest advice to parents published today.

◾ Dr. Spock's commonsense theory recognized that
- each child is an individual
- parents need to be flexible
- babies should eat when hungry rather than on a schedule
- children should be respected as human beings
- parents need to give children "firm leadership"

Rudolph Dreikurs

Rudolph Dreikurs and Vicki Soltz wrote *Children: The Challenge* in 1964. This book provided a step-by-step program for coping with childhood problems. Dreikurs identified four goals of misbehaviour:

- attention seeking
- power seeking
- revenge seeking
- displaying inadequacy

He asks parents to change their usual responses to these behaviours. He recommends that parents and caregivers catch children being good, offer choices, look for and reinforce positive behaviour, stay out of power struggles, and offer encouragement.

The success of his approach has influenced the work of others including Don Dinkmeyer, Sr., Gary D. McKay, and Don Dinkmeyer, Jr., whose *Systematic training for effective parenting* (S.T.E.P), republished in 1997, has been used for parenting training in Canada since the 1970s. In *Winning at Parenting ... Without Beating Your Kids*, Barbara Coloroso (1989) uses Dreikurs' theory to describe how children "con" their parents into doing their chores for them (displaying inadequacy), giving them more attention (attention seeking), and refusing to cooperate (power seeking).

The following material is adapted from Dreikurs and Soltz's (1964) publication *Children: The Challenge*:

Figure 15.2
Parents need to be aware of the goals of the child's misbehaviour when deciding what to do.

Dreikurs' Theory of Misbehaviour

Goal of Misbehaviour	Parent feels...	Parent's Response	What to Do Instead
Attention seeking Child wants attention or service (e.g., acts out or acts silly)	• Annoyed • Angry	• Raised voice • Negative attention • Slap, swat, glare • Reminds and coaxes the child	• Ignore the behaviour • Give attention to good behaviour instead • Use effective listening skills
Power seeking Child wants to be the boss (e.g., says no when asked to do a chore)	• Provoked • A desire to gain the upper hand	• Enters a power struggle • Enters a no-win situation	• Say nothing! • Count to 10 • Walk away • Offer choices that give the child control where possible

(continued)

Goal of Misbehaviour	Parent feels...	Parent's Response	What to Do Instead
Revenge seeking Child wants to hurt the parent's feelings (e.g., sulks, slams door, says, "I hate you!")	• Hurt • Insulted	• Wants to get even • Gets back at the child • Makes threats	• Let the child cool down and then talk • Stay calm • Use "I messages"
Displaying inadequacy Child withdraws, gives up (e.g., says, "I can't do it")	• Despair • At a loss about what to do	• Cajoles the child • Steps in and does the task for the child	• Teach problem solving • Encourage small steps • Use effective listening skills

Figure 15.3
Dreikurs' theory has influenced other child behaviour theorists.

Children seem to know exactly how to "push a parent's buttons" to get a response. When a parent or caregiver is able to anticipate their goals and sidestep the conflict, the child is treated with dignity and respect. Dreikurs asks parents to use strategies that encourage positive behaviour rather than wait until confronted by misbehaviour.

Figure 15.4
Parents need to know when to intervene in a conflict.

❖ Connections

1. Describe situations in which children misbehave to achieve each of the four goals in the chart adapted from Dreikurs' work. Give at least two specific ways that parents can respond in each situation that treats the child with dignity and respect and results in more positive behaviour.

Diane Baumrind

Diane Baumrind (1971) identified and described various parenting styles. Her study, "Current Patterns of Parental Authority," which examined how middle class parents interact with their children, was published in the journal *Developmental Psychology Monographs*. In the study, Baumrind observed children's responses to different parenting styles. She identified three distinct **parenting styles**, or ways parents act toward their children: authoritarian, permissive, and authoritative. She also determined that one's style of parenting has a long-term effect on children, and noted that authoritarian and permissive do not usually have very positive outcomes.

Baumrind's Theory of Parenting Styles

Parenting Style	Parenting Behaviour	Effect on Children
Authoritarian	• Uses commands and authority • Disciplines with force or physical punishment, or both	• Lower self-esteem • Less advanced moral reasoning • Higher levels of aggression
Permissive	• Overlooks misbehaviour • Has little control • Allows the child to make his or her own decisions	• Less self-control • Less oriented toward achievement • More unhappiness
Authoritative (Democratic)	• Sets limits • Provides rationales • Expects mature behaviour and dialogue • Uses encouragement rather than punishment	• Higher self-control and more independence • Cooperative • Achievement oriented • Positive social and psychological adjustment in adolescence

Figure 15.5
Baumrind's research contributed to a growing parenting movement that advocates democratic or authoritative parenting practices instead of spanking, physical punishment, and permissive parenting.

Figure 15.6
Keeping the lines of communication open with children allows them to voice thier feelings and encourages cooperation.

❖ Checkpoints

1. What are some of the reasons that people have different parenting styles?
2. Interview a parent of adult children to learn how their parenting changed as their children matured. How closely does their story reflect Galinsky's six stages of parenthood?
3. Why have parenting techniques changed since the 1900s. What changes have occurred in society? In families?

The Importance of Democratic Parenting

In shared parenting, two parents care for and guide the child, and each parent may have a different style. Where stepparenting is involved, more parenting styles are added to a family situation. Conflict can arise between a permissive parent and an authoritarian parent. It is very difficult to present a united front to children when parents have conflicting styles. Parents need to support each other and recognize that their approaches may not be identical. Talking about their parenting philosophy and style, and taking steps so that both move toward an authoritative or democratic style, can help resolve conflicts.

Democratic parents are generally self-confident, relaxed, but firm in their management. They consistently set limits on behaviour and are very clear in their expectations. The underlying belief is that children are responsible members of a social group who need clear guidelines. Clear explanations make it easy for children to understand and accept limits and the consequences of their actions. By building self-worth through respectful interaction, children learn to develop self-control. Democratic/authoritative parenting requires thought and effort but maintains the dignity of both parent and child.

The Role of Communication in Democratic Parenting

Keeping the lines of communication open with children allows them to voice their feelings and understand their own emotions. Effective communication strategies include active listening and the use of "I" messages. Clear dialogue encourages cooperation rather than confrontation. Teaching problem-solving techniques and conflict resolution will allow children to work through their own problems and interpersonal conflicts, and gain confidence. Children feel confident when they are contributing family members who are expected to take responsibility for their own actions. If they have this effective internal image of themselves, they are more likely to demonstrate positive behaviour on a regular basis.

Barbara Coloroso

Barbara Coloroso is well known as an expert and entertaining speaker on parenting issues, teaching, school discipline, conflict resolution, and justice. She has also written several books that have addressed many challenging questions for parents including *Winning at Parenting... Without Beating Your Kids* (1989) and *Kids Are Worth It* (1994).

In *Winning at Parenting* (1989), Coloroso's approach is to make parenting theory understandable and accessible to parents. Instead of authoritarian, permissive, and authoritative, she uses the terms brick wall, jellyfish, and backbone. **Brick-wall families** are inflexible and controlling and use punitive parenting strategies. In **jellyfish families**, anything goes, and limits to acceptable behaviour are not clear. However, in **backbone families**, flexibility mixes with limits. Within the framework of a backbone family, the child develops a "backbone." This "backbone," which becomes the child's moral sense of what is right and wrong, enables children to like themselves, think for themselves, and see that problems are never too big to solve (Coloroso, 1989).

Coloroso advocates backbone parenting that involves setting limits, allowing children to take responsibility for their actions, and giving them options for solving problems. A child who faces manipulation and control by a parent or other person who is "bigger" will respond in three ways: fright—obeying out of fear; fights—attacking the adult or taking his or her anger out on others; flight—running away either mentally or physically. Besides hurting a child's dignity, physical punishment teaches a child that if you are bigger, you can hit.

Instead of hitting, she recommends using "reasonable consequences" that are Reasonable, Simple, Valuable as a learning tool, and Practical (R.S.V.P.). If the consequence does not fit the problem, it is unreasonable. Grounding a child for two weeks because he or she slammed the door and broke the glass is not reasonable or practical, nor does it solve the problem or teach the child anything. The child who is expected to clean up the glass and replace the window has solved the problem and learns not to slam a door in anger.

Figure 15.7
Barbara Coloroso is a well-known speaker on the topic of parenting skills.

Elements of Barbara Coloroso's Parenting Theory

The following list is adapted from Barbara Coloroso's book *Kids Are Worth It* (1994):

- Kids make mistakes.
- Mistakes are for learning.
- Children can make responsible choices from an early age.
- Let children make choices unless the issue is life threatening, morally threatening, or unhealthy.
- Teach a child how to think, not what to think.

- Never treat a child in a way you would not want to be treated.
- Discipline should leave both parent and child with their dignity intact.
- We need to celebrate with our children.
- The essence of parenting is time, affection, and optimism: parenting is not an efficient vocation, it takes **time**; children need **affection** daily: a hug, a smile, a joke; **optimism** helps families through the everyday ups and downs.

Barbara Coloroso believes that the parent's job is to empower and influence children, not control them. Teaching children to make their own decisions enables them to become responsible citizens who can stand up for themselves while respecting the rights of others. She encourages parents to look at their own style of parenting, and if they find they are unhappy, explore ways to do it differently the next time they are in a particular situation, because "kids are worth it."

In 1998, the Ontario Government commissioned a report to study the importance of helping children realize their full potential. The Honorable Margaret Norrie McCain and Dr. Fraser Mustard, who served as co-chairs of the study, released their report *Early Years Study* in 1999. The report, which was published by the Children's Secretariat, deals with many aspects of parenting, including parenting style. The table below illustrates their findings on the relationship between parenting styles and the prevalence of children with difficulties.

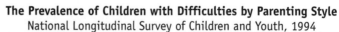

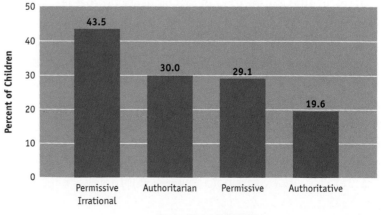

The Prevalence of Children with Difficulties by Parenting Style
National Longitudinal Survey of Children and Youth, 1994

Figure 15.8
The analysis represented in the chart shows that Ontario children in a good parenting structure (authoritative) had fewer difficulties than children in a poorer parenting situation (permissive-irrational).

❖ Checkpoints

1. What are the characteristics of democratic parents?
2. Compare "brick wall," "jellyfish," and "backbone" parenting.
3. In your own words, describe the goals of a child's misbehaviour.

T. Berry Brazelton

T. Berry Brazelton, a medical doctor and a leading expert on child development created a scale simply called **"The Brazelton"** that is used worldwide to measure potential and compare individual differences in infants at birth. The scale measures things like sensitivity to sound and light, response time to different stimuli, and activity levels. Brazelton relates this to a child's temperament, and he believes that the sooner parents know what kind of temperament the child has, the sooner they can respond appropriately and accept the child for the person he or she is.

Basic Temperaments Identified by Brazelton

The Passive Child
The **passive child**, often called a content child, is not as demanding or easily aroused as others and enjoys a cuddle. A passive child sleeps well, and does not cry readily.

The Sensitive Child
The **sensitive child** cries easily, may be upset by sounds, light, or sudden movement, reacts to any change in the environment, and may not want to be touched or cuddled.

The Active Child
The **active child** does not sleep long and is happy with movement, noise, action, and play. Bouncing may be preferred to cuddling.

A parent who is expecting a calm, quiet, playful, cuddler may be totally unprepared for one who fusses easily, does not sleep, will not calm down when overwrought, or resists cuddling. In his book *Infants and Mothers*, Brazelton (1983) describes the active baby, the quiet baby, and the average baby, and follows their development through the first year. He advises parents to follow the child's lead and find what works best to comfort and interest the child. Music, movement, subdued voices, a certain touch, a ritual, or something visual may be just the thing that makes life easier for parent and child, and determining this will help to promote the child's unique development.

The Goal of Positive Parenting

Positive parenting draws from many theories and combines many parenting practices, but it is essentially parenting that respects children for their individual natures. It allows parents and children to have fun together and develop a relationship based on enjoyment and mutual respect. Positive parenting builds on a foundation of love and affection, promotes mutual confidence and trust, and creates a feeling of belonging.

Effective parenting does not include nagging, scolding, preaching, or overcorrecting. Positive parenting is done with children, not to children. It honours the parental roles to teach, lead, and guide the child to become the best he or she can be. It is founded on the concept of nurturance, which involves comforting, playing with, and teaching a child. When a parent starts off parenting an infant or small child in a positive way, it becomes easier to continue positive parenting throughout the child's development.

Positive and Maladjusted Parent-Child Relationships

The research on parenting clearly indicates that early attachment and good parenting, which are respectful of the child and encourage learning, contribute to positive parent-child relationships. A child's temperament also influences the parent-child relationship, but an early awareness of individual differences in children can allow parents to foster a close relationship that suits the child's temperament. A positive parent-child relationship contributes to a child with an authentic self-image, a good capacity to withstand stress, and the ability to progress well in school.

Recent studies, such as the Statistics Canada study (1998) cited on the next page, indicate that maladjusted parent-child relationships are a result of poor parenting practices. Inconsistent parenting, belittling, and little or no acknowledgment of accomplishments are negative influences on development and contribute to behaviour problems in children. The Statistics Canada study, released in 1998, recognizes that "positive parenting is the greatest gift." In fact, the study noted that positive parenting outweighs negative circumstances such as poverty, the hardships encountered by single parents and teen parent families, and even divorce. Positive and effective parenting is the hope of the future.

Figure 15.9
Early attachment and good parenting contribute to positive parent–child relationships.

"Positive Parenting Is the Greatest Gift"

The following material appeared as part of a Consumer Information page on Internet provider istar's homepage:

A recent Statistics Canada study states that children's well-being is more dependent on positive parenting than financial security. Parenting style is the single biggest factor affecting children's behaviour, according to the report. Income and social disadvantage is more than offset by positive parenting in both single- and two-parent homes. The study, developed jointly by Statistics Canada and Human Resources Development Canada, monitored children's development and measured factors that positively or negatively influence children's development. The survey, which began in 1994, is a comprehensive study of 23 000 Canadian children under the age of 12 years, providing a picture of their physical, emotional, and academic lives over several years. The report revealed that poor parenting practices, such as inconsistent or arbitrary (changeable or erratic) punishment, venting anger at the children, or withholding praise for achievements, appear to be a better predictor of behavioural problems than living in single-parent, teen-parent, and lower-income families. The data shows that the majority of Canadian children are healthy, well-adjusted, and progressing well in school. It also shows, however, a significant number of children living in difficult circumstances such as low-income households, marriage breakdowns, and bad parenting. About 20 percent have behavioural problems such as physical or verbal aggressiveness or emotional problems such as depression.

Help for Maladjusted Children

Maladjusted children and their families require special intervention. Positive parenting is difficult for those who never experienced it themselves, and it may require a great deal of guidance by counsellors or therapists. Family counselling and parenting education helps families regain balance. In very difficult cases where child safety is an issue, children may be removed from the family by social services. Children may require therapy sessions to give them the skills and the support needed to survive negative parenting practices. Sometimes therapy will continue into adulthood.

Figure 15.10
Art therapy is one intervention that may help maladjusted children.

Career Capsule

ART AND MUSIC THERAPIST

Tasks and Responsibilities

Art and music therapists use creative processes to help children express their feelings about issues that are generally too difficult to verbalize. They help children identify their feelings and become more self-confident in discussing them. These feelings often concern difficult issues such as behaviour management problems or the abuse of a child by the people around them. Art and music therapists have knowledge of child psychology and psychological therapies, and they work with other professionals in the treatment of a child. As a result, the stress levels in the client can often be reduced in a calm, secure, and age-appropriate atmosphere.

Art and music therapy is often structured so it appears to be spontaneous. The therapist creates situations that allow children to unlock their feelings through art or music. The therapist is trained to work with the child using therapies appropriate to the child's level of development. Treatment often requires an initial assessment and formulation of a treatment plan designed for the patient's needs. Reports to the child's family and other health-care professionals are part of this job.

Work Environment

Art and music therapists usually work in clinics or in offices where they maintain a private practice. Sometimes they interact with other therapists such as child psychologists and social workers in the treatment of a child. Workplaces include hospitals, private practice, shelters, schools, and correctional institutions for older children.

Some therapists find it beneficial to schedule appointments for times when school is out. This

means that they frequently work in the evenings and on weekends. This type of work, like most health care work, can be emotionally exhausting.

Education and Aptitudes

It is important to have good communication and interpersonal skills for this career. Patience, compassion, and a strong interest in helping children are also essential. Most people who become art or music therapists also have a strong initial interest in art or music and a sincere love of children. Since the career is emotionally draining, a strong sense of self and self-confidence will help you be more successful.

To become a qualified and recognized therapist, a student must have an undergraduate university degree with an emphasis on social work, or psychology and the training and skill area of art, music, drama, or the like. Following graduation, a therapist must complete a clinical internship of at least 1000 hours before applying for admission to the appropriate professional associations.

Techniques for Parents and Caregivers

The days when Dr. Benjamin Spock's' advice was the primary guideline for parents are long gone, although parenting authorities continue to come and go. Entire shelves in libraries and large sections of bookstores are devoted to parenting advice, child-rearing advice, and child development information. Authorities agree that children should not be spanked, and recommend a number of alternatives. Not all techniques are suitable for all families or for all situations, and parents and caregivers need to determine which techniques suit their parenting philosophy. Through careful consideration, they are able to choose the techniques they are comfortable using and that will most benefit their child.

Effective Techniques for Parents and Caregivers

By learning a variety of successful caregiving or parenting practices, individuals develop a repertoire of possible strategies from which to choose. Young people can practise some of the techniques as they baby-sit, supervise children, or act in a leadership role with children. Comfort with a variety of approaches that maintain a child's dignity means that parents or caregivers can experiment with or choose appropriate techniques in difficult situations.

Distract and redirect: Beginning at an early age, distracting the child by offering an acceptable alternative helps avoid conflict. If a child grabs someone's hair, gently open the hand and replace the hair with a toy. If a child is arguing with his or her siblings, offer both children a diversion, for example, "Look, there is a fire truck going down the street. Come and see it!"

Have a childproof/child-friendly home: Move breakables out of the child's reach, put safety covers on electrical outlets, and keep poisons out of the child's reach. Children are born without knowing what they can and cannot touch. Childproofing reduces the necessity to say "no" and makes it less frustrating for parent and child. A child-friendly home has safe places to play, unbreakable cups and dishes to use, and washable surfaces, and is generally accessible to curious and active children.

Set limits: Clearly explain the boundaries, limits, or expectations, and follow through consistently. Limits should be logical, reasonable, and well-understood. For example, "You must use the car seat and seat belt every time" or "I expect you to sit down in the shopping cart every time." Remember, limits change as children develop new skills. "Wear your helmet when you ride your bike." When children follow through on their own, point out their success to them: "You remembered to wear your helmet. That's great!"

Do not argue about rules or limits: Effective parents and caregivers do not have a lot of rules because the more rules there are, the more rules must be enforced. Important rules, however, should not be subject to negotiation. This is especially true when dealing with safety issues. A parent can state firmly, "I am not going to argue with you about that."

Establish routines: Children find comfort in the sameness of routine. A bedtime ritual becomes something to look forward to if it involves something enjoyable, like a bedtime story or a back rub. "First you have a bath, then you put on your pyjamas and brush your

■ Effective techniques for parents and caregivers:
- distract and redirect
- have a childproof/child friendly home
- set limits
- do not argue about rules or limits
- establish routines
- provide transition time
- teach and train
- give encouragement
- offer choices

Figure 15.11
Trained routines are used throughout life.

teeth. We read a story, then you have a good sleep." The sameness of the routine can be followed when away from home as well. The familiarity makes it comfortable and easier to follow.

Provide transition time: Adults automatically give themselves time for transition from one event to another by mentally thinking about what they need to do next. A child needs transition time, too. "Go to bed right now!" should not be the first indication that it is bedtime. Telling children that they will need to get ready for bed in ten minutes allows them time to make the mental adjustment.

Teach and train: Children need to learn essential skills and habits such as how to brush their teeth, how to use toilet paper, how to speak politely to a grandparent, or how to say "please" and "thank you." This teaching takes time, and a parent must model it until a child can internalize it. Teaching should be done before the skill is actually needed, but not until the child is capable of accomplishing it. Ultimately, it takes more time to correct an untrained child than it does to teach him or her in the first place.

Give Encouragement: A child learns how to be successful in small steps, from getting back up after falling down, as well as from being able to make a mistake without belittlement or embarrassment. Encouragement gives the child the courage to move forward. Statements such as "I like the way you tried to put your shoes on all by yourself," or "That is a good place to put your blocks" give a child the confidence to do it again.

Offer choices: Letting children make choices within reasonable limits from a very young age not only gives them a sense of control over a situation, but helps them accept responsibility for making choices. They also learn to recognize when they have made a bad choice. "Do you want your milk in the elephant cup or the alligator cup?" takes the focus off a struggle over having to drink the milk, while giving the child a measure of control.

Natural consequences result directly from the child's behaviour. For example, if the child goes outside without mittens on a cold day, the natural consequence is very cold hands. Without nagging, the child will likely make the right choice the next time. However, if the child's personal safety becomes a concern, a parent should not allow the natural consequence to play out. Helping a child problem solve the situation lets him or her imagine the consequence without having to live it.

Logical consequences are established by the parents and relate logically to the behaviour. For example, if children's shoes get muddy, they have to clean them. Or if children do not come to the table on time, they will have to get their own dinner. It is important to ensure that the logical consequences are not punitive and offer a solution to a problem rather than a punishment for misbehaviour.

Time-in is an act of inclusion rather than exclusion. For example, when a child misbehaves, the parent sits with the child, calmly discusses the child's feelings, and teaches the child to problem solve. This helps the child cope with the disruption and also confirms that the parent still loves the child.

■ Time-in is an act of inclusion rather than exclusion.

Time-out removes a child from the problem situation, giving him or her time to calm down or rethink behaviour. The recommended length of time for time-out is one minute per year of age up to five minutes. Sometimes, children who are used to this technique will give themselves a time-out when they need to calm down and start over.

Humour can be used to diffuse anger, redirect a child, and turn a tense situation into a lighter moment. The tense silence following the breaking of a dish can be broken by blaming the incident on a fictitious character.

Offer love and comfort after dealing with misbehaviour. Parents or caregivers need to reinforce that misbehaviour is unacceptable but never tell children they are bad. Children are often upset by their misbehaviour and need to know they are still loved. A parent who refuses contact, displays continued anger, or uses the silent treatment shows disapproval for the child, not the behaviour.

For Better or For Worse® by Lynn Johnston

Figure 15.12
Why does the child in this cartoon need comfort?

Today, parents and caregivers show an active interest in reading about child development research. Parenting books and magazines are bestsellers in many bookstores, and there are many popular Web sites on the Internet. It is important to rely on a variety of authoritative resources for parenting information. Parents need to consult professionals in the community as well as other parents to help them decide what information to use in raising their own children. A parent needs to feel comfortable with the parenting techniques used. What works for one parent may not work for another; likewise, what works with one child may not work with another. A parent may need to try several different approaches to find what works best for the situation and the child in question.

❖ Checkpoints

1. Identify the temperament types in your own family.
2. What are the goals of positive parenting?
3. Outline the benefits of "childproofing."
4. Explain which of the effective parenting techniques you feel would be best to use in the following situations:
   - A six-month-old grabs his mother's earring
   - A two-year-old bites a playmate
   - A five-year-old uses inappropriate language
   - A ten-year-old steals from a store

Discipline from Infancy to Adolescence

Discipline may have seemed straightforward in the past when parents set the rules and children were punished if they disobeyed. Some children were thought to need a "good spanking" to set them straight, while others were on their best behaviour so as to avoid punishment. This kind of authoritarian parenting was generally accepted in a world that had one way of doing things. In pioneer days, a parent would instruct the child in the everyday tasks, and the child would follow the instructions. Children grew up and repeated the pattern with their own children. Parenting styles have changed for many reasons. Research, education, changing laws, rebellion against authority and physical punishment, changing gender roles, and a developing awareness of how parenting affects children are some of the factors that have contributed to changing parenting practices. It is no longer acceptable to discipline children through punishment.

■ *Is it ever okay to use physical punishment to discipline a child? Most experts and child welfare authorities say 'No.' And they add that corporal punishment doesn't work in the long run and can hurt a child's emotional development.... Parents will say it (physical punishment) didn't harm them. But they sometimes don't recognize the emotional scars that have been left and the way they react to people with power.*
— The Hope for Children Foundation

371

Children need discipline so that, as they grow into adolescence, they develop **self-discipline** and take responsibility for their own actions. Taking responsibility for their actions, however, can begin with little things, such as picking up toys when playtime is over, and become more complex as the child grows up. The goal of discipline is to guide children until they are able to rely on their own inner discipline.

Age-Appropriate Discipline

The guidance and discipline needed to encourage inner discipline and responsibility begins in infancy and changes with each stage of development through to adolescence, as shown in the guidelines of the Age-Appropriate Discipline chart. The goals of inner discipline in the chart's final column are goals only that may or may not be achieved, depending on individual circumstances.

■ To be effective, discipline needs to be:
- given by an adult with an affective bond to the child
- consistent, close to the behaviour needing change
- perceived as "fair" by the child
- developmentally and temperamentally appropriate
- self-enhancing, that is, ultimately leading to self-discipline

— The Canadian Paediatric Society (2002)

Age-Appropriate Discipline

Stage	Parental Guidance or Teaching Needed	Inner Discipline
Infant (0–6 months)	• Respond consistently to your child's needs • Use comforting to calm crying • Establish predictable rituals for bathing, feeding, and bedtime	• Calms self down from crying • Gives in to sleep when tired • Anticipates the order of things from consistent routines
Baby (6–18 months)	• Follow consistent routines • Engage the child in play • Teach words and use words • Encourage safe exploration • Childproof the home • Set limits (such as use a car seat every time) • Teach essential skills, such as stair climbing, nose blowing, hand washing, petting animals, saying please or thank you • Offer choices (red pyjamas or blue ones)	• Cooperates with routines • Spends longer periods of time amusing self • Communicates wants or needs with gestures or single words • Begins to use words • Begins to internalize limits
Toddler (18 months–3 years)	• Distract and redirect impulsivity • Teach child how to complete simple chores • Enlist their cooperation • Encourage hygiene, self-feeding, dressing, toileting, one step at a time • Model politeness, gentleness, sharing	• Starts to gain control over impulses • Is able to ask for help • Handles frustration • Takes the initiative to complete everyday tasks like dressing, tidying up • Cares about the feelings of pets, other children

(continued)

Stage	Parental Guidance or Teaching Needed	Inner Discipline
Pre-school and Kindergarten (3–6 years)	• Reinforce safety rules and limits • Use "time-in" and discussion to focus on changing behaviour • Ignore annoying behaviour, model expected behaviour, and acknowledge good behaviour • Give them chores they can handle • Let them learn from small mistakes	• Stops and reacts appropriately when there is danger • Recognizes and imitates appropriate behaviour • Takes responsibility for small chores without reminders • Begins to anticipate the consequences of behaviour
School Age (6–10 years)	• Acknowledge their contribution to the family • Discuss and agree on standards for chore completion • Discuss and agree on limits for television watching, homework completion, time spent on the Internet or with friends • Expect polite, respectful behaviour • Use natural and logical consequences • Encourage problem solving	• Takes pride in being able to help out at home • Self-motivated to do chores, complete homework • Develops interests and hobbies • Anticipates and accepts consequences • Demonstrates self-control
Preteen (10–13 years)	• Discuss and agree on increased kinds of responsibility • Allow them more freedom in their clothing and appearance choices • Discuss changing sexuality and sexual responsibility • Celebrate puberty • Allow them to resolve conflicts in their interpersonal relationships • Be there when they need to talk, vent, or have a good cry	• Takes responsibility for helping out at home • Develops a sense of self • Uses self-talk for confidence • Stands up to peer pressure • Accepts his or her changing body and takes the resulting responsibilities • Understands and controls changing emotions
Adolescent	• Keep the lines of communication open • Discuss and agree on acceptable behaviour and continuing contribution at home and in the community • Allow them to handle problems and take responsibility for steps that lead to their independence (getting a part-time job, a driver's licence, schooling) • Encourage the qualities you admire such as maturity, sense of humour, ability to get along with others	• Takes responsibility for actions at home and outside the home • Discusses concerns with others • Takes steps for independence • Sets personal limits • Cares about and contributes to the well-being of others • Uses problem-solving skills • Takes responsibility for self

Figure 15.13
Parents can encourage their child's inner discipline.

The following material, which appears on Family Service Canada's Web site, is based on an article by Vanessa Petrilli *"The Starting of Violence."*

What's Wrong with Spanking? PLENTY!

Top 10 List

1. It sets a bad example: "When angry, hit." Parents need to show children how to express anger and resolve conflict in a peaceful way.

2. Spanking and hitting are forms of violence. The word spanking has a cute ring to it. It is more pleasing to say "Do you want a spanking?" than to say "Do you want to get hit or hurt?" The hurting and hitting of children by adults is not cute. It is hurtful.

3. It can be habit forming: you start to do it without even thinking. Most adults have learned not to hit adults when they are angry. We can also show self-control when we are angry with children.

4. Spanking and hitting perpetuates an unfair double standard. Adults are protected by law from any form of assault. Children are people too!

5. It promotes a poor self-image. People (children) do not feel worthwhile if their body is not respected (that is, if they are hit).

6. It creates an atmosphere of fear. Children do not learn well when they are fearful of being hit for making a mistake.

7. It does not help children to learn self-discipline. The strongest element in discipline is a child's love for the parent. When a parent uses harsh methods to teach children right from wrong, the child develops feelings of resentment and hatred, which get mixed up with the love feelings a child has for his/her parent. This all adds up to confusion for the child and he/she may misbehave to try to clear up the confusion. The child is not asking to be hit, but asking for clear, consistent limits to be set.

8. It perpetuates a vicious cycle by indicating to children that it's O.K. to hit and hurt smaller people (including siblings).

9. Parents need to put themselves into children's shoes. How would adults feel if a boss or spouse hit them to correct them?

10. People are not for hitting! Adults need to be helpers, not hurters of children.

Discipline is teaching children, not hurting them.

Achieving Self-Discipline

Reward and punishment do not help children to achieve self-discipline. Both are external controls that a child comes to depend on. Soon, rewards will be expected for everything, whereas punishment may lead to retaliation through misbehaviour that becomes more and more disturbing. Self-discipline comes from inside. It is a feeling of self-control and personal confidence. A person with self-discipline does not need to rely on others for direction or approval.

Self-discipline can be shaped and encouraged from infancy. Parents and caregivers who are overly protective and hover over their children every minute do not allow them to develop and call on the inner resources needed to develop **self-control**. As children grow, they need opportunities for **taking responsibility** in small ways. Letting children make simple choices and complete simple chores is just the beginning. Having a role in the daily workings of a family gives children a sense of importance and place, and allows them to contribute with supervision until they are able to take on the responsibility themselves.

Figure 15.14
Children begin to learn self-control by taking responsibility for household tasks.

What the experts say

OTTO WEININGER

Otto Weininger is the author of Time-In Parenting, Toronto: Rinascente Book Inc., 2002. He answers the following questions:

What is punishment and what role does it play in teaching children self-discipline?

Punishment is a negative consequence applied to a child who has either deliberately or unintentionally failed to follow the rules—sometimes even when the child did not know the rules. Discipline should not be punishment and punishment is certainly not effective discipline.

*   Hitting is punishment.
*   Yelling is punishment.
*   "Time-out" or isolation can be punishment.
*   Some "logical consequences" can be punishment.
*   Some best-selling parenting programs can be punishment.

The only thing that punishment teaches is how to avoid more punishment. Some parents or caregivers may feel it necessary, but it has no effect other than a negative one on the development of self-discipline.

How can parents and educators help children acquire self-discipline in the family and later in school?

First and foremost, discipline occurs in a loving, supportive, developmentally appropriate, and kind environment. Parents and teachers need to take "time in" with children to work through the problems of discipline. When emotional needs are met, and children and parents are bonded to each other, children are motivated to discover and adopt the rules of appropriate behaviour.

Self-discipline will develop when these conditions are met:

*   The rules and expectations are clearly known and understood by children, according to their age and stage of development.
*   The rules are consistently applied, yet are not so rigid that they cannot be changed for specific circumstances and special occasions.
*   The expectations are reasonable—when they reflect what is necessary for harmonious living—not arbitrary impositions of adults.
*   The rules are child-friendly and child-centred.
*   The expectations are agreed upon, as best as possible, by all the affected persons, including children.
*   The expectations are modelled by adults.
*   Rules and policies are in agreement with the positive prevailing values of the culture and do not reflect unattainable ideals.

Parenting Wisdom

One of the most frustrating aspects of raising a family is sibling rivalry. Advice to parents regarding fights and arguments between siblings is not to get involved. Often, fights break out to get a parent to take sides or step in to alter the other child's behaviour. Separating children or taking sides encourages this behaviour, causing them to fight more. Feelings of anger toward a brother, sister, or even a parent are part of growing up. Parents are advised to acknowledge their children's feelings but tell them they need to work out a solution between themselves. Parents may need to use time-in with both children to outline how they expect them to resolve their differences. They will need to use their **negotiation** skills by talking to each other until they can come to an agreement they can both live with. The skills they develop are necessary in many other relationships throughout life.

Children make mistakes, and they need parents who will encourage them to sort out their problems and learn from them. **Self-talk**, in which they mentally provide encouragement for themselves, is a skill parents can teach children to develop confidence.

Parents need to have faith in their children. Sometimes the hardest part of encouraging self-discipline is to let children do things their own way. As children become more competent, parents need to reduce the number of limits they set so that children can set **personal limits**. At some point, they will have to decide how they spend their time and what they need to accomplish. Children cannot anticipate or even **accept consequences** for their behaviour if their parents are always reminding them what to do or stepping in and rescuing them. If their behaviour results in a consequence that they can handle, it gives them the power to make better choices, think for themselves, and move toward true self-discipline, which comes from within.

Figure 15.15
Although siblings may be rivals, they can cooperate and have fun together.

❖ Checkpoints

1. What is self-discipline, and how can parents help children achieve it?
2. What are the advantages for children and parents of using time-in?
3. Outline the benefits of self-talk, and give an example.

Chapter Summary

Chapter Highlights

- Parenting practices differ from one family to another, from one child to another, and from one stage of life to another.

- Parenting theory has evolved over time. Several important theorists have contributed to the kind of parenting practices that are advocated today.

- Dr. Spock was the first to affirm management over physical punishment.

- Diane Baumrind defined parenting styles and favoured authoritative (democratic) over authoritarian (strict) and permissive styles.

- Rudolf Dreikurs developed a theory of misbehaviour that showed parents how to encourage positive behaviour rather than negative behaviour.

- Barbara Coloroso combines both Baumrind's and Dreikurs' theories into practical advice that makes sense for parents.

- T. Berry Brazelton, who also advocates positive parenting, recognized the role of temperament in child rearing.

- Effective parenting, or positive parenting, is the single most important factor in how children turn out.

- Parenting theories have led to the development of a variety of techniques that parents and caregivers can use with children and that do not advocate spanking, force, or punishment.

- Discipline does not include punishment, but is focused on child guidance.

- As children move from infancy through adolescence, the kind of discipline needs to change with them to achieve the ultimate goal of self-discipline.

- Parenting is a continuous learning experience.

Review and Extend Your Learning

1. Interview the parents of a school-age child. Find out if their parenting style has changed as their child has grown up. How do the results of your interview compare with the descriptions in the sidebar on page 355? **(K/U)** **(T/I)**

2. Observe several parents to determine their parenting style. From your observations, compare the impact of the different styles of parenting (permissive, authoritarian, and democratic) on the behaviour of young children. **(T/I)**

3. Illustrate each point listed in Barbara Coloroso's parenting theory by providing a concrete example. **(C)** **(A)**

4. Write an opinion paper about Dreikurs' theory of misbehaviour. Discuss whether the theory can help parents avoid the struggles that often occur with children. **T/I** **C**

5. This chapter describes 15 effective parenting techniques. Choose eight of these techniques, and explain why each is useful or how it can be helpful for parents. **K/U**

6. Imagine yourself as a parent. Using the guidelines for age-appropriate discipline, describe five different child-rearing situations and how you would handle them to help your child achieve self-discipline. **A**

7. While you are baby-sitting or interacting with young children in a playground, try out some of the techniques recommended for parenting and disciplining young children. Try offering choices using "time-in," setting limits, or encouraging independence. Report on the effectiveness of your actions. **K/U** **T/I** **C** **A**

8. Describe techniques for enabling and empowering children and adolescents through the development of self-discipline. Analyze how these techniques contribute to the development of self-discipline. **K/U** **T/I**

Research Opportunities

9. Conduct a library or Internet search to learn more about the research of one parenting theorist (e.g., Dreikurs, Baumrind, Coloroso). Design a Web page or use a word processor to produce an information package. Your presentation should simplify and clarify the theory for other students. Include concise titles, an interesting layout, and appropriate graphics or clip art.

10. Read or view a biography or autobiography of an interesting person (who may or may not be famous) and report on the kind of parenting that shaped their life. Providing evidence from the biography/autobiography to support your view, identify whether the parenting was positive or maladjusted.

11. Check parenting magazines, parenting "how to" books, and the Internet to investigate parenting techniques. Report on other techniques that have been used successfully for shaping children's behaviour while keeping their dignity intact.

Issue Analysis

Dave and Hannah waited several years to start a family, which allowed them time to travel, establish their careers, and set up a household. They had learned to live with each other's strengths and weaknesses in a compatible way. When their children arrived less than two years apart, they were suddenly thrust into parenthood. What they were not prepared for was their very different styles of parenting. Hannah felt that Dave was too lax. He let the children do whatever they wanted. She, on the other hand, felt they should have strict rules and rigid routines. She felt annoyed when he gave in to them. He thought she was too controlling and did not give the children enough freedom to figure things out for themselves. Each felt that the other was not supporting their efforts to be a good parent.

marital and their parenting relationship. What changes would Dave and Hannah need to make to resolve their differences and present a united front?

1. Conflicting parenting styles is an issue for many parents that may affect both their

2. What are the advantages and disadvantages of being raised by two parents with very different parenting styles?

Unit 7 Children in the Global Community

This unit examines the challenge of raising children in today's society and the pressures of society, school, and media on the lives of children and families. Social and legal responsibilities for the safety and well-being of all children are examined. You will consider the importance of a shared commitment to children in Canada and around the world for the future well-being of children everywhere.

KEY INSIGHTS:

- Parents in today's society face many issues and challenges.
- Caregivers and those who work with children support parents in protecting children from violence and harm.
- Parents need to recognize the positive and negative influences of school and media on older children and adolescents.
- Parental involvement can influence the role of schools and media in human growth and development.

- Parents and society share responsibility for our children.
- Social services share social and legal responsibilities for children with parents and others involved in children's lives.
- There are times when families need the help of social-service organizations when raising older children and adolescents.
- Initiatives promoting shared responsibility for children between parents and society contribute to the future well-being of children and the ultimate health of a country.

Unit at a Glance

The Role of Society
in the Lives of Children

**By the end of this chapter,
you will be able to:**

- describe society's role in the lives of children and families

- identify and describe the issues and challenges that concern parents, caregivers, and others who interact with children in society

- evaluate society's expectations of and support for parents, caregivers, and people who work with children

- analyze the causes and consequences of violence toward children, and assess their impact on families, caregivers, and those who work with children

- analyze the challenges of balancing work and family

Important Terms

bullying

Canadian
  Multiculturalism Day

cycle of violence

homeless families

independence

joint custody

mandatory child support

National Aboriginal Day

patterns of violence

personal safety

Rights of the Child

Saint-Jean-Baptiste Day

school-age programs

sexual harassment

social policy

street proofing

working poor

Chapter at a Glance

What Social Concerns Do Parents Face?

There was a time when children stayed at home in the care of their family until they reached the age of five or six and the beginning of school. The family may have introduced them to their religious institution and neighbours, but on the first day of school they set off by themselves. It marked the separation between the years of family influence and the beginning of society's influence. Going to school for the very first time was a big step for young children, the first in a number of steps away from the family toward independence.

Today, however, interaction with the world outside of the family begins earlier in life. Many parent caregivers return to paid employment within the first year after a baby is born. Children go to child care, nursery school, and other homes, usually in the company of other children, and adults who are not their parents. A child entering junior kindergarten has already come in contact with the world outside the family through child-care situations, as well as through exposure to television, peers, and other social situations.

Today's fast-paced, complex world can be a source of concern for parents. Will their children be safe? Will they get along with others? Will they be well-cared for when their parents are not there? What will they learn about the world, and how much control will the parents have over what happens from now on?

One of the goals of parenting is for children to achieve **independence**, to take responsibility for themselves, and to do things on their own. Many of the skills that are taught at home help children to become more and more independent. They begin with small steps toward independence, such as making choices about clothing, doing chores, and helping others in the family. There are many successes to celebrate along the way. Successes such as not crying when being dropped off at child care, playing with a friend, independently riding a tricycle down to the corner and back, walking to school alone for the first time, are all important steps toward independence. At the same time that parents encourage independent behaviour, they must also teach children about some of the dangers that exist in the world.

As children become involved in the world outside of the family, they encounter many different people and situations. Respect for others begins at home. Parents and family members who model consideration for others regardless of race, colour, religion, or social standing, teach their children the importance of respect. Children need to be respected as well. According to Dorothy Law Nolte's

■ One of the goals of parenting is to help children reach responsible independence.

Figure 16.1
Accomplishing tasks, such as riding a bike by oneself, helps children to achieve independence.

famous poem, "Children Live What They Learn, if they live with kindness and consideration, they learn respect." (See page 343 to read this poem.) Being treated as important family members who are able to contribute to the functioning and well-being of the family allows children to develop the positive sense of self they need, both to help them respect others, and to be respected themselves.

Ensuring Children's Safety Outside the Home

A major concern for parents as their children approach school age is their children's **personal safety**. Is it safe for a child to cross the street? Will it be safe to walk to school? Does the child know what to do if a family member, neighbour, or stranger acts in a suspicious way? Will the child be picked on at school or will the child pick on others? Dr. James Garbarino, an expert in the field of family and community violence and trauma in child development, notes that "When children feel safe at home they are ready to grow. When safe in the neighbourhood, children are ready to play, explore, and form relationships with other children. When they are safe at school, they are ready to learn."

Ensuring Children's Safety

Every year in Canada, parents hear reports of children being approached by suspicious people, abducted, or sexually molested. A quantitative study conducted by Millward Brown in November 1995 for Stay Alert, Stay Safe, based on 1500 households, indicates that protection from abduction is the number one priority for child safety in Canada. However, Statistics Canada reports that very few children are abducted in Canada. "In 1996, about 56 000 children under the age of 18 were reported missing in Canada ... Over three-quarters (78 percent) of these children were runaways. Abductions accounted for less than 1 percent... In 1996, almost 1000 children (in Canada) under the age of 16 were victims of attempted or completed abductions. Parental abductions accounted for 62 percent of all abductions, and non-parental abductions accounted for the remaining 38 percent."

What accounts for the discrepancy between parental fear of abduction and the relatively low numbers of children who are abducted? When a child is abducted, the media know that the story will increase television viewing rates and sell newspapers. No parent wants to experience the horror of having a child abducted or

Figure 16.2
The safety of children in the community is a major social issue.

molested. One abduction story strikes fear into the hearts of many. The outside chance that their own children might be abducted leads parents to take steps to protect them. **Street proofing** is the term used to describe programs that teach children how to take action if faced with the possibility of abduction or sexual molestation.

Stay Alert, Stay Safe is a national street-proofing program that has been used in schools and community settings across Canada. The program's mission "is to develop an ongoing, national street-proofing program actively involving both children and adults, that aims to make them aware of and alert to potential dangers, by building situation understanding and, more importantly, children's confidence in handling such situations" (2001, p. 1).

The program uses two safety rabbits, Bert and Gert, to get present information to children. Their key messages are:

- Street proofing is a positive, fun thing to learn; it's not meant to be scary. Its purpose is to make you stronger and more powerful.

- People you know as well as people you don't know can be dangerous.

- Learn to rely on your own instincts—a feeling deep down inside of you. Learn the difference between feeling comfortable and uncomfortable.

- It's okay to say no to adults.

- Your body is your own and it's okay to not want to be touched. When you feel afraid or [uncomfortable], talk to someone you trust.

- Be especially careful if someone asks you to keep a secret; adults should not ask kids to keep secrets (p. 1).

The Stay Alert, Stay Safe program encourages good communication between parents and children so that parents can make use of teachable moments whenever a child has questions that need to be answered. Rather than frighten children, the program aims to encourage them to trust their instincts and be confident about asking for help when they need it. Street proofing from this perspective is not about following rules that may or may not guarantee safety; instead, it is about working with parents, children, and communities to create an atmosphere in which children generally feel safe.

Many communities produce information sheets for parents on how to ensure their children's safety in the community. All families within communities are encouraged to work together to keep children safe. There are many Block Parent programs in communities across Canada.

Street-proofing works with parents, children, and communities to create an atmosphere in which children generally feel safe.

Block Parent Program of Winnipeg Inc.

The following tips are taken from a Web site operated by the City of Winnipeg's Block Parent Program:

Street Smart Tip #1

Do your children know the safe places in your neighbourhood?

Talk to your children about where they can get help:
- a trusted neighbour
- a store that is open
- a Block Parent Home

Street Smart Tip #2

Do your children know what to do if someone grabs them?

They should twist, turn, and scream as loudly as they can! Teach your children that under the right circumstance; it's all right to say "NO!" to an adult or an older kid.

Street Smart Tip #3

Do your children know what to do if they are being followed or bothered by someone?

They should run for:
- home
- the nearest group of people
- a store that is open
- any house
- a Block Parent Home

Street Smart Tip #4

Do not label your children's clothing, toys, or school bags where their names will be in plain view.

Children might not be as cautious if a stranger calls them by their name.

Street Smart Tip #5

Do you know who your children's friends are?

Keep a list of their friends' names, addresses, and phone numbers.

Street Smart Tip #6

Do your children know what to do if they are home alone?

Make sure your children know:
- not to tell anyone at the door or on the phone that they are home alone
- who to call if they need help

Education is the first step to safety.

Figure 16.3
A Block Parent sign

Bullying

As children get older, they need to know about other threats to their personal safety and how to respond. **Bullying** is a major concern in both elementary and middle schools, and it continues to be a problem in high school. Bullying is the result of negative actions directed at one child by one or more children, repeatedly and over time, with the intent to hurt or embarrass. Bullying behaviour includes pushing, slapping, hitting, rude gestures, verbal threats, teasing, taunting, and exclusion. Bullying is a no-win situation: both victims and bullies face problems with self-control and social acceptance, which may continue well into the future. Bullying is a social issue that requires the efforts of parents, schools, and society as a whole to take action towards intervention as well as prevention.

What Causes Bullying?

A number of different factors, including family, individual, school, and lack of supervision, have all been identified as contributing to the problems of bullying.

Family factors: A number of child-rearing styles predict whether children will grow up to be bullies. In *Conflict Resolution: The Partnership Way*, authors B. Weinhold and J. Weinhold (2000) note that a lack of attention and warmth toward the child, together with poor supervision and the modelling of aggressive behaviour at home contribute to a child becoming a bully. Modelling of aggressive behaviour means imitating others who use aggression, such as parents' physical and verbal aggression toward their children or each other. Studies are exploring the connection between witnessing wife assault, particularly by male children, and witnessing bullying behaviour in peers. Studies, such as those conducted by P. Jaffe, D.A. Wolfe, and S.K. Wilson, authors of *Children of Battered Women* (1990), indicate that all types of aggressive behaviours are elevated in children who witness violence toward their mother by a father or male partner.

Individual factors: Children who are active, impulsive, and lack self-control may be more inclined to develop into bullies. Although there are many strong, physically adept boys who never bully, boys' physical strength compared to age peers also seems to be a characteristic that is associated with bullying.

School factors: As reported in *Bullying: Information for Parents and Teachers* by M. Sudermann, P.G. Jaffe, and F. Shieck (1996), many school associations are researching bullying and ways to prevent it. Social context and supervision at school can play a major part in the frequency and severity of bullying problems. While teachers and administrators cannot control individual and family factors that contribute to a child's inclination to bully, bullying problems can be greatly reduced in severity by appropriate supervision, intervention, and school climate.

Lack of Supervision: Supervision of children is of prime importance. Just as low levels of supervision in the home are associated with the development of bullying problems in individual children, so too are low levels of supervision at school, particularly on the playground or in the schoolyard, as well as in the hallways. The appropriateness of adult intervention when they see bullying or are made aware of it is also very important.

Figure 16.4
Bullying is a negative situation for all involved.

Figure 16.5
Appropriate supervision and intervention at school can greatly reduce bullying in the schoolyard.

Bullying: Myths, Facts, and Strategies For Reducing It

The following material is excerpted from *Bullying: Myths, Facts and Strategies for Reducing It*, an online resource produced by The Family Centre, an Edmonton, Alberta organization.

Bullying is not a harmless right-of-passage. Bullying harms the bully, the victim, and the bystander. The good news is that parents and teachers need not feel powerless to change this harmful dynamic. Below are some myths surrounding bullying and the facts that can help us help children to develop healthier peer relationships.

Bullying Myths	Bullying Facts
Bullying is a normal part of childhood and adolescence and is relatively harmless.	Bullying can contribute to long-term mental health problems in both the bully and the victim. If bullying is severe, pervasive, and long term, it can have catastrophic results such as homicide and suicide.
Bullies outgrow their aggressive behaviour.	Bullying in young people can evolve into sexual harassment, spousal/partner abuse, and/or child abuse.
Only boys bully.	We notice boys' bullying behaviour more often because it tends to be physical. However, girls (and increasingly boys) use social exclusion, and verbal and emotional abuse to hurt their victims.
The only way to stop bullying is to teach the victim to fight back.	Bystanders, teachers, and parents are three of the most powerful agents in the bullying dynamic. When adult or peer bystanders say "no" to aggression, it sends a powerful message to the bully. Victims need to learn assertiveness skills—meeting aggression with aggression just makes matters worse.
Bullying only happens in isolated, out-of-the-way areas such as alleys or ravines.	In one study carried out by Canadian researchers Debra Peplar and Wendy Craig, interviews with children indicated that bullying often takes place in areas supervised by adults, such as the playground, hallways, and classrooms in schools.

Strategies to support the building of pro-social skills in the child/teen who is bullying

• Be aware of how your child/student handles aggression, and validate and reward assertive versus aggressive behaviour.

- Be aware of your own aggressive behaviour—be a positive role model.
- Change the way your family/classroom/school handles discipline. Children who bully require discipline that is non-violent and logical.
- Never excuse your own or the child's/student's name-calling, intimidation, teasing, or taunting. Remember: No one ever asks for it.
- Provide opportunities for your child/student to feel good about him/herself by being of service to others.
- Limit the amount of violent popular culture your child/student is exposed to. Discuss violence he/she is exposed to.
- Ensure adequate supervision for all ages. Children/teens who bully are demonstrating a lack of critical thinking and good decision-making skills.
- Nurture your child's/teen's capacity to feel empathy. Children and teens who bully demonstrate a lack of empathy for others.

❖ Checkpoints

1. Explain why independence is one of the goals of parenting.
2. What accounts for parents' fears of abduction?
3. What are the goals of an effective street-proofing program?
4. Identify adult behaviours that a) promote bullying, and b) prevent bullying.

❖ Connections

1. Think about the first time you really felt independent. What were you doing that made you feel this way? In what ways did your family and your community help you to achieve this level of independence?
2. Find out about Block Parent programs. Report on how the programs are run and describe how they help parents and children. Locate the program nearest you.
3. Conduct a Web search to find out more about Debra Pepler and Wendy Craig's research on bullying. Summarize your findings in the form of a report.

Career Capsule

CHILD AND YOUTH WORKER

Tasks and Responsibilities

Child and youth workers help troubled children and teenagers understand and deal with personal and social problems. These problems may involve the home, school, peers, substance abuse, or dealings with the law. Child and youth workers plan and run treatment and residential facilities for their clients where stress is reduced and the children have a chance to grow and mature. Some facilities offer programs to treat addictions such as drug abuse.

Child and youth workers often work shifts in a residential facility, because the children must be supervised 24 hours a day. They work with clients in individual and group settings. Frequently, the job involves conflict resolution and intervention in angry confrontations between residents. Tasks also include helping individual clients modify their behaviour, change their attitudes, and develop living skills.

Work Environment

A child and youth worker works wherever children and teenagers with problems are found—in residential facilities, emergency shelters, social service agencies, treatment facilities, private (foster) homes, and even schools. Since children in residential facilities require round-the-clock supervision, shift work may be required. Provincial governments and community and government agencies in the social service sector usually employ child and youth workers.

Some workers can expect to divide their time between an office and visiting clients in the field. Part-time workers may work only evenings or weekends, or perform their duties on an "on-call" basis. Child and youth workers working in a residential facility must work the night shift on a periodic basis. Working conditions can involve high stress.

Education and Aptitudes

The minimum amount of education and training for a position as a child and youth worker is a two-year community college diploma. To advance in this career, you require a bachelor or even a master's degree from a university. In some provinces and territories, it may be possible to obtain employment in this field directly out of high school by completing an apprenticeship.

This occupation requires good conflict resolution and communication skills, along with empathetic detachment. It is essential to be able to solve problems quickly and effectively. Good crisis management skills and the ability to stay calm are also essential aptitudes for this type of work. Personal maturity and the ability to be objective with emotional issues is very helpful. Most agencies require a police background check with a clean record as a condition of employment.

Sexual Harassment

Sexual harassment is another issue that threatens personal safety. **Sexual harassment** can take the form of name-calling, including homophobic comments, suggestive gestures, sexual innuendo, and comments of a sexual nature intended to embarrass or put down the person at whom they are directed. It happens on the playground, on the school bus, in the hallways, and in the classrooms. Sexual harassment may begin in the early grades with teasing and rude comments, and it often continues because victims are reluctant to report it. For children and teenagers to be able to help stop sexual harassment, they must be taught to recognize it and encouraged to report it. Sexual harassment is a violation of human rights and under some circumstances may also be a criminal offence.

In addition to sexual harassment, four other sexual offences can involve children and adolescents. These are all federal offences under the Criminal Code of Canada: sexual assault, sexual interference, sexual exploitation, and child pornography. Although children and adolescents must be made aware of the dangers, graphic descriptions can create fear and give them more information than necessary. An early childhood discussion about the relationship between feelings of comfort and appropriate and inappropriate touch, as well as a thorough knowledge of the proper names of all body parts, is an effective way to start protecting children from sexual offences.

Protecting Children and Adolescents from Internet Dangers

Children and teenagers regularly "surf the net" and can quickly become involved in visiting Web sites with materials that are injurious to their self-esteem and moral well-being. Many parents of younger children purchase screening programs that lock out Internet sites with questionable or injurious materials, such as hate messages and pornographic images.

Teenagers, however, often have much more freedom to roam on the Internet. They may inadvertently or intentionally visit sites dealing with subjects that degrade other human beings, and that present emotionally unhealthy images. Parents must have frank and open discussions with their growing children about the hate and pornographic material that exists on the Internet. They must make their children aware that this type of material is especially degrading and hurtful to the people depicted or involved in its production.

Figure 16.6
While screening programs can block out questionable materials, parents should still monitor their child's use of the computer.

Parenting Skills

Internet Safety Tips for Parents

In recent years, the need to protect children from unsuitable sites and potentially dangerous situations has become an important issue. The provincial government of British Columbia, through its Ministry of Education, has published a report that helps parents to ensure that their children are using the Internet in the best possible way. The following material is excerpted from *Internet Safety Tips for Parents*, published in 2001 by the Province of British Columbia.

General rules for ensuring Internet safety

✓ Educate yourself about the Internet.

✓ It's important to be knowledgeable about the Internet, because even if you don't have a computer at home, your child can access it at school, at a friend's house, or at your public library.

✓ Create a family agreement for Internet use, including hours of use, which sites can be accessed, and which ones shouldn't be.

✓ Place your computer in a central, open location, like the living room, so Internet use can be supervised.

Guiding your child online

✓ Look at the sites your child visits.

✓ Look into software or online services that filter out offensive material. Check with your Internet service provider (ISP) for any blocking features they might offer.

✓ Consider installing a children's search engine, like Yahooligans.

✓ Create a special folder of "bookmarks," or "favourites," for your child on your computer's browser.

Preserving your family's privacy

✓ If you have a Web site, avoid putting your children's pictures on it.

✓ Teach your children to never give out identifying information about any family member. This includes names, addresses, phone numbers, e-mail addresses, passwords, or credit card numbers.

✓ Encourage them to tell you if anyone is pressing for personal information.

✓ Teach your children that talking to a stranger on the Internet is no different than talking to a stranger on the street.

Minimizing possible risks

✓ Talk to your children about potential online dangers such as giving out personal information to strangers. Chat room acquaintances are strangers and your child should never arrange to meet them in the real world unless you give permission or know who they are.

✓ Better yet, if your children are young, steer them away from chat rooms. Older children should only participate in chat rooms you approve of.

✓ If your child starts receiving phone calls from strangers, or places calls to people you don't know, get to the bottom of it immediately.

✓ Tell your children that if someone harasses them online, says something inappropriate, or makes them feel uncomfortable in any way, they should tell you, their teacher, or a trusted adult.

Contact the police immediately if your child receives child pornography, has been sexually solicited, or has received sexually explicit images from an adult.

■ Parents and caregivers should be aware of and immediately report any inappropriate activities toward children.

All Canadians must be aware that since 1993 Canada has a new Child Pornography Law. This law defines child pornography as including photographic, film, video, or other visual representations depicting people under age 18 engaged in sexual activity. This also includes paintings, drawings, and written materials. It is an offense under the Criminal Code of Canada to make, distribute, sell, and importantly, possess such materials in Canada. The law is designed to protect children under the age of 18 from being sexually exploited by pornography and pornographers.

❖ Connections

1. A commonly used folk wisdom states, "It takes a village to raise a child." How does this statement relate to the idea that parenting and child safety are a social concern?

2. Share your reflections regarding the role of adult supervision in protecting children from harm in our society.

■ *It takes a village to raise a child.*
— Folk Wisdom

Parents become more aware of social concerns as their children become more involved in society as a whole, and as society also sees children as its responsibility. Parenting is not a job done in isolation, but rather within the supportive framework of a community and society at large.

Figure 16.7
Many federal laws affect children, parents, and caregivers.

The Role of Society in the Lives of Children

The laws of the land influence the role of parents and guardians in society. Parents and guardians are legally and socially responsible for providing adequate food, shelter, care, and education for their children. Community programs and social agencies are available to support and assist parents when circumstances make it difficult for them to fulfill their obligations.

Laws Governing Parents and Children

Laws exist at both the federal and provincial levels that regulate children and parents in society. Legislation governing child protection, child care, and school attendance occurs at the provincial/territorial level, while legislation involving more global concerns, such as child labour and child welfare, resides at the federal level. Children are both a national asset and the hope for the future of the country. As a democratic society, children and parents must be part of the political agenda.

Canadian Federal Laws

Family Law Act
•   governs marriage and the dissolution of marriage

Criminal Code of Canada
•   specifies that parents, foster parents, guardians, or heads of a family must provide the necessities of life for children under the age of 16, and that they will face penalties if they fail to do so
•   determines the nature of child pornography and penalties for possessing it

Canada's Charter of Rights and Freedoms
•   outlines the rights of parents and children

Labour Laws
•   include child labour protection

Young Offenders Act
•   protects the legal rights of children under the age of 18 charged with criminal offences

Provincial Law

Provincial and territorial legislation further defines the rights and
responsibilities of parents and children. The provinces and territories
determine how the educational process is funded and enforced. They
register births, deaths, and marriages. They are also responsible for
many jurisdictions including health care, education, welfare, housing,
and children and family services. The excerpt from Saskatchewan's
Action Plan for Children is an example of a recently developed social
policy that illustrates the range of government programs and services
provided by the provinces and territories.

Saskatchewan Action Plan

What Is Saskatchewan's Action Plan for Children?

The Government of Saskatchewan, as part of its social
programs initiatives, has developed the Child Action
Plan, a major interdepartmental initiative of the
Government of Saskatchewan. The following material
appears as part of the Saskatchewan's Social Services
home page.

The plan represents the cooperative effort of nine
government departments:

- Saskatchewan Education
- Saskatchewan Post-Secondary Education and
  Skills Training
- Saskatchewan Health
- Saskatchewan Intergovernmental and Aboriginal
  Affairs
- Saskatchewan Justice
- Saskatchewan Municipal Affairs and Housing
- Saskatchewan Social Services
- Saskatchewan Women's Secretariat
- Saskatchewan Northern Affairs

The Child Action Plan is a provincial strategy to
enhance the well-being of Saskatchewan children,
youth, and families. It provides a process for working
together and means that government, communities,
organizations, and individuals are encouraged to develop
common approaches to children's issues. By working in
co-operation, we ensure that resources are used more
effectively and are appropriate for the community.

Prevention and earlier intervention is a key focus
of the Action Plan. There is very strong evidence to
show that every dollar spent on preventive programs
significantly improves the quality of life for young
children. Studies also show it saves six to seven
dollars later on in areas such as social assistance,
remedial education, and losses to crime. Prevention
involves short-term costs for long-term savings.
With strong prevention approaches, the need for
long-term intervention is reduced.

Support to vulnerable children, youth, and families
is another key focus of the Child Action Plan. With
our country's current economic situation and our
complex social issues, many Saskatchewan families
are facing serious challenges. They must have access
to the services they need to improve their lives. The
Child Action Plan supports the services they need and
those services are based in their community.

Social Policy and Social Services

Human Resources Development Canada (HRDC) is the federal ministry responsible for social policy. Strategic Policy, the name of the
centre where policy development takes place, is made up of a number

of branches that work together to research, develop, and manage policy. The social policy branch provides "strategic policy analysis on a broad range of challenges facing Canadians in the areas of social policy and income security" (Government of Canada, 2003).

Canada's **social policy** outlines what is legal and permissible regarding social security and social service programs. It also outlines Canada's plan of action for ensuring the welfare of its citizens. The social policy branch develops policies and benefits for seniors, persons with disabilities, and poor and homeless persons, as well as families and children. Some of the policies and benefits that have been developed for families and children include The National Child Benefit, The National Children's Agenda, Understanding the Early Years, and support of low-income families with children in the transition from welfare to work.

Social policies developed at the provincial level provide rules and funding for child-care centres, hospitals, public health units, and a number of other public services that are important for parents and children. Recent groundbreaking research shows the importance of the early years in child development. This has encouraged both federal and provincial governments to develop policy for programs and funding that influences the health, well-being, and learning potential of every child.

Community Services

Community services are also in place to support families and children. They may be supported by local funds or by some federal or provincial grants, or completely funded through private or charitable donations. Organizations such as local YMCAs and YWCAs, the Children's Aid Society, Parents Without Partners, and Big Brothers and Big Sisters provide programs and services designed to assist parents in creating positive home environments that foster optimum human development.

Every community is different. To find out exactly what is available for parents and children in your community, check your local planning council, United Way office, hospital, newspaper, telephone directory, or community notice boards for public service listings, announcements, advertisements, and news stories. As part of your own contribution to the community, you may decide to volunteer for a community project or program that benefits parents or children.

Figure 16.8
Community services may provide projects or programs that foster community health and well-being.

Case Study: Community Service: Dads Do It Differently

"Are we almost there, Dad?" Rory asks excitedly. "There" means "Dads and Kids Day," the Saturday morning community service initiative at the high school put on by the Grade 11 Parenting classes. On one Saturday of each month, a different activity is planned just for dads, stepdads, or surrogate dads and their children. In December, they made candle-holders out of tree branches, and baked cookies. In January, they built a slide by packing snow into a large wedge shape, high at one end and low at the other, and misting it with water until it froze into a great surface to slide down. Now it is June, and their last activity for the year is washing cars. The staff parking lot is zigzagged with hoses and littered with buckets and sponges. Children sponge down doors and wheel covers, while fathers reach high to clean the roof.

"What's your mom doing right now?" a student asks a six-year-old girl who is wielding a green sponge.

"Oh," she answers wisely, "she's getting some peace and quiet!"

Finally, the hoses are drained and rolled up, buckets are put into trunks, and the dads and their children gather around a barbecue, for the hot dogs and dripping Popsicles.

"I hope you do this again next year," one father comments to the supervising teacher, while others nod in agreement. "It made me feel like a kid again!"

Questions

1. Considering a similar model, what activities would you recommend that are suitable for families in your school area?
2. How might you advertise the program and organize your class to help out on a Saturday? What obstacles might you face in designing a similar program for your community?
3. What is the value of this kind of community service program for families in your neighbourhood?

❖ Checkpoints

1. Describe how sexual harassment threatens personal safety.
2. List and describe the social issues and policies that are governed by federal law.
3. What are community services? How can they help families with children?

Parenting Challenges in Today's Society

Parenting is a social activity. Parents compare their children with other children, and their challenges with those of other parents. Many social influences shape how individual parents see their roles and fulfill their responsibilities. Religion and culture define a variety of possibilities. Individuals' background, beliefs, and place in society influence how much authority parents have over their children, whether one or both parents work outside the home, who spends the most time with the children, and what household and parent-child activities each parent is responsible for.

Figure 16.9
Many important transitions in family life are observed with a religious ceremony.

What does your culture or religion expect of men and women in terms of child discipline, child care, family income, and authority? What is expected of teachers, religious or cultural leaders, and male and female children within their families and in society? Because Canada includes so many races, cultures, and religions, there is an interesting range of beliefs regarding parenting and raising children. Some children may find their family traditions restrictive, and may adopt new traditions when they have children of their own, while others will find ways to incorporate their family history into the families they establish.

Protecting Culture and Religion

Canada has a rich and diverse cultural heritage. For many Canadians, religion is an important and meaningful aspect of their lives. Over the years, many families came to Canada from various countries to avoid religious persecution. Religious freedom is considered a right in this country. Many families continue to enjoy a strong communal identity through their religion. Many of the important transitions in family life including marriage, birth, and death are often observed with a religious ceremony. Religious principles define and protect the sanctity of family in society.

Aboriginal cultures in Canada have had to struggle to prevent the loss of their cultural and spiritual roots. Native and Inuit communities across Canada are reclaiming their heritage through Native language programs and a renewal of spiritual and traditional knowledge. Preserving Aboriginal culture is an important research focus at the University of Victoria in British Columbia. The following excerpt from their online publication *The University of Victoria's Canada Research Chairs Strategic Research Plan (2000)* describes the reason for and purpose of this research:

> As Aboriginal populations, environments, and cultural traditions continue to be eroded by the forces of the global economy, the protection of these rich, diverse resources has become critical. Uncovering and preserving unique cultural knowledge and experiences such as language, literature, art, traditional knowledge of ecology and environmental management, and governance requires innovative research that relies on the ability to draw from numerous perspectives. The University of Victoria is exploring the forces that influence the formation of cultural knowledge on a global scale, and also has special interest in the indigenous cultures of British

Columbia and Canada. How the literary traditions of Canada's indigenous peoples relate to those of other Aboriginal peoples, and how the wisdom and traditional knowledge of cultural groups can be integrated into Canadian society are current research topics. Approaching from a perspective within the community, as well as from the outside, we are working on finding ways of enhancing the quality of life of indigenous peoples and supporting the capacity for development of indigenous communities. (2000, p. 6)

Canada recognizes the diversity of Canadian families and the importance of preserving religious and cultural identities. There are three national days of celebration that mark cultural heritage. **National Aboriginal Day** is celebrated on June 21, the day of the summer solstice, because of its symbolic importance for Aboriginal people. This day celebrates the remarkable accomplishments of the Inuit, Métis, and members of the First Nations and their contribution to the building of Canada. **Saint-Jean-Baptiste Day** on June 24 is celebrated in honour of Saint-Jean-Baptiste, the Patron Saint of French Canadians. It is a day to celebrate the linguistic and cultural heritage of Francophones and to recognize their contribution to the building of this country. **Canadian Multiculturalism Day** on June 27 is celebrated as part of the annual Celebrate Canada group of events. It provides an opportunity to recognize the contributions of the many diverse communities in Canadian society. Although none of these days is a statutory holiday, each day represents an opportunity to honour Canada's rich cultural heritage.

Figure 16.10
National Aboriginal Day recognizes the important contributions of Inuit, Métis, and members of the First Nations.

Challenges of a Changing Society

Society has changed a great deal over the past one hundred years. At the beginning of the last century, Canada was still largely an agrarian, farming, or rural society. The family farm was a common picture with both parents at home, working in many different capacities as a production unit. Children who were old enough went to a local school, usually after completing morning chores, and returned at the end of the school day to complete more chores before settling down to finish any schoolwork for the next day. Families were large, and the farm provided their food and their livelihood.

In towns and cities, the picture was not all that different as many families were involved in a family business. Often, both parents worked in the business in a similar way that families worked on the farm. The family grocery, the family hardware store, the family gas station, were all owned and operated by parents and their children. As manufacturing grew and flourished, this type of production economy in the early 1800s gave way to a wage economy. Factories required labourers and attracted those who wanted a steady income. By the 1950s, a man could earn enough money at a factory job to support a wife and family, and to pay for a mortgage, a car, and a family vacation every year. Families left the farm and moved to the cities where men went to work for wages, and women stayed at home to care for young children, clean the house, and have dinner prepared when the wage earner returned home for the evening. In poorer families, however, women also had to work to help make ends meet.

The standard of living rose throughout the 1960s as the Canadian economy flourished. The face of society changed. The advent of the birth control pill and rapidly changing views about the role of women in society meant that women were no longer solely childbearers and homemakers. They had smaller families, higher levels of education, and were needed and increasingly accepted by the labour market.

During the 1970s, the standard of living continued to rise rapidly. The cost of living rose substantially and one family income was no longer sufficient to pay for the rising expectations and the associated costs of homes, cars, vacations, and all the goods and services that families were consuming. Two-income families became the norm, and women joined professional ranks in careers that were once only available to men. Divorce became more prevalent, as well as more socially accepted.

Life expectancy increased so that grandparents lived longer and sometimes required help from their children. This caused the creation of a "sandwich generation" in which parents cared for the many needs of their children as well as their parents. Life became much more complicated for men, women, children, and families, leading to a number of social issues that continue to face families today.

Sandwich-generation parents often care for aging parents, grandparents, or both. Geriatric diseases, mental illness, and physical disabilities in aging grandparents often pose additional challenges for working parents.

Figure 16.11
Over the past 40 years, standard of living and life expectancy in Canada has increased significantly. One of the results has been the creation of the sandwich generation.

Balancing Work and Family

Two-income families face a number of challenges. Time management is one of their main concerns. It is a challenge to get children to child care or school, provide nourishing meals for everyone, keep the home reasonably clean and in good repair, and still have time for interests, activities, and hobbies. Women who leave the home for paid employment find they have two jobs—one away from home, and the other doing the work required in the home at the end of the day. Men take more responsibility for housework and child care than they did in the past, but recent census data outlined in the news article from *Canadian Press*, published on March 17, 1998, shows that they continue to lag behind women in these areas.

Census results show women do most unpaid housework

TORONTO (CP) — Housework, child care, and caring for seniors have finally come out of the closet.

Statistics Canada has released results of the first census in the world that asked people about the amount of unpaid, unrecognized work they do inside their homes.

And, as predicted, it showed women are doing most of that work even though most of them work outside the home as well.

The 1996 census found 92 percent of Canada's 11.8 million adult women report doing housework, compared to 85 percent of men; 42 percent of women look after children, compared to 34 percent of men; and 19 percent of women are looking after seniors, compared to 14 percent of men.

And in every category, women spend longer hours at those tasks.

A quarter of women spend 30 hours or more on housework and two-thirds of women with full-time paid jobs spend 15 hours or more a week looking after their children.

At the extreme end, 18 percent of wives with a full-time job spent 60 hours or more caring for children. That doubled to almost half of wives without a full-time job.

Options for Working Parents

To meet the needs of their family, parents may vary the amount of time spent working outside the home. Two incomes can provide a better lifestyle for a family in some ways, but it may also mean sacrificing family time together. Working alternate shifts may be a solution, allowing the parent who is not working to be home with the children at the beginning and end of the school day. This can help reduce the amount of money needed for child care.

In some situations, when neither parent is available before or after school, **school-age programs** at schools or community centres can provide care for children who are not old enough to stay home alone. Part-time work by one or both parents is another option that allows them to be at home with their children more often, while still providing much needed income. Sometimes parents can job share or take turns working and staying home when their children are small, which allows one parent to be with the children at all times.

Figure 16.12
While two incomes may provide a better lifestyle in some ways, it can also present challenges to other family needs and functions.

The options for working two-parent families are far greater than for lone-parent or low-income families. Parents who do not have enough income from one job may have to work two jobs, overtime, or double shifts just to make ends meet. A lone parent does not have as much choice, and generally must work full-time to provide income for the family. In these cases, having reliable and affordable child care makes working that much more possible.

Signs of a Family Friendly Workplace

While workplaces are generally adult environments, they affect children of parents who work outside the home, as well as youth who have entered the workforce.

Parents have concerns about the availability and quality of child-care services, as well as about balancing and integrating their work and family lives. It is important for parents to be available for their children at key times, such as for school events or when children are sick, and for children to understand and feel connected to their parents' work lives.

Most youth are keen to find jobs, and many begin some form of employment while in their early or mid teens. Key workplace issues for youth relate to how well the transition is managed from home and school to part-time or full-time work.

Child and youth friendly workplaces address the needs of parents, youth employees, and families as a whole through supportive policies, programs, and practices. The following material was published in 2000 by the BC Council for Families in the publication *Family Connections 8*.

What are some things that make communities child and youth friendly with respect to workplaces?

- employers who pay fair wages and abide by the labour code
- major employers who provide workplace child care, including facilities for nursing mothers; smaller employers who provide information and support in finding child care
- major employers who have good parental leave policies
- major employers who promote, allow, or support job sharing and flexible working hours
- major employers who provide information and support on parenting issues (for example, through on-site educational workshops)
- employers who allow parents to bring their children to work (for example, in cases of emergency, as well as for learning purposes), and who hold family events
- employers who support community programs for children and youth
- employers who ensure that working hours and conditions do not interfere with the schoolwork of their young employees
- workplace policies that address discrimination and sexual harassment, developed with the input of employees
- community information and support for youth seeking employment, especially for those from minority groups or those who face other barriers to employment

Talking Parenting

Janit Porter, Doctor of Chiropractic; Mother of Noah 16 months and Daniel 3

I love to spend time with my children, but I also love what I do. I do not think I would be a good mother if I were not able to still practise.

I have set up my office in a renovated house so that our home is above it. That way I have been able to breast-feed both of my children. I do not spend time in the car on the road and I am always there in case of emergencies. My children know that. I also have a very helpful husband, a wonderful nanny, and a supportive office staff who I consider as part of the family.

It takes a village to raise a child. I believe that children need the influence and nurturing of all the people around them, not only their parents. You do not own your children. I am grateful every day for the role that my family and the patients that I care for play in caring for my children.

Like most first-time parents, I read a lot of information, sometimes too much information. Over the past two years, though, I have found that the most practical and valuable parenting information has come from my patients. If I am not sure about something, I just ask one of the mothers in my practice. I love to talk to the older mothers in particular because, after so many years, they tend to have a more relaxed attitude about raising children and do not panic about the little things. So other peoples' experiences have helped me figure out how I want to deal with my children. You take all the information you have at hand and do what feels right for you, what you feel comfortable with. It has worked so far.

Figure 16.13
Janit, Noah, and Daniel

Child Care

Besides having more responsibility for the care of children during the hours outside of work, studies show that women also take more responsibility for finding quality child care that meets the individual needs of their children while they are at work. Often, because women are viewed as the second-wage earner, they are responsible for arranging child care when they return to work following a maternity or parenting leave. Many communities have a shortage of licensed child-care spaces, and children are put on waiting lists sometimes even before birth.

Public child care is available to any child, regardless of his or her family situation. A public child care is licensed by the province or territory, and must meet rigorous standards. Public child care also offers the benefit of subsidized care for low-income families; however, these spaces are limited and often have long waiting lists. Private child care is not regulated in the same way. Examples of private child care include baby-sitting in a private home, or baby-sitting that is provided for a few

Figure 16.14
Finding reliable child care may be difficult. Parents must make sure their child is safe while in the care of others.

hours a week by a community group. Often private child care is found through word of mouth, and because it is not licensed, is usually more informal. The private care provider may decide to give up child care without notice, so a parent can be left scrambling to find other care.

The question of who will care for the children is a major concern for every family with young children. There are many factors to consider, whether it is finding a reliable baby-sitter for a few hours from time to time, or a daily caregiver while both parents work.

Cost: The amount parents spend on child care often makes the cost of raising children highest in the early years. In some cases, it may cost nearly as much for child care as a parent earns working at a part-time or minimum wage job. With the additional high cost of transportation to and from work, some women may choose not to work at all for the small amount of income they have left over. In cases where the family income is quite low, some families are eligible for subsidized child care, with the government paying for all or part of the child-care cost.

Quality: It can be a challenge to find child care where the environment is caring, encourages learning, includes physical activity, and meets the developmental needs of every child. Not every child-care situation suits every child or is in harmony with the values of the parent. It takes time to find the right place, and if it does not work out, someone, usually the woman, must start to look all over again.

Safety: Parents must be assured that their children are safe when they are being cared for. Police records of sexual offenders and police checks for child-care workers have made a positive difference. Child-care workers should have certificates indicating that they have completed basic first-aid training and safety training. Fire drills and enforcement of safety procedures should be ongoing in every child-care situation.

Location: Child care must be accessible and close at hand. Driving children to a child-care situation halfway across a large city can add unnecessary stress and travel time to the day. Those who have access to child care close to their work or directly in the workplace benefit from that convenience. More businesses are discovering that having a child-care facility on the premises is beneficial and increases their employees' productivity.

Backup child care: When a child is too sick to go to a child care centre, a parent must have a backup caregiver or take a day off from work. Not all employers allow parents time off for the emergency care of a child without the parent losing a day's pay. One way to face this challenge is through a relative, neighbour, or friend who is available as a backup caregiver.

BETWEEN FRIENDS   *BY SANDRA BELL LUNDY*

Figure 16.15
It can be difficult to juggle both parenthood and work when children are sick.

❖ Checkpoints

1. What are sandwich-generation parents?
2. How can parenting partners work together to balance work and family?
3. If you had a child that required child care, what cost, quality, safety, and location factors would be important to you?
4. Who in your family and community can you rely on for backup child care if you need it today?

❖ Connections

1. Investigate the child-care options in your community. Determine the locations and describe the type of care that is provided.
2. Research three of the major employers in your community and determine if they have a family friendly workplace. Present your findings in a comparison chart.

Divorce, Custody, and Child Support

During the 1960s and 1970s, Canada's divorce rate rose steadily, especially after a change in divorce laws made it easier to obtain a divorce. Hollywood movies and television programs contributed to the view that divorce was the answer when the glow of romantic love faded. In Canadian society, marriages are often based on love and companionship, rather than the economic partnerships that form the basis of arranged marriages. Divorce rates have decreased somewhat in the past decade, but are still substantially higher than they were prior to the 1960s. Divorce is a fact of life for many children in our society.

There is less trauma when parents make every effort to make the divorce amicable, and talk with their children about it. However, children of all ages still experience negative emotions and uncertainty when their families break apart. Family counselling can help families avoid divorce, and it can help families survive divorce.

What the experts say

ANNE MARIE AMBERT

Anne Marie Ambert, a Sociology Professor at York University, is the author of "Divorce: Facts, Causes, and Consequences," published by the Vanier Institute of the Family. She answers the following question:

How does divorce affect children? Does the effect vary with age?

Research shows that at all age levels, children of divorced parents have higher rates of emotional, behavioural, social, and academic problems than children in two-parent families. The age of the child at the time of divorce is one of the factors that will determine the impact that separation will have on the child. If parents divorce when their child is 20 years old, for example, that child is less likely to be affected by the diminished economic circumstances of either parent. Poverty is more likely to affect preschoolers,

especially if the mother gains custody, because almost 60 percent of single mothers live below the poverty line. However, it should be noted that "there really is no good time for parents to divorce."

The impact of divorce varies with the age of the child.

Infants: Although the brain of an infant is developing rapidly, they do not have the cognitive capacity to understand divorce. However, they are keenly aware of how their parents are feeling and sense the turmoil that a divorce is likely to cause. Infants are also developing a sense of trust in the world and are keenly aware of stress. Parents are likely to be highly stressed during divorce proceedings and cannot help but transmit this stress to their child. As a result, the infant is likely to have trouble sleeping and cry more often.

Toddlers: Children at this age will sense the change in their lives that a divorce will bring. The parents' lives may become chaotic, and this will confuse toddlers. As a result, they may regress to earlier behaviours—for example, wanting to nurse or have their bottle back. Parents are advised to go along with this behavioural regression because demanding the more mature behaviour may make the problem worse. On a positive note, if one parent has always been the primary caregiver and is able to continue to function well in this role, most toddlers will not really notice the absence of the other parent.

Preschoolers: The preschool child may be more severely affected by divorce than an older child because they are most at risk for the long-term consequences of poverty. New research clearly indicates that poverty during the early childhood years hinders cognitive and verbal development in the long run. Readiness to learn and future school success are very dependent on these factors.

On an individual level, as a consequence of the divorce, preschoolers have been observed to become more clingy than usual, have more temper tantrums, and experience sleep disorders. Parents can help their children through these times by comforting the child and helping them regain their sense of control after a tantrum.

Young School-Age Children (ages 6 to 7): Children in the primary years of elementary school often feel that they are to blame for their parents' divorce. " If only I hadn't done that bad thing, Mommy would still love Daddy," could be a typical reaction for a child of this age. These children sometimes struggle with guilt and may withdraw into a fantasy world where their parents are still together. They sometimes set up a "parent trap"—for example, "Dad wants to talk to you on the telephone"—in hopes that it will be the magic that will bring parents back together.

Other young children act out in a way that is out of character for them. Acting out may have serious consequences at school and set the stage for a downward progression in school success. When this is coupled with the family experiencing financial hardship, life chances can be seriously affected.

Older School-Age Children (ages 8 to 12): Preteen children show a great deal of variability in their reaction to a divorce. Some may talk to their parent(s) about the divorce, but many do not.

Many will not even discuss it with their peers. Despite this outward show of indifference, these children may be holding in feelings of anger and shame. In many cases, the custodial single parent must move to more affordable housing after a divorce, and the children lose their familiar peer group as a result. This is a serious loss for most older school-age children. Schoolwork may be the first to suffer after a divorce, and this has long-term consequences for future success.

Teenagers: Going through puberty makes teenagers volatile at the best of times, and a divorce in the family adds a significant amount of stress and frustration to their lives. Teenagers will tend to turn to their peer group for support and stress relief rather than their parents. A teen may display his or her frustration through delinquency or sexual promiscuity.

For adolescents, a particularly difficult situation arises when the custodial parent loses the opportunity to communicate with and supervise them because they are working to "make ends meet." Adolescence is already an age when "temptations" toward deviance abound and a youth who lacks parental support may succumb to detrimental peer pressures. Schoolwork may suffer accordingly. Adolescent girls whose parents have separated are at particular risk of becoming sexually active and more often than others become pregnant.

On a positive note, teenagers whose parents divorce may already have positive success at school, be well-established, and continue this pattern. They often will have part-time jobs and not be so affected by the lowering of family income.

Although research shows that at all age levels, children of divorced parents have higher rates of emotional, behavioural, social, and academic problems than children in two-parent families, there are several cautions in interpreting the above troubling information. The first is that, among an unknown number of children, some of what appear to be negative effects of divorce already existed before parental separation. It is important to study how the children were before the divorce.

The second important point is that whatever statistics you read concerning the negative outcomes of children "of divorce," they do not apply to the majority of children affected by divorce. What these statistics indicate is that children of divorced parents have a greater risk of developing problems than children whose parents remain together. But these statistics also indicate that a majority of children of divorce do not experience developmental problems.

Nevertheless, I do not wish to err in the opposite direction and shrug off the negative effects of divorce. They are real and costly for children, parents, and schools, as well as the welfare and health-care systems. Students who wish to know more about my research into the effects of divorce on children are advised to read my full paper on the subject.

In most cases, children continue to live with their mother, although they now have more say about with whom they will live after a divorce. **Joint custody** means that children spend time with both parents, and both parents continue to take responsibility for parenting decisions. Following a divorce, the standard of living for a mother and her children often decreases, while it increases for the father. Single mothers do not always have the highest paying jobs, and they continue to be the ones who take primary responsibility to feed, clothe, and shelter their children.

As of May 1, 1997, changes to the federal Divorce Act now enforce **mandatory child support**. According to Malcolm C. Kronby, author of *Canadian Family Law* (2001), "There is a schedule of guideline amounts for each province, with small variations of amount for each income level. For example, the table amount of child support for an Ontario resident who earns $40,000 annually and has one child is $345 a month. For $50,000 and three children, it is $917 a month" (p. 73). If it is the father who has custody, the mother is expected to pay the monthly child support, calculated on the basis of her earnings.

Separation agreements drawn up before the legal divorce generally take these child support tables into consideration, and also indicate whether the support continues until the child is 18 or 21 years old. To protect their rights and interests, both parents have their own legal counsel in the case of separation and divorce.

Increased Media Violence

Another social challenge for parents is children's increased exposure to violence in society. Even parents who curtail their children's television viewing cannot control the number of violent images that occur in television programming. Subtle and hidden violence occurs in electronic games, cartoons, television programs, and children's videos. Graphic violence appears in news reports, advertising, music videos, and computer games. Parents may feel helpless about their children's exposure to violence; however, they can talk to children about what they see and how they feel when they are exposed to violent images. Parents may need to eliminate violent programs and the related toys that generate violent behaviour from their homes. They can also reduce exposure to violence by monitoring what their children are exposed to in their child-care situations and at school.

Poverty

Government cutbacks to social services and welfare have led to families with children becoming increasingly dependent on community services and food banks. The number of **working poor**—that is, families who are working but whose income is at or below the Low Income Cut-Off Line (LICO)—has increased. Single income or lone-parent families are more likely to experience poverty than are two-income families, but other factors also contribute to poverty. Job loss, disability, health problems, drug addiction, and alcohol dependency all contribute to loss or misuse of income.

Poverty is not always visible. Families may still be able to clothe their children to look like other children with clothes from organizations such as Good Will, Amity, or the Salvation Army. Their children may continue to attend school, but they may be hiding hunger. "I forgot my lunch" or "I'm not hungry" may cover up the fact that a family's money has run out before the end of the month.

The most obvious indicator of poverty is when a family loses its home. A growing number of **homeless families** are moving in to community shelters, or having to live on the streets. The cost of housing can be prohibitive, especially in large cities. Having to pay both the first and last month's rent to acquire rental housing can prove to be too much for homeless families. Subsidized housing and programs such as Habitat for Humanity that assist families with housing acquisition are not always available. Local and provincial governments continue to address the housing issue, and to try to keep families off the streets.

Figure 16.16
Programs such as Habitat for Humanity help families with a low income acquire affordable housing.

The following article by F. Berkoff appeared in *Canadian Living* in March 2002:

Mouths to Feed

Here is a sad and sobering fact: although, by all standards, Canada is a rich nation, many of its residents cannot afford to maintain a healthy diet.

The latest National Population Health Survey from Statistics Canada shows that in 1998 and 1999, a lack of money forced almost 2.5 million people (about eight percent of Canadians) to compromise the quality of their diet or the quantity of food they ate at least once. During that same period, an additional half-million people worried that they would not have enough to eat because they did not have enough money. The survey also found that about 600 000 people received help from food banks or other charitable agencies in the year before the survey.

However, children in these households were not necessarily undernourished: adult caregivers often tend to sacrifice their own diet to save their children from hunger. "This confirms previous research that showed that low-income women are trying their very best to feed their kids despite a lack of money," says Debbie Field, executive director of FoodShare in Toronto. Field adds that this study also confirms that the number of households that are vulnerable to hunger is much higher than previously thought.

Protecting the Rights of Children in Society

In 1979 during the International Year of the Child, the United Nations began to consolidate previous work on a declaration of the rights of the child. It examined the plight of children worldwide, and found that children were not treated equally or justly. Parents were not always able to protect their children, provide for their needs, or keep them safe. Children could not always be protected from exploitation, violence, or abuse in countries where they had no rights. The United Nations determined that parents needed help protecting their children, so they outlined the responsibilities of parents and nations to protect and uphold the rights of every child. In 1989, The United Nations Convention on the **Rights of the Child** was ratified. By 1995, one hundred and eighty-five countries, including Canada, had ratified these rights for children.

The United Nations Convention on the Rights of the Child defines a child as any human being under the age of 18. Laws that a ratifying government passes must, without discrimination, respect and follow the rights of children as outlined by the Convention. All children, regardless of race, gender, class, ability, or disability, must be treated exactly the same. The best interests of children must be kept in mind, and governments must provide and carry out the laws that maintain the rights and safety of all children.

According to the Convention, governments must respect the rights and duties of parents and guardians, and at the same time take responsibility for the survival and development of every child. Children have the right to life and to the basic necessities of life, such as food and shelter. Children have a right to a name, a nationality, and an identity, and a right to know their parents, be cared for by their parents, and live with their parents unless their parents are abusing them.

The actual Convention contains 50 articles that detail at great length all aspects of child rights. Canada has adopted the rights of the child, and has added and rewritten some laws to accommodate them. However, the government cannot ensure that the rights of children is upheld without the support and work of families, caregivers, and anyone in a career, occupation, or place in society that involves children.

❖ Connection

1. Talk to school-age children to find out if they know about their rights. Produce a simple yet interesting pamphlet that gives children the information they need to know about the rights they have, and how to get help if they feel their rights are being violated.

In Canada, the area where children's rights are threatened most is in violent situations. Doctors, school personnel, staff in religious institutions, social agencies, and police are responsible by law in some provinces and territories for reporting cases of child abuse, neglect, and violence. Anyone who lives and works with children must know his or her legal responsibilities when it comes to identifying, reporting, and ending violence against children.

Violence Toward Children

Violence toward children is rarely an isolated incident. Research indicates that circumstances leading to **patterns of violence** in families have a history. Children who were abused by their parents often grow up to repeat the same behaviour with their own or other children.

The **cycle of violence** from one generation to the next continues unless someone recognizes that he or she has a tendency toward violence, and takes steps to stop it. When it comes to raising children, however, stress and anger can trigger violence in even the most well-intentioned person. Counselling, access to a help-phone line, and anger management training can make a positive difference by helping to break the cycle of violence.

The following article was published by Health Canada, and reprinted in their online magazine *Health! Canada* (February 2001):

Family Violence — It hurts everyone

Family violence and abuse can happen anywhere, to anyone. Violent and abusive people and their victims live in small towns and big cities, are at every level of income, are all ages, and come from every religious and ethnocultural background.

Abuse is a betrayal of trust in an intimate relationship. Abuse can be physical, sexual, emotional, or all three. Neglect and financial exploitation are other aspects of abuse.

Sobering statistics
Figures from surveys conducted in the last five years illustrate the extent of family violence in Canada:

- Seven percent of people who are married or living in a common-law relationship experience some type of violence by a partner.
- Women are three times more likely than men to be injured by spousal violence, and five times more likely to require medical attention.
- Children and youth under 18 years of age make up 60 percent of all sexual assault victims and 20 percent of all physical assault victims.
- Parents are more likely than other family members to commit violent acts against children and youth.
- Older adults are more likely to experience emotional and financial abuse than physical or sexual violence.
- In the past 20 years, one-third of murder victims were related to their killers.

Children are not only abused and mistreated in their families, but may experience violence in many different situations. Sexual assault, physical abuse, witnessing domestic violence, and experiencing emotional trauma and neglect all represent forms of violence that affect children in some way. Convicted child abusers include members of the clergy, teachers, baby-sitters, scout leaders, coaches, neighbours, relatives, and people in general who have been entrusted with caring for children. Recognizing and reporting violence is everyone's responsibility.

Indicators of Abuse and Violence

Anyone who interacts with children should know the signs and symptoms of abuse in children. Caregivers, doctors, teachers, neighbours, and others who see children on a regular basis may be the first to recognize abuse. Physical abuse is sometimes the easiest to identify because it leaves marks. However, assaults can be aimed at places that are usually covered with clothing. Children in the normal course of a day may fall, hit their head, or break a bone, but repeated injuries, unusual bruising, burns, or lacerations, may lead one to suspect abuse. Children who have been abused may exhibit unusual fears. They may cringe at a touch or a loud noise. They may not want to go home at the end of the school day, and at the same time they may be afraid to say anything that might implicate their parent. Withdrawal, anxiety, depression, self-destructive or aggressive behaviour, and delayed development may be indications of a child suffering from emotional harm.

Reporting Responsibilities

Some provinces have legislation that regulates the reporting of violence toward children. In Ontario, the Child and Family Service Act recognizes that "each of us has a responsibility for the welfare of children." It states clearly in Section 72 (1) that members of the public, including professionals or others with official duties with respect to children, have an obligation to report promptly to a children's aid society if they suspect that a child is or may be in need of protection. The person making the report of observed or suspected abuse must make the report themselves; they must not rely on any other person to make the report for them. In addition, if a person has already reported, observed, or suspected abuse once and the behaviour continues, they are responsible to make further reports. A child in need of protection is a child who experiences physical, sexual, and emotional abuse, as well as neglect and risk of harm.

Those persons who work closely with children have a special responsibility to report suspicions of abuse or violence. Due to their particular responsibility, failure to report is an offence, and they are liable on conviction to a fine up to $1000 or a prison term of up to one year. The following professionals are affected by this law:

- health-care workers, including physicians, nurses, dentists, pharmacists, and psychologists
- teachers, principals, social workers, and family counsellors
- priests, rabbis, and other members of clergy
- operators and employees of day nurseries, youth and recreation workers, peace officers, coroners, solicitors, service providers and their employees, and any other person who performs professional duties with respect to a child

Even if information is obtained in confidence, all professionals or people who perform official duties involving children must report that a child is in need of protection.

False Reports of Abuse

Occasionally children, adolescents, and adults report that they have been abused when no abuse has occurred. Children sometimes make up stories to get attention or to hurt an adult they know. Reports may turn out to be malicious and designed to ruin the reputation of an adult connected in some way to the child. Malicious reporting does not happen frequently, but when it does occur, the damage done to the

Figure 16.17
Professionals, such as child-care workers, speech pathologists, and social workers, must report suspected cases of child abuse to the local Children's Aid Society.

accused is enormous. Reputations and careers can rarely be salvaged after a false report. Individuals should never give the impression that they do not believe a report of child abuse. Once the report is made, it is up to the justice system to determine if the accusation is false.

Effects of Violence

Violence toward children has lasting effects. Children who suffer abuse may have lasting emotional scars. Some can carry on with a normal life with the help of counselling, but others experience various difficulties with relationships, violence, or crime, and some may even resort to suicide. Family breakdown often results when violence occurs. Divorce may be a necessary step to protect children from a violent parent, or it may result from the trauma that a family experiences, even when the abuse is perpetrated by someone from outside of the family.

The Criminal Code of Canada regulates assault, sexual abuse, mental cruelty, or any form of harm or violence against children. Whether or not a person is convicted, charges alone may be enough to damage his or her reputation. Teachers may never teach again, and caregivers have a police record that prevents them from ever caring for children again. Therefore, making a false accusation can ruin innocent lives. Those who are convicted are sent to jail, with the hope that they can be rehabilitated. However, many people leave prison, only to commit more violence against children in some other community or family. Laws must continue to protect children from violence.

❖ Checkpoints

1. What is joint custody?
2. Define the term "working poor."
3. Describe the indicators of child abuse.

❖ Connections

1. Watch a television program that is often watched by children eight to ten years of age. Evaluate the program for the number and types of violent incidents it depicts. Determine if the program contains too much violence. Give reasons for your opinion.
2. Outline the procedure to follow for someone who suspects child abuse in your community.

Chapter Summary

Chapter Highlights

- Parents grow increasingly aware of a number of social concerns as their children become more involved in the world outside the family and take their first steps toward independence.

- The personal safety of children outside the home is critical.

- Street proofing children is an important step in protecting them so that they can recognize and take action against danger.

- Bullying and sexual harassment require action on the part of schools and parents.

- Parenting is not done in isolation. Society as a whole takes responsibility for children.

- A number of laws, social policies, and social and community services are available to protect, direct, and support parents.

- As society continues to change at a rapid pace, a number of social challenges affect children and families, including balancing work and family, finding quality child care, divorce, custody, and child support, dealing with media violence, and a growing concern for poverty and homelessness.

- Governments assist parents in protecting children's rights.

- Canada has adopted universal rights of the child drawn up by the United Nations, and has enacted laws to protect children's rights.

- Violence against children is one area where parents, caregivers, and those who work closely with children, can take action to uphold children's rights. Recognizing and reporting children who are in need of protection, and becoming educated are important steps toward ending violence against children.

Review and Extend Your Learning

1. What might be the adverse effects on children of poorly planned or overzealous street-proofing programs? **T/I**

2. Re-examine the factors that cause bullying. Write a brief overview of the strategies that parents and school officials can use to help avoid bullying. **K/U** **T/I** **C** **A**

3. Prepare a presentation for parents of elementary school children to educate them about the issue of bullying. **K/U** **C**

4. Investigate provincial or territorial legislation related to the legal rights and responsibilities of parents and children in your home area. **T/I**

5. Families face many challenges. Which ones should caregivers or those who work with children be aware of? Give a rationale for your choices. **K/U** **A**

6. Investigate child care for infants and toddlers at three facilities in your community. Make a chart comparing the three facilities in terms of cost, quality, safety, location and convenience, and your values and beliefs. **K/U** **T/I** **C** **A**

7. Analyze the connections between divorce and poverty. Describe the impact that each of these situations has on children. **T/I**

8. Evaluate the causes and consequences of violence toward children. Identify the impact that violence has on families, caregivers, and those who work with children. **K/U** **T/I**

9. Prepare a short research questionnaire to determine what children know about violence and how it has affected them. Compile the results of your inquiries. Report your findings to the class. **T/I** **C**

Research Opportunities

10. Conduct a Web search for Canada only, using the words "social services" and your province or territory. Investigate the social programs in your region that protect children—for example, laws relating to education, child-care centres and day nurseries, and child and family services. What social programs, laws, or social policies exist to protect children up to age 6, from ages 6 to 12, and from ages 12 to 18? In your opinion, are children well-protected by your provincial or territorial government, or do changes need to be made?

The World Beyond the Family

By the end of this chapter, you will be able to:

- analyze the role of child-care providers in meeting the challenges of balancing work and family

- identify the role and functions of schooling in our society and in relation to family life

- investigate and interpret the contributions that schools make to the socialization of individuals throughout life

- identify how the media can be seen as agents of socialization

- evaluate the influence of the media on parents, children, and adolescents

Important Terms

agent of socialization
audiovisual technology
breakfast programs
censorship
curriculum
defiance of authority
display media
electronic media

formal education
informal education
mentor
online learning
print material
private school

public school
social conventions
stereotype
truant
violence in school

Chapter at a Glance

How Do Schools and Media Influence Parents and Children?

Parents and children cannot escape the influence of schools and the media. From the time a child is six years old, school takes up seven hours of the day, five days of the week, for almost ten months of the year. Children are also expected to do schoolwork at home, beginning as early as the first grade.

Children have access to a variety of media:

- **print materials** such as books, magazines, catalogues, and newspapers
- **audiovisual technology** such as television, radio, and video
- **electronic media** such as computers, Internet, electronic messages, and interactive games
- **display media** such as store displays, window displays, billboards, and signs

New information, values, and ways of thinking and acting continuously bombard Canadian children.

From morning until night, school and media bombard children with information, values, and ways of thinking and acting that represent a much bigger world than the child's immediate family. For the most part, parents accept and encourage the influence of schools and media because of their many positive contributions to a child's development. At school, teachers instruct in **social conventions** such as taking turns, waiting in line, thinking before you speak, being kind to others, and saying please and thank-you. Schools provide a ready-made peer group. Professionally trained teachers encourage interaction and a sense of belonging. Children learn the rules and practise the essential behaviours that they need in society. They follow the steps that lead to independence. However, not every experience at school is positive, which raises concerns for many parents.

Parents welcome the educational potential of electronic media. Its influence begins before children begin school and continues throughout their lives. Child-centred programs on video and television teach very young children words, songs, and important concepts as they watch, sing along, repeat, and imitate. Educational programs for older children introduce them to art, mathematics, crafts, activities, and drama. At the same time, however, children who have access to programming that is captivating and often of low quality become the target of high-impact advertising. Parents and caregivers need to find a balance between the positive and negative influences of school and media on the socialization of their children.

School as an Agent of Socialization

■ If I could choose what schools would teach, what would I include?

School is an **agent of socialization** because of its role in teaching children the ways of society. People often ask what "schools should teach." Some believe schools should teach only the basics such as reading, writing, and arithmetic. Others feel that schools should teach more about everyday life and how to face social problems such as AIDS, sexuality, poverty, violence, commercialism, and family breakdown. Some argue that schools should encourage every child to reach the highest possible academic achievement, while others argue that schools were meant to train individuals for jobs at all levels of society.

A Brief History of Schooling

Historically, school as we know it has existed for only a short time. Not that long ago, children did not attend school in a formal sense. They were educated by parents, tribal elders, clergy, tutors, or private teachers if the family was wealthy. Some were trained by an artisan, local craftsperson, or tradesperson who took on an apprentice. Before there were books or print materials, direct instruction of a particular skill was the norm. Counting and mental arithmetic were used for basic business transactions, while reading and writing were the privilege of the church, the state, or the elite.

Before the invention of parchment by the Egyptians, records were carved in wood or etched in stone. History was preserved by word of mouth. The oral tradition of telling, retelling, and remembering stories was valued. Reading and writing slowly made their way into society as writing on parchment and paper allowed words to be recorded and preserved. The wave of human migration from the Mediterranean regions throughout Europe encouraged more people to learn how to read and write. Written messages sent with travellers from one region to another became a way of sending and sharing news, long before newspapers were invented.

The first books were written by hand. Later, a primitive form of printing was used to produce books and papers by carving the letters from blocks, dipping them in ink, and then pressing them by hand onto paper. It was a long and difficult process. Books were rare, costly, and not readily available for the average person. The invention of the printing press in the 1400s made it possible to mass-produce books, newspapers, handbills, and magazine-type publications. As more print materials were produced, it became important to learn to read.

Figure 17.1
During the Middle Ages, all records and recorded history were done in longhand with quills and ink.

Although education continued to be individual and private, the availability of reading materials made the teaching of groups of people easier.

During the Industrial Revolution as manufacturing became mechanized, fewer workers were needed. Children and youth were no longer needed in factories, and they became a problem for society. Schools became the answer. In Canada, cities, towns, and even rural communities set up **public schools** paid for out of taxes, allowing all children to receive an education. Reading, writing, arithmetic, and the natural sciences were the main subjects, but as the world became more complex, other subject areas were added to the curriculum. **Private schools**, supported by tuition fees paid for by parents who wanted a particular kind of education, already existed and continued to be available. Today, both public and private schools continue to teach children academics, as well as what is acceptable in the community.

❖ Checkpoints

1. What are the "ways of society" that are taught by schools?
2. What is an agent of socialization?
3. What are the differences between public and private schools?
4. How did the invention of the printing press contribute to formal schooling?

Rules and Regulations Governing Schooling

Before their children begin to attend school, parents need to have some knowledge of school rules and regulations. In Canada, the provinces and territories are responsible for public education. Once a child is enrolled in school, parents are responsible for the child's attendance, and they can be charged if the child becomes **truant**, or stops attending regularly.

Education in Canada: Who is responsible for what?

The provincial or territorial government is generally responsible for

- setting policies and guidelines for school trustees, directors of education, principals, and other school board officials
- developing the curriculum and setting requirements for student diplomas and certificates
- preparing lists of approved textbooks and other learning materials

School boards are generally responsible for

- determining the number, size, and location of schools; building, equipping, furnishing, and maintaining schools and the programs for special education, elementary, and secondary education
- preparing an annual budget and managing funds allocated by the province
- developing policies for safe arrival programs for elementary schools (bussing and transportation)

- hiring teachers and other staff
- helping teachers improve their teaching practices and performance
- enforcing student attendance, and ensuring schools abide by the Education Act and its regulations

Each principal is generally responsible for

- determining the organization of the school, ensuring ongoing maintenance of the school buildings, and administering the school's budget
- ensuring curriculum delivery and assessment practices in compliance with provincial policies
- admitting and placing students, maintaining student records, and ensuring report cards are sent to parents
- ensuring student supervision and school discipline, and developing a code of conduct
- assigning teachers to classes, assisting and supervising them, and recommending the appointment, promotion, demotion, and dismissal of teachers

Teachers are generally responsible for

- preparing lesson plans and teaching classes
- encouraging students in their studies, and evaluating student work and progress
- supervising student behaviour and maintaining classroom discipline
- demonstrating good citizenship and respect for all groups of people

Students are generally responsible for

- attending classes, completing schoolwork, and taking examinations
- exercising self-discipline and behaving courteously toward both their teachers and their fellow students

Parents are generally responsible for

- sending their children to school "ready to learn" (early parenting influences school readiness)
- ensuring their children attend school; typically, attendance is compulsory between the ages of 6 and 16

❖ Connections

1. As a student, reflect on the responsibilities that each group or person has for your education. If it were possible, would you change, add, or remove any of these responsibilities from any person or group of people? Explain your reasons to a group of your classmates.

■ *Children who enter elementary school with "ready-to-learn" skills are less at risk of having difficulties at school, leaving school before high school graduation, becoming involved in criminal behaviour, and becoming addicted to tobacco, alcohol, and other drugs.*
— Ontario Coalition for Better Childcare

Isn't that nice. His first day at school and already the principal would like to have a consultation with us ...

Figure 17.2
Why are these parents about to be surprised?

Case Study: Parents Not Doing Their Job

Ann Landers was a syndicated columnist whose advice columns were carried in hundreds of newspapers. This letter originally appeared in *The Toronto Star* on January 5, 2002.

DEAR ANN:
I am a grade school teacher. I think parents have forgotten their job when it comes to preparing their children for school. May I please use your column to give them some reminders?

It is the job of parents to make sure their child comes to school clean, fed, dressed, and on time.

It is the job of parents to make sure their child comes to school prepared with books, paper, pencils, and other supplies.

It is the job of parents to make sure their child completes all homework assignments.

It is the job of parents to teach their child respect, courtesy, responsibility, and good manners.

What does the teacher do? It is the teacher's job to prepare your child academically and provide a good foundation for future educational growth. It is the teacher's job to provide challenging and interesting assignments and projects.

It is hard for me to do my job when children show up late, without supplies or homework, and with a poor attitude. I do not get paid enough to be a mother to all these children. Parents, please, do your job so I can do mine. – Teacher

DEAR TEACHER:
Thanks for sitting in my chair today. Parents, pay attention!

By permission of The Eppie Company and Creators Syndicate, Inc.

Questions
1. Do you agree or disagree with the teacher? Explain why.
2. How do the teacher requests relate to a child being "ready to learn?"
3. Develop an argument either for or against the teacher's position. Debate your position with a classmate who takes the opposing view.

Formal and Informal Education

Formal education is regulated by the government and follows a pre-scribed **curriculum** or specific courses of study. It takes place in a particular setting, with qualified teachers or instructors. **Informal education** takes place outside of schools. Children learn a great deal from their parents on a daily basis. Parents model desired behaviour, instruct in various skills, and guide children in what they need to know to get along in their family and in society. They learn much from their siblings, friends, and other peers.

Children also learn informally from many different people in settings outside the family. Youth workers such as swim coaches, dance or skating instructors, playground and program leaders, and guides provide important life lessons while modelling acceptable behaviour. Anyone can benefit from the informal role played by a **mentor**, a person who plays a key role in advising or guiding you. A mentor may be a good listener, someone you admire and want to be like, or someone you look up to. You may have a mentor who helps you become a better athlete, student, or worker. Even parents can have mentors who help them become more confident parents. There are no official guidelines for mentors, but their role as informal teachers is very important.

Figure 17.3
Everyone involved with education has specific responsibilities.

❖ Connections

1. Compare what you learn from formal education with what you learn from informal education. How do formal and informal education prepare you for the future?
2. Identify some of the mentors who have taught or guided you in your life. Which of their qualities would you like to have? Why?

The Lifelong Influence of Schooling

Across Canada, students are required to attend school until the age of 16. Most occupations require at least a high school diploma, but learning continues in many different ways throughout life. Some people choose to go into post-secondary education after high school, while others may choose to go directly into the workplace. Both offer opportunities for lifelong learning. Many adults continue to take courses as their jobs or careers change. New hobbies or changing interests may also lead them to learn new skills. As the saying goes, "You are never too old to learn!"

Career Capsule

ELEMENTARY SCHOOL TEACHER

Tasks and Responsibilities

The elementary school teacher teaches children from kindergarten to Grade 8. Most elementary teachers teach a wide variety of subjects to their class, but some are specialists in areas such as mathematics, music, or physical and health education, and teach children from multiple classes.

Teachers are responsible for covering the curriculum specified by the province or territory in which they work. Their job is to plan interesting and innovative ways to teach this material and to assess student learning. Teachers write detailed reports and meet with the parents to tell them how well their child is doing. When a child has trouble learning, the teacher plans remediation and works with specialists brought in to help the child. Teachers are also expected to model and teach their students good social values, attitudes, and life skills along with the academic curriculum.

Work Environment

Elementary class sizes in Canada can range from 20 to 30 students. Teachers usually work alone and spend much of their day teaching and talking with students. They also supervise the schoolyard during recess and lunch periods. Maintaining discipline, conflict management, and problem solving are necessary skills in this environment.

Teachers work during the school day, and many take work home as they prepare lessons and grade student work outside school hours. To do an effective job as an elementary school teacher requires a minimum of 50 hours per week. Teaching is time-consuming and can be stressful.

Education and Aptitudes

Prospective teachers must love children and be interested in learning themselves. Good communication skills are essential. A calm, patient, and empathetic person tends to make a good teacher. Skills in dealing with other teachers, support personnel, and parents are additional essential attributes of a successful teacher.

In Canada, an undergraduate degree and a concurrent or subsequent teaching degree are required and generally take five years to complete. Many teachers go on to earn post-graduate degrees in education or to take additional qualification courses to upgrade throughout their careers.

Schools and Social Issues

Schools must keep up as society changes. Some of the social issues that make their way into the classroom are children whose first language is not the language of instruction, children in joint-custody arrangements, or children who do not have enough to eat.

Hunger has become a social issue that schools face on a regular basis. Children who come to school without breakfast have more difficulty concentrating and fall behind in their learning. Schools and communities have joined forces to provide breakfast programs for hungry children. **Breakfast programs** provide more than just added nutrition and a good start to the school day. They also provide social interaction and life skills. Helping prepare, serve, clean up, and share are an integral part of school breakfast programs.

Violence has also escalated in our society, and reports of school shootings, though less frequent in Canada, have led to growing concern for safety in schools. **Violence in schools** has many underlying causes. Sometimes schools and society as a whole feel at a loss for solutions. "Safe school" policies may include the use of peer tutors or peer mediators, motivational speakers, and self-esteem exercises. Another approach is to bring programs such as Crime Stoppers into the school, so that suspicious behaviours can be reported without identification of the person reporting.

Figure 17.4
Many students benefit from school breakfast programs.

What the experts say

STU AUTY

Stu Auty, President, The Canadian Safe School Network from an article published by Orbit *magazine.*

Are schools safe places for parents to send their children?

Ontario schools are still safe places for the vast majority of our children, but we need to recognize that a generation of kids has been attending school under far different circumstances than those experienced by their parents or teachers. Whether it is fear of being bullied in the schoolyard or of being confronted with a weapon during a conflict, times have changed. Kids, too, realize that it can be risky to tell their parents, teachers, or even police of their concerns for fear of physical reprisal. School administrators speak of a new category of students who are truant because of a fear of attending school. Weapons, gangs, female violence, bullying, and harassment are all common issues for schools, but with a harder edge. Some school boards have even created budget lines for uniformed security services, and virtually all accept and value municipal police as allies in creating safe schools.

Solutions are as yet illusive, and trends are moving in a direction that can be unsettling. We know that it is important to provide a climate where kids avoid "street" solutions and feel comfortable in coming forward with their problems. We also know that strategies that work are not necessarily readily available. Adults don't always know how to enter a child's or a teenager's world and fix it, and raising false expectations can sometimes cause more damage than good. So we need to stay engaged as we work toward solutions that make as much sense to kids in schools as they do to us as parents and educators.

The Canadian Safe School Network, born out of the efforts of the earlier Task Force, is attempting to keep focused on the problems—and solutions—of safe schools through conferences, research, and a variety of public advocacy efforts.

Another social issue at all levels, including colleges and universities, is **defiance of authority**. There was a time when teachers and administrators held positions of respect and had some power to control defiance from students. A number of social factors have led to the undermining of authority in society as a whole.

A growing "anything goes" attitude in movies and television programming favours characters who get laughs for rudeness, who are admired for having outspoken attitudes, and who rarely take responsibility for their own behaviour. Being polite and respectful still needs to be taught and valued for people of all ages in our society. Being polite and respectful comes from training that society expects parents to give their children at home. It is part of sending a child to school "ready to learn."

■ Schools today must be able to respond to our rapidly changing society.

Is there a solution to the growing number of social problems that present themselves in schools at all levels? Valuable programs such as English as a Second Language (ESL), special education, and peer tutoring provide individual students with the tools to succeed, while parent associations are finding creative ways to support students, schools, and programs. **Online learning** brings the classroom into the home via the Internet, so that many more Canadians can continue their education without having to give up a much-needed job. Schools cannot help but respond to a changing society and to the educational needs of people of all ages.

❖ Checkpoints

1. How should schools respond to hunger, violence, and defiance of authority?
2. Write and perform a rap that outlines the characteristics of a "safe school."
3. What are the benefits of online learning?

Media Pressures Facing Parents and Children

Media has a huge influence on shaping identity and defining what is acceptable in society. By the age of eighteen, many children will have spent more hours watching television than they will have spent in school, yet people often deny the influence of the media. You might hear someone say, "Oh, I really don't pay any attention to advertising. It certainly does not affect me." Yet if you look at their clothing, personal grooming products, the food they buy, and the beverages they drink, you may see evidence to the contrary. Advertising uses media because of its powerful influence on everyone. Media and advertising are selling more than products; they are selling lifestyles.

Targeting Children

Parents need to pay particular attention to the ways in which their children become targets of marketing, advertising, and the media. Children quickly learn the names of all the licensed products that flood the market after the release of the latest movie, cartoon, or children's program. Parents contribute to this trend. Before they can walk or talk, babies are sporting slippers, diapers, and sleepers emblazoned with popular characters and company logos. With every seasonal event from going "back to school" to Christmas toy launches, or from valentine cutouts to Halloween costumes, children are encouraged to want the newest and most popular products. Last year's lunch box or outfit simply will not do.

Studies have shown that children actually determine who they will accept and who they will not accept, beginning as early as nursery school, based on who wears what or who has the latest toy. Parents are pressured by their children and the media to keep up with the most recent trends in clothing labels or collectible toys. Childhood is the perfect time for advertisers to target parents and children because children grow out of their clothing and change their interests very quickly. As soon as they need a bigger size or learn a new skill, the marketers are ready with a new product or a new version of an old product. Is it any wonder that it costs well over $150 000 to raise a child to age 18!

Figure 17.5
Even children in nursery school have been shown to be affected by media advertising.

❖ Connections

1. Analyze different kinds of advertising directed at children. Report on the techniques used by advertisers when promoting products to children.
2. Design a note-page poster warning parents "about advertising."
3. Write a critical reflection that addresses whether parents of young children should boycott "licensed" products.
4. Bring a photo or an actual item to class of a product or logo that was in style when you were younger. What happened to that product line?

Case Study: Children and Television

Janna, 36, and David, 38, have four children, Sue and Savannah, ages 3 and 4, and Derek and Matthew, ages 14 and 15. Janna began to notice that a lot had changed since she had her first two children in her early twenties. They had been a handful, and they did not have a lot of money in those days, but they had had a lot of fun. Weekends in the summer were spent camping, hiking, and bike riding, and in the winter they had spent a lot of time outdoors or going to the boy's hockey games. Perhaps it was being older or perhaps it was because these two were girls, but things definitely seemed different.

Janna decided to keep a journal of all their activities for the week. She noted Dave's extra-long hours—three days out of five at his new job—how many times they ate at fast food restaurants, and the number of hours they all watched television. What became obvious was that on most days, from the time the children came home from preschool until they had to take their bath, the television was on. The girls watched cartoons on Saturday mornings, and in the afternoon they watched their videotapes. Janna even noticed that when they watched television they hardly moved, and she felt guilty about the number of times she found herself bringing them snacks that were eaten without taking their eyes off the screen.

It was time to take action. With her notes in hand, she talked to David about their options. One was to get rid of the television altogether. He pointed out that they had their favourite shows, too, and that not all television is bad. She felt they had developed very bad habits that needed to be corrected in a drastic way. "Let's just try giving up television for two weeks and see how it goes," she suggested.

The first week was difficult. The girls sulked and wailed. Since the boys both had part-time jobs, it was a little easier for them, but they still complained. David was on edge. Janna felt exhausted trying to fill up the time with other things. But by the end of the week, Dave and Janna noticed that the girls were going to sleep better at night. They even got out toys they had not played with in a long time. On Saturday Janna let them help her clean the bathroom, not caring if they got covered in suds or left streaks. They went for a walk in the afternoon and helped

make macaroni for supper. On Sunday it rained so they made cookies, and then Dave helped them put together their puzzles.

The second week went better. The children began to play more games on their own and spent a long time doing some elaborate pretend play. Both Dave and Janna read to their children more in the evenings, and even though Dave did sneak a look at a ball game one night, the television stayed off the rest of the time. They listened to music more, and they talked more to their children and to each other. It had been a success, but now they have to decide what to do next.

Questions

1. How did turning off the television affect the quality of life for this family?
2. Do you agree with the statement "not all television is bad?" Explain.
3. What options do families have for taking control over the programs that children watch on television?

Media Representation

Media comes in many different forms. Magazines full of glossy advertising are placed strategically at checkout counters, proclaiming how to lose weight quickly or offering advice for relationships, families, parents, and homeowners. What kind of a lifestyle are they selling along with their flawless models, their bizarre story lines, and their unrealistic body images?

Television programming is packaged into time segments that often have as many advertising minutes as content. Television, movies, and music videos bring a vision of an unrealistic world into our homes 24 hours of the day. Movies shown in the theatre are uninterrupted by advertising, yet advertisers pay moviemakers large sums of money to have their products used throughout the film. Television and movies distort reality by speeding up the action, by cutting, splicing, and editing, by using special effects, computer imaging, and close-ups, and by simplifying life and relationships. Because we see characters again and again, it is tempting to believe that what they represent is real, when in fact it is far from reality.

Computers bring us instant gratification by making things happen at the click of a mouse. Computer technology is a growing area of concern for parents. Access to pornography, propaganda, gambling, and the

Negative Media Messages

Media is persuasive; it motivates children to behave like adolescents and adolescents to behave like adults. Organizations such as Media Watch Canada and the National Clearinghouse on Family Violence investigate the representation of society in the media and possible effects on children and adolescents. Stereotyping and media violence are two such concerns.

dangerous contacts children and adolescents can make are concerns. No matter what form media takes, it has the power to alter thinking, behaviour, and value systems. A parent's best defence is to be aware, to be critical, and to monitor children's exposure to all forms of media.

❖ Connections

1. Analyze some current magazine advertisements that are aimed at both children and parents. Describe the audience they are targeting (e.g., the age group) and the "lifestyle," as well as the image that they are promoting.

2. Many movies are not made for children, yet they watch them and learn from them. How can parents control what children see?

3. Make a list of 101 things parents can do with their children besides watching television. Print the list in the form of an attractive information poster for parents.

Media Stereotyping

In 1994, MediaWatch published its "Front and Centre" study, which questioned how people were portrayed on Canadian television. The study found as follows:

> In general, dramatic programming was found to include a much higher percentage of people from diverse racial and ethnic backgrounds than did the news. However, women from diverse racial and ethnic backgrounds fall far behind their male counterparts in both types of programming, becoming almost invisible as either reporters or sources in newscasts.
>
> When women from diverse racial and ethnic backgrounds do appear in dramas, they are likely to be cast in minor roles that have been traditionally played by women or are stereotypical in nature. In newscasts, they appear in more domestic than foreign stories. Women from diverse backgrounds are usually interviewed in the context of a racially or culturally specific story and are likely to be identified as mothers or victims of violence. (p. 3)

This particular study observed the number of times specific genders and cultures were represented in Canadian television shows. The topic of media stereotyping is a concern for a number of organizations, including Media Awareness Network, a Canadian non-profit organization that promotes media and Internet education by producing online programs and resources. Among many topics of concern to the organization is the issue

Figure 17.6
Computers can connect children to many aspects of the world at the click of a mouse. Parents must be aware of and limit what children are exposed to in the media.

Stereotypes

To establish character identities quickly, writers for movies, television and advertising often use stereotypes. A **stereotype** is a fixed image of a person or group. Stereotypes generally conform to a pattern of dress and behaviour that is easily recognized and understood. Often, a judgement is made about the person or group being stereotyped. That judgement may be positive or negative. Generally, stereotypes are less real, more perfect, more exaggerated, and more predictable than their real-life counterparts.

Figure 17.7
Computer games often depict unrealistic and violent images that children find captivating.

of stereotyping. The material excerpted below, from the network's Web site, explains why media stereotypes exist and what parents can do to lessen their influence.

Media Awareness Network

Media stereotypes are inevitable, especially in the advertising, entertainment and news industries, which need as wide an audience as possible to quickly understand information. Stereotypes act like codes that give audiences a quick, common understanding of a person or group of people—usually relating to their class, ethnicity or race, gender, sexual orientation, social role, or occupation.

But stereotypes can be problematic. They can

* reduce a wide range of differences in people to simplistic categorizations
* transform assumptions about particular groups of people into "realities"
* be used to justify the position of those in power
* perpetuate social prejudice and inequality

More often than not, the groups being stereotyped have little to say about how they are represented.

Ethnic and Visible Minorities

Anyone who examines North American entertainment and news media will notice that members of ethnic and visible minorities are inadequately represented in entertainment and news media, and that portrayals of minorities are often stereotypical and demeaning.

This tendency is particularly problematic in a multicultural country like Canada, where 15 per cent of the population are immigrants and visible minorities comprise 25 to 51 percent of the larger urban centres. Toronto is the first city in the Western world in which the majority of inhabitants are people of colour. "Without much fuss," says historian Gwynne Dyer, "we've become the most spectacularly diverse country in the world." Why, then, have the media not kept pace?

Women and Girls

Ideas of what women should look like and how they should act change over time. The (size-12 sex goddess) *ideal* woman of the 1950s who spent her on-screen time breathlessly trying to marry a millionaire may have yielded to the trials and tribulations of the neurotic, ultra-thin professional woman. But not much has really changed.

Many media activists argue that producers should be called to account, and that images of women should be forced to be more realistic.

Christina Kelly, editor of *YM*, made headlines when she announced that the magazine would no longer run stories on dieting and would include pictures of bigger models. Media activist Jean Kilbourne applauded the move, saying, "Any magazine that purports to be for girls and young women, dieting has no place in it. This is a step in the right direction... It would be wonderful if some other magazine editors would be equally as courageous."

Media Awareness Network encourages parents to take the following actions to stem the influence of media stereotyping:

* Explain how everything they see on TV (even news and documentary programming) is a reality that has been created by producers, directors, cine-matographers, actors, editors, advertisers, and others—and they bring to it their own points of view, biases, and commercial interests.
* Ask (your kids) what points of view are most often seen on TV (i.e., middle class, male, western society, etc.)? Whose views are not being heard and what cultures and lifestyles are not being shown? Why? Explain how, through these omissions, television can teach that some people and ideas are more important than others.

Talk about whether TV characters look and act like real people.

* Do people on TV look like people in real life? What are the differences?
* How do they feel about the lives they see portrayed on television? Do they envy some aspects of the lives of people on TV? Are they content with their own lives?
* Do they want to look like the people they see on TV? Is this realistic?
* Do kids on TV act like kids do in real life? Should they?
* With young children, talk about "make-believe" and the difference between real life and TV.

Media Violence

Parents are also concerned about the effect of media violence on children, because there is so much violence in the media today. Music videos, movies, video games, and everyday television programs contain many violent images including abusive language, sexual assault, beatings, shootings, and stabbings. In an article prepared for the National Clearing House on Family Violence, "The Effects of Media Violence on Children," Dr. Jane Ledingham (2002), Director of the Child Study Centre at the University of Ottawa, cites a number of studies that link television violence to aggression in children.

According to research cited in Ledingham (2002), in an important study carried out in Canada, children were found to have become significantly more aggressive two years after television was introduced to their town for the first time (Kimball and Zabrack, 1986). Children who prefer violent television shows when they are young have been found to be more aggressive later on, and this may be associated with trouble with the law in adulthood (Huesmann, 1986). Strong identification with a violent TV character and the belief that the TV situation is realistic are both associated with greater aggressiveness (Huesmann and Eron, 1986). In general, boys are more affected by violent shows than are girls (Lefkowitz, Eron, Walder, and Huesmann, 1977).

Ledingham also points out that parents should be concerned about the cumulative effect of violence on children. Parents should be available to talk with their children about what they are seeing and allow them to express how they are feeling.

Media and Lifestyle

Media also defines lifestyle in the images it presents and the way of life it promotes. Sex in movies and on television is portrayed as normal and inevitable, while sexually transmitted infections (STIs) and responsible birth control are rarely considered.

Alcohol is both advertised and illustrated as commonplace. Sports magazines carry more alcohol and tobacco ads than any other type of magazine. Beer and wine ads portray alcohol as an essential part of having a good time. Movies and television programs are rarely without alcohol, making its consumption appear ordinary and normal. Tobacco, on the other hand, cannot be advertised on television, yet tobacco companies spend millions for magazines, print, and display

■ A number of studies link television violence to aggression in children.

media. More smokers are finding their way into movies and television programs. Children are targeted using cartoon images and by co-opting the language of the adolescent culture. Tobacco companies encourage youth to smoke by equating smoking with adulthood.

Media creates a consumption culture with needs and wants beyond what is necessary for survival. The "desire to have" is created to get people to spend, including growing numbers of children at progressively younger ages. Things rather than relationships often define the quality of life. Lifestyle is also affected by how we interact with various media. Spending more than twenty hours a week in front of a television, video game, or computer screen is contributing to growing numbers of obese children, adolescents, and adults, as are the high-calorie fast foods and snacks that have become part of our culture.

Media Censorship

■ Media defines lifestyles and often presents unrealistic images for children to absorb.

Over the years, parents have tried to have books banned from schools and libraries because of their content and have sometimes been successful at the local level. Various groups and organizations have called for the **censorship** or banning and curtailing of different kinds of media without much success. Freedom of speech is a right in the democratic world, and media censorship infringes on this right. In Canada, the *Canadian Charter of Rights and Freedoms* came into law on April 17, 1982. Section 2 (b) of the Charter guarantees "freedom of thought, belief, opinion, and expression, including freedom of the press and other media of communication." However, hate propaganda or hate literature and sexual obscenity are not included in our freedoms of expression. Children are also protected by the Child Pornography Act, which was unanimously passed in the House of Commons in 1993, following several years of debate.

The CRTC (Canadian Radio-Television Telecommunications Commission) contributes to the censorship of the media by providing guidelines for radio and television programming, and by revoking a licence to broadcast if a radio or television station does not follow the regulations noted in the CRTC section.

Canada has laws governing obscenity, but artistic expression is open to interpretation and debate. Canada has banned tobacco advertising from television. There is no similar ban on violence in the media, so the responsibility for censorship lies with each parent.

The Canadian Radio-Television Telecommunications Commission (CRTC)

The Canadian Radio-Television Telecommunications Commission was established in 1968. It is an independent public authority that reports to Parliament through the Minister of Canadian Heritage.

The CRTC has as its main objective access for all Canadians to reliable telephone and other telecommunications services. As part of this objective, the CRTC ensures that Canadian television programming reflects accurately and fairly Canadian society and diversity. The organization monitors 3300 broadcasters (e.g., television, cable, radio, pay and speciality television stations) and almost 80 telecommunications carriers (all major Canadian telephone companies).

The following points are taken from acts of the CRTC that govern general broadcasting regulations, pay television regulations, and specialty services regulations:

A licensee shall not distribute or broadcast programming

a) that contains anything in contravention of the law;

b) that contains any abusive comment or abusive pictorial representation that, when taken in context, tends to or is likely to expose an individual or a group or class of individuals to hatred or contempt on the basis of race, national or ethnic origin, colour, religion, sex, sexual orientation, age, or mental or physical disability;

c) contains any obscene or profane language or obscene or profane pictorial representation.

Parental Involvement in Schools and Media

Because schools and media are so influential in the socialization of children, it becomes increasingly important for parents to stay involved in all aspects of their children's lives. Children can benefit from the ongoing involvement of parents in their schools and in their daily interaction with media.

The Parent-School Connection

Not every parent will be able to find time for parent-teacher associations or parent councils. Not every parent will be able to volunteer at their child's school or chaperone school trips, but all can make sure their children attend school regularly, and help them organize all the details of getting out the door or to the bus on time. Every parent can monitor their children's growth and development by taking time before or after school to find out about their accomplishments. Showing interest in a child's performance or speaking positively about school and about the child's teacher helps build confidence. Listening to the child's problems with a teacher, classmates, and peers is important. Children need to talk about what they consider their "issues."

There are many ways to connect with the school. Letters, notes, telephone calls, and even e-mail to the teacher can keep the lines of communication open. Parent-teacher interviews demonstrate to both the child and the teacher that what happens at school is of major

Figure 17.8
Parents can help children see how media can be a positive influence in their lives.

importance. School defines a large part of a child's life. You can recognize this by making a place at home for completing homework and reviewing the school day.

Making the Most of Media

Media has many positive uses that parents can maximize. Print materials can be used to encourage children to read and to make connections between objects and ideas. Electronic media such as computer and telephone technology can inspire creativity, promote research skills, and open up a world of interesting topics and activities. Audiovisual technology brings the world into the home and opens the door to new learning. All of these forms of media are also used to promote many positive elements. Through the media, children are encouraged to make healthy choices, understand the consequences of poor decisions, and experience some of the best that human beings have to offer. To provide balance, safety, and security, however, parents must be involved in a child's use of media resources.

Parents can pay attention to the lyrics of the music their children listen to and supervise the movies and television that they watch. Talking to children about what they see and hear and what messages are getting through to them can help children think more critically about what they are exposed to. Limiting television by deciding what to watch as a family provides some measure of control. Raising questions about why violence was used, how individuals are depicted, or what the advertising is really saying will go a long way toward giving children the critical thinking skills they need to examine media images. Perhaps the biggest challenge for parents is to provide activities that are just as compelling and enjoyable as the media.

Children under the age of seven or eight do not distinguish between the program and the advertisement. Many children believe everything that they see. Parents need to use the language of media to educate children. Parents can help children better understand by pointing out what an advertisement is and what it is trying to sell. They can also ask children to look for the special effects, the edits, and the close-ups. Showing children just how big the toy really is, when it looks huge on the television screen, can help children to distinguish between the television screen and reality.

Parents can also point out the positive uses of media. Watching news programs together and finding news locations on a map of the world can help children better understand the world. Looking for educational programming that explains how things work can be fun and beneficial to learning. Showing respect and amazement for the power of the film to evoke feelings, teach, and create and re-create can teach children to be aware of their own feelings when watching a program. Pointing out instances where media agrees with your beliefs and family values, as well as where it differs, can help children to think about and better understand the family's values. Media is a tool that, like other tools, can be used or misused.

❖ Checkpoints

1. What is censorship? What is its role?
2. How does media censorship protect children?
3. How can parents take action to maximize the important influence of school in their children's lives?
4. How has media had a positive influence on your knowledge of the world?

The Effects of Media Violence on Children: What Parents Can Do

The following material is adapted from Dr. J. Ledingham's article "The Effects of Media Violence on Children," published by the National Clearinghouse on Family Violence Health Canada.

- Don't panic. Remember that watching one television show or playing one computer game with some violent content is not going to irreversibly damage your child. What matters most for young children is the cumulative effect of what they watch and the general viewing habits that they develop.
- Make rules and stick to them, but allow for some flexibility.
- If possible, start early in influencing your children's exposure to television and electronic media.
- If you want to reduce the amount of violent content they are exposed to, make rules about what your children see, not how much they see.
- Make sure that you can live with the rules you set and that you are ready to enforce them. The important thing about any media use agreement is how consistently you implement it. Keep it as simple as possible.
- Make video technology your ally. You cannot watch every program with your children or preview all the shows they might want to watch. However, young children are often happy to watch their favourite videotapes over and over again; you can

let them watch a tape you have already seen instead of worrying about what is on television at that specific time.
- Make lists of games and programs you consider acceptable.
- Consider investing in an electronic device or computer program that can limit television watching, or Web site selection.
- Give your children attractive alternatives to TV and video games. Enrolling them in regularly scheduled community programs or making a routine of outdoor excursions or indoor crafts will reduce the number of arguments about television and teach children how to enjoy a broader range of activities.
- Adapt your approach to the age of your child. Involve older children in determining the rules.
- Talk to your children about violent images and get them to tell you how they see them. One of the most powerful ways of keeping children from being affected by media violence is to get them to tell you how children can be fooled or hurt by what they see or hear.
- Be prepared for the possibility that, for your children's sake, you may have to change your own media use habits. Decide how you feel about violent content. Be aware of what you watch when your children are around and decide whether you can and should reconsider your choices.

Chapter Summary

Chapter Highlights

- Parents continue to play a significant role in the lives of children and adolescents who spend more hours at school and in contact with the media.

- Schools are a fairly recent phenomenon in society and add to the socialization process, which began at home, by enforcing rules and expecting children to behave in socially acceptable ways.

- The provinces and territories regulate public education with different groups, including students and their parents, taking on different responsibilities.

- Schooling and its role in socialization continues throughout the life cycle as growing numbers of people return to school for various reasons throughout their lives.

- Schools need to address an increasing number of social issues such as hunger, violence, and defiance of authority as the face of society continues to change.

- Media and advertising have a powerful influence on socialization, particularly by targeting children through the promotion of toys and clothing featuring the latest popular characters.

- Media takes many forms and promotes particular stereotypes and lifestyles, which have a negative influence on children and adolescents.

- *The Canadian Charter of Rights and Freedoms* allows the media a great deal of freedom of expression.

- Parents concerned with the role of schools and media in their children's lives need to ensure that they stay involved to protect their children.

Review and Extend Your Learning

1. Before the beginning of formal schooling, what was the purpose of education? How has the purpose of education changed over time? **K/U**

2. Of all the people involved in the education process, who has the greatest responsibility for student learning? Support your answer with examples. **K/U** **T/I** **A**

3. The list of responsibilities of teachers seems relatively short. Interview a teacher to get a more detailed list of their responsibilities. **T/I** **C**

4. Consider the negative impacts of the media. For each, provide a concrete example as well as a strategy to combat that particular negative impact. **K/U** **T/I** **A**

5. What are the positive aspects of the media? Design a checklist that parents can use to help them capture the positive aspects of media for children. **K/U** **A**

6. Prepare an information pamphlet for parents outlining strategies for helping their children achieve in school. **K/U** **C** **A**

7. Conduct research to determine what parents think about television. Find out if they monitor or limit television viewing in any way. Share your findings with the class. **T/I** **C**

Issue Analysis

Analyze a variety of media such as television sitcoms, magazine advertisements, movies, music videos, and Internet sites, and determine how individuals and families are represented. Questions you might ask about what you are seeing, reading, or hearing are as follows:

1. How are people being depicted? Are males and females depicted the same or differently?

2. Could a man be substituted for a woman in the ad or program, or a woman for a man, with no change in meaning?

3. How are families represented? What roles do men play? What roles do women play?

4. What are the values or beliefs that are presented?

5. Are consequences discussed for behaviours such as unprotected sex, smoking cigarettes, or drinking alcohol? Is drinking during a pregnancy shown?

6. Is there evidence of violence, and if so, what kind, and how much?

7. What do you find most realistic and most unrealistic about the presentation?

8. Who is the intended audience, and would it be suitable for children?

9. Is the violence in society a reflection of violence in the media, or is violence in the media merely a reflection of violence in society? What is your answer to this question?

Planning for the Future: Investing in Children

By the end of this chapter, you will be able to:

- identify society's expectations of parents, caregivers, and people who work with children
- evaluate society's support for parents, caregivers, and people who work with children
- identify the issues that concern all who interact with children in society
- describe the role society plays in the lives of children and families
- explain the diverse global influences on children and families, and evaluate their impact on human growth and development
- explain why social challenges need to be viewed and understood in an integrated framework
- describe how social service agencies support children and families when problems arise

Important Terms

child-care centre
crisis counsellor
disciplinarian
electronic technology
emerging initiative

family care
family counselling
flex hours
globalization
grief counsellor

licensed family care
life-saving technologies
nanny care
parental leave

post-traumatic
 stress disorder
provider
relationship counsellor
social services

Chapter at a Glance

How Do Parents and Society Share Responsibility for Children?

In the past, families were entirely responsible for the care, education, and religious training of their children. Families were isolated in agricultural and rural Canada, and society as a whole had little to do with what went on in the family. Children who had special needs were cared for by the family with no outside help. When women were needed in the fields, older children, or extended family, cared for younger children. It is clear that in most parts of Canada, all of that has changed.

To begin with, families have changed a great deal in recent decades. The majority of women in Canada work at occupations outside the home for their personal and family income, as well as for personal satisfaction. More families than ever before are struggling with poverty, not always because of unemployment, but often because of low wages and job insecurity. Many families do not have close relatives to call on for child care, since their own parents and siblings have jobs, and their neighbours have their own busy lives.

Society is responding to the changing needs of families. It is more responsive to the growing number of women in the labour force, the increase in the number of fathers caring for children, and the critical importance of child development in the early years of life. Society is sharing more of the responsibility for children, as evidenced by **emerging initiatives** from government, business and industry, and communities. These initiatives are new policies and procedures that support parenthood and families and that address the needs of children and their working parents, but there is still much to achieve.

The federal government has changed the provisions for maternity and parental leave. Recent legislation allows the mother or the father to take parental leave for a full year following the birth of a child or adoption. Parents may divide the **parental leave** so that one parent is with the child while the other works. However, only parents who have worked long enough at one job and have paid the required number of employment insurance premiums are eligible. Part-time workers and those with a history of job changes are not eligible.

Provincial governments legislate the provision and licensing of child care to provide the best possible options for parents, yet most children are in unlicensed, private in-home care without regulations.

The business world is also responding to the needs of parents and young families. Some family-friendly workplaces provide valuable

Figure 18.1
Parents can now take up to 12 months of leave.

Figure 18.2
The long-term benefits of quality child care outweigh the costs.

options for working parents. On-site child care and job sharing programs allow parents to spend more time with their children and still maintain their place in the work force. A few businesses also have policies that provide parents with "personal days" to provide care for children who are sick, and with **flex hours** that allow parents to determine which part of the day fits their child's schedule best. However, many of these initiatives are often available only in the corporate world, and are often the first "frills" to be cut when companies downsize. The majority of working parents do not have these advantages.

Local communities recognize that they, too, have much to offer parents and children. Recreation departments, churches, cultural organizations, and other community initiatives offer child-care programs and special activity programs for children to attend before and after school, on professional development days, during school breaks, and during summer holidays. In spite of these initiatives, however, many parents still struggle to find child care that meets their needs.

We still have a long way to go in Canada to meet the needs of every family and every child. There is still a lack of accessible, affordable, quality child care. Child development services are not always easily accessible, as they are scattered under many different local, provincial, and federal jurisdictions. The reluctance to develop universal policies and programs may be tied to the long-standing belief that children are the private responsibility of parents. However, society benefits in the long run by investing in children and contributing to their care and development.

Both Canadian and American studies report a payback for investing in quality child-care programs for children under age five. A study by Gordon Cleveland and Michael Krashinsky (1998) at the University of Toronto reported a payback of two dollars for every one dollar invested in quality child-care programs. Similarly, a study by A. Starr cited in *Business Week* (Starr, 2002) indicates a payback of four dollars for every dollar spent on quality preschool programs for poor children in the United States.

Not all child-care programs provide economic payoffs. Publicly funded, universal, regulated child care as described in the excerpt by Dr. Susan Prentice (2000) is essential in all provinces and territories. Quality preschool programs also provide children with developmental advantages as noted in a study by Rebecca Marcon (2000), reported in *Early childhood research and practice*. She followed the

Case Study: The Case for Public Child Care in Manitoba

The following material is excerpted from an article by Dr. Susan Prentice, "The Case for Public Child Care in Manitoba" (2000):

Manitoba entered the 1990s as a national leader in child care. That distinction is now gone. The child-care system has suffered through more than a decade of attrition and been forced to absorb major cuts in both federal and provincial funding. As a result, there is now only one child-care space for every ten Manitoba children under twelve. Those spaces that are available are too expensive for too many parents, and the quality of service has been compromised.

While the story in Manitoba has been one of steady decline, governments elsewhere have recognized child care for the important investment that it is and now treat it as a public responsibility. Quebec has had a popular and successful five-dollar-a-day program in place for several years, and the BC government recently announced that it will soon begin the process of implementing a publicly funded child-care system.

In the 15 member states of the European Union, between 75 and 99 percent of all preschool children aged three to six years are in educational child-care programs, whether or not their parents are employed.

These public models are based on the belief that child care is a public good—something on which experts in economics, health, education, social services, and social perspectives agree. Research shows that high-quality child care enhances all children's healthy development, is a support to all families regardless of their labour force status, and is a precondition for women's equality. Child care promotes school readiness, helps build healthy communities, helps reduce poverty, creates jobs, facilitates economic self-reliance, contributes to the lifelong good health of children, and aids in the building of safer communities. Researchers also point out that inclusive early childhood services strengthen appreciation for diversity and promote equity among classes, levels of ability, racial and ethnic groups, and generations, and, therefore, strengthen social solidarity.

That Canadians recognize these qualities from their own lived experience is confirmed regularly in opinion polls. To take just one recent example, a 1998 Environics poll found that 76 percent of Canadians believe a child-care system should be available for all families, with the costs shared by governments and families.

There are sound economic reasons to support public investment in child care. Recent studies demonstrate that $2 of social benefits flow from every $1 invested in child care. The Vancouver Board of Trade has concluded that "the economic payback" from investing in early childhood care "is spectacular."

Questions

1. What support does Dr. Susan Prentice give for investing in publicly funded universal child care for children in Manitoba?
2. Investigate whether child care has been given more attention and more dollars across Canada since this report was published.
3. Research child-care providers in your area. How much does licensed child care cost in your community? What accounts for the cost?

progress of 183 children from the time they entered preschool at age four to the end of third grade. She found that "children's later school success appears to have been enhanced by more active, child-initiated early learning experiences." In contrast, she found that their progress "may have been slowed by overly academic preschool experiences that introduced formalized learning experiences too early for most children's developmental status" (p.1). Investment in quality early childhood care for all children is essential.

Figure 18.3
Parents have a legal responsibility to meet the many needs of their children.

Social and Legal Responsibilities for Living and Working with Children

With the increased involvement of society in the lives of families and children, there is a corresponding sense that society should define what is expected of parents, caregivers, and those who work with children. Anyone who plays a role in the lives of children must be aware of their legal responsibilities and the legal rights of children, and they should have an understanding of what can be expected of children at various stages of their development. Living up to the expectations of the public when caring for children is part of the responsibility.

Expectations for Parents

What do we expect of parents in our society? Parents have a legal responsibility for the physical, economic, educational, emotional, and safety needs of their children, but they also have a social responsibility for their children. They are expected to be loving and nurturing, mature and responsible, and to provide positive role models for their children. Above all, they are expected to be wise **disciplinarians**. Parents whose children behave badly or inappropriately or come into conflict with the law become the easiest targets for criticism in our society. Parents are expected to produce perfect children who are able to contribute to society. However, effective parenting skills are learned; they are not inborn.

❖ Connections

Many adults in our society think that parenting should be taught in schools and that students should have some parenting education to graduate from high school. Since you are taking a parenting, family studies, or human development course, reflect on the following:

1. Before I took a parenting course, I did not know that...
2. Since I started taking the parenting course, I am now aware that...
3. After I have finished this course, I expect to be able to...
4. I think students should (or should not) have to take a parenting course because...

Expectations for Caregivers

Child-care workers, baby-sitters, day-care personnel, and other care-givers are among the lowest paid workers in our society, yet they are expected to provide the best care possible next to parents themselves. Caregivers have to walk a fine line between being affectionate and not replacing parents affection; using discipline without being too strict, or too lenient; and providing a positive learning environment while being mindful of care and safety. They are expected to have some training, either as parents of their own children or through early childhood education courses. Having first-aid training and safety training are very important, though not mandatory, while caring for the children of others. Most provinces and territories have legislation that governs how caregivers are to conduct the business of child care. More importantly, however, caregivers are expected to meet the high standards that parents have for someone who acts as their substitute in providing care and education for their children.

Expectations for Others Who Work with Children

There are many people who work with children in their occupations, some in a professional capacity and others in an informal capacity. Doctors, dentists, child psychologists, speech therapists, teachers, hairdressers, fast-food service workers, photographers, and optometrists are just a few of the many people who come into contact with children every day. Some of them have specific training in child development, while others may just have a commonsense under-standing of children. Parents and society as a whole have very specific expectations for professionals such as doctors or child psychologists because of their specialized training. They also expect others who work with children to be professional, attentive to the needs of chil-dren, and able to interact with children in an appropriate, considerate, careful, and caring fashion.

The safety of children from violence, abuse, and neglect is the business of anyone who comes in contact with children through their employment. Many professionals such as teachers, child-care workers, clergy, and doctors, because of their special role with children, are legally responsible for reporting any suspicion of child abuse, and are subject to fines if they do not report. All people working with children need a thorough knowledge of child development, and a solid founda-tion in parenting skills and techniques.

What Parents Expect from Caregivers—ACCESS

Attentiveness to health and safety, and the physical and emotional needs of children

Communication regarding the child's day, development, and individual concerns

Competence in exercising authority and appropriate discipline

Enthusiasm for working with children and contributing to their development

Structure in planning activities and establishing daily routines

Supervision of all activities, social interaction, and play

Figure 18.4
All people who work with children need a thorough knowledge of child development.

Children are a national resource. They become the future of our society. Parents, caregivers, and those who work with children in any way have an enormous social responsibility for the health, well-being, and optimum development of all children.

❖ Checkpoints

1. What recent changes have been made to the parental leave policy?
2. What evidence supports this statement: "We still have a long way to go to meet the needs of all parents and children in Canada."
3. List and explain the obligations that parents have for their children.
4. Describe the expectations that parents have of caregivers.

The Social Obligation of Child Care

Child care has only recently been viewed as a social obligation. Historically, child care has been available to parents in Canada in some form since the late 1800s, with the establishment of kinder-gartens and nursery schools. Some employers in larger centres in the early 1900s were farsighted enough to provide child supervision for the women they hoped to attract into their employ. However, regu-lated child care did not exist until the 1940s, when the Ontario Day Nurseries Act was passed in response to the needs of mothers working in factories and ammunition plants while their husbands were at war. The legislation was the first of its kind in Canada and addressed both child care and child development. The purpose of child-care centres governed by this act was to supervise children while contributing to their development.

Because child care is somehow seen as a working mother's responsibility, it has not been given the attention or the funding it deserves. Given the number of children in child care in Canada and the amount parents collectively spend, the abstract for the article "A Profile of the Childcare Services Industry" (Stafford, 2002), prepared for Service Industries Canada, indicates that child care is a concern for all Canadians.

A Profile of the Child-Care Services Industry

Abstract:
The child-care services industry in Canada is unique in that it is entrusted with a precious resource: close to 1.4 million children. Child-care providers assist with the daunting tasks of promoting child development, ensuring children's safety and well-being, and maintaining responsive relationships with individual children.

This paper examines the child-care services industry in Canada and is divided into three basic parts. First, the article studies the demand for child-care services, including the $3.5 billion spent by households for these services. The financial characteristics of the industry and the roles played by the non-profit sector and government fee-subsidy and grant programs are examined next. And the final section looks at some of the characteristics of the child-care workforce.

Souce: Statistics Canada, Stafford, J. *A profile of the childcare services industry*, Catalogue No. 63F0002XPB2002040, http://www.statcan.ca/english/IPS/Data/63F0002XPB2002040.htm

Child-Care Options

Parents need accessible, affordable, quality child care. What are their options? According to Child and Family Canada, parents have three options for non-parental care of children aged 0–12 :

- in a child's home, usually referred to as **nanny care**
- in a caregiver's home, usually referred to as **family care**, which may be licensed or unlicensed
- in **child-care centres**, on a half-day, full-day, evening, or overnight basis in the following categories: infant care (usually under 12–18 months); toddler care (usually 12–18 months to 2.5–3 years); preschool care (usually 3–5 years); and school-age care (usually 5–12 years)

Family care may or may not be licensed by the province, while a child-care centre operates under provincial regulation.

> ■ **Three options for non-parental child care:**
> 1. Nanny care
> 2. Family care
> 3. Child-care centres

Home-Based Child Care

Family care is an arrangement in which a person cares for five or fewer children in a private home. Caring for more than five children in addition to the caregiver's own children requires a licence. Because family care is usually not regulated or supervised, parents share the responsibility of ensuring their children receive quality care with the caregivers they employ.

Advantages of Family Care

Family care is informal and provides care for a small group of children that encourages a parent-caregiver partnership. Family care is provided in a family-like setting for infants, toddlers, and preschoolers, as well as school-age children. Children from the same family can be cared for together, often in their own neighbourhood, close to school and friends. Hours of care can be flexible to suit the needs of individual families.

❖ Connections

Parents and caregivers should set up an interview before agreeing on a family caregiver.

1. What questions might parents want to ask caregivers before deciding to place a child in their care?

2. What questions might caregivers ask the parents before accepting a child into their care?

Unlicensed Family Care

Anyone can offer unlicensed care for a child in their own home. The affordability, convenience, and availability may lead many parents to choose unlicensed care. Many caregivers provide wonderful care that meets all requirements of a licensed situation, but that is not always the case. Parents cannot be assured of the health, safety, or quality of unlicensed care. Five children is the legal maximum for unlicensed care, but some have been known to exceed that limit some or all of the time. There is also no guarantee that a caregiver will continue to provide care year after year. Some caregivers choose to offer care only for a few months of the year or only while their own children are not yet in school. Others make it their life's work. Parents need to consider all the consequences of choosing unlicensed care for their children.

Licensed Family Child Care

Licensed family care involves licensed agencies that recruit individual caregivers who care for up to five children, not counting their own, in their own homes. These caregivers, usually called **providers**, are supervised by home visitors employed by the agency. The agency itself is inspected by the department or ministry responsible for child care. The agency that supervises the home caregivers also provides support and resources.

Providers receive

• information regarding child development, first aid, safety, health, and nutrition

• suggestions for activities that are suitable for the ages of the children

Figure 18.5

Some family care situations are supervised by provincially licensed home child-care agencies. The agency arranges for the training of people who want to care for children in their own home. The agency provides support and advice, and it monitors the care to ensure that it fulfills provincial requirements. This helps licensed caregivers provide quality child care, which includes the following:

• a caregiver with knowledge and understanding of children's needs

• parent involvement in the overall child-care experience

• appropriate settings and routines

• a stable arrangement

- recruitment of parents who need child care
- help with fee collection and record-keeping, and policies for holidays and vacations
- access to a toy and equipment lending library

If available, some parents will choose licensed family care over public programs because it is supervised and supported by an agency, yet still offers the comforts of a home.

❖ Connections

Are you thinking of becoming a home caregiver in the future? Find out about the guidelines in your province. For example, Ontario has published a complete reference book called *A Child Care Guide for Home Caregivers* that is available online from the government Web site. It offers practical information to assist caregivers in setting up safe, healthy in-home care that provides a stimulating environment.

1. What are the advantages and disadvantages of being a home caregiver?
2. Using *A child care guide for home caregivers* or a similar reference specific to your area, devise a business plan for operating a family child-care business.
3. Where in your community could you find low-cost, safe equipment and supplies for your family child-care business?

Child-Care Centres

Child-care centres are governed by provincial legislation. Centres could be set up in schools, factories, businesses, communities, homes, or any other approved facility. Subsidies may be available for low-income families, but quotas may apply.

Advantages of Licensed Child-Care Centres

Although the actual centre may have large numbers of children of different ages attending, they also have a high number of qualified staff available. Because they are regulated, parents can expect that their child will receive an acceptable standard of care. Families are also assured of regular government inspections of the child-care operation.

Regulations require nutritious meals and snacks; specified health and hygiene procedures; programming to ensure optimal development through fine- and gross-motor activities, rest, and outdoor play;

Who Regulates Child Care in Your Province or Territory?

For guidelines for family child care and child-care centres in your province, territory, or reserve, contact the following:

Prince Edward Island: Health and Community Services

New Brunswick: Department of Family and Community Services

Nova Scotia: Family and Children's Services

Newfoundland: Department of Health and Social Services

Quebec: Ministry of Health and Social Services

Ontario: Ministry of Community and Social Services

Manitoba: Department of Family Services

Saskatchewan: Department of Social Services

Alberta: Department of Health and Social Services

British Columbia: Ministry for Children and Families

Yukon: Health and Social Services

Northwest Territories: Department of Health and Social Services

Nunavut: Department of Health and Social Services

First Nations Living On Reserves: First Nations Child and Family Services (administered by First Nations, in cooperation with provincial or territorial authorities)

Figure 18.6
Regulations governing licensed child-care centres assure parents that government standards will be met.

We have a long and wide body of research which concludes that children benefit from being in good quality preschool programs with trained staff. This is true whether or not their mothers are in the workforce and it's true regardless of the socio-economic status of the parent.
— Kerry McCuaig

language, social, and cognitive development; nurturing; safety, including fire and health inspections, and criminal reference checks for all staff. The environment must also meet the standards for proper lighting, fencing, playground structures, and security. Regulations also ensure that no corporal punishment will be used.

After-School Care

Parents of school-age children who require care outside school hours may choose programs that are run by either licensed or unlicensed providers. Parents will want to ensure that acceptable standards for behaviour are maintained and that after-school snacks, active play, and an opportunity to complete schoolwork are provided. Both home-based care and child-care centres can provide quality programs for all children up to the age of twelve, whether or not parents work.

❖ Checkpoints

1. Why did the Day Nurseries Act come into existence?
2. What government body licenses child care in your community?
3. Identify the advantages and disadvantages of licensed and unlicensed child care.

Social Services: A Community of Caring

Sometimes things go wrong in families and they need the help of **social services** or family services that are provided by taxes and charitable donations.

Examples of Agencies that Support Families in Times of Need

- **First Nations Child and Family Services** provide support for registered First Nations families living on reserves.

- **Alcoholic's Anonymous, Gamblers Anonymous, Overeaters Anonymous** help those with addictions.

- **Women's Shelters and Children's Aid Societies** respond to domestic violence, child abuse, and neglect.

- **Catholic Family Services, The Mennonite Relief Committee, Salvation Army, Teen Challenge Farms, and other religious organizations** provide debt counselling, assist with shelter, food, and clothing needs, and provide a wide range of personal and relationship counselling.

- **Government Services** such as Family Services and Social Services can provide subsidized child care, financial assistance, retraining, and health care.

- **Community Resource Centres, Early Childhood Centres, and Public Health Units** provide advice and education for parents and caregivers about the health and developmental needs of children.

- **Parents Without Partners, Big Brothers/Sisters** provide support for lone-parent families and their children.

- **Homes for Young Mothers Without Partners** provide support for unmarried teens who are pregnant or who have recently given birth.

- **Homeless Shelters** exist to provide shelter and relief to homeless individuals, families, children, and teens.

Every province, territory, and community has a variety of social services to assist families. Public libraries, government Web sites, and telephone listings, as well as medical clinics, community centres, pharmacies, high-school guidance centres, and even post offices, have information about the social services available in a particular area.

What the experts say

BRUCE RIVERS

Bruce Rivers, M.S.W., R.S.W., Executive Director of the Toronto Children's Aid Society (CAS); President of the Child Welfare League of Canada, a national advocacy and membership organization focused on the needs of vulnerable children and youth

What are the main changes that have occurred in the field of child welfare, and what social changes would make it easier for you to do the job of protecting children?

Demands for child-welfare services in our city have been steadily growing by 10 to 15 percent for each of the last five years and can be attributed to three major factors:

- tougher child protection legislation and a stronger emphasis on everybody's duty to report concerns about child abuse or neglect to the CAS or the police

- heightened public attention and media focus on child safety through gut-wrenching cases of child neglect

- a series of socioeconomic stressors that are combining to erode many parents' capacity to cope with their parenting responsibilities on a day-to-day basis

Each day at the CAS we receive about 150 new calls or referrals for help from the community. The information we collect is extensive and, when collected, it starts to paint a picture that is both informing and fundamentally disturbing. Most striking is that about 75 percent of the children and families we work with are living at or below the poverty line. Most of the families are young, single mother-led; about 53 percent or 6 out of 10 families we serve are receiving some form of social assistance; and only 24 percent were living in assisted housing. Of the families we worked with, 670 were homeless last year.

To these social and economic indicators, add the fact that close to 60 percent of the parents we work with are struggling with a significant emotional or mental illness at a time when psychiatric supports and waiting lists are long. In addition, in 40 percent of the families we work with, domestic violence is commonplace, and substance abuse is prevalent in about 50 percent of them. Add all these factors up, and the lens of child welfare starts to focus on what we describe as toxic family situations—toxic in terms of the health and welfare of the children.

During the past century, through our work with children, youth, and their families, we have learned a whole lot. Ninety percent of the families we work with do not set out to harm their children. Simply put, they live as an adult what they learned as a child. A couple of years ago, Health Canada esti-mated the cost of supporting an abused child to be as much as one million dollars over a lifetime. Our agency did a study involving 100 families where the caregiver was a substance abuser. We found that 84 percent of adult users were victims of child phys-ical abuse and that 76 percent had been sexually abused as a child.

Children with a history of sexual abuse are seven times more likely to become alcohol- or drug-dependent, and ten times more likely to attempt suicide. Our prisons are filled with adults who were victims of physical and/or sexual abuse. Up to 85 percent of female prisoners were victims of child abuse, and it is estimated that it costs one hundred thousand dollars per year to keep each of these women in jail.

We know that children and youth learn what they live. Of the parents we work with, 65 percent report that their parents abused them when they were chil-dren, and most report that they were not exposed to positive parenting in their growing-up years.

In 72 percent of the physical abuse cases that come to the attention of CAS, the abuse has resulted from disciplinary sessions and episodes that have grown out of control. I know it is controversial, but if there was ever an argument for questioning the use of corporal punishment with children and youth, it is that disturbing statistic. The time has arrived to challenge our thinking in this regard.

The research is clear when it comes to violent and racist family environments. They are a breeding ground for future violence and racism, as children learn from their caregivers how to form relationships, how to interact with others, and how to react and solve problems. In a study of children who witnessed violence in their own homes, 60 percent acted out with their brothers and sisters, and 30 percent were violent with their friends and their peers.

The most important responsibility in the world is that of being a parent, yet it is the one job that we are often least ready for and capable of taking on. The CAS joins many in society, including teachers, school boards, social welfare agencies, parent support groups, judges, police officers, and others in its belief that parenting and child-development courses ought to be mandatory in all Ontario' schools to enhance or com-pensate for whatever experience we acquire through our own childhood. Many young parents, for instance, have absolutely no idea how fragile infants are. Over the past two years, we logged 34 cases of Shaken Baby Syndrome (SBS). Some children recovered, many did not, and two are dead. If there was ever an argu-ment for parent education, this solidifies it in my view.

In looking ahead for the children and youth of our country, we have to mobilize our resources and energy to break the cycle of abuse and violence. We have to take a multifaceted approach that probes the need for sound social and economic policies that affect chil-dren. We have to challenge our beliefs around some fundamental issues, like the use of corporal punishment with children. We have to make parenting courses universal and mandatory in all our schools.

We have to invest in prevention and act on all that we know about the early years of a child's life by supporting programs and interventions that will strengthen the nurturing and care those young children receive before age six. And we must never forget those who have already fallen victim and are suffering and traumatized.

❖ Connection

1. Investigate social services available in your community. As a class, make a poster or booklet that summarizes the services that are available, who they serve, and how to access or contact each service.

Family Counselling

Ann Landers was a well-known newspaper columnist who was often consulted about personal and family problems. When there was no easy answer or if the person needed professional help, she always recommended counselling. A counsellor is a qualified professional who will listen to personal and family problems and help find solutions. When the problem involves a spouse, a partner, a child, in-laws, or other relatives, **family counselling** could be very helpful. Often, families seek counselling when they have an immediate problem or crisis. When families experience a crisis such as the loss of a job, a bankruptcy, accident, or disability, they could benefit from talking to a **crisis counsellor**, who can help them take the necessary steps to regaining control. When relationships break down between couples or between parents and children, a **relationship counsellor** can listen to both sides and mediate a solution, or help them agree on how to move forward. Sometimes a death in the family can be very difficult, and a **grief counsellor** can provide the understanding and support that families need to help survive the loss. Family doctors, religious leaders, local health clinics, or local Mental Health Associations can provide information on how to locate a suitable counsellor.

Children and Grief

Sometimes a child's first experience with death is the death of a pet. This provides parents with the opportunity to talk with the child about death and what it means. Children take things quite literally,

Figure 18.7
Hospitalization of a family member—child or parent—can be very traumatic for all members of the family.

so care must be taken in the words that are used. If you are not careful, they may spend days "looking for the big fish bowl in the sky." Children cannot be protected from death by not talking about it. Eventually everything dies—plants, animals, and people.

Children also experience grief in some of the traumatic separations from someone they love. They may experience intense feelings of loss or grief from a divorce, the prolonged illness of a primary caregiver, their own separation from their family, as in foster children, prolonged absence for family visitation, enrolment in a residential program or camp, or through a prolonged stay in hospital.

Feelings and emotions are a significant part of the grieving process. Children need to know that parents feel sad when someone dies. It is normal and acceptable to feel sad or lonely. If the death is that of a parent, sibling, or friend, children may feel that they may have been responsible in some way and will need to be reassured.

Talking about the cause of death helps them understand that there is a reason people die, which may help them voice fears about their own death or the death of someone else close to them. Many families find that religious and spiritual rituals can be comforting. A child who has never attended a funeral service before needs to be prepared for what to expect. They should be told what people do at a funeral, how they should behave, and that some people will be crying. Reassure them that it is okay for them to cry as well.

Creating positive memories, having a ritual like taking flowers to a cemetery, and talking freely about the person who died is far better than ignoring the death or pretending that it is not important. Parents who are not comfortable talking to their children about death can get books from the library or ask a relative, religious leader, community hospice worker, or funeral director for help. Grief counselling can be helpful for the whole family, especially if a parent's own grief is preventing him or her from supporting children in their grief.

Families and Children with Special Needs

Figure 18.8
Though children with special needs require more resources and social support, their love and unique character adds immeasurably to their families.

In the past, babies who were born with life-threatening complications or who experienced trauma at birth rarely lived beyond the first weeks or months of life. Today, with an increase in the number of **life-saving technologies** such as incubators, respirators, feeding tubes, and medication, children can survive a wide range of complications, including premature birth and extremely low birth weights, birth defects, trauma, injury, and disease. As life expectancy increases for infants who at one time would have died, parents are often faced with raising a child who has developmental challenges, a learning disability, physical exceptionality, chronic illness, or inherited disease.

Recently, The Vanier Institute of the Family reported that between 5 and 20 percent of Canadian families have children with disabilities. This means that at least 400 000 and possibly more than 1.5 million families have children with disabilities. Disability is more than an issue involving individual children. It is a family and societal issue. Additionally, it should be understood that "children with disabilities make a positive difference in the lives of their families and all who know them" (McCloskey, 2002, p. 2). Canadians need to focus not just on disabilities, but on the abilities that go with them.

Talking Parenting

The following excerpt is taken from "Family Voices: Living with Disability" (2002), published by The Vanier Institute of the Family:

Rhonda Grant of Regina

In many ways, we are a typical family of four. We have a seven-year-old daughter and a four-year-old son. What makes us atypical is that we have lived in five provinces and a territory, and that one of our children has Down syndrome.

Having lived on both coasts and several points between, one thing that has been strikingly evident is the inconsistency in services, policies, and education available to children with disabilities in different regions of the country. This can be very frustrating and, more importantly, damaging when you consider the importance of early intervention in children. Time lost can never be regained. There needs to be a standard of practice across Canada.

Emphasis on inclusive education needs to be heightened. The benefit of including children with disabilities in a classroom with their non-disabled peers is circular. When children experience individuals with disabilities in a classroom—their first real exposure to a diverse society—they will appreciate their individuality and not question their value as citizens when they grow up and become decision-makers. As a society, we need to understand the "big picture" long-term benefits of supporting families and children with disabilities.

■ *Jessica (my cousin) is three years old and as bright as the sun. Her eyes sparkle like stars every time I see her, and her smile always lights up the room. Jessica is special to me because she was born with Down syndrome and she has made me realize how warm and loving she is.*
— Chris, 13, *Transition*

■ *Our fifth boy has autism... Sam is falling short of his potential... I see large gaps in the supports he receives. For instance, in spite of a severe communication disorder, he saw a speech pathologist for only twenty minutes a month last year. Twenty minutes. I find these things frustrating. I find them intolerable. I find them in contravention of Canada's laws concerning universal health care... Sam's little brother says Sam should be a librarian when he grows up because he loves books and keeping things in order, and he's pretty quiet. I hope he can.*
— Teresa Blair, *Transition*

Raising a child with special needs means a variety of challenges. Increased medical intervention will be a lifelong concern and may involve daily medication, physical and occupational therapies, hospitalization, and even repeated surgery. The physical care of children with special needs may require special equipment, specially designed furniture, and perhaps a highly sanitary, germ-free environment. Extra effort to encourage learning and development may require special classes, special education, and one-on-one assistance. A child with special needs may require the full-time care of one parent, plus the help of all family members. Siblings of children with special needs learn very early to accept their brothers' or sisters' limitations and to find ways to interact with them and even assist with their care. Although the attention may be focused on the child with the special needs, they soon become "just family."

Parents sometimes need outside help, above and beyond the medical profession. Not every community has a children's centre that can provide programs and assistance. Families may have to move closer to facilities that can provide care, or they may find it necessary to travel long distances to receive the services they need. Local services, caregivers that are specialized in serving children with special needs, or social workers that provide activities and assistance for the child also fill a need.

Some communities have "day away" programs staffed by volunteers who provide care for a child with special needs to give parents a needed break. Every situation involving children with special needs is different. One of the most helpful strategies is to find a support group of parents who are experiencing similar challenges. If there is not a group close by, parents can locate groups through children's hospitals or through the Internet, or they may start their own group. Sometimes the best way to help themselves is to help others.

❖ Checkpoints

1. Identify the social agencies that could provide assistance for a single parent living below the poverty line.
2. How might a relationship counsellor help families?
3. Describe the effect that life-saving technologies have had on families.

Career Capsule

OCCUPATIONAL THERAPIST

Tasks and Responsibilities

Occupational therapists aid people who have physical, mental, and emotional problems or developmental delays. Some deal mainly or exclusively with children.

They plan and implement programs for children to help them develop their motor skills and reach developmental milestones. Children with learning disabilities or pervasive developmental delays can be aided by an occupational therapy program to develop self-confidence and learning strategies. Being an occupational therapist involves a lot of hands-on physical activity. The result is improved life skills so that the child can live a more independent life or become integrated into the school system.

An occupational therapist usually works with a client's doctor, physical therapist, and/or social workers or psychotherapists to plan and evaluate programs for the client. Administrative duties are also very important. The records kept by occupational therapists are often used in legal proceedings having to do with the evidence of rehabilitation or degree of disability of their client.

Work Environment

Children's occupational therapists find work in hospitals, schools (for example, for deaf or blind children), private practice, community centres, and the homes of their clients. Some night and weekend work may be required to meet the needs of individual clients. The work is often physically and emotionally draining. Rewards in the form of increased patient mobility, independence, and life skills and improved mental health are a major reason occupational therapists value their work.

Education and Aptitudes

Occupational therapists require excellent communication and interpersonal skills. Occupational therapy is a demanding career requiring a high energy level and good problem-solving skills. The ability to be patient, compassionate, and optimistic is essential to ensure that the programs being planned and used will work for the client.

A four-year undergraduate bachelor's degree in occupational therapy is the starting point for an occupational therapist. Following that, a master's degree in physical or social sciences is recommended for advancement in this career. To work in Canada, the graduate must complete the licensing examination from the Canadian Association of Occupational Therapists.

Global Child Development Challenges

Globalization refers to a growing awareness that we belong to a much bigger picture than just our own family, community, or country. It also has a negative connotation when the world becomes accessible for exploitation. Transnational corporations have endangered families around the world in their bid for larger markets and a bigger share

■ *A nation that neglects its children neglects its future.*
— Dr. Fraser Mustard

of the global economy. Television, satellite communications, and worldwide computer connections have brought the entire world into our homes. Through **electronic technologies** such as short-wave radio, news wire services, television, and the Internet, we become familiar with the lives of children and those who live and work with children around the world.

Children in other countries experience serious hardships and grim realities. They are victims of war, famine, overcrowding, poverty, child labour, and malnutrition. They suffer incredible physical and emotional trauma, yet their resiliency is amazing. Many children of war not only have experienced the fear of attack and the horrors of witnessing death and destruction, but also have lost their homes and their family members. Very young children end up in orphanages, refugee camps, or on the streets struggling for their survival. Fear, anxiety, and nightmares haunt them for years afterward, much like the "shell shock" that soldiers experience during wars. Medical practitioners, psychotherapists, and psychiatrists often refer to these as **post-traumatic stress disorder**.

In many countries of the world, the level of poverty is much more severe than it is in Canada. Lack of running water, overcrowded conditions, and homelessness are common in many places. In some countries, families live in city dumps so that they can forage for a living in the garbage of the wealthy. Famine occurs when crops and food production are lost because of drought or excessive flooding in many regions, resulting in malnutrition and starvation and the death of adults and children alike. AIDS is an epidemic that is ravaging families and children around the world.

Children do their best to survive, and many work for a few cents a day in shocking conditions, risking their eyesight, hearing, life, and limbs in countries where no child labour laws protect them. Still others turn to prostitution, stealing, or begging to secure their daily survival.

It is difficult to predict what the future holds for children who experience these realities. Individuals, governments, and many organizations question what can be done to improve the plight of children around the world, including Canada.

Figure 18.9
Poverty is a global concern for children everywhere. In many countries, the level of poverty is much more severe than it is in Canada.

Social Economic Factors and Human Development

In the 1990s, Canadian researchers Daniel Keating, Clyde Hertzman, Margaret McCain, and Fraser Mustard explored social and economic factors as they relate to human development. The nurturance that children receive early in life has a profound influence on their health, well-being, and competence later in life. Families who experience a decline in their socioeconomic status are less able to provide the nurturing that their children require.

However, studies in neuroscience and brain development indicate that children in poor economic situations who received stimulation early in life have improved levels of development in spite of their economic situation. "People who are reared in poor early parenting circumstances are more likely to be poor parents and repeat the cycle. They are not all poor parents, by any means, but those who are poorly nurtured themselves have a harder time learning parenting skills without any models from their own childhood. Parenting support can help fill the gap" (McCain and Mustard, 1999, p. 45). Programs and parental support that allow for a nurturing, interactive environment can promote development across all income levels and enhance the future well-being of society.

Social change and upheaval are not restricted to North America but are a global reality. Global conditions have increased the demands on families with young children and their need for assistance with child care and parenting support. Without an investment in children today, an entire future generation will experience a loss in health, well-being, and productivity. Social institutions and policies need to change around the world to address human development issues.

Planned programs are needed to provide sensory stimulation for young children and support for parents, particularly those with low incomes. Increased resources for early child development and government policies that put children first are needed to ensure the future well-being of every nation.

Initiatives that will assist countries in preparing themselves to meet new global challenges for parents and children might include adopt-a-grandchild programs, community resource centres, accessible parenting education, and improved access to child care and early childhood education programs. Nurturing, sensory stimulation, human interaction, and confident parenting must be provided and encouraged for all children everywhere.

■ *People who are reared in poor early parenting circumstances are more likely to be poor parents and repeat the cycle.*
— McCain and Mustard

Investing in Early Childhood and Parenting Programs

Currently, many concerns about children in our own society need to be addressed. Child care, early childhood education, and parenting education continue to be the focus of many interest groups who recognize the importance of investing in children. According to The Ontario Coalition for Better Child Care, the result of investing in children is a direct reduction in social costs.

Reduced Social Costs

The Canadian government is beginning to provide funding for early childhood programs because of the payback they afford in reduced social spending including health care, child welfare, education, police, and prisons. Children who attend quality early childhood development programs that offer child-centred play and learning opportunities arrive at school "ready to learn." They show advanced language and math skills, are better able to concentrate on school work, make less use of later remedial programs, are better able to follow adult direction, and are more empathetic to their peers. These benefits are consistent among all children, whether or not there is a parent in the home full time.

❖ Connections

■ One result of investing in children is a direct reduction in social costs.

1. At the First Ministers Meeting in Ottawa in September 2000, the federal government and the provinces and territories set a national children's agenda, the Early Child Agreement, and committed $2.2 billion dollars to the provinces and territories from 2000 to 2005 for early years initiatives. This agreement committed the provinces and territories to spend their share of the money on any or all of the following areas:

   • promote healthy pregnancy, birth, and infancy
   • improve parenting and family supports
   • strengthen early childhood development and care
   • strengthen community support for improving early child care and development

   Find out what has happened in your province or territory with the money coming from the federal government's Early Child Agreement. Which of the four areas of the agreement has your province or territory concentrated upon? Evaluate your province or territory's current progress on this agreement. What can you as a citizen and possible future parent do to encourage more progress?

   Studies continue to provide evidence of the growing need for
child care, early childhood education, and support for families with
young children. Taken together, the evidence makes a compelling
argument for the need for support.

Comprehensive Child-Development Programs

Kerri McCuaig and Dan Keating Discuss Universal Child Care

In spite of the growing evidence for it, universal
child care and universal child development programs
have not received the support they are due. Many
areas and sectors have yet to provide adequate support. There are success stories, however. According
to McCuaig and Keating (2000), two prominent
Canadian authorities on children's issues, the
province of Quebec is providing a comprehensive
child-care program. Quebec provides maternity and
parental leave benefits for employed and self-
employed parents that replaces 70 percent of their
earnings. Their school boards provide full-day
schooling, before and after school care, and holiday
care for children five and older. For children from
birth to age four, children's centres provide either a
group or a licensed home setting, with flexible
hours, that costs parents only five dollars per day.
Subsidies are provided for low-income families.
Demand for the programs by mothers who are not in
the work force, as well as by mothers who are, suggests that Quebec's programs provide more than
child care; they help children develop.

An Integrated Framework

McCuaig and Keating argue for comprehensive programs across
Canada. When children's services are spread out across several different
ministries and organizations, they are far too difficult for parents to
access. If families had to worry about only one child, there would be
less confusion, but the reality is that they often have two, three, or
more children, all needing different kinds of care and different services.
If all services were brought together under one umbrella, then parents
would find them much more accessible. The payoff for children and
families would be that the focus would shift to child development and
its positive long-term effects on society. McCuaig and Keating believe
that early childhood development services could combine forces to
address all the issues that relate to early child development, as shown
in the graphic on page 458.

■ The payoff of an integrated
framework of children's services
would be concentration on children's
development. This would create
positive long-term effects for society.

An Integrated Framework

Figure 18.10
Some of the many elements that contribute to healthy early childhood development.

The Essential Role of Parenting Education

Parenting education as a school subject is fairly recent in Canada, and it has followed a number of social changes. Parenting roles have changed over the past several decades. By the 1980s, it was becoming the norm to have a father in the delivery room assisting with the birth of his child. Parenting styles were shifting away from the authoritarian models, and male and female roles were changing in the workplace and the family.

In schools across Canada, subjects that had long been designed for male or female students began to open their doors to students of both genders. Child-development courses that had been included under home economics expanded, with a coeducational focus.

During the late 1970s and early 1980s, courses such as "Parent Effectiveness Training" (PET) and "Systematic Training for Parenting Effectiveness" were offered across Canada in response to a changing society and a growing demand for some instruction in parenting techniques. Today, the benefits of parenting education are becoming more evident. There has been a decline in physical punishment, a growing concern for the optimal development of children, and an increase in involved parenting by men and women.

Talking Parenting

The Importance of Parenting Education

Beverley Murray, Professional Home Economist and Consultant in Private Practice

Unless they make a conscious decision to change, parents provide the same parenting to their own children that they received. The vast majority of parents want the best for their children. But if they do not have effective skills and knowledge on which to base their parenting practices, they will rely on "instinct" and so "the sins of the father will be visited upon the children" generation after generation.

Parenting education is an effective way for the younger generation to acquire knowledge and skills that will provide their children with a better developmental environment than they themselves experienced. This will benefit the children directly in helping them become better adjusted, happier, and more productive adults. The ripple effect will continue to positively affect their own children and those in each successive generation. With parenting education for all, each generation of parents will continue to improve their knowledge and skills; thus, they will be able to keep up-to-date with best practice.

All of Canadian society will also benefit directly from parenting education programs. Better parenting will reduce the need for child-support programs, improve the health of people of all ages, reduce the social and economic costs for the larger society, and increase the productivity of its citizens and the society as a whole.

It is important that all corners of Canadian society recognize and support the importance of parenting education so that every child is well-nurtured, and parenting is a valued activity undertaken by well-prepared adults and a supportive community. The skills and knowledge of effective parenting are needed not only in the home. Every adult who interacts with a child has an effect on that child's development positively or negatively. The closer the emotional connection, the greater the effect. Even those adults who do not have direct contact with children affect the lives of children by the decisions they make in schools, communities, and all levels of government.

Figure 18.11
Beverley Murray

■ All of Canadian society will benefit directly from parenting education programs.

Figure 18.12
Parenting education opens your eyes to the possibilities of being the best parent you can be for your children.

❖ Checkpoints

1. What have been the negative effects of globalization on children and families?
2. How could children across Canada benefit from each of the four areas of the Early Child Agreement?
3. Describe the immediate and long-term benefits of parenting education.

Parents and potential parents who have had formal parenting education will be aware of the many challenges that come with the job of parenting. They will have learned how to contribute to the healthiest pregnancy, the best possible birth experience, and the most critical years in the life and development of their children. They will have learned a variety of ways to teach and encourage children, and they will have a repertoire of parenting techniques to choose from. Parenting education opens your eyes to the possibilities of being the best parent you can be for your children.

If you are one of those who has chosen parenting education, congratulations! You have touched the future.

Chapter Summary

Chapter Highlights

- Rapid changes in families and society have made children everyone's responsibility.

- Parents, caregivers, and others who work with children have both legal and social responsibilities for children.

- The area that is currently of greatest concern in our society is the obligation to provide affordable, accessible, quality child care for all children in Canada.

- The two main types of child care available are family care and child-care centres. Not all family care situations are licensed, but all child-care centres must be licensed.

- Social services are responsible for providing a "community of caring" for families who experience a family crisis, family breakdown, or a death in the family.

- Families with children who have special needs require services that provide essential care and assistance beyond what the family can provide.

- Each child and each situation involving special needs is different and requires unique strategies. Funding and support from government, organizations, volunteers, and other parents is critical.

- Children around the world face many challenges, including war, famine, poverty, child labour, and other life-threatening conditions.

- Globalization has brought the plight of children around the world to our attention. Initiatives that place children first and contribute in a positive way to their early development will reap rewards in the future.

- There is a need to invest in children by providing universal, affordable child care and early education, and to consolidate social programs to make them more accessible to parents and children everywhere for the benefit of our future society.

- We can make a difference in the lives of children by recognizing the importance of parenting education.

Review and Extend Your Learning

1. Compare and contrast the legal obligations and social expectations of parents and caregivers. **T/I**

2. At least one expert has said that poor child care is worse than no child care in terms of its effect on children. Do you agree or disagree? Explain your reasoning. **K/U T/I**

3. Parents should always choose a child-care provider or service with the same parenting philosophy as they have. Write a one-page paper explaining why this is important. **K/U T/I C**

4. Compare the benefits of family care and child-care centres. Why would parents choose one over the other? **K/U T/I**

5. Spend some time with a person with special needs in your community or classroom. Use your experience to recommend and evaluate strategies for dealing with a child with special needs in a real-life setting, such as going to a ball game, playing at the park, going for a swim, playing games, going shopping, or helping out in a special education classroom. **K/U T/I C A**

6. Using information from the interview with Bruce Rivers and other evidence provided by your own research, write a proposal to address the issues that still exist in the provision of child care today. **T/I C A**

7. Refer to Beverley Murray's essay, and then write an advertisement to convince members of the public why parenting education is absolutely essential. **C A**

8. There are "many ways in which children and adults with disabilities make a positive difference in the lives of their families and all who know them" (Donna McCloskey, *Transition*). Explain this statement by focusing on the abilities of individuals with disabilities. **K/U T/I C A**

Research Opportunities

9. "Nanny care" is care provided for your child(ren) by a caregiver in your own home. Research the costs, advantages, and disadvantages of nanny care. Compared to family care or a child-care centre, is nanny care a worthwhile option?

10. Try to gain work experience in the social service sector. Social services are funded by government and private contributions. Volunteering at a community centre, answering phones for a social service provider, working in a child-care centre, or supervising children while their parents attend community meetings can be valuable experiences for anyone interested in working in the social service sector.
    - Find out who provides social services in your community.
    - Find out how you could volunteer or arrange a work experience placement with their organization.
    - Arrange to receive a record of the hours during which you volunteered.
    - If you anticipate using your volunteer employer as a reference, make sure you ask for their permission to do so.

11. Review the literature on a specific childhood disability. Organize your review of literature using the following headings:
    - Characteristics
    - Care and nurturance of children
    - Rewards and challenges for families

    Remember to include an introduction, conclusion, and a list of the references cited in your review.

12. Conduct an Internet search of sources such as Statistics Canada, Sign on For Kids, or The Canadian Council on Social Development, which provide statistics that reflect the state of the family and children in Canada today. Gather statistics about the participation of mothers in the work force, the number of children needing child care, the number of children in child care, and the number of child-care programs that promote early development. Use these statistics to develop an argument for improved funding of child care and improved social support for parents of young children.

13. Using the Internet, find out where parenting or human development courses are taught in other schools across Canada. At what grade level is parenting taught? What are these courses called? Use push pins to locate your findings on a map of Canada.

Appendix

The following pages are excerpted from *What a child will be depends on you and me: A resource list for a child's first five years.* The kit is published by Invest in Kids, a national not-for-profit foundation that is dedicated to the healthy social, emotional, and intellectual development of children aged zero to five.

THE ESSENTIALS OF DEVELOPMENT

Emotional Development means developing a full range of emotions, from sad to happy to angry, and learning to handle them appropriately. This leads to deeper qualities — sympathy, caring, resilience, self-esteem, assertiveness and being able to rise to life's challenges.

Will a child stay in an emotional shell or emerge sunny-side up?

These are the hard-boiled facts. Responsive, loving relationships foster positive traits like self-esteem, trust and empathy. If tiny tots feel safe and secure, they learn to meet life's challenges with confidence and enthusiasm. Let's get cracking.

Will a child be well-grounded or blown away by the winds of change?

A tiny sprout can only learn how to weather life's challenges with our nurturing and support. You see, resilience stems from the comfort and encouragement we give children in the first years of life. With cuddles, kisses and words of reassurance, little ones discover how to bend when they need to, how to adapt to change and how to bounce back from disappointment. Let's all help our children stay firmly rooted.

Social Development means being able to make friends and get along with others, work as part of a team and be a good leader, all of which are built on self-confidence, cooperation and trust.

Will a child lie and vegetate or blossom intellectually?

Well, that all depends on the seeds we plant during the first five years of a child's life. Simple things like talking, singing and reading to a child from the day of birth will have a lasting impact on her potential. Intelligence doesn't grow on trees. But it certainly grows on love and supportive stimulation.

Cognitive Development means being able to communicate, to think both creatively and abstractly, to pay attention and to solve problems, and develop keen judgment and a lifelong readiness to learn.

COMFORT, PLAY AND TEACH: THE ESSENTIALS OF CAREGIVING

Kids don't come with a handbook or a set of instructions for parents and caregivers. The research shows that there is no single approach. No magic potion will transform all of our children into happy resilient adults. But there are approaches with proven results. There are THREE ESSENTIALS OF CAREGIVING that get children off to a good start.

COMFORT:

Infants and children are born with a very limited capacity to comfort themselves. They need us to comfort them when they are sick, tired, upset or otherwise frustrated. During the first five years, they need adults to gradually teach them how to handle their emotions and how to seek help when they need it.

PLAY:

Play is important for children. Play is the major way young children learn about themselves and others. During the first five years, children need parents and care-givers to provide opportunities for play and at times to join in with the child in joyful, free, spontaneous moments of fun.

TEACH:

Children are born with almost no capacity to know what is safe and important. In the years before age five, they need parents and caregivers to provide routines and rules to maintain safety and respect for others. Parents and caregivers also need to provide consistent consequences and moral guidance, suitable for the age and temperament of each child. Children are also born with a limited ability to stimulate themselves intellectually. They need parents and caregivers to teach them how to think, solve problems and communicate.

Most of these essentials take place in ordinary, everyday activities at home or daycare.

Practically all adults are good at one of the three essentials. It is not crucial for each caregiver to be the "best" at all three. Children in families in which these essentials are shared among parents and other caregivers do fine.

The important thing to remember is that children need exposure to all three of these essentials.

YOUR CHILD FROM BIRTH TO 6 MONTHS

From newborn to baby:
The most important developmental achievements

Social

Typically Can:
- Respond to own mirror image
- Offer toy to another person
- Smile socially at another person
- Try to imitate facial expressions and gestures

Emerging Skills:
- Is disturbed by strangers
- Recognizes the word "no"
- Is able to "call out" to parent for help
- Enjoys interactive games like peekaboo

Language

Typically Can:
- Cry
- Coo, chuckle, gurgle when happy
- Begin to make vowel and consonant combinations
- Utter consonants such as f, v, th, s, sh, z, m, n
- Vary volume, pitch, rate of utterance

Emerging Skills:
- Begins to babble
- Responds to some words (e.g., "no no")
- Imitates two or three familiar gestures such as pat-a-cake
- Turns in response to name

Gross Motor

Typically Can:
- Lift head and pull to sitting position when hand held
- Turn from back to stomach and from stomach to back
- Turn head freely
- Sit with slight support
- Sit in chair and bounce

Emerging Skills:
- Takes weight on feet when held in standing position
- Takes early stepping movements
- Gets into creeping or crawling position
- Appears to be dancing when straightens one leg at a time in upright position

Cognitive

Typically Can:
- Enjoy examining and banging objects
- Remain alert 2 hours at a time
- Create changes in objects by looking at them upside down or further away

Emerging Skills:
- Searches for a toy that is covered up
- Remembers that an object is hidden and searches for it
- Looks for dropped object
- Begins to enjoy clowning around
- Uses several senses at once

Emotional

Typically Can:
- Begin to quiet down on his/her own after getting upset
- Express many emotions: sadness, anger, happiness and excitement
- Check out parent and touch face as if memorizing it
- Show mood changes that tend to be rapid

Emerging Skills:
- Has a special toy that always goes to bed with him/her
- Sleeps for longer periods at night

Fine Motor

Typically Can:
- Move toy from hand to mouth
- Hold toys placed in both hands
- Bang spoon placed in hand
- Grasp table
- Reach for and grasp objects with whole hand

Emerging Skills:
- Transfers toy from one hand to the other
- Releases toy by dropping
- Throws toy purposefully
- Holds two blocks and looks for a third
- Rotates wrist to turn and manipulate object

YOUR CHILD FROM BIRTH TO 6 MONTHS

Games and activities for you and your baby

COMFORT

Seeing your face or a familiar face, feeling your touch and hearing your voice give your baby feelings of warmth and security and a sense that this new world is predictable, responsive and kind.

Cuddling your baby helps satisfy your baby's need for closeness and comfort.

Watching you during daily activities provides your baby with pleasure, entertainment and comfort.

Baby massage calms and soothes while communicating love, comfort and security to your baby.

PLAY

Peekaboo games help babies develop memory for objects and people. The "I'm going to get you" game is another game parents can play that is guaranteed to delight and bring squeals of joy.

Rocking and jumping games, such as bouncing your baby gently on your lap while you listen to music on the radio or TV, entice your baby into music and rhythm, engaging his or her whole body.

TEACH

Rhymes and songs give pleasure and comfort, especially when given by a familiar voice in a lyrical and repetitive chant. Use any opportunity such as diapering, feeding or bathing as a chance to sing to your baby.

"Shake-Shake" toys that make a noise give your baby lots of stimulation and pleasure. This encourages your child to reach for new objects to see what noise they will make.

The years before five last the rest of their lives.™

Prepared by Dr. Sarah Landy of the Hincks-Dellcrest Institute, Advisor to Invest in Kids Foundation.

YOUR CHILD FROM 6 TO 18 MONTHS

From dependence to independence:
The most important developmental achievements

Social

Typically Can:
► Feed self but is still messy
► Imitate others
► Drink from a cup
► Not share
► Fight limit setting
► Remain "egocentric" and think the world exists for him/her

Emerging Skills:
► Pulls on pants
► Plays alongside another child

Cognitive

Typically Can:
► Point to body parts
► Begin to pretend play
► Initiate activities
► Realize things exist when they are out of sight

Emerging Skills:
► Sorts and matches things
► Distinguishes colours and shapes
► Begins to understand the passing of time and the meaning of "when we go home," "not now" and "tomorrow"

Language

Typically Can:
► Say a few words
► Use gestures as well as to show he/she wants something
► Understand simple instructions
► Follow one command

Emerging Skills:
► Listens to a story
► Sings songs
► Understands far more words than will say

Emotional

Typically Can:
► Be very curious and "gets into things"
► Become more of an individual
► Be reluctant to change
► Be subject to mood swings and tantrums

Emerging Skills:
► Concentrates on a task for some time
► Shows concern for others

Gross Motor

Typically Can:
► Walk alone
► Walk up and down stairs with hand held
► Throw a ball
► Sit down from standing
► "Dance" to music
► Ride on small-wheeled toys

Emerging Skills:
► Steps backward
► Steps sideways
► Begins to run
► Jumps and climbs
► Seats self on a small chair

Fine Motor

Typically Can:
► Place 10 cubes in a cup
► Grasp items with thumb and forefinger
► Target small objects
► Stack three to four blocks
► Turn page of a book
► Scribble
► Fill and empty containers

Emerging Skills:
► Folds paper
► Attempts simple puzzles
► Copies simple lines drawn on paper

YOUR CHILD FROM 6 TO 18 MONTHS
Games and activities for you and your baby

COMFORT

Exploring feelings using pictures of people showing different emotions helps your child understand and show concern for others.

Using encouraging words — such as "good for you" or "you're doing a good job" — provides security and helps your child develop confidence and independence.

Establishing routines at bedtime, bathtime, or mealtime helps your child predict what comes next and feel secure.

PLAY

Movement games contribute to your child's sense of separateness and of his or her own body's strength. Dancing to music, using riding toys, doing jumping jacks and performing the actions to games such as "Follow the Leader" and "Simon Says" and to songs such as "If You're Happy and You Know It" foster many skills and self-awareness.

TEACH

Language activities such as reading books or singing songs, nursery rhymes and verses introduce your child to familiar words and sounds. Bounce your child on your lap while you sing the songs and play the games. Making animal and other familiar sounds and linking them to pictures will help your child associate animals and objects with the sounds they make.

Songs and rhymes should be fun and be repeated often since your child will gradually become familiar with tunes and words heard frequently.

Finger plays help your child pay attention to the rhythm of the words, and he or she will love imitating the actions. Some favourites you may know are "Hickory, Dickory, Dock," "Eensy, Weensy Spider," and "Where is Thumbkin?"

The years before five last the rest of their lives.™

Prepared by Dr. Sarah Landy of the Hincks-Dellcrest Institute, Advisor to Invest in Kids Foundation.

YOUR CHILD FROM 1 ½ TO 2 ½ YEARS

From early toddler to the terrific twos: The most important developmental achievements

Social

Typically Can:
- ▶ Play alongside another child with enjoyment
- ▶ At times, get frustrated and bite, hit or pull hair
- ▶ Recognize self and family in photograph
- ▶ Be aware of sex differences

Emerging Skills:
- ▶ Shares a piece of food
- ▶ Takes turns in a song or game
- ▶ Begins to be toilet trained

Cognitive

Typically Can:
- ▶ Understand "today" and "soon" but not "yesterday"
- ▶ Name parts of the body
- ▶ Engage in pretend play with others

Emerging Skills:
- ▶ Counts up to five
- ▶ Matches familiar objects by choice
- ▶ Understands the concept of one
- ▶ Groups things by form and size

Language

Typically Can:
- ▶ Point to at least one body part
- ▶ Name some pictures in a book
- ▶ Repeat words
- ▶ Use two- to four-word sentences
- ▶ Follow simple commands

Emerging Skills:
- ▶ Sings simple songs
- ▶ Use personal pronouns such as "mine," "me," and "you"
- ▶ Expresses feelings verbally (e.g., "I'm mad")
- ▶ Uses size words correctly

Emotional

Typically Can:
- ▶ Be away from parents for a short time without being too upset
- ▶ Show fears and be able to be settled down
- ▶ Demand own way for much of the time
- ▶ Be attached to cuddly or favourite toy
- ▶ Be unhappy about any changes in routine

Emerging Skills:
- ▶ Learns to listen and follow simple directions
- ▶ Names several emotions and identifies them in others

Gross Motor

Typically Can:
- ▶ Run without falling
- ▶ Walk backward and sideways
- ▶ Climb over furniture
- ▶ Walk upstairs alternating feet
- ▶ Walk along a line

Emerging Skills:
- ▶ Kicks a ball
- ▶ Walks a few steps on tiptoe
- ▶ Throws and retrieves objects
- ▶ Jumps in place, both feet off the floor
- ▶ Pedals a tricycle

Fine Motor

Typically Can:
- ▶ Take lids off jars
- ▶ Fit jars and squares inside of each other
- ▶ Draw vertical line
- ▶ Build tower of five blocks
- ▶ Complete simple inset puzzle

Emerging Skills:
- ▶ Clutches pencil with whole hand
- ▶ Holds brush and paints on paper
- ▶ Uses small scissors to cut
- ▶ Strings beads
- ▶ Imitates folding paper in half

YOUR CHILD FROM 1 ½ TO 2 ½ YEARS
Games and activities for you and your toddler

COMFORT

Turn-taking games or songs such as "Bumping Up and Down in My Little Red Wagon" will help children understand the right way to take turns with others while also fostering a sense of cooperation.

Make time for your child to share feelings and reactions about his or her day. You may need to help with some words as your child's vocabulary grows.

PLAY

Pretend play: Provide a corner equipped with props where your child can "make-believe." Occasionally join in these pretend games. For some children, these role plays help them explore and express their feelings.

Sensory games: Stimulate your child's sense of touch by letting him or her feel things like a brush, prickly rubber toy, sponge, sandpaper, or velvet. Have him or her match and name textures and objects. Put them in a bag and have the child find and name them.

Creative activities: Activities done with crayons, paint, paper and other art materials offer a fun experience for your child. These activities will encourage eye-hand coordination and fine motor skills, and give your child a sense of control.

TEACH

Sorting: Encourage your child to sort things by colour, shape, size, and texture.

Rhyming games: Let your child expand his or her vocabulary. Try to label familiar objects and actions, and sing familiar songs. Use picture books to label objects while also fostering an enjoyment for books. Remember to give your child a chance to use all the new words.

Action songs: "Head and Shoulders" and "If You're Happy and You Know It" help children become familiar with body parts.

The years before five last the rest of their lives.™

Prepared by Dr. Sarah Landy of the Hincks-Dellcrest Institute, Advisor to Invest in Kids Foundation.

YOUR CHILD FROM 2 ½ TO 3 ½ YEARS

From terrific twos to delightful threes:
The most important developmental achievements

Social

Typically Can:
- Join in associative play with a group of peers
- Show empathy if not overwhelmed
- Complete toilet training
- Cooperate with dressing and undressing
- Enjoy being in a play group

Emerging Skills:
- Shares toys
- Cooperates in putting toys away
- Takes turns
- Plays games with simple rules

Language

Typically Can:
- Use a vocabulary of about 900 words
- Use language to get what is wanted
- Use language to express feelings
- Respond to simple instructions
- Use plurals and personal pronouns "I," "you," "me"
- Repeat three numbers
- Use five-word sentences
- Name pictures of familiar things in picture book

Emerging Skills:
- Asks "what," "where," "who" questions
- Uses parts of speech correctly
- Plays with words in silly rhymes
- Uses new and unfamiliar words

Gross Motor

Typically Can:
- Run 15 metres in under 10 seconds
- Climb on jungle gym and other equipment
- Kick a ball
- With hand held, jump from height of 20 centimetres
- Stand on one foot with momentary balance
- Throw a small ball
- Get up from squatting position without help

Emerging Skills:
- Does standing broad jump for 30 centimetres
- Jumps off ground with two-footed jump
- Hops on one foot for a few steps
- Uses pedals to ride tricycle and steers to avoid obstacles
- Catches a large ball with arms extended
- Skips six times imitating another person

Cognitive

Typically Can:
- Sort objects by colour and size
- Classify objects by purpose (e.g., to play with, to wear)
- Name one or more colours
- Count three objects
- Say name and part of address
- Understand time intervals better (e.g., today, tomorrow, yesterday)

Emerging Skills:
- Counts up to 10 and understands number concepts up to three
- Uses increasing number of pronouns and prepositions with understanding
- Understands "its time to"

Emotional

Typically Can:
- See things from another person's perspective
- Control aggression and tantrums at least part of the time
- Be less upset by limits and discipline
- Understand and follow simple rules
- Be settled after nightmares more easily
- Sleep through night

Emerging Skills:
- Is much more even-tempered and cooperative with parents
- Keeps room and toys in order
- Continually grows in independence and self-esteem
- Expands pretend play into rich, connected themes
- Uses pretend play to gain control of frustrating and frightening experiences
- Plays out adult roles in play

Fine Motor

Typically Can:
- Copy a circle from a drawing
- Build a tower of nine blocks
- Place round, square and triangular blocks in a form board
- Complete easy puzzle
- Copy bridge of blocks from model

Emerging Skills:
- Handles scissors and cuts out
- Copies a cross
- Pulls up zipper but cannot do buttons
- Screws lids on jars
- Carries liquids in cup
- Puts on shoes but cannot tie laces

YOUR CHILD FROM 2 ½ TO 3 ½ YEARS

Games and activities for you and your child

COMFORT

Making a family album with a page for each member of the family can help your child develop a sense of belonging. Attach pictures of events or their favourite food, colour or activity to each page.

The Art Park: Find a wall or door where your child's favourite artwork can be "parked." All of you will feel pride in these wonderful creations.

PLAY

Children love building and creative activities using blocks or cardboard boxes. You and your child can have a building centre with a variety of building materials including blocks, boxes and cardboard. Don't forget: knocking down can be as fun as building up.

Messy play with water, clay, mud or sand is fun too. Other activities include making and creating things with his or her hands. Scissors, crayons and paints and paper are important tools for the preschool child.

TEACH

Cooperative games that involve other children such as "Tag" or "Simon Says," provide an opportunity to play with others while following simple rules.

Matching and naming pictures by faces, colours, shapes, sizes and feelings help your child begin to put objects into different classes and enhance the beginning of abstract thinking.

Reading activities shared by you and your child provide a chance to enjoy familiar and new stories, and to introduce new words.

Counting games and songs can be part of the daily routine or can be more formal, with games and songs such as "Five Green and Speckled Frogs," "Alice the Camel" or "Three Little Monkeys."

The years before five last the rest of their lives.™

Prepared by Dr. Sarah Landy of the Hincks-Dellcrest Institute, Advisor to Invest in Kids Foundation.

YOUR CHILD FROM 3 ½ TO 4 ½ YEARS

From observer to explorer:
The most important developmental achievements

Social

Typically Can:
► Begin to grasp concept of sharing
► Show attachment to one playmate
► Enjoy games with rules
► Show interest in sex differences and may undress with other children
► Enjoy dramatic play with others
► Take turns
► Stop napping

Emerging Skills:
► Shows concern for younger or hurt person
► Is a team leader
► Plays cooperatively in a group

Language

Typically Can:
► Play with language and make up new words
► Use average vocabulary of 2,000 words
► Use correct grammatical structure
► Talk about imaginary conditions
► Use negatives (e.g., "I don't want to go")
► Understand "on top of" and "under"
► Carry a tune
► Use plural nouns (e.g., "dogs")

Emerging Skills:
► Asks questions with "why" and "how"
► Recites nursery rhyme or sings a song
► Uses past, present and future verbs (e.g., "talked," "talk" and "will talk")
► Understands "top," "middle" and "bottom"
► Says most speech sounds accurately
► Is 80% understandable to people outside the family
► Uses five- or six-word sentences
► Speaks with grammatical correctness

Gross Motor

Typically Can:
► Walk on tiptoe for three metres
► Balance on walking board
► Ride tricycle without bumping into things
► Enjoy throwing and catching games
► Move to music in rhythm
► Walk up and downstairs alternating feet
► Toss bean bags into holes in targets

Emerging Skills:
► Bounces on trampoline
► Carries out rudimentary galloping
► Jumps down from half-metre height

Cognitive

Typically Can:
► Point to six common shapes (e.g., star, triangle)
► Understand "nearest" and "longest"
► Recall events in recent past
► Begin to match pictures in simple lotto games
► Understand difference between reality and fantasy
► Count to five
► Distinguish something alive from an object

Emerging Skills:
► Shows interest in written words and letters
► Follows three simple instructions
► Understands complete sentences
► Understands number concepts to 10
► Sorts objects by colour, shape, size
► Names five colours

Emotional

Typically Can:
► Control frustration and anger much better
► Experience positive self-esteem and feel good about themselves and what they do
► Talk about feelings such as hunger, tiredness, illness
► Comply with requests from parents a greater percentage of the time
► Concentrate for up to 20 minutes
► Show strong interest and feelings for family
► Persevere on a difficult task for longer

Emerging Skills:
► Shows desire to fit into routines of home
► Carries out small chores to fit into family and be responsible
► Shows self-reflection (e.g.,"What I said isn't nice")
► Understands and has positive and negative feelings about another person

Fine Motor

Typically Can:
► Put large & simple jigsaws together
► Cut with children's scissors
► Paint with a large brush on large paper
► Manipulate clay
► Draw a person with three parts
► Fold paper

Emerging Skills:
► Buttons and unbuttons buttons
► Cuts on line with scissors
► Carries cup without spilling liquid in it
► Strings small beads to make a necklace

YOUR CHILD FROM 3 ½ TO 4 ½ YEARS
Games and activities for you and your preschooler

COMFORT

Sharing feelings and experiences from daily events with your child will develop an increased sense of trust.

Pretend play with your old clothing allows children to use their imagination and pretend to be grown up. Encourage pretend play by having dress-up clothes available and helping children to make up a play or a puppet act. Exploring different roles can promote a sense of security, which is so essential during the early years.

PLAY

Active games such as "Tag" and "Mother May I" encourage children to have fun running and rolling, both indoors and outdoors. Four-year-olds need opportunities to run, climb, gallop and jump. Outdoor time and just "getting the wiggles out" can be great for all the family.

Quiet activities such as painting, cutting, building with cubes, doing puzzles and printing letters increase attention span and fine motor skills.

TEACH

Encourage your child to talk about feelings by
• Sharing likes, dislikes and feelings
• Talking about big and little, fast and slow, near and far
• Having a child tell all she or he can about himself or herself
• Pausing in a story and asking how the person may be feeling
• Reading stories regularly

Books, language games and storytelling continue to be important as your child's language expands. If these can reflect a child's interest, they will be especially inviting. Try to be patient in answering children's endless questions. Together you and your child can create a storybook with pictures and words of his or her own.

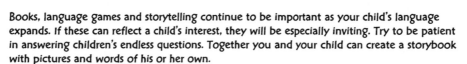

The years before five last the rest of their lives.™

Prepared by Dr. Sarah Landy of the Hincks-Dellcrest Institute, Advisor to Invest in Kids Foundation.

YOUR CHILD FROM 4 ½ TO 5 ½ YEARS

From explorer to discoverer:
The most important developmental achievements

Social

Typically Can:
- Play cooperatively with two to five children
- Enjoy going visiting
- Be quite competitive
- Enjoy group play and circle time
- Become embarrassed to be seen nude
- Make friends easily
- Show social skills of giving, sharing and receiving
- Show concern for children in distress

Emerging Skills:
- Develops an interest in team sports and activities
- Has sleepovers with friends
- Begins to plan social times with friends

Language

Typically Can:
- Use vocabulary of 2,200 to 3,000 words
- Enjoy using big words
- Remember name and address
- Speaks fluently and with grammatical correctness
- Use sentences of at least five to six words
- Be 90% understandable to people outside the family

Emerging Skills:
- Remembers birthday
- Understands left and right

Gross Motor

Typically Can:
- Use adult-like posture to throw and catch a ball
- Walk up and downstairs alternating feet without support
- Broad jump up to one metre
- Skip on both feet or gallop
- Walk along six-centimetre balance beam
- Throw a small ball six metres
- Jump to touch something
- Jump a 30-centimetre hurdle
- Balance on either foot
- Run on tiptoe

Emerging Skills:
- Hops distance of 15 metres
- Accompanies music with body movements (e.g., slow, heavy, soft, like a bear)
- Touches toes without bending knees

Cognitive

Typically Can:
- Think out plan before making something
- Name a coin correctly
- Count objects past 10
- Attend to an activity for up to 20 minutes if interested
- Remember a play theme overnight
- Name five colours
- Remember stories and TV jingles
- Distinguish between three and four sizes
- Maintain mood of calm and quiet much of the time
- Sort objects by colour, shape, size

Emerging Skills:
- Understands number concepts
- Writes numbers up to five and some letters
- Understands calendar and clock
- Puts things in categories
- Knows days of week, months, seasons
- Remembers past events more clearly
- Spells out very simple words

Emotional

Typically Can:
- Be industrious and enjoy being busy making things
- Exhibit more confidence and self-assurance than last year
- Accept authority, ask permission and respect rules
- Ask to marry opposite sex parent
- Begin to feel shame and guilt if he/she disobeys
- Loves to giggle and tell jokes and riddles
- Is aware of rules and tells others about them
- Integrate negative and positive views of self and others
- Have bad dreams and nightmares

Emerging Skills:
- Develops habits and mannerisms: biting nails, pulling clothes, blinking, etc.
- Has an imaginary friend

Fine Motor

Typically Can:
- Draw a person with most parts included
- Copy, square, circle and rectangle
- Building 10 cube tower
- Do seven- to eight-piece puzzle
- Hold pencil between thumb and forefinger
- Use same hand consistently
- Draw letters and numbers
- Cut and paste
- Wash hands and face
- Dress if he or she has plenty of time
- Print name
- Feed self with little mess using fork and spoon

Emerging Skills:
- Ties shoelaces and bows
- Does up buttons and fasteners
- Copies triangle

YOUR CHILD FROM 4 ½ TO 5 ½ YEARS
Games and activities for you and your child

COMFORT

Safe haven: Give your child the opportunity to be independent but at the same time provide him or her with security. Your child needs to know that if a mistake is made, he or she can come to you for help and comfort.

Special helper: Ask your child to help with family tasks around the house.

Special times calendar: Create a calendar on which you and your child can note special events that are important for all family members.

PLAY

Activities that encourage exploration, such as cooking, provide opportunities for children to experiment with different materials. Talk to your child about the changes that occur.

Keep a "creative box" of scrap odds and ends, crayons, and glue and give your child the chance to be creative.

TEACH

Letter and number games introduced in daily routines can be ideal for fostering your child's understanding of simple counting, adding and spelling. For instance, count the number of settings at the table, or think of all the words that start with the first letter of your child's name.

Interactive games such as "I Spy" can be lots of fun and develop your child's observation skills and awareness of his or her environment.

Cooking experiences provide a natural opportunity for children to learn about concepts such as measuring, mixing or time.

The years before five last the rest of their lives.™

Prepared by Dr. Sarah Landy of the Hincks-Dellcrest Institute, Advisor to Invest in Kids Foundation.

Glossary

A

abortion the intentional termination of a pregnancy

abstinence in this instance, refraining from having sexual intercourse

acquiescence the state of being consenting or accepting, such as changing your behaviour because someone asks you to

active child a child who does not sleep long and is happy with movement, noise, action, and play

active labour second stage of labour in which a woman experiences noticeable contractions for a full minute every two to three minutes

active listening listening that involves the use of nods and smiles, asking questions, and using "I" messages to respectfully let children know how you feel about their behaviour

active play play that involves movement, interaction, and manipulation

adolescence the stage of development between childhood and adulthood

agent of socialization a person or organization, such as school or family, that plays an important role in teaching children the ways of society

age-appropriate a child's behaviours that reflect his or her age; the term is also used to describe toys, activities, and games that reflect a child's age

aggressive child a child who interacts with the environment through energetic and forceful responses

amniotic fluid the cushioning fluid that surrounds the embryo or fetus

anarchy the absence of law

androgynous name a name that does not connote gender, for example, Sean, Michael, Dana, and Shannon

anthropology the study of the lives and cultures of human beings

anxious ambivalent infant an infant who turns away from or avoids the touch of a parent who has returned after an absence

anxious avoidant infant an infant who shows resistance, anger, or hostility when a parent returns after an absence

APGAR scale a scale that measures and assesses the condition of a newborn to determine if medical assistance is required

associative play a social type of play where children play with others and share toys

attachment a strong connection to another person; special affection or kindness for another

audiovisual technology forms of media such as television and video, and electronic sources such as computers, Internet, electronic messages, and interactive games that bring together representations of sight and sound

authoritarian parenting a restrictive parenting style that uses commands, authority, and discipline with force or physical punishment

authoritative parenting a flexible parenting style that sets limits, provides rationales, expects mature behaviour and dialogue, and uses encouragement rather than punishment

autonomy the state of being self-directing, making your own decisions and moral choices

axon the part of a nerve cell that carries impulses away from the main part of the cell

B

backbone family a family that mixes flexibility with limits

beginning family the stage during which mate selection and the birth or adoption of a first child signify the start of a new family

biological clock in this instance, an expression that defines the process that may influence people to have children

birth canal the vagina during the birth process

birth defect an abnormality present from birth

birth plan an outline of preferences that parents and practitioners have for the birth

blastocyst the beginning of a human embryo; a ball of cells consisting of an inner cell mass, a cavity, and an outer layer

boarding school a school that provides lodging and food during the school term for all or some of its students

bonding the formation of a close relationship between people; for example, between a parent and child

brain wiring connections in the brain

Braxton Hicks contractions contractions that occur during mid- to late pregnancy, when the uterus tightens from time to time; does not signal labour

breakfast program the provision of breakfast by schools and communities for hungry children

brick-wall family a family that uses punitive parenting strategies and is inflexible and controlling

bride price a token or goods given to the father of the bride by the groom as a form of payment for the bride

bullying negative actions directed to one child by one or more children, repeatedly and over time, with the intent to hurt or embarrass

C

caesarean delivery a method of delivering a baby through a surgical incision made in the wall of the mother's abdomen and uterus

Canadian Multiculturalism Day a yearly event, celebrated on June 27, that is part of the Celebrate Canada group of events

capillaries tiny blood vessels that connect arterioles and venules

cell differentiation the process when cells are programmed for a particular function

censorship the practice of banning or repressing materials or ideas considered objectionable

chattel a possession or property such as furniture and animals

child abuse non-accidental physical injuries, emotional abuse, sexual molestation, and/or incest inflicted on a child by a parent or adult

child labour work done by a child in a business or factory

child-care centre a centre that offers child-care supervision plus programs for children to the age of 12, governed by provincial legislation

childhood the stage of development between infancy and adolescence

childproofing the act of making surroundings safe for a child

chromosome genetic material that carries coded information that determines heredity

cognitive development the evolution of factual knowledge and understanding

cognitive intelligence the possession of and ability to use factual knowledge and understanding

cognitive science the study of how we learn

communication blocker a strategy, such as blaming, sarcasm, the use of insults, and name-calling, that inhibits communication

compromise occurs when two people in conflict are fairly close to agreement and decide to compromise—give up some of what they each want—to settle a problem

conception the moment when the sperm and egg unite

concrete operations the stage (between the ages of 7 and 12) identified by Piaget when children understand the relationship between objects and actions

consensus building the use of problem-solving strategies to accomplish a win-win solution, where both parties feel somewhat successful

contraception the intentional prevention of conception

contracting family a family that is becoming smaller; for example, when older children begin to leave the family

cooperative play a type of social play where participants understand and accept rules and work together toward a common goal

counter culture opposite viewpoints or rejection of values and mores of the mainstream society

covert rule a rule that is implied or understood without being explicit, such as passing food to the head of the house before taking food yourself

criminal behaviour behaviour that results in breaking the law

critical period a time frame during which certain features or conditions become important to a situation

crisis counsellor a qualified professional trained to help people take control after a crisis such as bankruptcy, accident, or disability

culture the arts, beliefs, habits, institutions, and other customs that together are considered as being characteristic of a particular community, people, or nation

curriculum a set of courses and programs offered at school

cycle of violence a pattern of abuse or violence that continues from one generation to the next unless someone takes steps to stop it

D

daughter nuclei the two identical nuclei that form from the division of a single cell, creating two completely new cells, each containing 46 chromosomes

defiance of authority the act of opposing an influential person or organization

democratic parenting a flexible parenting style that sets limits, provides rationales, expects mature behaviour and dialogue, and uses encouragement rather than punishment

dendrites multiple branches at the ends of axons in the nervous system that connect to new targets

development the process of growth and change

developmental psychologist a social scientist who studies human development and the details of physical, social, emotional, moral, and intellectual (or cognitive) growth and development

dilation in this instance, the widening or expanding of the cervix during labour

disciplinarian   a person who disciplines others

discipline   a trained condition of obedience or self-regulation

display media   eye-catching materials set up to communicate information to a large audience; for example, billboards, signs, window displays

dowry   goods or property given to the groom's family in return for marrying the bride

E

early labour   the first phase of labour, beginning with very mild contractions and continuing until the cervix has opened to three centimetres

effacement   the thinning of the cervix during labour to permit widening or expanding

egalitarian   shared authority, where power is divided between the adult leaders of a family

electronic media   computers, the Internet, electronic messages, interactive games, and telecommunication technologies

electronic technology   a telecommunication service, such as short-wave radio, news-wire services, television, and the Internet

embryo   the term used for a developing organism in the womb from the time it is implanted in the uterus until it takes the basic human shape of a **fetus**

emerging initiative   in this instance, a new policy or procedure that addresses the needs of children and their parents

emotional abuse   the act of ignoring or belittling a child's needs for love and belonging

emotional development   the maturation and evolution of emotions, social skills, identity, personality, and morals

emotional intelligence   an individual's ability to recognize and identify their own emotions; recognize, identify, and respond to the feelings of others; and solve emotional problems

emotional literacy   the ability to identify, express, and talk about feelings

empathy   the ability to understand another's feelings

empathy belly   a small sack constructed of fabric and weights, worn by a non-pregnant person to simulate the size and weight of a pregnancy

encouragement   favourable comments that affirm behaviour, giving the child the courage to act in the preferred way in social situations

environmental deprivation   the notion that one has been deprived of opportunities and stimulation needed for growth and development

episiotomy   the incision made in the vaginal opening to allow the baby's head to exit the mother's body

ethics   professional standards or rules of conduct or behaviour

expanding family   the phase of family life when second and subsequent children are born and grow to adulthood

external conflict   discord that starts when the needs, wants, or values of one person conflict with those of another person

exuberant play   a type of play that requires plenty of space, such as a gymnasium or outdoor play area

F

failure to thrive   inability to grow or develop as a result of neglect

family   "any group of two or more persons, who bond together over time by ties of blood or mutual consent, birth and/or adoption and who, together, assume responsibilities for the functions of families" (The Vanier Institute for the Family)

family care   care provided for children in the caregiver's home

family counselling   assistance from a professional trained in helping people resolve problems that are personal or involve family members such as a partner or children

family development   the evolution of ever-changing relationships between and among family members over time

family home child care   a stay-at-home parent who provides care for their own child or children and a few other children

family life cycle   identifiable stages of family life, such as the young single, new couple, family with young children, family with adolescent children, launching stage, and family in later life

family meeting   a scheduled time when families get together and follow an agenda to get input from every family member to determine responsibilities and make important family decisions

family of orientation   the family into which you were born, or the family that nurtures, provides for, and instructs you

family of procreation   the family that you generate in the future; the one you will nurture, provide for, and instruct

family studies   the interdisciplinary study of individuals and their families using anthropology, sociology, and psychology, along with the social sciences of economics and political science; also includes some aspects of the humanities disciplines of religion, philosophy, law, and education

family violence   intentional use of damaging behaviours—ranging from physical abuse to emotional abuse, blackmail, threats, manipulation, and other controlling behaviours—by one family member against another

feedback   the response to a message, which completes two-way communication

Fetal Alcohol Spectrum Disorder   also known as **FASD**; the conditions it covers are all caused when alcohol is consumed in pregnancy

fetal blood   blood carried by the umbilical cord from the fetus to the placenta

fetus formed from the embryo at the end of the eighth week after conception, resembles the basic human shape with arm and leg buds, a trunk, distinct head, and formed organs

fine-motor skills skills that involve the use of small muscles, such as those needed to cut with scissors

flex hours schedules that allow parents employed outside of the home to determine which part of the work day fits their child's schedule best

fontanels soft parts of the newborn skull where the bone has not yet filled in

formal education officially regulated instruction, which follows a prescribed curriculum, and takes place in a particular setting, with qualified teachers or instructors

formal operations the stage (beginning around the age of 12 to 14) identified by Piaget when one becomes capable of logic, deductive reasoning, and abstract thinking

full term the quality of being born on or near the due date of pregnancy

G

generational cycle of violence a repeat in adulthood of abuse witnessed or experienced as children in their families

genetic loading a state that occurs when both parents pass on a specific gene

globalization in this instance, a growing awareness that we belong to a much bigger element than our own family, community, or country

grief counsellor a trained professional who will help people deal with the sense of loss and related feelings following the death of a family member or other person

gross-motor skills skills that involve the use of large muscles, such as sitting up

growth spurt a rapid increase in growth often accompanied by an increase in appetite

H

homeless family a family without a home; it can be a temporary or longer-term situation

human development the lifelong patterns of physical, social, emotional, intellectual, moral, and spiritual maturation

human ecology the interdisciplinary study of individuals and their families and environments

hypothesis an assumption or predicted outcome to a research question

I

imaginative play dramatic play that brings together several kinds of play at the same time, for example, playing house, taking on adult work roles, or make-believe play outside on the climber, in the sandbox, or with cardboard boxes

independence in this instance, a child's ability to take responsibility for his or her actions and making correct choices

infant reflex an instinctive automatic reactions to stimuli

infertility the incapacity of a man or a woman to reproduce

informal education learning that takes place outside of an organized school program; learning that may occur from interaction with friends, family, community, and media and lead to self-discovery

informed consent in this instance, written approval or permission from a person to conduct a study after being informed of all aspects of the research

informed decision-making the act of carefully weighing the advantages, disadvantages, and consequences of the decision

intellectual development the maturation of mental processes such as learning, imagination, memory, and perception

interdisciplinary study human inquiry based on a combination of disciplines

internal conflict a state where a person experiences opposing feelings arising from dealing with two sets of competing demands

internalization in this instance, the motivation to choose right over wrong for inner satisfaction and not for an external reward

J

jellyfish family a family in which limits to acceptable behaviour are not clear

joint custody a situation when children spend time with both parents, and both parents continue to take responsibility for parenting decisions

K

kibbutz a form of communal living in Israel

L

lanugo soft downy hair that covers the body of a fetus or newborn

latchkey kid a child who spends part of the day at home alone before or after school, and carries a house key to let himself or herself into the family home

left-brain dominant a condition in which the brain is influenced by its left side, which is the centre for logic and mathematics

licensed child care caregivers who are registered with the government, and are governed by strict regulations

licensed family care individual caregivers recruited by licensed agencies, with each caregiver looking after up to five children

life-saving technologies in this instance, technologies such as incubators, respirators, feeding tubes, and medication to help children survive a wide range of complications, including premature birth and extremely low birth weights, birth defects, trauma, injury, and disease

lifestyle   the routines and practices of a person's life including things such as job, income, where and how you live, friendships, leisure activities, and more

limits   clearly defined boundaries and behaviours

listening face   a facial expression that indicates attentiveness, shows warmth, and uses eye contact

logical consequences   results or effects that relate logically to the behaviour; for example, if you get your shoes muddy, you clean them

M

major decision   a decision that may require a substantial outlay of money, or that may alter the life of one or more family members

majority rule   a vote to resolve simple conflicts within a group such as what movie to see

malnutrition   a state that is caused by a lack of food nutrients needed for normal growth and development

mandatory child support   as of May 1, 1997 the federal Divorce Act enforces financial support of children by non-custodial parents

manipulation   handling objects and learning from the involvement of the senses

maternal blood   the blood of the mother, which does not mix with fetal blood

matriarchy   a culture in which the mother is the ruler and authority figure of the family or tribe

mediation   a process where an unbiased third party asks questions that keep both parties calm and focused on reaching a solution

mentor   a person who plays a key role in advising or guiding someone; a good listener, someone to admire or imitate

metamessage   the meaning behind the message

midwife   a person who provides care before and during childbirth

minor decision   a decision that does not involve a significant outlay of money, and that does not affect anyone's life in a critical way

mitosis   cell division

mixed message   a verbal communication in which the words do not match the body language and tone of voice of the speaker

molecule   in this instance, a substance, such as oxygen, vitamins, minerals, carbohydrates, proteins, or fat, that is essential for fetal growth and development

moral dilemma   a situation involving a choice between two courses of action, where there are moral considerations in support of each course of action

mother tongue   the first language you learn

motor development   development that depends on muscle development and progresses from head to toe, and from large muscles to small muscles

multiple intelligences   intelligence exhibited through different aptitudes

N

nanny care   care provided for your child(ren) by a caregiver in your own home

National Aboriginal Day   a yearly event, celebrated on June 21 (the day of the summer solstice), that recognizes the remarkable accomplishments of the Inuit, Metis, and First Nations people and their contribution to the building of Canada

natural consequences   in this instance, an effect that results directly from the child's behaviour; for example, if the child goes outside without mittens on a cold day, the natural consequence is very cold hands

negative socialization pattern   a situation in which unacceptable behaviour is modelled, unacceptable behaviour is accepted, and negative feedback is given

neglect   a form of child abuse in which children do not receive the necessities of life, such as food, shelter, hygiene, a safe environment, supervision, and love and affection

negotiation   the back-and-forth discussion that allows two parties to reach a decision or solution acceptable to both

neonate   a newborn human infant

neuron   a specialized cell that is the main functional unit of nerve tissue

neurotoxin   a toxin, such as alcohol, that permanently destroys brain cells

nickname   a shortened or alternate version of the name given that sometimes can be a sign of affection or a source of great embarrassment

non-verbal communication   using body language or gestures, eye contact, facial expressions, and posture to convey a message

norm   accepted ways of society

numeracy skills   knowledge of numbers and number concepts

nurturance   the sum of environmental factors, such as love and care, that act on an individual; the act or process of raising or rearing children

nurturing relationship   a relationship in which people, in this case children, are allowed the safety and security needed to grow and develop

O

observation protocol   a formal tool for recording observations, focusing on a list of questions to ask, or a list of details to which you need to pay attention

one-way communication communication that occurs when one person talks or sends out messages, but does not receive a response

online learning the act of taking educational courses via the Internet

onlooker play a situation when children watch other children play without joining in

overstimulation bombarding the senses with too much information

overt rule a rule that is clearly stated, and easy to challenge and change

P

parallel play a type of play when children play side-by-side with different toys or activities with little or no interaction, each child intent on their own activity

parent a father or mother; one who produces offspring or the person who has full responsibility for a child

parental leave partially paid leave from one's employment for an eligible parent for up to one year following the birth of a child or an adoption

parenthood a stage of life that involves the care and nurture of children; the job of raising children including meeting the needs of children before and after they are born and nurturing, teaching, and guiding children throughout their lives

parenting participation in the act of raising children

parenting philosophy a set of guidelines or beliefs that sum up what parents feel is the best approach to use with their children

parenting style an approach to raising children identified as either permissive, authoritarian, or authoritative/democratic

passive child a content child, not demanding or easily aroused, who enjoys a cuddle, sleeps well, and does not cry readily

paternity the relationship of father to child

patriarchy a culture in which the father is the ruler and authority figure of the family or tribe

patterns of violence the notion that violence in families repeats itself in the next generation

peer group any group made up of other people of the same age

peer helper a student who counsels, supports, or tutors other students

permissive parenting a parenting style that overlooks misbehaviour, has little control, and allows the child to make his or her own decisions

personal limits limits set by a child for himself or herself

personal safety protection from assault, molestation, sexual harassment, or threat to one's physical or mental well-being

physical abuse the act of physically hurting a child or adult that may result in marks, burns, or fractures, as examples

physical development growth and maturation of the senses, muscles, and motor skills

placenta a blood-rich organ that grows in the uterus only during pregnancy and that provides nourishment to the fetus and removes waste products

placid child a child with a calm, peaceful, and quiet disposition

play therapy a method used by child psychologists to discover hidden emotions, frustrations, fears, anger, and hostility in children

positive feedback responses (verbal or non-verbal) that encourage or reward behaviour

positive learning experience in this instance, an experience that helps a child to learn through positive responses from a parent or caregiver

post-traumatic stress disorder a range of symptoms that signify a state of shock following a stressful or traumatic experience

poverty not having enough money or resources to meet the necessities of life

premature born six or more weeks early or weighing less than 2.5 kilograms

prenatal health care checkups during pregnancy by a medical doctor or midwife trained to pinpoint any problem and offer the necessary guidance for a healthy, full-term pregnancy

preoperational period the second of four developmental stages as defined by Jean Piaget, that begins when a child is two and ends when she or he is approximately seven years old

primary research the study conducted and reported by the person doing the research

print material reading materials made of paper and ink, such as books, magazines, brochures, instruction manuals, newspapers

private child care licensed or unlicensed care provided by an individual or organization

private school a school supported by tuition fees paid by parents who want a particular kind of education for their children

progenitor one who produces offspring

provider a licensed caregiver who offers the child-care resources needed by parents

pruning in this instance, the atrophy or dying off of neuron connections that were not reinforced in early brain development

psychology the scientific study of behaviour and the human mind

puberty the age at which a person reaches reproductive maturity

public child care licensed care run by the municipality and open to all

public domain something open to use by all people, such as television, newspapers, or radio

public school   a school paid for out of taxes and government funding, allowing all children to receive an education with a full curriculum

punishment   a deliberate act against a person, a reprimand or harsh penalty

putative father   the male responsible for getting the female pregnant

Q

qualitative research   research that is not based on numbers or statistics, but which gathers evidence on the quality of life in human terms

quantitative research   experimental research that results in data such as numbers, measurements, and statistics

quickening   the fetal movement felt by a mother around the fifth month of pregnancy

quiet play   a type of play in which a child plays alone or with a very small group

R

regression   the return to a level of behaviour that is more common to an earlier stage of development

reinforcement   repeated acknowledgement and encouragement of a preferred behaviour until that behaviour becomes second nature to the child

relationship counsellor   a trained professional who helps people resolve problems in their close relationships, as between partners or between parents and children

research question   a question that a social scientist hopes to answer through research, and which suggests what research method would be the best one to use

resiliency   the ability to overcome problems and manage life effectively

responsibility   in this instance, the many things that parents are accountable or answerable for, including the provision of adequate food, shelter, care, and education

right-brain dominant   a condition in which the brain is influenced by its right side, which is the centre for creativity and language

Rights of the Child   a United Nations declaration that all children, regardless of race, gender, class, ability, or disability, be treated exactly the same

rite of passage   religious and cultural beliefs, rituals, or ceremonies that mark a significant change in status or the start of a new stage in life

role model   a person someone admires and wishes to model his or her behaviour after

rooming in   when the mother and child stay in the same room day and night immediately after birth

S

Saint-Jean-Baptiste Day   a yearly event, celebrated on June 24, that recognizes the contributions Francophones have made to the building of Canada

scientific method   the format followed to write up science experiments, including purpose, hypothesis, method, results, analysis, and conclusion

school-age program   a school or community centre program that offers before or after school care for school-age children who are not able to stay at home alone

secondary research   research that involves recording or reporting what other researchers have already discovered

secure infant   an infant who is comfortable with a parent who returns after an absence

self-control   the ability to control one's feelings and actions

self-discipline   the ability to control and regulate one's behaviour

self-talk   an act of mental rehearsal; the ability to develop confidence by mentally providing encouragement for oneself

sense of autonomy   a state of or a desire for independence and self-determination

sense of trust   a feeling of reliance that forms through attachment with a significant other; feeling confident that one's needs will be met

sensitive child   a child who reacts intensely to stimulation and change in the environment

sensorimotor period   the first of four developmental stages as defined by Jean Piaget, that begins at birth and lasts until two years of age

separation behaviour   a stage of behaviour many children go through if left by their parents between eight months and three years, including protest, despair, and detachment

sexual abuse   the act of forcing a sexual act upon someone

sexual harassment   threats to personal safety taking the form of name-calling, suggestive gestures, sexual innuendo, and comments of a sexual nature intended to embarrass, or put down the person at whom they are directed

Shaken Baby Syndrome   symptoms of trauma that indicate the rough handling or deliberate shaking of an infant which may result in permanent brain damage or death

shared authority   a situation where power is divided between the adult leaders of a family

sibling rivalry   feelings of resentment, jealousy, and competition that may arise between two or more siblings

social convention   a general agreement or custom such as taking turns, waiting in line, thinking before you speak, being kind to others, and saying please and thank you

social development   the evolution of knowledge of how people interact, play, share, take turns, or talk socially

social policy a policy established by one of three levels of government that determines what is legal and permissible regarding social security and social services programs

social science the study of human society, thought, culture, and behaviour

social services agencies funded by government or private contributions that provide subsidized child care, financial assistance, retraining, and health care to people in the community

socialization an ongoing process that teaches individuals the ways of society

socially acceptable behaviour behaviour that is customary or expected in society

sociology the systematic study of human relationships within social organizations

solitary play a type of play where people play by themselves; for example, babies playing with their feet or toddles waking up from a nap and amusing themselves with an activity centre on the side of the crib

spina bifida a congenital defect in which the spinal column or part of it is malformed, partially exposing the spinal cord and meninges

stereotype a fixed or oversimplified image or opinion of a person or group of people

stimulation the state of being stimulated or excited

stimuli information received from one or more of the five senses and processed by the brain

stranger anxiety an emotion sometimes experienced by infants around eight to ten months of age, where they become shy or fearful around strangers

street proofing the term used for programs that teach children how to take action if faced with the possibility of abduction or sexual molestation

style guide a collection of rules and guidelines governing the appearance and use of written information

sudden infant death syndrome also known as **SIDS**; the unexpected death of an apparently healthy infant, usually during sleep

symbolic play a spontaneous type of play that children of all ages enjoy, involving the use of toys or objects to represent something entirely different. For example, a hairbrush pushed around on the floor is symbolic of a car or train.

synapses connections between neurons that allow the flow of electrical impulses

T

taking responsibility being accountable for your choices, behaviour, actions, and relationships

talk starter a phrase, such as "Do you mean that…", that encourages conversation

temperament the combination of physical, mental, and emotional qualities that make up a person's nature

teratogen a chemical substance that causes birth defects

"The Brazelton" a scale that measures potential and compares individual differences in infants at birth in areas such as sensitivity to sound and light, response time to different stimuli, and activity levels

theory an explanation or view of events, behaviours, or situations that make them easier to organize and understand

thwarting authority deliberately disregarding laws of government or social organizations

time-in an act of inclusion rather than exclusion; for example, when a child misbehaves, the parent sits with the child and calmly discusses the child's feelings and teaches him or her to problem-solve

time-out the removal of a child from the problem situation giving him or her time to calm down or rethink the behaviour

toxoplasmosis a disease caused by parasites that can damage the internal organs and nervous system during the early stages of pregnancy; the parasite lives in cat feces and unpasteurized milk

transition a change or passing from one condition, place, form, stage to another

transitional labour the final phase of labour, in which the cervix dilates to ten centimeters and stronger, longer contractions occur closer together

trophoblast the outer layer of the ball of cells that reaches the uterus after conception; the layer that attaches to the uterine lining

truant one who is absent from a required obligation, such as a student who stops attending school

two-way communication communication with feedback

U

umbilical cord the cord that carries fetal blood from the fetus to the placenta

V

verbal communication communication that involves the use of words as in talking and listening, or sending and receiving written messages

vernix a cheesy wax-like coating that covers the fetus to protect the skin

violence in schools the use of physical force causing injury or destruction that happens on school property

W

working poor families or individuals who are employed, but their income is at or below the Low Income Cut-Off Line (LICO)

Index

Credits

Photo Credits

Unit 1 Banner, p. 2: left to right: © Steve Smith/SuperStock, © Francisco Cruz/SuperStock, PhotoDisc, © Royalty-Free/CORBIS/MAGMA, © Comstock IMAGES; **p. 3:** Eyewire; **p. 5:** top right: Courtesy of Eva Meriorg, bottom left: Courtesy of Robert Glossop; **p. 7:** PhotoDisc; **p. 8:** © Bluestone Productions/SuperStock; **p. 10:** PhotoDisc; **pp. 13, 17:** © Royalty-Free/CORBIS/MAGMA; **p. 21:** Courtesy of Tina Morrison; **p. 23:** © James Leynse/CORBIS SABA/MAGMA; **p. 24:** PhotoDisc; **Unit 2 Banner, p. 27:** left to right: © Comstock IMAGES, © Royalty-Free/CORBIS/MAGMA, PhotoDisc; **p. 29:** ©ThinkStock/SuperStock; **p. 30:** © CP Picture Archive; **p. 33:** © Archivo Iconografico, S.A./CORBIS/MAGMA; **p. 34:** © Bettmann Archive, F2563; **p. 35:** National Archives of Canada, Ottawa (Accession No. 1990-568-1)/C-010688; **p. 39:** National Archives of Canada/C-004239; **p. 42:** © Comstock IMAGES; **p. 43:** Courtesy of Kathy Lynn, Parenting Today; **p. 44:** © Comstock IMAGES; **p. 45:** © Francisco Cruz/SuperStock; **p. 50:** PhotoDisc; **p. 51:** Chip Henderson/Index Stock Imagery; **p. 52:** Courtesy of Eva Meriorg; **p. 53:** © ThinkStock/SuperStock; **p. 54:** PhotoDisc; **p. 57:** © Jim Craigmyle/CORBIS/MAGMA; **p. 58:** top left: PhotoDisc, bottom left: Courtesy of Laura Tryssenaar; **p. 59:** © Royalty-Free/CORBIS/MAGMA; **p. 61:** © Comstock IMAGES; **p. 62:** Eyewire; **p. 64:** Courtesy of Ashleigh Poole; **p. 66:** Bill Lai/Index Stock Imagery; **p. 69:** © Royalty-Free/CORBIS/MAGMA; **pp. 73-75:** PhotoDisc; **p. 76:** Eyewire; **p. 77:** PhotoDisc; **p. 78:** Courtesy of Marta Kivik; **p. 79:** PhotoDisc; **p. 80:** © Royalty-Free/CORBIS/MAGMA; **p. 81:** PhotoDisc; **p. 83:** Al Harvey/Image Network Inc.; **p. 84:** Chuck Carlton/Index Stock Imagery; **p. 87:** HIRB/Index Stock Imagery; **p. 88:** © Peter Turnley/CORBIS/MAGMA; **p. 89:** CP/Kelowna Courier/Gary Nylander; **p. 90:** Courtesy of Pedro Barrata; **Unit 3 Banner, p. 93:** left to right: PhotoDisc, © Bananastock/SuperStock, Eyewire; **p. 95:** PhotoDisc; **p. 97:** Courtesy of Thu Thuy Caya; **p. 99:** © Royalty-Free/CORBIS/MAGMA;

p. 100: © Royalty-Free/CORBIS/MAGMA; **p. 101:** top right: Dave Mager/Index Stock Imagery, bottom right: PhotoDisc; **p. 102:** CP PHOTO/Winnipeg Free Press/Ken Gig; **p. 104:** Dick Hemingway; **p. 106:** top left: PhotoDisc, bottom left: Antony Nagel Mann/firstlight.ca; **p. 107:** PhotoDisc; **p. 111:** top right: © Royalty-Free/CORBIS/MAGMA, centre right: Don Stevenson/Index Stock Imagery; **p. 118:** Chris Minerva/Index Stock Imagery; **p. 120:** © Royalty-Free/CORBIS/MAGMA; **p. 123:** top right, Courtesy of Laura Tryssenaar; bottom right: Eyewire; **p. 124:** Eyewire; **p. 126:** © Royalty-Free/CORBIS/MAGMA; **p. 128:** © Bluestone Productions/SuperStock; **p. 131:** PhotoDisc; **p. 132:** Graham French/Masterfile; **p. 134:** Eyewire; **p. 136:** © Comstock IMAGES; **p. 137:** PhotoDisc; **p. 143:** Courtesy of the MacIntyre family; **Unit 4 Banner, p. 147:** left to right: © Pixtal/SuperStock, PhotoDisc, PhotoDisc; **pp. 149, 152, 155:** PhotoDisc; **p. 156:** © Image Source/SuperStock; **p. 158:** top: FOR BETTER OR FOR WORSE © UFS, Reprinted by Permission, bottom left: © ThinkStock/SuperStock; **p. 160:** PhotoDisc; **p. 161:** Courtesy of Jessica Pegis; **p. 163:** Frank Siteman/Index Stock Imagery; **p. 164:** Courtesy of Johanne Ewing; **pp. 166, 169:** PhotoDisc; **p. 170:** © Comstock IMAGES; **p. 171:** Mark Segal/Index Stock Imagery; **p. 172:** Omni Photo Communications Inc./Index Stock Imagery; **p. 178:** PhotoDisc; **p. 180:** © ThinkStock/SuperStock; **p. 181:** Myrleen Cate/Index Stock Imagery; **p. 183:** Eyewire; **p. 186:** © Royalty-Free/CORBIS/MAGMA; **p. 187:** © Bryn Colton/Assignments Photographers/CORBIS/MAGMA; **pp. 191, 193:** PhotoDisc; **p. 195:** ADAM@HOME © 1997 by Universal Press Syndicate. Reprinted with permission. All rights Reserved.; **p. 196:** Courtesy of Jeanne Kennedy; **p. 197:** Courtesy of Bonnie Buxton; **p. 199:** Courtesy of the Allen Family; **p. 201:** Kindra Clineff/Index Stock Imagery; **Unit 5 Banner, p. 205:** left to right: PhotoDisc, © Royalty-Free/CORBIS/MAGMA, © Royalty-Free/CORBIS/MAGMA; **p. 207:** © Royalty-Free/CORBIS/MAGMA; **p. 209: Copyright ©**

BOB SCHUCHMAN/Phototake—All rights reserved; **p. 211:** all images: Courtesy of Laura Tryssenaar; **p. 212:** © Royalty-Free/CORBIS/MAGMA; **p. 213:** Courtesy of Eva Meriorg; **p. 214:** PhotoDisc; **p. 217:** FOR BETTER OR FOR WORSE © UFS, Reprinted by Permission.; **p. 219:** Courtesy of Eva Meriorg; **p. 220:** © 1997 TIME Inc. reprinted by permission; **p. 221:** PhotoDisc; **p. 224:** © Royalty-Free/CORBIS/MAGMA; **p. 230:** Courtesy of Dr. Andrew Meltzoff; **p. 236:** © Owen Franklin/CORBIS/MAGMA; **p. 237:** Courtesy of Linda Silver; **p. 241:** top: Lennart Nilsson/Albert Bonniers Forlag AB, *A Child Is Born*; **p. 246:** top: Oxford Science Films; centre: Oxford Science Films; bottom: Lennart Nilsson/Albert Bonniers Forlag AB, *A Child Is Born*; **p. 247:** Lennart Nilsson/Albert Bonniers Forlag AB, *A Child Is Born*; **p. 248:** FOR BETTER OR FOR WORSE © UFS, Reprinted by Permission.; **p. 249:** © John Henley/CORBIS/MAGMA; **p. 255:** © Royalty-Free/CORBIS/MAGMA; **p. 257:** Getty Images/Per Eriksson/The Image Bank; **p. 263:** PhotoDisc; **p. 264:** Courtesy of Mary Cunningham; **p. 267:** both images: PhotoDisc; **p. 268:** Eyewire; **p. 269:** © Royalty-Free/CORBIS/MAGMA; **p. 270:** Brand X; **pp. 271-272:** PhotoDisc; **p. 274:** © Royalty-Free/CORBIS/MAGMA; **p. 275:** PhotoDisc; **p. 276:** Rubber Ball Productions; **p. 277:** © ASTIER FREDERIK/CORBIS SYGMA/MAGMA; **p. 279:** top right: Courtesy of Anne and Mark Brown, bottom right: PhotoDisc; **p. 280:** SW Production/Index Stock Imagery; **p. 282:** PhotoDisc; **p. 286:** top left: T.Bonderud/Firstlight.ca, bottom left: Courtesy of Carol Crill Russell, Invest in Kids; **p. 289:** Matthew Borkoski/Index Stock Imagery; **p. 290:** PhotoDisc; **p. 291:** © Royalty-Free/CORBIS/MAGMA; **p. 292:** Courtesy of Mary Cunningham; **pp. 293-295:** PhotoDisc; **p. 296:** all images: PhotoDisc; **p. 297:** Jesse Parker/firstlight.ca; **p. 299:** Steve/Mary Skjold/Index Stock Imagery; **p. 300:** © Tony Arruza/CORBIS/MAGMA; **p. 302:** © Jennie Woodcock, Reflections Photolibrary/CORBIS/MAGMA; **p. 306:** PhotoDisc; **p. 308:** Getty Images/Barros & Barros/The

Text Credits